THE ITALIAN NOVELLA

ROUTLEDGE MEDIEVAL CASEBOOKS
Christopher Kleinhenz and Marcia Colish, Series Editors

The Chester Mystery Cycle
A Casebook
edited by Kevin J. Harty

Medieval Numerology
A Book of Essays
edited by Robert L. Surles

Manuscript Sources of Medieval Medicine
A Book of Essays
edited by Margaret R. Schleissner

Saint Augustine the Bishop
A Book of Essays
edited by Fannie LeMoine
and Christopher Kleinhenz

Medieval Christian Perceptions of Islam
A Book of Essays
edited by John Victor Tolan

Sovereign Lady
Essays on Women in Middle English Literature
edited by Muriel Whitaker

Food in the Middle Ages
A Book of Essays
edited by Melitta Weiss Adamson

Animals in the Middle Ages
A Book of Essays
edited by Nona C. Flores

Sanctity and Motherhood
Essays on Holy Mothers in the Middle Ages
edited by Annecke B. Mulder-Bakker

Medieval Family Roles
A Book of Essays
edited by Cathy Jorgensen Itnyre

The Mabinogl
A Book of Essays
edited by C.W. Sullivan III

The Pilgrimage to Compostela
in the Middle Ages
A Book of Essays
edited by Maryjane Dunn
and Linda Kay Davidson

Medieval Liturgy
A Book of Essays
edited by Lizette Larson-Miller

Medieval Purity and Piety
*Essays on Medieval Clerical Celibacy
and Religious Reform*
edited by Michael Frassetto

Hildegard of Bingen
A Book of Essays
edited by Maud Burnett McInerney

Julian of Norwich
A Book of Essays
edited by Sandra J. McEntire

The Mark of the Beast
*The Medieval Bestiary in Art, Life,
and Literature*
edited by Debra Hassig

The Book and the Magic of Reading
in the Middle Ages
edited by Albert Classen

Conflicted Identities
and Multiple Masculinities
Men in the Medieval West
edited by Jacqueline Murray

Imagining Heaven in the Middle Ages
A Book of Essays
edited by Jan Swango Emerson
and Hugh Feiss, O.S.B.

Anna Komnene and Her Times
edited by Thalia Gourna-Peterson

William Langland's *Piers Plowman*
A Book of Essays
edited by Kathleen M. Hewett-Smith

The Poetic Edda
Essays on Old Norse Mythology
edited by Paul Acker and Carolyne Larrington

Regional Cuisines of Medieval Europe
A Book of Essays
edited by Melitta Weiss Adamson

The Italian Novella
A Book of Essays
edited by Gloria Allaire

THE ITALIAN NOVELLA
A BOOK OF ESSAYS

EDITED BY GLORIA ALLAIRE

Routledge
Taylor & Francis Group

LONDON AND NEW YORK

First published 2003 by
Taylor & Francis Books, Inc.

Published 2013 by Routledge
2 Park Square, Milton Park, Abingdon, Oxfordshire OX14 4RN
711 Third Avenue, New York, NY 10017

Routledge is an imprint of the Taylor & Francis Group, an informa business

First issued in paperback 2014

The Italian novella/edited by Gloria Allaire.
    p. cm. — (Routledge medieval casebooks)
Developed from papers presented at The world of the Novella sessions held at the 35th and 36th International Congresses on Medieval Studies, in 2000 and 2001, respectively, under the sponsorship of the Medieval Institute at Western Michigan University, in Kalamazoo. With additional original contributions.
Includes bibliographical references and index.

ISBN 978-0-415-93725-2 (hbk)
ISBN 978-0-415-86939-3 (pbk)

    1. Novelle—History and criticism—Congresses. 2. Italian fiction—History and criticism—Congresses. I. Allaire, Gloria, 1954– II. International Congress on Medieval Studies (35th : 2000 : Kalamazoo, Mich.) III. International Congress on Medieval Studies (36th : 2001 : Kalamazoo, Mich.) IV. Western Michigan University. Medieval Institute. V. Medieval casebooks

PQ4177 .I85 2002
853.009—dc21

2002069666

Contents

Preface   vii

Introduction   1

1. **Lies My Father Told Me: Boccaccio's *Novelletta*
   of Filippo Balducci and His Son**   15

   Ernesto Virgulti

2. **The Crisis of Word and Deed in *Decameron* V, 10**   33

   Susan Gaylard

3. **Master and Servant Roles in the *Decameron***   49

   Cormac Ó Cuilleanáin

4. **Telling Lies, Telling Lives: Giovanni Sercambi
   between *Cronaca* and *Novella***   69

   Myriam Swennen Ruthenberg

5. **Sercambi's *Novelliere* and *Croniche* as Evidence
   for Musical Entertainment in the Fourteenth Century**   81

   Cathy Ann Elias

6. **The Lover Praised by the Husband:
   A Courtly Tale between *Exemplum* and Novella**   105

   Maria Bendinelli Predelli

7. **Masuccio Salernitano's *Gusto dell'orrido***   119

   Michael Papio

  8. **Imitation and Subversion of Models
      in Agnolo Firenzuola's *I Ragionamenti***   **137**

      Manuela Scarci

  9. **Alterity and Sexual Transgression
      in the Sixteenth-Century Tuscan Novella**   **159**

      Domenico Zanrè

 10. **Animal Anxieties: Straparola's "Il re porco"**   **179**

      Suzanne Magnanini

 11. **The Motif of the Woman in Male Disguise
      from Boccaccio to Bigolina**   **201**

      Christopher Nissen

Contributors   **219**

Author/Title Index   **221**

Subject Index   **231**

Preface

The present volume developed from papers presented at "The World of the Novella" sessions organized by the Italians and Italianists group and held at the Thirty-Fifth and Thirty-Sixth International Congresses on Medieval Studies in 2000 and 2001, under the sponsorship of the Medieval Institute at Western Michigan University in Kalamazoo. Early versions of essays by Myriam Swennen Ruthenberg, Maria Bendinelli Predelli, and Christopher Nissen were read at the Thirty-Fifth Congress, and by Susan Gaylard at the Thirty-Sixth Congress. (Cathy Ann Elias's essay was originally presented at a separate session at the 1998 Congress.) The papers generated much lively discussion, the impetus of which prompted me to solicit additional original contributions on the Italian novella and its development across the centuries. Sincerest thanks go to my colleagues and co-organizers, Sharon Dale and Leslie Zarker Morgan, and special gratitude is due Maria Bendinelli Predelli, who initially conceived this session topic and who later suggested additional possible contributors.

Other contributions in this volume were first presented at equally prestigious conferences. An early version of Michael Papio's study on Masuccio Salernitano was read as part of a session entitled "Transformations of the Novella" at the Modern Language Association Convention held in Toronto, December 29, 1997. Ernesto Virgulti read a shorter version of his essay for the Learned Societies Conference held at the University of Alberta (Edmonton), May 25, 2000. I wish to extend our collective thanks to the organizers of these important venues for scholarly exchange. Essays by Cormac Ó Cuilleanáin, Domenico Zanrè, Manuela Scarci, and Suzanne Magnanini are original and are presented here for the first time.

Warm appreciation is also due Christopher Kleinhenz, general editor of the Routledge Medieval Casebooks series, for his enthusiastic interest in making this project a reality. Finally, thanks must be extended to Anne Davidson and her editorial staff at Routledge for their patience and assistance in the final stages of preparing this book.

Introduction

The novella, a short prose form that grew out of medieval *exempla* and didactic literature, developed through the centuries to both embrace and influence other narrative genres. A major stock in trade of Italian narrators from the late thirteenth to the seventeenth centuries, its roots can also be traced to the moralizing anecdotes and folk wisdom included in popular sermons, *fabliaux,* and parables. From its humble beginnings in the terse medieval assemblage called *Il Libro di novelle e di bel parlar gentile* (anachronistically better known as *Il Novellino*), this flexible genre would later furnish the raw material for the highly structured *Decameron* of Giovanni Boccaccio, thereby endowing Italian art prose with its stylistic model par excellence, according to the pronouncements of Pietro Bembo in his *Prose della volgar lingua*. Always associated with the *borghesia* of Florence and Tuscany, the form is well known for its verbal wit and practical jokes as well as for its acute sense of observation with regard to human activities and contemporary social reality. Characters include people from all walks of life—artisans and aristocrats, Saracens and the clergy, men and women, young and old—portrayed within an equally wide variety of situations. The pleasures of narration are united with the traditional component of moral edification to produce a literary entertainment that is not immune from intense examinations of psychological motivation or biting critiques of human behavior.

The content of novellas includes material drawn from courtly tales and chivalric romance, from the Bible and hagiography, from written and oral sources, and, later, from folk and fairy tales as in the cases of Giovanfrancesco Straparola and Giambattista Basile. The style is frequently compared to that of oral delivery or storytelling, a process emphasized in those novella collections that use a frame tale that features a group of characters who exchange stories for their mutual amusement. Novella production flourished in the latter half of the Trecento, continued throughout the Quattrocento, and enjoyed a new upsurge in the Cinquecento in the wake of Pietro Bembo's positive appraisal of Boccaccio's *Decameron*. Humanists did not escape the fascination of this vernacular genre, which they attempted to elevate by composing original novellas in Latin or by translating famous examples into that more erudite language. Given Bembo's stamp of approval, it is not surprising to find novellas being written either singly or in collections in northeastern Italy. Italian novellas provided plots and characters for playwrights during the High Renaissance and exerted international influence on authors such as Lope de Vega, William Shakespeare, and Pierre Boaistuau, who frequently reworked their basic narrative situations.

Although novellas are typically relegated to literary anthologies under the rubric of *la prosa minore* or viewed as an inferior cultural eddy that paralleled the more illustrious current of Latin humanism, the impact and influence of *la novellistica* should not be underestimated. Far from being a literary curiosity with a negligible readership, the novella was an inevitable response to the demands of a booming vernacular book culture already in the early Trecento. A century before Poggio Bracciolini set out on his book-hunting expeditions, and a century and a half before Vespasiano da Bisticci opened his famous *bottega* for the production of luxurious codices, there was a vociferous demand for reading material in the vernacular. Literacy in medieval Italy was much higher and was achieved earlier than in other European countries, and, on that score, populous and prosperous Florence and Tuscany outdistanced other cities and regions of the peninsula. In fact, the chronicler Giovanni Villani, writing in approximately 1338, boasted that about 80 percent of all Florentine children were taught to read, and "artisans and even laborers kept account books."[1] Similarly, we must recall that Boccaccio says he wrote his *Decameron* "as support and diversion for . . . ladies in love."[2]

The growth of a new genre that suitably met the narrative needs of a new linguistic culture should not surprise us. At the time of the *Tre Corone* and even slightly earlier, the commercial enterprises of the new merchant culture demanded intellectual skills such as the ability to read and write in the local vernacular, the capacity to understand basic mathematics in order to maintain accounts, and even some knowledge of foreign languages and customs to ensure the success of international business ventures. The increase of pragmatic literacy paved the way for a new mode of nonprofessional, lay reading—reading for pleasure—that differed from the traditional reading practices of legal, ecclesiastic, or university scholars.[3] As literacy increased, so did the demand for literary works written in the corresponding vernacular.

Here I wish to emphasize the connection of the term *novella* not only to the verb *novellare*, "to narrate, recount, tell stories," but also to the noun that indicates "novelty." The very newness of this genre reflected the newness of its language and the culture that gave it birth: the Tuscan vernacular. It is not correct to assume, as is sometimes the case, that the novella was the origin of the modern "novel." Considering the present-day English term, that might indeed seem a logical trajectory of development, but one must realize that the modern "novel," a lengthy fictional narrative in prose, actually had its predecessor in the French *roman*, a lengthy prose narrative written in a language other than Latin. Unlike the course of development predicated on the deceptive English noun, the etymologically accurate derivation is conserved by the terms used in present-day French (*roman*) and Italian (*romanzo*) to signify the modern novel.

This very novelty of a popular language used by people in their everyday activities contributes to the vernacular genre's wit and vivacity, its quick rhythm and lively responses as opposed to the slower pace and tempo of classical erudition. The novelty of its characters and plots are as fresh as its language and syntax. Despite the debts of style and structure owed to Boccaccio's *Decameron*, later novella writers are not exempt from introducing their own innovations: the form can be reworked and revitalized to suit the narrative needs of a particular readership. The contributors to this volume, a distinguished group of international scholars, bring new and varied approaches to bear on novellas by the master— "Ser Giovanni Boccadoro" as Masuccio Salernitano once humorously invoked him—and also explore the ways in which the "minor authors" stretched the elastic boundaries of the genre to reflect the contemporary mores and political situations with which they and their readers were familiar.

Even though the *Decameron* repeatedly served as a model for later novella writers who often enacted particular innovations on its components, the exemplary book itself can be viewed as a remarkable break with the literary canon of Boccaccio's own day. In Ernesto Virgulti's essay on the well-known, humorous Introduction to *Decameron*, Day IV, a *novelletta* narrated by Boccaccio's authorial persona is reinterpreted not as a moralistic lesson against sexual desire but as a lesson on the very futility of attempting to extinguish that natural impulse. Virgulti traces the tale's predecessors and apologues as found in medieval tracts, sermons, and *exempla*, and then proceeds to demonstrate how Boccaccio does something radically different by recrafting the originally misogynistic material into a defense of women precisely through a knowing application and interrogation of the power of language. As has been suggested, the *Decameron* can even be considered the first major European feminist text. Indeed, seven of the *Decameron*'s ten narrators are women, one of whom suggests the flight into the countryside; women participate in the storytelling; and Boccaccio dedicated the work to ladies in love. Despite the importance given to women in this text, surprisingly little criticism has been devoted to the subject. Beyond questions of structure and content, Virgulti astutely examines the relationship of language and gender, a condition that was already present in Dante's day: the inferior status of the *fiorentin volgare* directly paralleled that of women in fourteenth-century Florentine society. In a striking linguistic move, Boccaccio deliberately adopts the marginalized language to create a scathing parody of the antifeminist *exemplum* and at the same time to effect a brilliant defense of women. His manipulations of language enable his young protagonists to outmaneuver the traditional rhetoric of their repressive elders while at the same time providing the (female) reader with a "serious message about the deceptive power of language," an argument that will return in essays by Susan Gaylard and Myriam Swennen Ruthenberg.

The link between language and gender relations is probed still further in the next essay; here, Susan Gaylard looks at the interplay of words and deeds, *fatti* and *parole*, a well-known theme that runs throughout the *Decameron*. Day V, Story 10, the midpoint of the work and one of the few tales that address the issue of sodomy, has been studied with respect to its structural position and theme, yet its full significance can only be understood by reading it with Day VI, Story 1 as its logical complement. As Teodolinda Barolini has pointed out, the associations *women: idle speech and passivity (parole)* and *men: deeds and activity (fatti)* are crucial to the sexual poetics of the *Decameron*. A close examination of this topos within the two complementary tales at the book's center again reveals a strikingly feminist move on Boccaccio's part. Here, traditional gender roles are decidedly inverted as female characters appropriate the "male" activities of using time wisely and converting words into deeds, while the male figures are portrayed as verbally and sexually impotent. In a play on both the Aristotelian and Christian paradigms of creation and generation, the males—whether heterosexual or homosexual—are here incapable of shaping their material into proper form. The metanarrative of Day VI, Story 1 reveals intricate metaphorical connections between the concepts of words and (sexual) deeds with narrating and horseback riding. "Storytelling and sexual intimacy are correlated through the metalanguage of theatrical chivalric gestures" to reveal deep connections between V, 10 and VI, 1. "The very idea of agency through words," a notion fundamental to the proper functioning of the text as *Galeotto* and to the project of writing itself, comes under examination.

Agency of another kind is examined in Cormac Ó Cuilleanáin's "Master and Servant Roles in the *Decameron*." In numerous tales, servants (or nonservants in disguise) act as helpers or go-betweens to attain the often indecorous ends of their masters. The lightly sketched ancillary figures of servants frequently complement those of masters to foreground the latter and to portray the full spectrum of human behavior. However, the master-servant paradigm not only functions on the literal level of plot and character, but is also used by Boccaccio for practical, logistical, and even metaphorical effects. Although these characters are often nearly invisible in Boccaccio's narrative economy, his text offers hints of the harsh realities of medieval life in which servants held a fixed place in "the chain of social being." Their worth was both real and symbolic, extending beyond their domestic responsibilities to the social aggrandizement they conferred upon their masters. Within the historical context, Ó Cuilleanáin analyzes the notion of efficient service within the context of the plague, perceptively noting that "[o]ne of the signs of social collapse in Florence of 1348 had been precisely the aggravation of the servant problem." The obsession with practical order and decorum is embedded into the frame story of the *Decameron*. Ó Cuilleanáin then goes on to construct a taxonomy of the master-servant relationships within the novellas themselves. The complicity of maidservant-mistress or manservant-master is reenacted not only in erotic settings but sometimes in violent, criminal ones. Faithful maidservants act as replacements for their mistresses in bed, while the fidelity of menservants might be tested when they are ordered to commit murder. Finally, the essay draws an analogy between the master-servant relationship and that of reader-writer. "The writer . . . depends upon the goodwill of his patrons almost as much as a . . . domestic servant depends upon the goodwill of his master. The creation or performance of cultural entertainment can even be seen as a parasitic activity, dependent for its very being on the consumer who judges it."

The deceptive potential of language, already discussed by Virgulti with respect to the Introduction to *Decameron*, Day IV, is also the theme of a unique novella by Luccan chronicler and novella writer Giovanni Sercambi, one that can be extended to the entire novella genre and, indeed, to the project of writing itself. Although Sercambi's works have long since been edited, scholars tend to focus either on one genre or the other. In "Telling Lies, Telling Lives: Giovanni Sercambi between *Cronaca* and *Novella*," Myriam Swennen Ruthenberg successfully interfaces Sercambi's historiographic and narrative praxes. Her essay demonstrates "how a unique, first-person autobiographical fragment inserted toward the end of the *Croniche*" engages the reader in "an intricate game of author-narrator-subject identity hide-and-seek" that culminates in a metanovella in chronicle format nested within *Il Novelliere*. At a time when notions of literary genres were still in flux, Sercambi consciously blurred the boundaries between what we would term autobiography, chronicle, and fictional narrative. In order to vent his personal frustrations with the government he had helped install, Sercambi filters autobiographical data through the fictional format of the novella and ultimately inserts himself as the dual persona of author and third-person protagonist into the centrally positioned *Exemplo* 79. In this dark metanovella that at once adopts the tropes of chronicle and inverts those of novella, the author both "reconfirms his authority as maker of the book" and demonstrates himself to be "the able interpreter of both physical . . . and linguistic signs." In this *exemplo*— the moralistically loaded term that Sercambi gives many of his novellas—the activity of *novellare* is interrogated and shown to be ultimately fallible and subject to misinterpretation. In fact, the dynamic tension between *narrare* and *notare*—storytelling and writing authentic history, fiction versus fact—vibrates throughout Sercambi's fascinating body of work.

Although Sercambi's texts have long been known to literary scholars, their value as a testimony for medieval performance practice has eluded musicologists.

In an original contribution to both the study of Italian novella and to that of medieval music, Cathy Ann Elias sifts through Sercambi's novellas and chronicle to discover precious bits of musicological evidence. Taking as her point of departure Howard Mayer Brown's study on musical descriptions in the *Decameron*, Elias takes issue with his conclusion that "monophonic ballate were far and away the principal—indeed, the only—poetic form set to music and performed by and for the upper classes" in the Quattrocento. Brown's argument, which hinged on the notion of simplicity, suggested that early ballatas reflected the style and length of laude and could therefore have been learned and even performed by amateur musicians. Whereas Boccaccio did not include any music for texts he mentions and, in fact, himself authored the texts specifically for the *Decameron*, there is extant music for many of the pieces that Sercambi mentioned in his writings. (Even though Sercambi was writing some twenty years after Boccaccio, the productive period of the composers mentioned spans the lives of both writers.) With musical evidence in hand, Elias points out that none of the ballatas in Sercambi supports Brown's simplicity hypothesis: one in particular is long and complex. Evidence in Sercambi also shatters the notion that amateur musicians who belonged to the élite of Luccan society would have had only the necessary skills to sing monophonic pieces. Of the eleven texts in *Il Novelliere* for which music survives, only one is monophonic. Furthermore, Sercambi's narrative descriptions prove that a variety of performance possibilities existed in the same historical moment. Not only did the aristocrats listen to and enjoy these pieces, but they themselves sung them in various groupings: same gender, mixed gender, children only, or mixed girls and boys. Sercambi also indicates how and when instruments were used as well as when dancing was part of the entertainment. As a parallel to the secular use of music, Elias also uncovers information regarding the use of *moralità* (didactic songs) by the *religiosi*, specifically the penitential Bianchi movement. These descriptions in Sercambi furnish an interesting literary corollary to the work of historian Daniel Bornstein. Finally, Sercambi's writings offer proof of the transmission of texts and music from Florentine composers throughout Tuscany, revealing a period of active cultural exchange despite political and regional differences.

Essays by Maria Bendinelli Predelli and Christopher Nissen present unedited texts that are pertinent to the discussion of how the novella developed and its effect on other genres in later centuries. The first of these presents the discovery of a novella-like narrative from Manuscript C43 of the Biblioteca Augusta in Perugia. This rather innocuous dialectal reworking of a courtly tale that circulated in Europe was copied in the mid-fifteenth century, but it still preserves traces of the original narrative. Bendinelli Predelli identifies two Latin analogues—*exempla* by Walter Map and Giraldus Cambrensis, which are datable to the late twelfth century—and two novellas by Ser Giovanni Fiorentino and Masuccio Salernitano. With regard to the topic of magnanimity in courtly relations, there is even an echo in Boccaccio. Similarities in the tales and thematic evidence suggest a Provençal troubador source from which the material could have been transmitted to both England and Italy. Although the overall plot structure remains the same, changes in narrative details permitted the story's adaptation to different social contexts. The misogyny and moralizing of earlier clerical versions is refashioned within the narrative norms of the *cantare* genre. The Perugian manuscript version tackles the issue of overcoming sexual desire, a theme examined with respect to the *Decameron* in Virgulti's essay, but this recently discovered text unites the chivalric virtue of the knight with the moral necessity of the monk.

Whereas Bendinelli Predelli's theoretical perspective uses a backward look at courtly and chivalric virtues to interpret her text, the next essay casts its glance forward to the early Romantic period. Michael Papio's essay brings modern theories on the sublime, the horrible, and the grotesque to bear on *Il Novellino* by Masuccio Salernitano. What Crocean critics such as Mario Fubini considered nonpoetic narrative "perversions" are, in fact, "an extremely useful point of departure" for studying the development of the novella tradition. As other contributors to this volume will argue, an author's success as a *novelliere* and the worth of his or her text must not be measured against the aesthetic yardstick of Boccaccio and the *Decameron*. Unlike Boccaccio or Sercambi, both fourteenth-century Tuscans, Masuccio was writing in another place and time: the more repressive Aragonese Naples of a century later. Whereas Boccaccio rewards the cleverness of underlings who subvert authority, Masuccio instead punishes his characters' attempts to step beyond the bounds of social, familial, or political obligations. Masuccio's monstrous and perverse characters and their repulsive behaviors are a "striking innovation in the evolution of fifteenth-century prose." He still aims to entertain his readers, but "whereas Boccaccio applauds the triumphs of the underdog, Masuccio finds amusement in his debasement and derision." As with Gothic tales of later centuries, the reader experiences an aesthetic pleasure "from a sort of flirtation with death and taboo." Transgressive sexual unions, violent murders, and brutal rapes enacted upon the nobler protagonists by the unsavory characters "provoke forceful aesthetic and psychological responses in the reader." Masuccio's "estrangement of reality" at once creates a unique style of narrative and invigorates the genre by endowing it with a new satirical power.

As in the case of Masuccio, various other post-Boccaccian writers of novellas have not received adequate critical attention due to the Crocean prejudice that dismissed them as poor imitations of the master. This critical misrepresentation has noticeable implications for the novellas written in the Cinquecento, many of which contain apparently inexplicable departures from the normative Boccaccian material. Rather than dismissing such anomalies as narrative violations, the reasons for their inclusion must be sought in the political, social, and cultural circumstances that existed at the time of their composition. Essays by Swennen Ruthenberg,

Elias, and Papio indicate how inherited material could be reshaped according
to the narrative exigencies of authors working in different regions: Florence was
not Lucca, was not Naples. The next two essays, by Manuela Scarci and Domenico
Zanrè, demonstrate the impact that political turmoil can have on the writers of a
single city or region working at different periods in history. Their studies, as well
as those by Suzanne Magnanini and Christopher Nissen, contribute to the growing
critical interest in reevaluating the novella tradition of the Cinquecento.

Florentine *letterato* Agnolo Firenzuola first studied law, then pursued an
ecclesiastical career, and even attained the rank of abbot before dedicating himself to literary pursuits. The apparent breach of decorum—that an ex-churchman
could produce immoral and even bawdy tales—scandalized his nineteenth-
century critics thereby causing the rest of his output and his true purpose for writing to be adumbrated. As often happened when Romantic Age aesthetics met
medieval and Renaissance texts head on, honest critical assessment bowed to the
personal tastes and biases of the critics. In her essay, Manuela Scarci seeks to
restore Firenzuola's work to its true position in literary history, recalling that he
"was the first to readopt the model of *Decameron* in its totality," but hastening to
add that "far from being a passive appropriation" of another author's literary
material, Firenzuola's project possessed much broader cultural implications.

Early print editions and past critical practice further damaged the integrity of
Firenzuola's incomplete *I Ragionamenti* by separating the frame dialogue on love
from its tales. The intended meaning of the novellas can be established only by
reading the accompanying dialogue as a reference point. The fact that the licentious novellas seem to contradict the loftier Neoplatonic dialogue must not be
seen as a failure to maintain a coherent structure but as a deliberate move on the
part of the author. Scarci asserts that "every component has its exact opposite
somewhere else . . . in a *mise en abyme* type of composition. . . . [T]he dialectic
interaction of opposites [is] far too numerous and systematic to be merely casual."
Such deliberate "contradictions" demand recognition as "structural ironic inversions" that have as their external reference point the linguistic and philosophical
models promulgated by Pietro Bembo, the theorist whose ideas had such a large
impact on the literature of the Cinquecento.

By invoking the theories of irony and parody articulated by Wayne C. Booth
and Mikhail Bakhtin, Scarci urges a reinterpretation of *I Ragionamenti*: its negative reception can be blamed on the failure of critics to recognize its author's parodic intent. Reading in this light, one notes that the members of Firenzuola's
brigata explicitly mock the high status given to Petrarch's language by Bembo. In
attacking Bembo's fundamentally platonic system, Firenzuola turns to other classical authorities (Horace, Cicero) to defend modern innovations and quotidian
language. The theoretical oscillations within Firenzuola's text—apparent weak-
nesses to many critics—in fact reflect the author's unwillingness to restrict his
linguistic expression according to a particular, codified mold. Nor does he pro-

pose an alternative solution of his own to the *questione della lingua*: "He disavows the validity of the first system by delineating the exigencies of the other while, at the same time, he confirms it by refusing to develop and articulate fully his own." Whereas Firenzuola deliberately keeps the Boccaccian model before his reader's eyes, his departures from it appear as ironic mockeries of Bembo's preferences. Notably, Firenzuola omits the plague from his frame story—precisely the portion of the *Decameron* lauded by Bembo for its solemn language. A second jibe at Bembo concerns the latter's idealization of platonic love. As a challenge to this tenet, Firenzuola sets against Bembo's idealization the very earthy sexual relationships of the *Ragionamenti* novellas. Far from being detachable, independent narrative units, the novellas are saturated with ironic inversions of Bembo's norms and serve as the ultimate site of the author's parodic strategies.

In addition to the overdetermined borrowings from Boccaccio, Firenzuola's compositional process mixes genres and uses conventional elements of novella in nontraditional ways. In his hands, the originally didactic purpose of the early novella that developed out of the *exemplum* takes on a highly ironic spin. The erotic novellas not only subvert the recognized Neoplatonic theories of Love, but also run counter to the author's "own" direct discourse on the subject as expressed in the dialogue portion of the text. By reading the novellas with the dialogue as Firenzuola intended, one recognizes that their presence "is tantamount to a rebellion against a given artistic code." Firenzuola's apparently superficial linguistic innovations, therefore, were designed "to have repercussions on the entire cultural apparatus of his times."

Domenico Zanrè's essay highlights the same intent to undermine the cultural mainstream, but he expands the topic to include evidence from another Florentine author, Antonfrancesco Grazzini. Zanrè chooses to examine the novellas of these two men within the theoretical framework of alterity, sexual transgression, and transformation. Whereas past criticism posited that such acts reflected the sadomasochistic or homosexual inclinations of the authors themselves, Zanrè uses approaches from the fields of gender studies and queer theory to show that such a psychobiographical approach is simplistic and misleading. He argues instead that such instances of nonconformity aptly reflected the authors' marginalized positions outside officially sanctioned cultural institutions such as the Accademia Fiorentina.

In Firenzuola's novella collection, *I Ragionamenti*, overt similarities in framing device, *brigata*, setting, and lexicon reveal the *Decameron* as Firenzuola's unmistakable model. His tales are filled with traditional motifs of mistaken identity, cross-dressing (including the false-servant ploy), and discovery. However, "Firenzuola chooses to treat the *cornice* as a forum for the discussion of contemporary [literary] issues" such as the nature and meaning of love, the Petrarchan *canzone*, and the *questione della lingua*. A further departure from the Boccaccian model is the fusion of elements from Renaissance drama to the more traditional novella motifs.

Grazzini's questionable political acquaintances caused him to come under suspicion by the authorities. This, in addition to his frustration with Cosimo I's takeover of the academy he had helped to establish, goes far to explain the violence and cruelty perpetrated on the representatives of authority in his novellas. His collection *Le Cene* was written during this period—the first of these "dinners" takes place precisely on the day when the Accademia degli Umidi was dissolved by ducal decree—and allowed him to give voice to his dissension. In Grazzini's tales, pedants, lechers, and randy clergymen are not only tricked and humiliated, but they are also physically tortured or even castrated as punishment for their sexual incontinence. The violent *beffe* directed against members of the cultural establishment are, in effect, a form of "literary catharsis . . . [that] allowed him to give vent to his frustration at his lack of success in the cultural life of the city." Zanrè's conclusion suggests a narrative function for the novella far removed from Boccaccio's *Galeotto* ("go-between") destined to provide solace to lovesick ladies and argues yet again the necessity of revising the inaccurate critical judgements too often passed on post-Boccaccian novellas and their authors.

Just as social and political turmoil can help to explain the remarkable innovations in the novellas of Firenzuola and Grazzini, upheavals on an even larger scale—the voyages to the New World and the Reformation—combined to produce a scientific, philosophical, and theological climate in which the classical authorities were reinterpreted in light of these events. This was the period in which Giovanfrancesco Straparola wrote his *Le piacevoli notti*, perhaps the first novella collection to include popular fables and fairy tale elements. Thanks to the presence of folkloristic elements in his tales, Straparola's work captured the attention of numerous folklorists (notably, German) in the 1960s and 1970s. Yet, as Suzanne Magnanini points out in her essay, the standard folkloristic or formalistic analysis of these tales imposed upon them "a cross-cultural uniformity through a reduction of the narrative to the most basic elements . . . [which stripped] the work of its details and peculiarities." Beyond their usefulness for folklorists, Straparola's tales have awakened little interest among Italian literary critics, who typically value them only in comparison to Boccaccio. As we have seen with other authors studied in this volume, a proper interpretation of any text demands careful examination of broader literary, historical, and social contexts in order to understand its author's intent and the cultural resonance it would have held for its readers.

The presence of folk and fairy tale motifs such as monstrous births or the animal bridegroom were, in Straparola's day, supported by early modern scientific discourse. Unlike the Ovidian metamorphoses or Plinian hybrids that populated the medieval imaginative landscape, these monsters were the bizarre engenderings of new varieties of interspecies copulation held to be entirely within the realm of possibility. Analogous accounts were presented as medical fact in

French, Spanish, and Italian treatises and academic lectures. Given the new teratalogical canon that emerged in the sixteenth century, the sin of bestiality
(coupling with an animal) became a special preoccupation that stood out from
other types of sexual transgression. Beyond serving as a marker of adulterous
relationships, as abnormal offspring did for the Middle Ages, the resultant
hybrids "were destabilizing radicals within the carefully constructed system of
classification erected in order to make sense of the surrounding world and
humankind's position within it." In the early modern world, the birth of such creatures went beyond the notion of sinful generation to raise thorny questions regarding infanticide or, if the unfortunate creatures survived, baptism and legal rights.
Magnanini argues that ultimately "the monster must undergo a double erasure":
whether by the intellectual reasoning process or by actual physical transformation, its bestial qualities must be cancelled out so that biological and social order
are restored.

Sixteenth-century theories of monstrous births also went beyond Aristotelian
notions concerning the passive, secondary role of the female in generation and
beyond the misogyny of the Church to attach an especially insidious blame to the
female body for its role in permitting the realms of fact and fiction to become
blurred. Here we have come far from Boccaccio's "ladies in love" confined to
their rooms or his female characters who daringly attempted to assail the male
province of "deeds" and actions. In Straparola, certain female characters are
shown as all too capable of committing dangerously rebellious sexual acts. Their
overstepping of "natural" decorum by shunning the proper human male partner
and taking on a more active role in procreation is implicitly rebuked as their acts
go alarmingly awry. In the denouement of one of Straparola's tales, it is the male
character who "removes the final traces of the disorder created by the female
body."

Christopher Nissen's essay traces instances where women physically disguise that body, from the novellas of Boccaccio—notably the tale of Zinevra and
Bernabò (*Decameron* II, 9)—to later examples by Ser Giovanni Fiorentino, Sercambi, Antonio Pucci, and Masuccio, and thence to a recently discovered female
prose writer of the sixteenth century, Giulia Bigolina. Although only two of her
narratives are extant, in them "the motif of the male disguise attains its fullest
expression and becomes a vehicle for the reexamination of the status of women
and the roles of the sexes in society." The expedient of a heroine disguising herself as a man derives from ancient Greek romance and can be categorized according to its function within a text. The male disguise can be assumed as protection
during travel or flight, to attain amorous ends or to effect practical jokes, even to
rescue men in danger. Such a disguise facilitates the heroine's "movements in
male-dominated social spheres" and sometimes even endows her with remarkable
powers that would otherwise be denied to her. Whereas the woman-in-disguise
motif was extremely popular in Renaissance literature and drama, Giulia Bigolina

takes its use over the top, both in terms of frequency and complexity, in her two surviving texts. The first occurs in the novella "Giulia Camposanpiero," a title not without autobiographical implications. Its heroine, portrayed in real-world terms, is a clever wife who adopts male disguise to rescue her husband. However, Bigolina's lengthy prose narrative *Urania* represents a tour de force of the motif.

In this unedited text (considered a novella by A. M. Borromeo despite its length), the heroine assumes no less than three male personae and even takes on the name of her own faithless lover. A secondary female character who is smitten with the false "Fabio" dresses as a man for a time and accompanies her. Pretending to be a merchant from Bologna, Urania eventually conveys her own tale of misfortune to the real Fabio. Finally, in a plot twist worthy of Shakespeare, this woman dressed as a man must convince a Wild Woman that she really is a man and obtain a kiss without being mauled in order to free her beloved from death and win him as her husband.

Bigolina's use of the male disguise is not confined to the level of plot and character. Instead, her heroine appropriates the masculine tropes of melancholy and madness due to love. Echoing the spurned heroes of chivalric romance, Petrarch, and perhaps even Jacopo Sannazaro, the broken-hearted heroine Urania does not remain confined to her chamber à la Boccaccio's *Decameron*, but flees into the countryside to seek a solitary cure for her suffering. In her male disguise, the female protagonist also acquires male authority and not only participates in but also dominates two diegetic *questioni d'amore*. The motif takes an innovative (and ironic) didactic turn as Urania becomes a teacher and instructs real male characters in proper behavior toward women. It is perhaps not necessary to add that, through her cross-dressed female character, Bigolina herself acquires a mouthpiece for her own participation in these popular debates on the nature of love.

To conclude, the essays in this volume repeatedly demonstrate that the novella, long considered a "popular" form because of its language and subject matter, should not be shunned as an inferior literary product. The very nature of its vernacular language and the access to the everyday world that it grants to the reader make the novella the perfect vehicle for critiquing a given society. Although this genre seems an ideal one for offering a realistic representation of human life and relationships in a given time or place, departures from the narrative norm can serve as a means for prompting the reader to reexamine the role of the individual in that society. Despite the changes the genre underwent through the centuries—longer length, evolution of a frame story, greater complexity of plot and characters, incorporation of new material such as the fairy tale, and participation in contemporary intellectual debates and new scientific discourse—the original impulse of the *exemplum* to instruct has never been fully supplanted by the novella's desire to entertain.

Notes

1. Cited in Samuel Kline Cohn, Jr., *The Laboring Classes in Renaissance Florence*, Studies in Social Discontinuity (New York: Academic Press, 1980), 12. For a discussion of the accuracy of Villani's claims, see Paul F. Grendler, *Schooling in Renaissance Italy: Literacy and Learning, 1300–1600* (Baltimore: The Johns Hopkins University Press, 1989), 71–74.
2. Giovanni Boccaccio, *The Decameron*, trans. Mark Musa and Peter Bondanella (New York: Penguin Books/New American Library/Mentor, 1982), 3.
3. On the different modes of reading, see Armando Petrucci, *Writers and Readers in Medieval Italy. Studies in the History of Written Culture*, ed. and trans. Charles M. Radding (New Haven, Conn.: Yale University Press, 1995), 132–44.

1

Lies My Father Told Me: Boccaccio's *Novelletta* of Filippo Balducci and His Son

Ernesto Virgulti

Giovanni Boccaccio's little story of Filippo Balducci and his son, also known as *la novelletta delle papere,* is found in the Introduction to Day IV of the *Decameron.* Because it is not narrated by the *brigata* of storytellers, but by the author himself, the *novelletta* is technically not part of the *Centonovelle.* The story is told as part of the author's defense against the accusations of his critics, who have found his work objectionable on several counts; most of these involved his predilection for women, to whom he dedicates the *Decameron.* Thus, prior to analyzing the Balducci tale, it is necessary to briefly examine the nature of the accusations of Boccaccio's critics and detractors, as well as the author's response to those charges, especially since they concern his female readership. Given the importance of women in Boccaccio's text, this essay would be seriously wanting if it did not include at least some brief remarks on the social conditions of the author's female public and, in particular, their role and significance in the *Decameron.* Since the "lies my father told me" are lies that Filippo Balducci tells his son about women and carnal desire, I shall also make some mention of sexuality and deception, but only as they relate to the *novelletta* and to the other stories under consideration. It would be clearly impossible to attempt even a cursory treatment of the topics of sex, lies, and women in the *Decameron,* for each of these would merit at the very least a book-length analysis.

Although the focus of this essay is the *novelletta delle papere,* one of the shortest of the collection, I could not isolate this story from the other novellas without seriously compromising its meaning, its function, and its relation to the whole work. I shall therefore briefly consider its affiliation with the tale that immediately precedes it, that of Rustico and Alibech (*Dec.* III, 10), and with some that follow it, particularly the novella of Tancredi and Ghismonda (IV, 1). There remains one last point to make regarding the direction of this essay. The *novel-*

letta of Filippo Balducci and his son is set against the backdrop of Florence and carries a distinctive Boccaccian trademark; however, the story is not entirely original. Boccaccio appropriated the basic plot from one of the apologues belonging to the *exemplum* tradition. Naturally, in the hands of the master storyteller and architect of the novella genre, the original parable undergoes such a significant transformation that the original message and intent is no longer recognizable. Therefore, in examining the structural and thematic components of the tale, it is essential to compare it to earlier versions of the parable that could have served as Boccaccio's sources. Only then will we be able fully to grasp the innovative aspects and revolutionary nature of Boccaccio's writing.

Those who are familiar with Boccaccio's *Decameron* know that women play a prominent and instrumental role in his work, so much so that some critics have proclaimed that it is "the western world's first major feminist text"[1] and that "it represents the start . . . of female emancipation."[2] To be sure, Boccaccio's tales offer us a number of memorable paradigms of female virtue and intelligence: the Marchesana di Monferrato, Gostanza, Ghismunda, Madonna Oretta, Madonna Filippa, and Griselda, to name a few. Surprisingly, however, relatively few critics have addressed this question of the role of women in *Decameron*, and no comprehensive study on this topic exists.

Equally important and prevalent in the world of the *Decameron* is the role that sexuality and deception play. Not only are these elements individually present in the great majority of the novellas, but in at least two instances (Days III and VII) sexuality and deception come together to form the main storytelling theme of the entire Day.[3] We must also recall that the very first tale of the collection features a virtuoso—and perhaps pathological—liar, Ser Ciappelletto (or Cepparello), whose duplicity and crafty verbal ability convince a gullible friar-confessor that the dying scoundrel is worthy not only of absolution but also of sainthood. By strategically placing this comically absurd story about the canonization of a shamefully corrupt prevaricator, "the worst man that ever lived," at the beginning of the *Decameron*, Boccaccio is evidently informing us that his work is radically different from that of his predecessors and must be read and interpreted as such.[4]

As he states in the *Proemio*, Boccaccio dedicates his work to gracious ladies ("vaghe donne")[5], particularly those who have experienced the vicissitudes of love. Following the dedication is a brief description of the condition of upper-middle-class and noble women. Although men enjoy great freedom and a variety of activities to help dispel their melancholy thoughts of love (hunting, fishing, riding, gambling, business, etc.), women are deprived of such outlets or opportunities. They are forced to conceal their amorous desires and sorrows, and they are relegated to the solitary, narrow confines of their chambers: "Esse dentro a' dilicati petti . . . tengono l'amorose fiamme nascose; . . . nel piccolo circuito delle loro camere racchiuse dimorano" (*Proemio,* 10). Moreover, women are subjugated by figures of authority such as fathers, mothers, brothers, and husbands:

"ristrette da' voleri, da' piaceri, da' comandamenti de' padri, delle madri, de' fratelli e de' mariti" (*Proemio,* 10).[6] In order to repair the wrong done to women by Fortune and to come to the aid of all ladies in love ("in soccorso e rifugio di quelle che amano" [*Proemio,* 13]), Boccaccio offers these oppressed, lovelorn ladies his *Centonovelle,* intended to provide not only consolation and entertainment, but also useful counsel: "parimenti diletto . . . e utile consiglio" (*Proemio,* 14). From the outset, we can see that Boccaccio identifies and establishes women as his primary, but not exclusive, reading public.[7] If Boccaccio intended to educate or provide "utile consiglio" to his readers, then it is doubtful that he would have excluded men,[8] for, as we shall see, the *Decameron* targets misogynistic male attitudes. We can conclude that among the potential recipients of the work, which includes the literati of the time,[9] Boccaccio reserves a special place for his *vaghe donne,* positing them as his "implied readers"[10] and inscribing them as such into his text.

Women play an important part not only in the text's reception, however, but also in its production. In claiming that he is not the inventor of the tales but merely the scribe, Boccaccio delegates the formulation and narration of the stories to the ten members of the *lieta brigata,* seven of whom are women. Moreover, it is the women—specifically Pampinea—who decide to flee the plague-ridden city of Florence in 1348 and seek refuge in the bucolic countryside, where they will spend time telling tales to one another. The function of the *brigata* of storytellers is to set the narrative machine in motion. Women not only constitute the first level of readership in Boccaccio's text; they are also the generating force behind the storytelling itself.

Another point involves the question of language and its relation to women. Boccaccio's decision to write his major work in the *fiorentin volgare,* instead of the loftier Latin, was determined, in part, by his female readership and, in part, by the novella genre that he intended to codify. Latin was the language of learned men and established literary traditions, whereas the vernacular's position was not unlike that of women. The father of the Italian language himself confirms this. In his famous letter to Cangrande della Scala, Dante draws an interesting parallel between gender and the vernacular, stating that his *Commedia* is written in the *locutio vulgaris,* the manner in which even women speak.[11] However, perhaps it was precisely the inferior status of the Florentine vernacular and its relation to women that most appealed to Boccaccio. In like manner, the novella genre that he had chosen was considered an inferior, popular art form with respect to the literary canons of its times: Francesco De Sanctis goes so far as to call it "un genere scomunicato."[12] Such a genre had to adopt an appropriate and representative language. In codifying the novella, it was doubtless Boccaccio's intention to elevate the status of both the novella genre and the vernacular language to a level of literary respectability. As *lingua emergente,* the Florentine vernacular became the most appropriate choice not only for Boccaccio's new genre but also for his new, bourgeois reading public.

To be sure, Boccaccio's preoccupation with women and his break with the literary canons of his time provoked a strong reaction from the literary intelligentsia of the fourteenth century, among them his dear friend Francesco Petrarca. In a letter to Boccaccio dated 1372 to 1373 (Seniles XVII, 3), Petrarca expresses his disapproval of the *Decameron's* lewd content, language, and style "for the common herd and in prose" as well as its intended female readership, "those who seemed likely to read such things."[13] Although they were written a number of years after the *Decameron's* composition, Petrarca's comments are indicative of the type of reception that the literati of the time gave to Boccaccio's text. The reaction of certain fellow scholars to whom Boccaccio had circulated some novellas (presumably those of the first Three Days) prior to the text's completion was so unfavorable that the author felt compelled to suspend the storytelling after the Third Day and incorporate a defense of his new work. Anticipating further criticism at the time of writing and aware that he was breaking new literary ground, Boccaccio includes a response to his would-be critics and detractors partway through his text.

In the Introduction to Day IV, Boccaccio addresses five charges. The first three relate to his fascination with women and his writing for a female audience; the fourth challenges his ability to earn a living writing such fruitless stories; and the last allegation questions the veracity of the novellas and the author's reliability. Boccaccio answers these charges individually after he narrates his *novelletta* of Filippo Balducci; however, I shall anticipate and briefly consider his response to the first three charges concerning women before examining the *novelletta*. The author pleads guilty to the first allegation that he is too fond of women and that he delights in pleasing and consoling them (*Dec.* IV, Intro., 5). His detractors charged that it is not fitting for a man of his age—thirty-seven—to discuss or try to please women: "a ragionar di donne o a compiacer loro" (IV, Intro., 6). Boccaccio's response to this second accusation is that there are innumerable examples from antiquity of distinguished men who, in their declining years, delighted in the beauty of women. Interestingly and by no coincidence, however, the examples he cites are three contemporary poets of the new Italian vernacular literature: Guido Cavalcanti, Dante Alighieri, and Cino da Pistoia (IV, Intro., 33–34). The third charge, like the second, has broader implications. He has been told that he should remain with the Muses in Mount Parnassus and write more serious literature, rather than waste away his time writing trifles and frivolities for idle ladies. To this, Boccaccio replies that the Muses are in fact women, and women—not Muses—have been for him an infinite source of inspiration: "le donne già mi fur cagione di comporre mille versi, dove le Muse mai non mi furono di farne alcun cagione" (women have already been the cause of my writing a thousand verses, whereas the Muses have never caused me to write any at all [IV, Intro., 35]). In addition to upholding his ardent predilection for women and acknowledging their role and importance in his work, Boccaccio is defending the merits of his new novella genre, one that his detractors consider frivolous and ethically lacking. The author's caustic response can be seen as both a rejection of established literary traditions and a vindication of the aesthetic quality of his work, which is aimed at a new, less elitist reading public.[14] Raffaello Ramat has rightly observed that there is too much diversity and therefore no possibility of dialogue between Boccaccio and his detractors, who are advocates of an old culture and an old civilization.[15] In his previous works, Boccaccio did indeed subscribe to classical models and literary conventions, but the *Decameron* for the most part severs all ties to that tradition. As a testament to a changed cultural and socioeconomic reality, his new text employs an innovative form and a language not only representative of, but also accessible to, a broader reading public. The *Decameron* is very much a new work of *poesia,* inspired by women, the same earthly Muses who inspired the new vernacular works of Guido, Dante, and Cino.

Let us now examine the *novelletta* of Filippo Balducci and his son and its relation not only to the author's defense but to the *Decameron* as a whole. Since the story is narrated prior to addressing the five allegations levelled against him, it follows that, in addition to its other significance, the *novelletta* was designed to play a part in the author's response to his critics. As mentioned, this is the first and only time that Boccaccio emerges from behind the screen of his ten storytellers to personally narrate a tale.[16] Either for reasons of humility or to avoid comparisons with the tales told by the *brigata,* however, the author deems his little novella to be incomplete: "non una novella intera . . . ma parte d'una" (IV, Intro., 11). Despite Boccaccio's claim, the *novelletta* is in my view exemplary and flawless in its brevity, structure, and balance. The following is a summary of the essential aspects of the story.

After the death of his wife, dejected and deprived of the woman he adored, Filippo Balducci decided to withdraw from Florentine society and devote himself completely to the service of God, taking his young son of two years with him. Giving all his possessions to charity, he retired to a small, remote cave on Mount Asinaio, where he and his son spent their days fasting and praying. Filippo taught his son about God, the saints, and the glory of eternal life, taking great care not to let the boy see or hear about worldly things. For years he kept his son confined to the cave, away from anything that might distract him from his prayers and devotions. Occasionally, Filippo would leave the boy and go to Florence for errands. On the day of one of these trips, his son, who by this time was eighteen years of age, said to him, "Dear father, you are now an old man, and not as able to endure difficulty and work. Why don't you take me with you to Florence this once to meet your friends, those devoted to God, so that I, who am young and more capable of working, can then go to Florence for our needs whenever you wish, and you can remain here?" Confident that the boy had been adequately instructed in the service of God, Filippo took his son with him to Florence.

When he saw the magnificent palaces, churches, and all the wonders of Florence, the young man was filled with amazement, all the while asking his father what the many things that he was seeing for the first time were called. Coming upon a party of very lovely and ornately dressed young ladies, the boy asked his father what they were. Filippo replied, "My dear son, keep your eyes to the ground and do not look at them, for they are evil things!" (Figliuol mio, bassa gli occhi in terra, non le guatare, ch'elle son mala cosa! [IV, Intro., 21]). But the boy insisted on knowing what these things were called. Not wanting to arouse any carnal desire in the lad, the father did not tell him that they were called women. Instead he replied, "They are called goslings" (Elle si chiamano papere [IV, Intro., 23]).

Taking no further interest in anything else, the boy pleaded, "Dear father, I beg you to make it possible for me to have one of those goslings!" Astonished by this request, Filippo answered, "Be quiet: they are evil things." To which the young man replied, "Oh, is this what evil things look like? . . . I do not know what you are saying, nor why these are evil things. As far as I am concerned, I have never seen anything so beautiful or so pleasing as they are. They are more beautiful than the painted angels you have shown me so many times. Alas, if you care for me, make it possible for us to take one of these goslings home with us and I will give it something to peck" (. . . e io le darò beccare [IV, Intro., 28]). Greatly distraught, the father replied: "I won't allow it, for you do not know from where they peck!" (. . . tu non sai donde elle s'imbeccano! [IV, Intro., 29]). And saying this, Filippo realized that his intellect was no match for Nature, and he regretted having brought his son to Florence.

This amusing little tale about a young man's discovery of women and the awakening of his sexual desire has been rightly viewed by most critics as an example of Boccaccio's naturalism[17] and his rejection of medieval religious values. However, Boccaccio's celebration of the powers of Nature should not be viewed in purely sensual or hedonistic terms. Although he condemns the subjugation of natural instinct, Boccaccio does not necessarily sanction the liberal pursuit of sexual gratification. Characters such as Masetto da Lamporecchio (*Dec.* III, 1) and Rustico (III, 10), who seek only to satisfy their carnal desires, often end up entangled in their own debased, lascivious plots. Boccaccio's *novelletta* is much more than just a celebration of Nature. This modern apologue not only denounces any form of repression, especially when it involves the deceptive use of language and intellect, but it also takes aim at the whole medieval exemplary tradition and its purported universal truths. The question remains: Why does Boccaccio choose to narrate this story himself in the Introduction to Day IV, midway through the defense of both his work and his female readership?

It is my contention that Boccaccio intended to create a narrative parody of the charges levelled against him by his detractors. In the first place, the *novelletta* underscores the naturalness of the author's attraction to women and his writing for them. As he himself remarks to his gracious ladies, even an ignorant, uncivilized youth like the Balducci boy, raised on a wild, remote mountaintop, was immediately overwhelmed with desire the moment he cast his eyes on women: "come vi vide, sole da lui disiderate foste, sole adomandate, sole con l'affezion seguitate" (IV, Intro., 31). Like the boy, Boccaccio cannot deny the irresistible forces of Nature. The crude state of the young Balducci—imposed upon him by his father—calls to mind another rustic simpleton, Cimone, in *Dec.* V, 1. Cimone, whose name ("bestione") signified "brute" or "moron," was so hopelessly imbecilic and ill-mannered that his father had banished him to live in the country with the farm workers on their estate, not coincidentally the same motif of isolation present in the Balducci tale. One day, upon seeing the lovely Efigenia, Cimone was so awestruck that "his heart, into which no learning had ever penetrated, was now pierced by Love's arrow through Efigenia's beauty" (nel cuore, nel quale niuna dottrina era potuta entrare, entrata la saetta d'Amore per la bellezza d'Efigenia [*Dec.* V, 1, 16]). By means of a woman's beauty, Love succeeded in doing what no one had been able to do: awaken the lofty virtues concealed within him. Cimone was thus transformed from a muttonhead ("montone") into an intelligent, charming, well-mannered individual. If women have the power to stir a young hermit without sentiment ("un giovinetto senza sentimento") like Balducci, more wild animal ("animal salvatico") than human (IV, Intro., 32), or to metamorphose a moron like Cimone into an enlightened gentleman, then why is it so unusual for Boccaccio to be infatuated and inspired by them? Although he appropriates the Dolce Stil Nuovo notion of love as a force that elevates and ennobles man, Boccaccio does not view women as unattainable divine creatures or abstract concepts. They do not inhabit the metaphysical sphere, but—like his *novelle*—are part of the real world. In this sense, women represent the new narrative mode he is shaping, a genre firmly rooted in the social and cultural reality of his time.

Still other elements of the Balducci tale address the allegations of Boccaccio's detractors. Filippo's abandonment of society and its earthly pleasures, and his decision to retire to Mount Asinaio, mirrors that which Boccaccio's critics would have him do: namely, abandon his fair ladies and the worldly subject matter of his novellas, and retreat to Mount Parnassus with the Muses in order to write more worthy and morally profound literature. This suggestion, for the author of the *Decameron,* is as meaningless as the confinement and repression of Filippo's son. Boccaccio does not derive his inspiration from scholastic models or mythological deities, but, as we have seen, from the real world and real women: "le Muse son donne." Unlike the old Balducci, Boccaccio is unwilling to repudiate women, the city, its pleasures, and its culture. These are the very elements that nourish his storytelling imagination and that make up the world of the *Decameron.* Through Balducci, Boccaccio shows us the absurdity and hypocrisy of living isolated from society. Filippo realizes that his experiment in asceticism is a fiasco even before the "papere" incident. Other than God, the Saints, and eternal life—the only things his father taught him—the young Balducci has absolutely no awareness or knowledge of temporal matters. The moment he reaches Florence, the lad is filled with amazement and asks what every single thing is called. Ironically, the son's total ignorance is the result of his father's failure to teach him about the world. Once the naming of objects begins, Filippo's fate is sealed. We have only to await his final humiliation when he tries to deceive his son by denying the existence of women.

Like Filippo, Boccaccio's detractors, who would have him sever all ties with his ladies and the real world, have an extremely "confined" view of what is worthy of knowing and what constitutes creditable literature. The Balducci tale parodies the beliefs of a reactionary literary intelligentsia trying to maintain that only the morally and spiritually edifying universal truths of the *exemplum* tradition have merit. Filippo's failure represents a waning literary tradition's failure to communicate to a new generation of readers. Through his *novelletta,* Boccaccio exposes the shortcomings and obsolescence of exemplary models.[18] At the same time, he is making a case for a more realistic, pragmatic and socially relevant form of writing, one that is both a source of pleasure and useful counsel: "diletto . . . e utile consiglio" (*Proemio,* 14). In my view, the author's defense and the accompanying *novelletta delle papere* underscores Boccaccio's intention, on the one hand, to challenge the precepts and authority of medieval literary tradition, and, on the other, to give validity to his new narrative genre, a form that expresses and reflects the changing sociocultural climate of the second part of the fourteenth century.

Let me make a brief observation on Mount Asinaio, the remote mountaintop where Filippo keeps his son confined for sixteen years. As I shall later illustrate, the basic plot of the *novelletta delle papere* is taken from the *exemplum* tradition. Boccaccio's version, however, is infused with a number of realistic or historical elements that sets it apart from those of his predecessors. For example, the Balducci were in actuality a well-known middle-class Florentine family, some of whom, like Boccaccio's family, were agents of the prominent merchant-bankers, the Bardi (*Dec.*, 1:463, n. 1). As for Mount Asinaio, there is a mountain north of Florence called Senario, which in the Middle Ages was the site of a castle where bourgeois laymen would go for spiritual retreats.[19] In the mid-thirteenth century, the castle was turned into a monastery. Thus, Boccaccio's Tuscan readers could easily associate this mountain with holy hermits and religious retreats. Yet, instead of Senario, Boccaccio uses "asinaio" (from *asino,* "donkey" or "ass"), which means "donkey driver." This raises the interesting question: Did Boccaccio employ the term to designate Filippo "the donkey-driver" who leads his asinine son to a state of ignorant isolation, or is Boccaccio just trying to make asses out of his critics?

Having examined the apologue as part of Boccaccio's response to his detractors, let us now look at other aspects of the story itself. Perhaps the most comical feature of the *novelletta* is the unexpected reversal in the narrative, one of the structural trademarks of the *Decameron's* novellas. When asked by his son what the women are called, the astonished Filippo knows he must invent something. Having kept the lad confined and ignorant all his life, the father assumes he can deceive him. Filippo believes that by masking the truth, by calling the women "goslings" ("papere"), he can actually extinguish his son's sexual desire: "The father, not wishing to arouse any potential desires less than useful in the young man's carnal appetite, did not to want to name them by their proper name, that is, 'women' " (Il padre, per non destare nel concupiscibile appetito del giovane alcuno inchinevole disiderio men che utile, non le volle nominare per lo proprio nome, cioé femine [IV, Intro., 23]). Unfortunately, in the end, Filippo's renaming strategy not only proves to be ineffective; it backfires. The young Balducci unwittingly responds to his father's linguistic machinations (substituting "goslings" for "women") with his own linguistic device, a sexual metaphor expressing his latent desire to give one of the goslings something to peck: "io le darò beccare." The redesignation of an object, or the substitution of its signifier, does not change the signified or the referent, nor does it temper the instinctive desire on the part of the Balducci boy to "feed" the goslings. Although he does not know what the lovely and elegant ladies are called or where they "peck," the young man certainly knows what he wants and, like a child who has seen an amazing new toy or pet, he will not stop pestering his father until he is allowed to take home one of the goslings. Millicent Marcus has pointed out that, in trying to falsify the reality of women, the father inadvertently teaches his son about female sexuality: "Thus, Filippo's strategy of denial becomes one of disclosure through metaphor" (51). This little tale clearly underscores the futility and hypocrisy of any attempt to suppress natural instinct, either through confinement, repression, deception, or the falsification of reality. In order to fully appreciate the innovativeness of Boccaccio's tale, however, one must examine its provenance and compare it to earlier renditions.

The earliest known source of the tale is a parable found in the legend of *Barlaam and Josaphat,* attributed to St. John of Damascus, who authored the work around A.D. 600. One of the more faithful renditions can be found in Jacopo da Varagine's mid-thirteenth-century work, *Leggenda Aurea.*[20] The legend contains one of Boccaccio's possible sources: "The Parable of the Youth Who Had Never Seen a Woman." It tells of a king who is warned by astrologers that his newborn son will go blind if he sees the light of day before he reaches the age of twelve. The king orders an underground chamber to be built, where he keeps his son during those fatal years (a variant of the motif of confinement). At the end of the twelve years, the youth is finally taken out into the world where he is shown many beautiful things. Upon seeing some women pass, he is told that they are demons who lead men into error. Later, when asked by his father which things he liked the best, the boy answered, "The demons, who lead men astray!"

This parable, with its misogynistic portrayal of "women-as-demons" who lead men astray, circulated easily in medieval Christian culture, which already held a negative view of both women and adolescence. Undoubtedly influenced by, among others, St. Augustine, who dedicated a substantial portion of his *Confessions* to misspent youth and sins of the flesh, patristic writers and Christian apologists adopted a view of adolescence as a precarious, lustful age incapable of overcoming temptation. The parable in question clearly reflected the repressive teachings of the Church and monastic life in particular, where it was easily assimilated into collections of religious *exempla* by such authors as Jacques de Vitry, Vincent de Beauvais, and Domenico Cavalca. These versions, including a secular rendition in the anonymous *Novellino*,[21] are essentially similar, particularly in their treatment of women. In Odo of Shirton's *Narrationes*,[22] however, there is a short apologue titled "De heremita iuveni," which contains an interesting variant that links it to Boccaccio's *novelletta*. It is about a young hermit who comes to the city with an abbot. Seeing some women pass, the hermit asks what they are. The abbot replies that they are geese (*anseres*). Not surprisingly, of all the things the hermit sees that day, the geese are the most appealing. Back at the monastery, the abbot calls together his monks and uses this incident to prove how dangerous women are and how easily a young, innocent boy can fall into temptation. Other than the substitution of the traditional metaphor of "women-as-demons" for "women-as-geese," which Boccaccio appropriated, Odo's version does not significantly deviate from the others. The various religious *exempla* all have a common misogynistic theme.

What is revolutionary in Boccaccio's *novelletta* is that he takes the very same *exemplum*, intended to demonstrate the evils of women, and transforms it into something radically different from that of its predecessors. He creates a new fictional space for the parable in which the original meaning and intent become absurd and meaningless. To be sure, there are numerous examples in the storytelling world of the *Decameron* where the author rejects misogyny and the imposition of unnatural practices in the name of a higher morality. Filippo Balducci's failure to curb his son's normal sexual desire, first through confinement and then through the manipulation of language, reveals not only his own shortcomings but also the inadequacies of asceticism and, by extension, any form of repression. By creating a parody of the original *exemplum*, Boccaccio exposes the prejudices and biases of a literary tradition that was becoming weary and obsolete.

The implications of this *novelletta* do not end here, however, because the various components and tales of the *Decameron* are not distinct, disconnected units, but a series of interrelated structures. To isolate this or any other novella from the rest would severely limit the meaning and understanding of both the story itself and the work as a whole. For example, the confinement and repression of Filippo's son, which proves to be totally pointless and ineffective, mirrors the isolation of Boccaccio's aforementioned female readers, banished to their solitary rooms by domineering and overbearing parents, husbands, and brothers ("ristrette da' voleri, da' piaceri, da' comandamenti de' padri, delle madri, de' fratelli e de' mariti, il piú del tempo nel piccolo circuito delle loro camere racchiuse dimorano" [*Proemio,* 10]). To these ladies, to whom he dedicates his work, Boccaccio warns of the pitfalls of an isolated and constricted existence. The Balducci boy's gullibility and simple-mindedness might seem humorous and innocuous, but let us not be misled by the light, comic tone of the *novelletta*. As we shall see in the stories immediately following the tale, the results of a similar type of repression are disturbingly tragic. This is not merely a question of overprotective parents sheltering their children from the world's evils, but one of wider social oppression and domination. Balducci's remote mountain cave and the lonely bedrooms of Boccaccio's female readers thus become metaphors of subjugation and of social and cultural segregation. Although the author might not be able to offer his chambered ladies liberation, his stories do expose the consequences of confinement and deception. Unlike the credulous young Balducci, Boccaccio's readers should not fall prey to the authority and duplicity of an *asinaio* who will lead them to a state of ignorant isolation.

The confinement and repression of Balducci's son reflect the dismal social conditions not only of Boccaccio's female readership (and medieval women in general), but also of many of the *Decameron*'s female characters. Strategically placed in the Introduction to the Fourth Day, the *novelletta* appropriately serves as a narrative prologue to the tales that follow. As such, it foreshadows the subjugation of the tragic heroines of Day IV at the hands of male authority figures. A primary example is one of the most pitiable and ill-fated female figures in the whole *Decameron*[23]: Lisabetta da Messina (*Dec.* IV, 5), a young woman who is totally dominated by not one but three oppressive and uncompromising brothers. When they uncover a love affair between Lisabetta and one of their clerks, Lorenzo, the three brothers secretly arrange to murder their sister's lover in an isolated location. Lorenzo later appears to Lisabetta in a dream, telling her what happened and where he is buried. Arriving at the remote site and unable to transport the whole body, Lisabetta severs the head and brings it back to her room where she places it in a vase with basil plants. Upon discovering this gruesome herbaceous mixture, the brothers deprive Lisabetta of the only morbid and pathetic fulfilment she has left in her life: the pot of basil containing her beloved Lorenzo's head. As a result, Lisabetta is so anguished and grief-stricken that she dies weeping in her lonely bedchamber.

Some of the elements of the Balducci tale show even greater affinities with the novella immediately following it, that of Tancredi, Prince of Salerno, and his daughter Ghismonda (*Dec.* IV, 1).[24] Indeed, both Balducci and Tancredi are elderly widowers who attempt to completely dominate the lives of their only children. Whereas the *novelletta* creates a light and playful atmosphere, however, the tale of Tancredi and Ghismonda is dark, oppressive, and macabre, almost as if Boccaccio intended to create a chiaroscuro effect by juxtaposing the two stories. Filial protection and repression at the hands of the despotic Tancredi soon degenerate into brutal murder when he discovers that his daughter has been secretly involved with a man of a lower station, his own valet, Guiscardo. Motivated by an unusual sense of possessiveness and betrayal, the father has his daughter's lover killed and dismembered. He then has Guiscardo's heart brought to his daughter in a golden chalice. The heroic Ghismonda, in turn, responds by committing the ultimate act of rebellion against her father: she tragically takes her own life. In so doing, Ghismonda deprives her obsessive father of the very thing he loved so much and tried so desperately to protect.

The unfortunate tragic heroines of Day IV share a common bond not only with their male counterpart, the young Balducci, but also with the *Decameron's* isolated and repressed female readers whose condition is articulated in the *Proemio*. The difference is that the novellas of Ghismonda and Lisabetta represent the horrific extent to which obsessive parents and brothers will go in exercising control over the women in their family. The consequences of repression have gone far beyond comically deluding the innocent Balducci boy; they have deteriorated dismally into cold-blooded murder. It is interesting to note that in both the Balducci and Tancredi tales, the children respond appropriately and symbolically to the actions of their fathers. The young Balducci counters his father's linguistic machinations (substituting "goslings" for "women") with his own linguistic device, a sexual metaphor expressing his natural desire to "give the goslings something to peck." Ghismonda reacts far more tragically to the heartless murder of her lover by drinking a lethal potion from the very same chalice in which her father had placed her beloved Guiscardo's heart.[25]

Having examined the links between the *novelletta delle papere* and the novella that immediately follows it, let us now look at how the *novelletta* relates to the one that immediately precedes it, the story of Rustico and Alibech (*Dec.* III, 10). Interestingly, the Balducci tale functions cleverly as a bridge connecting the comic novellas of Day III and the tragic ones of Day IV, thus confirming my earlier assertion that the stories of the *Decameron* are structurally and thematically interconnected. Although the last story of Day III contains some of the same motifs found in the *novelletta* (ascetic life, natural instinct, deception through language), it deviates substantially from it on account of its erotic content. The protagonist is another young ingenue, Alibech, who, having heard about the merits and virtues of the Christian faith, arrives at the cave of the holy hermit Rustico in search of a way to serve God. Upon seeing the pretty young girl, Rustico is overwhelmed with carnal desire and devises a plan to possess her. After assuring himself that she is as innocent as she appears, the hermit disrobes and asks the girl to do the same. Under the pretext of serving God, Rustico tells the naïve Alibech that he has a "devil" who is tormenting him so much that they must put him back into hell ("rimettere il diavolo in inferno"). As with the elder Balducci, Rustico's strategy soon backfires. The young protégée becomes so eager and so diligent in the service of God that she wants to put the "devil" back into "hell" more often than Rustico is capable of resurrecting it.

Although the tale has no known antecedent, Boccaccio most certainly drew his inspiration from some of the religious apologues dealing with asceticism and the temptation of the devil. One such story is found in *Specchio della vera penitenza* (*The Mirror of True Penitence*) by Iacopo Passavanti (c. 1302–1357), a Florentine preacher and writer, and titled "Il monaco superbo tentato dal diavolo in forma di donna" ("A Prideful Monk Tempted by the Devil in the Form of a Woman").[26] It relates how one night the devil, who has assumed the appearance of a woman, presents itself cold, lost, and hungry at the cell of an arrogant hermit. Taking pity, the hermit, offers hospice. Once inside, the "woman" begins intently to seduce the hermit, who goes to embrace her, but she vanishes. The laughing and jeering of a multitude of demons is heard, and the hermit, now humiliated and sorrowful, prays for God's forgiveness.

As in the Balducci tale, Boccaccio's parody of the *exemplum* once again exposes the hypocrisy of celibacy and ascetic life. Any attempt to repress Nature will not only result in failure, it might even—as in Rustico's case—bring out the devil! Both the Balducci and Rustico novellas also supplant the misogynistic theme so prevalent in the religious *exemplum* tradition where the woman is portrayed as a demon or evil temptress. It is not Alibech but the "holy" hermit Rustico who is the deceitful seducer and corrupter of the innocent young girl. Moreover, like Filippo Balducci, Rustico manipulates language in order to deceive and to disguise the truth. The difference is that whereas Filippo uses metaphor as a means of repression in an attempt to extinguish his son's sexual drive, Rustico uses metaphor as a means of seduction, to satisfy his own sexual desires. In both cases, however, the treachery backfires, and we have the characteristic Boccaccian narrative reversal. In their own naïve way, the two young protagonists, the Balducci lad and Alibech, unknowingly outwit their elders and prove that they are just as capable of using metaphoric language. Unable to serve God as often as she would like, Alibech complains to Rustico, "As I have helped, with my hell, to subdue the pride of your devil, you would do well to help tame the fury of my hell" (cfr. *Dec.* III, 10, 29). Notwithstanding Filippo's attempts to deny the reality of women, his son still wants to take home a pet gosling and "give her something to peck." Analogously, under the guise of serving God, Rustico devises a "ceremony" that masks the reality of the sexual act. Ironically, Alibech proves to be much more fervent and devout than her mentor in the service of God. In both cases, lies are told to disguise the object of sexual desire. Interestingly, in the first novella of Day III, deception is effected not by linguistic misrepresentation but by the total absence of language. Masetto da Lamporecchio seduces a small convent of nuns using a different strategy: he pretends to be deaf and dumb. Like Rustico, however, Masetto is soon hoisted by his own petard when he finds himself incapable of satisfying the unbridled sexual cravings of the nine nuns.

Boccaccio's clever use of metaphor and acerbic parody clearly constitute the comic force behind the two novellas just examined. However, in addition to entertaining his female readers as he states in the *Proemio*, Boccaccio also wants to provide them with useful counsel ("utile consiglio"). Contrary to the opinions of

Boccaccio's detractors, his novellas are not useless frivolities ("ciance"), nor is his dedication to women a mere chivalric gesture or literary ploy. As parodies of the religious *exemplum,* the novellas of Filippo Balducci, Masetto (III, 1), and Rustico (III, 10) expose, in a derisive and farcical manner, the futility and hypocrisy of confinement, asceticism, and sexual repression. On the other hand, the tales that follow the Balducci story contain disturbingly tragic outcomes. The novellas of Ghismonda (IV, 1) and Lisabetta (IV, 5) indicate how the same repression, in the hands of obsessive authoritarians, can easily degenerate into brutal bloodshed. The *novelletta delle papere* thus stands at the center, bridging not only comic and tragic forces, but also readers and critics. Beneath the satirical and irreverent humor of Boccaccio's novellas lies a serious message about the consequences of subjugation and the deceptive power of language. The Balducci and Rustico tales underscore how figures of authority manipulate language in order to conceal the truth. By exposing the treachery of repressive forces and the unreliability of discourse, Boccaccio is cautioning all his readers—but in particular his confined female audience—against the gullibility and blind acceptance of any form of moral authority. For this reason, he discredits and supplants the *exemplum* tradition and its providential claims to morally profound universal truths. This is certainly a radical departure from the exemplary mode of Boccaccio's predecessors, but then the *Decameron* is a radical and innovative text that is ushering in a new, socially relevant literary form and a new age in history.

Notes

An earlier version of this essay was read at the Learned Societies Conference held at the University of Alberta, Edmonton, May 25, 2000.

1. Douglas Radcliff-Umstead, "Boccaccio's Idle Ladies," in *The Roles and Images of Women in the Middle Ages and Renaissance,* ed. Douglas Radcliff-Umstead, University of Pittsburgh Publications on the Middle Ages and Renaissance, no. 3 ([Pittsburgh, Pa.]: Center for Medieval and Renaissance Studies, Institute for the Human Sciences, 1975), 75.

2. Robert Hastings, *Nature and Reason in the* Decameron, Publications of the Faculty of Arts of the University of Manchester, no. 21 (Manchester, U.K.: Manchester University Press, 1975), 52; hereafter cited in text as Hastings.

3. Interestingly, even those who carried out the first structuralist analyses of the *Decameron* noted the frequency and prominence of sexuality and deception on the syntactic level or deep structure. For example, in his *Grammaire du* Décaméron (Approaches to Semiotics, no. 3 [The Hague: Mouton, 1969]), Tzvetan Todorov observed that the "state" of love is "l'état plus repandu dans le *Décaméron*"; however, "l'analyse syntactique des nouvelles permet de voir que il s'agit toujours d'un état presque physique; il n'éxiste pas d'amour platonique" (32). Most of the transformations or changes of state come about by means of either verbal modification or deception, or through some form of disguise.

4. For a metaliterary reading of the novella of Ser Ciappelletto, see Giuseppe Mazzotta's "The Marginality of Literature," in *The World at Play in Boccaccio's* Decameron (Princeton, N.J.: Princeton University Press, 1986), 47–74; first published in *University of Toronto Quarterly* 42 (1972): 64–81, and hereafter cited in text as Mazzotta; Millicent J. Marcus, *An Allegory of Form: Literary Self-Consciousness in the* Decameron, Stanford French and Italian Studies, no. 18 (Saratoga, Calif.: Anma Libri, 1979), 11–26, hereafter cited in text as Marcus; and Cormac Ó Cuilleanáin, *Religion and the Clergy in Boccaccio's* Decameron, Letture di pensiero e d'arte (Rome: Edizioni di Storia e Letteratura, 1984), 148–77. One of the first to underscore the metaliterary significance of the Ciappelletto tale was Guido Almansi, who uses the novella to formulate the central thesis of his *The Writer as Liar: Narrative Technique in the* Decameron (London: Routledge and Kegan Paul, 1975). He states that Ciappelletto "is not merely an artist and master of verbal inventiveness with a genius for deception, but also a negative print of the writer, who is the master of all deceptions. . . . [His] amazing ability to create a fictitious universe and seat himself at its centre on the throne of sainthood parallels the writer's ability to create the far larger fictitious universe of the *Decameron*. . . . Thus the first novella becomes an aesthetic model of literature as falsehood, and the artist as counterfeiter" (29–30; hereafter cited in text as Almansi).

5. In "Boccaccio's Dedication to Women in Love," in *Renaissance Studies in Honor of Craig Hugh Smyth,* ed. Andrew Morrogh, 2 vols., Villa I Tatti, no. 7 (Florence: Giunti Barbèra, 1985), Victoria Kirkham has interpreted Boccaccio's dedication to "idle women" in a more sensual manner. The *Decameron's* authorial voice, in Kirkham's opinion, "speaks not for the lovelorn, but for the lustful" (1:333). Moreover, "idleness presupposes love" and "leads to lust" (1:336). She also equates idleness with sloth and asserts that "love and leisure . . . may conceal a more menacing combination, lust and idleness" (1:338). Although I agree in part with Kirkham, it is necessary to point out that Boccaccio does not address his female readers as "idle women." According to Vittore Branca (*Dec.* 1:7, n. 9), the adjective "vaghe" used to describe women in the *Proemio* means "graziose" or "leggiadre" (fair, lovely, gracious, charming). In fact, at the beginning of the Introduction to Day I, the author addresses his female readers as "graziosissime donne." All citations and references to Boccaccio's *Decameron* are taken from the edition by Vittore Branca, 2 vols., Einaudi Tascabili, Classici, no. 99 (1980; reprint, Turin: Einaudi, 1992); hereafter cited in text as *Decameron.* All English translations of this and other texts are mine.

6. Boccaccio's description of the isolation and subjugation of women is accurate and has been validated by the recent research of social historians such as Daniel Bornstein, who writes: "In the late Middle Ages, women labored under the heavy burden of institutional and ideological disabilities. They were barred from political office; they were hampered by a host of legal restrictions; they were subjected to the authority of their male relatives; they were excluded from institutions of higher education; they were deemed physically, intellectually, and morally inferior to men" ("Women and Religion in Late Medieval Italy: History and Historiography," in *Women and Religion in Medieval and Renaissance Italy,* eds.

Bornstein and Roberto Rusconi, Women in Culture and Society [Chicago: The University of Chicago Press, 1996], 1). As Georges Duby and Michelle Perrot succinctly put it: "Women were long relegated to the shadows of history" (Introduction to *Silences of the Middle Ages*, ed. Christiane Klapisch-Zuber, A History of Women in the West, no. 2 [Cambridge, Mass.: Belknap Press/Harvard University Press, 1994], ix).

7. Janet Levarie Smarr offers interesting insights on the *Decameron*'s relation to women in her *Boccaccio and Fiammetta: The Narrator as Lover* (Urbana, Ill.: University of Illinois Press, 1986). However, Smarr's interpretation of Boccaccio's dedication is rather restrictive: "The audience is not merely women but women in love. Boccaccio even explicitly excludes other women" (171). Smarr goes on to say that, in Day IV, Intro., Boccaccio extends the dedication to include all persons in love: "Possibly, then, 'women' means anyone under the power of passion or ruled by appetite rather than reason" (172). Mazzotta provides us with another interpretation of the dedication to women: "Boccaccio's gesture of addressing the *Decameron* to the women of leisure is a coy claim and, concomitantly, an admission of estheticism and futility. . . . Boccaccio, therefore, clearly establishes in his introduction a state of tension between two types of literary mediation, the erotic mediation and the prophetic mediation" (57).

8. Although Boccaccio dedicates his work to women, Branca informs us that the *Decameron* was widely read by the male bourgeoisie, especially merchants ("Tradizione medievale," in *Boccaccio medievale e nuovi studi sul* Decamerone, 4th ed. [Florence: Sansoni, 1981]), 8–9.

9. Boccaccio is clearly aiming at a vast audience that includes not only women, but also the writers and intellectuals of his time. Why else would he include a defense of his work in the Introduction to Day IV? As Mario Baratto observes: "Un intellettuale che osserva, giudica, sceglie, opera una sintesi della realtà con strumenti che sono propri alla casta cui appartiene: non a caso, pur affermando di scrivere per le donne (ed è già il segno di una nuova richiesta di un pubblico più vasto), il Boccaccio sente il bisogno di difendere e di valorizzare la sua opera agli occhi dei dotti, dei letterati" (*Realtà e stile nel* Decameron, Nuova biblioteca di cultura, no. 34 [Vicenza: Neri Pozza Editore, 1970], 47; hereafter cited as Baratto).

10. In his now famous *The Rhetoric of Fiction* (Chicago: The University of Chicago Press, 1961), Wayne C. Booth coined the term *implied author* to designate the picture of the author constructed by the reader. I use Wolfgang Iser's term *implied reader* to designate the counterpart of the implied author; that is, the presupposed (or ideal) reader constructed by the work or the author. See Iser, *The Implied Reader: Patterns of Communication in Prose Fiction from Bunyan to Beckett* (Baltimore: The Johns Hopkins University Press, 1974), xii.

11. Epistola XIII, 10, "Lettera al Magnifico Cangrande della Scala" in Dante Alighieri, *Tutte le opere,* ed. Luigi Blasucci (Florence: Sansoni, 1965), 345.

12. For Francesco De Sanctis, the novella, like narrative romances, are "generi di scrivere volgari e scomunicati" (blasphemous, irreverent genres), and Boccaccio's *Decameron* is a revolution compared to the literary traditions of its time: "Non è una evoluzione, ma è una catastrofe o una rivoluzione" (*Storia della letteratura italiana,* 2 vols., I Grandi Classici [Florence: Salani, 1965], 1:327, 343).

13. In his letter to Boccaccio (XVII, 3), Petrarca acknowledges that he has not read the *Decameron* in its entirety, only the beginning and the end (*Letters of Old Age. Rerum senilium libri I–XVIII,* trans. Aldo S. Bernardo, Saul Levin, and Reta A. Bernardo, 3 vols. [Baltimore: The Johns Hopkins University Press, 1992]), 2:655.

14. Giorgio Padoan points out that Boccaccio's response constitutes the rejection of pompous and lofty literature, while at the same time affirming that "scrivere novelle è far opera di poesia" (to write novelle is to create works of poetry) ("Mondo aristocratico e mondo comunale nell'ideologia e nell'arte di Boccaccio," in *Il Boccaccio, le Muse, il Parnaso e l'Arno,* Biblioteca di "Lettere italiane," no. 21 [Florence: Leo S. Olschki Editore, 1978], 84).

15. Raffaello Ramat, "Introduzione alla 'Quarta Giornata'," in *Saggi sul Rinascimento,* Studi critici, no. 12 (Florence: La nuova Italia, 1969), 52; hereafter cited in text as Ramat.

16. Another rare cameo appearance by the author in a novella collection, with corresponding implications for the centrality of the author's message, occurs in Giovanni Sercambi's *Il Novelliere.* See the essay by Myriam Swennen Ruthenberg, chapter 4 in this volume.

17. Among the critics who view this tale as a celebration of Boccaccio's naturalism, see Aldo D. Scaglione, *Nature and Love in the Late Middle Ages* (Berkeley: University of California Press, 1963), 101–6; Baratto, 56–57; Hastings, 10–15; and Pier Massimo Forni, *Forme complesse nel* Decameron, Biblioteca di "Lettere italiane," no. 42 (Florence: Leo S. Olschki Editore, 1992), 59–60, hereafter cited in text as Forni. However, Scaglione rightly points out that Boccaccio's naturalism "is not the naïve, spontaneous, unconscious delight in detailed realistic representation which characterized so much of medieval realism. It is a conscious program, intellectually formulated and presented in a polemic, militant, aggressive tone, in explicit reaction to medieval prejudices" (104). Other readings of the *novelletta* include Marcus, 50–51; and Giancarlo Mazzacurati's "Rappresentazione," in *Lessico critico decameroniano,* eds. Renzo Bragantini and Pier Massimo Forni, Studi e strumenti (Turin: Bollati Boringhieri Editore, 1995), 293–99. Ramat (50–69) examines the *novelletta* within the context of Boccaccio's defense; and Federico Sanguineti looks at some of the tale's sources in his "La novelletta delle papere nel *Decameron,*" *Belfagor* 37 (March 1982): 137–46.

18. Ironically, as a result of Pietro Bembo's theorizing, Boccaccio's own text would later become an exemplary model with those very shortcomings. See Manuela Scarci's essay, chapter 8 in this volume.

19. See Charles Singleton's notes to Payne's translation of *Decameron,* 3 vols. (Berkeley: University of California Press, 1982), 3:852–53.

20. My summary follows the legend of Jacopo da Varagine's "S. Barlaam e Josafat," *Leggenda Aurea,* ed. and trans. Cecilia Lisi (Florence: Libreria Editrice Fiorentina, 1952), 815–32.

21. See Novella 14 in *Novellino e conti del Duecento,* ed. Sebastiano Lo Nigro (Turin: UTET, 1968), 87–88.

22. Odo's parable is found in Léopold Hervieux, *Les Fabulistes Latins, Vol. 4: Les Fables et les Paraboles d'Études de Cheriton* (Paris: Librairie de Firmin-Didot, 1869), 409.

23. The novella of Lisabetta da Messina (*Dec.* IV, 5) has been the subject of a number of studies. See, in particular, Mario Baratto and Mario Lavagetto, eds., *Il testo moltiplicato: Lettura di una novella del* Decameron, Le Forme del discorso, no. 31 (Parma: Pratiche Editrice, 1982), which contains five different perspectives on the tale (sociological, psychoanalytic, narratological, linguistic, and anthropological) by Baratto, Serpieri, Segre, Nencioni, and Cirese, respectively.

24. For critical readings of the novella of Tancredi and Ghismonda (*Dec.* IV, 1), see Luigi Russo, *Letture critiche del* Decameron, Universale Laterza, no. 66 (1956; Bari: Laterza, 1970), 156–62; also Marcus, 44–62; Mazzotta, 131–58; and Forni. The element of father-daughter incest was proposed by Almansi (133–57) and alluded to by Baratto, 180–95, and by Alberto Moravia in his essay "Boccaccio," in *L'uomo come fine,* I Satelliti Bompiani (Milan: Bompiani, 1964), 138–58.

25. Tancredi's "heartless murder" of his daughter's lover, Guiscardo, is similar to the type of vengeance carried out in the novella of Rossiglione and Guardastagno (*Dec.* IV, 9). Here the betrayed husband murders and disembowels his wife's lover, then deceitfully has a meal prepared with the extracted heart that he feeds to his wife. I examine the various versions of this tale in "The Medieval Legend of the Eaten Heart," in *Storytelling: Interdisciplinary and Intercultural Perspectives,* eds. Irene Maria Blayer and Monica Sanchez (New York: Peter Lang, 2002), 86–101.

26. See Iacopo Passavanti, *Specchio della vera penitenza,* in *Racconti esemplari di predicatori del Due e Trecento,* ed. Giorgio Varanini and Guido Baldassarri, 3 vols., I Novellieri italiani, no. 4 (Rome: Salerno Editrice, 1993), 2:602–6.

2

The Crisis of Word and Deed in *Decameron* V, 10

Susan Gaylard

The tale of Madonna Oretta, the first tale of Day Six, has received much critical attention as the midpoint of Boccaccio's *Decameron*, but the tenth story of the preceding day has not. And yet this novella is just as central as the one that follows it; indeed, if one counts the Author's tale in the Introduction to Day Four, the final story of Day Five is the fifty-first tale. This novella could thus even challenge the status of Madonna Oretta's story as a key to reading the *Decameron* as a whole—a parallel of *Purgatory* XVII, 51 of Dante's *Commedia*.[1] Roberta Bruno Pagnamenta observes the symmetry between the two central tales of the *Decameron*: whereas the first story of Day Six is about telling stories, the last tale of Day Five is about the fruits of storytelling.[2] This essay will argue that these two tales together, through the play of metaphors used to describe sex and storytelling, constitute a crisis at the midpoint of the work. Considering the ample critical attention directed to VI, 1, this essay will examine primarily V, 10 within the context of VI, 1.

The interplay between the notions of words and deeds through literalization and metaphorization is a common and noted theme throughout the *Decameron*. Teodolinda Barolini begins her discussion of the sexual poetics of the *Decameron* with the adage "le parole son femmine e i fatti son maschi" (words are female and actions are male), noting that the two categories necessarily contaminate each other by virtue of the fact that "fatti" is itself a *parola*.[3] Barolini reminds us of Boccaccio's insistence on the forced immobility of his supposedly female audience, who are physically *racchiuse* while they are by nature—at least according to Pampinea in I, Intro., 75—metaphorically *mobili*. By contrast, men have ample freedom to enjoy a variety of *fatti*: "a loro, volendo essi, non manca l'andare a torno, udire e vedere molte cose, uccellare, cacciare, pescare, cavalcare, giucare o mercatare" (*Proemio*, 12).[4] ([I]f they wish, they can take a walk and listen to or look at many different things; they can go hawking, hunting, or fishing; they can ride, gamble, or attend to business.)[5] The old woman in V, 10 echoes the author's assertion, insisting that women can do only one thing—sex—while men can do thousands of things.[6] Barolini, however, argues that the wide variety of metaphors used to describe sex in the *Decameron* allows "the one thing women do to take on the dimension of the many things men do" (196). Barolini concludes that the *Decameron* essentially reverses another proverb so that "le parole fanno fatti" (197). Barolini's hypothesis seems valid for the *Decameron* as a whole; however, it is my contention that, at the central point of the *Decameron*, the gendered categories of word and deed are both profoundly blurred and irremediably separate at the very point at which they should connect: the passage from the day of deeds to that of words.

In the *Proemio*, 10, Boccaccio states that women, "il piú del tempo nel piccolo circuito delle loro camere racchiuse" (most of the time limited to the narrow confines of their bedrooms), must seek pleasure from mere *parole*, through the stories they are being told. The Author's Conclusion affirms that women have as much time available to them to read the tales as they are unable to spend in amorous delights: they can take pleasure in reading when the pleasures of love are unavailable. Unlike these "idle ladies," men of letters read "non per passare ma per utilmente adoperare il tempo faticano" (Concl., 21) (not just to pass the time away, but to employ their time to the greatest advantage [Musa and Bondanella, 687]); therefore, for them, these tales of pleasure might well be a waste of time.

Robert Hollander has argued convincingly for an essentially modern and individualistic interpretation of the enigmatic concept of "utilità" in the *Decameron*.[7] According to his analysis, the stories describe all of us "exercising our wills in pursuit of the goods of the world as we perceive them good. In that pursuit it is *utilità* which we seek—that alone is *dolce* to us, whether it be money, power over others, sexual pleasure" ("*Utilità*," 227–28). Thus, we could understand the *utile consiglio* that—along with pleasure—Boccaccio's proem promises to young women in love as advice that might lead these women from being idle and closed in to using their time "to the greatest advantage" as men do. If this were the case, then these women, like the men, would ultimately have less time for reading: they would move away from Boccaccio's tales of pleasure to the pleasure of actions.

It is in this light that we can consider the alternative title of the *Decameron*: *Prencipe Galeotto*, a book of pleasure that is useful in that it might facilitate factual pleasure by moving the (female) reader from the realm of words to the (male) realm of deeds. The old woman of V, 10, herself a literal go-between or Galeotto, underscores the book's Galeotto function, echoing the wording of the Author's Conclusion as she insists that youth should not be wasted in stories:

> Di questo mondo ha ciascun tanto quanto egli se ne toglie, e spezialmente le femine, alle quali si convien troppo piú *d'adoperare il tempo* quando l'hanno che agli

uomini, per ciò che . . . quando c'invecchiamo, né marito né altri ci vuol vedere anzi ci cacciano in cucina a dir delle favole con la gatta. (V, 10, 20–21, emphasis added) (In this world, you've got to grab what you can get, and especially a woman, who needs, even more than men, *to take advantage of every opportunity that presents itself.* For . . . when we get old, no husband or anyone else cares to look at us; on the contrary, we are chased into the kitchen to tell stories to the cat [Musa and Bondanella, 371].)

The essentially male activity of using time to one's advantage, here claimed for young women, is in sharp contrast with women's eventual fate of telling tales with the cat, possibly an echo of the Tuscan proverb "dove son donne e gatti, son più parole che fatti."[8] Moreover, the idea that we each have what we can take from the world seems to anticipate Boccaccio's insistence in his Conclusion that the usefulness of his book depends on what each reader gets from it.

It is the old woman's (verbal) affirmation of her own power over men that leads the wife of the tale from the arguments wasted on her husband to a succession of enjoyable *fatti* with other young men. In a parallel of the author's claim to provide useful advice to adept readers, the old woman professes herself to be the most useful person in the world to her listener, as she claims a re-creative ability that is literally authorial:

[T]u non potevi a persona del mondo scoprire l'animo tuo che più utile ti fosse di me, per ciò che egli non è alcun sí forbito, al quale io non ardisca di dire ciò che bisogna, né sí duro o zotico, che io non ammorbidisca bene e rechilo a ciò che io vorrò. (V, 10, 22)

([T]here is no one in the world you could have revealed your thoughts to who could be more helpful to you than I, for there is no man refined enough to stop me from telling him what he needs, nor is there a man so uncouth and uncultivated that I cannot easily soften him up and bring him around to my way of thinking [Musa and Bondanella, 371–72].)

The old woman's claim to be able to create what she will, using words to mold and sculpt her material, inverts the gender roles of Aristotle's theory of generation. According to the Aristotelian paradigm dear to many late-medieval (male) writers, "the female always provides the material, the male provides that which fashions the material into shape" (II, iv, 738b).[9] The old woman's assertion of artistic authority also evokes the Christian paradigm of creation, both through God's molding of earth in Genesis 2:7 and through the (male) Word (John 1:1–3).

Robert Hollander has pointed out that, for Dante, the supreme creator was God.[10] According to Hollander, Boccaccio in polemic with Dante exalts Giotto's art, rather than God's, as supreme mimicry of nature (*Dec.* VI, 5, 5–6). Boccaccio then appropriates for himself the creative authority of a painter who can indeed depict Christ, the Word—and male—himself: "egli fa Cristo maschio" (Concl.,

6). In the final tale of Day Five, the old woman's feminine verbal reclamation of the Aristotelian paradigm is a clear parallel of Boccaccio's appropriation of authority, particularly since the supreme philosopher and "autore" for Dante (and much of the Middle Ages) was Aristotle.[11]

In her story, the *vecchia* advocates the wife's conversion from words into actions in the name of God: "Figliuola mia, sallo Idio, che sa tutte le cose, che tu molto ben fai; e . . . sí il dovresti far tu e ciascuna giovane per non perdere il tempo della vostra giovanezza" (V, 10, 15). (My child, God knows, for He knows everything, that you are acting for the best; . . . you and every other young woman should do it in order not to waste the opportunities your youth affords you [Musa and Bondanella, 371].) This Galeotto's injunction to the pleasure of actions over words is therefore justified in the name of the Word, which is action. Conversely, the author justifies the verbal pleasure of the *Prencipe Galeotto* in the name of the great writers, including Guido Cavalcanti and Dante Alighieri (IV, Intro., 33). In her brief manifesto, the old woman seems to appropriate both for herself and for the author an authority that would affirm the Galeotto function of the text.

A dichotomy between word and deed appears highlighted in the shift from an emphasis on actions in Day Five to words in Day Six. The rubrics to the two days indicate a change in agency. The topic of Day Five is "ciò che a alcuno amante, dopo alcuni fieri o sventurati accidenti, felicemente avvenisse" (lovers who, after unhappy or misfortunate happenings, attained happiness [Musa and Bondanella, 313]). By contrast, the rubric to Day Six is "chi con alcun leggiadro motto, tentato, si riscotesse, o con pronta risposta o avvedimento fuggí perdita o pericolo o scorno" (those who, having been provoked by some witty remark, have defended themselves with the same, or who, with a ready reply or some other shrewd move, have managed to escape danger, loss, or ridicule [Musa and Bondanella, 380]). This apparent movement from male-oriented actions to the "female" domain of words is an oversimplification, as is clear from the literal confusion of gender roles at the end of V, 10. The gender associations of the rubrics are explicitly negated at the beginning of Day Six, as Filomena declares that modern women are incapable both of using words to their advantage and of understanding witty remarks; her tale (VI, 1) is an exception to the rule.

The first tale of Day Six deals with verbal pleasure, as the knight offers to "carry" Madonna Oretta "on horseback" by entertaining her along the way with a story. This traditional chivalric gesture fails when the *cavaliere* is unable to impose appropriate verbal form on what is apparently delightful content. His audience and the object of his (metaphorical) chivalric attentions, Madonna Oretta, is able in one deftly handled sentence to bring the "horse" to a halt. The knight, who is said to be "molto migliore intenditor che novellatore," laughs at Madonna Oretta's *motto* and starts telling other stories.

Alan Freedman has pointed out that this ending is a travesty of Madonna Oretta's wit.[12] The lady asks to be set down from the horse, only to have the *cavaliere* underinterpret her words, excluding himself as the brunt of the joke.

Thus the male figure demonstrates the interpretative obtuseness that Filomena regrets is typical of maladroit modern women (VI, 1, 3). In the ninth story of the Sixth Day, the *cavalieri* underinterpret the witty motto of "Guido di messer Cavalcante de' Cavalcanti." This "great leader among horsemen" who, like Madonna Oretta, is really on foot, escapes because as a man he is able to act: his words are poorly understood by his audience.[13] By contrast, at the beginning of Day Six, Madonna Oretta has only words at her disposal and is therefore forced to remain a passive listener on the knight's "horse." Here the inept horseman—the antithesis of Cavalcanti—lacks both verbal and interpretative skill so that Filomena's story has no real resolution.

The metaphor of a horse for a novella, of a knight beguiling a lady with a tale so that she feels as though she were riding, recalls the prevalent use of riding and horse lexicon to describe intercourse elsewhere in the *Decameron* (III, 2; III, 4, 25; VII, 2, 34; VIII, 4, 32; IX, 10). Franco Fido notes the disparagement of the knight's sexual prowess in the comment about his swordsmanship as well as the ironic "antiorgasmo" produced in Madonna Oretta.[14] This *cavaliere* indeed lacks skill if he is unable to produce a comfortable trot on a palfrey, the type of horse used for travel and suitable even for a lady. V. A. Kolve has traced the traditional medieval association of the horse "with sexual prowess and freedom."[15] For example, in the *Roman de la rose*, Genius praises copulation in terms of *chevalerie*, that is, "horsemanship" as a means of reproduction. If it were not for the *chevalerie* of our parents, we would not now be alive: "Se ne fust leur chevalerie, / Vous ne fussiez pas ore en vie" (lines 19791–92).[16]

Moreover, Daniela Delcorno Branca has noted the significance of the two couples on horseback portrayed on the title page of a manuscript possibly produced under the guidance of Boccaccio himself (Paris, B.N., ital. MS 482).[17] Lancelot and Guinevere are depicted on the right, embracing—a metaphorical coupling; Galehaut ("Galeotto") and the Dame de Malehaut are on the left, holding hands. According to Delcorno Branca (163), the image offers a positive revision of the episode condemned in *Inferno* V, 137, by illustrating one of the rare happy moments of the Lancelot love story: the moment in which Guinevere has just conceded the Dame de Malehaut to Galehaut. In the initial below this miniature, the author is reading stories to a primarily female audience while Cupid hovers overhead, his bow drawn. It seems clear, as Delcorno Branca suggests, that the title page of this early manuscript offers a positive reading of the *Decameron*'s subtitle *Galeotto*: "il libro e chi lo scrisse."

This apparent simultaneity of Galeotto the book and its effects seems to indicate a close relationship between linguistic and sensual pleasure. If storytelling and sexual intimacy are correlated through the metalanguage of theatrical chivalric gestures, the connections between the Days, and particularly between V, 10 and VI, 1, appear much closer. Moreover, the verbal action of imposing form—in which both the knight and Madonna Oretta fail because she is unable to negate

form and content by imposing silence—connects the tale even more closely with
the protagonist of V, 10.

Pietro di Vinciolo at the end of Day Five indeed has some surprising points of
similarity with the knight at the beginning of Day Six. Pietro marries for the sake of
appearance, and therefore his marriage vows, like the knight's promise of a good
horseback ride, are *parole senza fatti*: a traditionally feminine failing, in the medieval
view. In both cases, the man's sexuality is under examination: Pietro because he
is homosexual, and the *cavaliere* because of the links among intercourse, riding,
and storytelling. Furthermore, both Pietro and the *cavaliere* tell a story within a
story. Unlike the knight, however, Pietro is capable both of telling someone else's
story and, more significantly, of imposing his own form on what becomes his story,
so that it too can be resolved under Fiammetta's rubric, "di ciò che a alcuno
amante . . . felicemente avvenisse" (the adventures of lovers who . . . attained happiness). The ending of the tale allows for a doubled, if not a tripled, interpretation, as it
fits the rubric from the point of view of the wife and presumably of the lover.

There are some significant differences between Pietro di Vinciolo and Boccaccio's apparent source in Apuleius.[18] In his *Metamorphoses* IX, 14–28, the
baker returns home early from the fuller's house, interrupting a tryst between his
wife and one of her lovers. She manages to hide the lover, and her husband
explains why he is home early: dinner was interrupted by the discovery of his
friend's wife's lover in the house. The baker's wife pretends to be horrified; later
it is discovered that she is herself hiding a lover in the house. The structure of the
story thus far appears identical to Boccaccio's version. The shocked Apuleian
baker, however, vigorously vituperates his friend's wife, saying

Nefarium . . . et extremum facinus perditae feminae tolerare nequiens fuga me pro-
ripui. Hem qualis, dii boni, matrona, quam fida quamque sobria turpissimo se
dedecore foedavit! Iuro . . . ego . . . me nunc etiam meis oculis de tali muliere minus
credere. (*Met.* IX, 23)[19]

(It was unspeakable and terrible . . . what that depraved woman did! I could not
endure it, and I rushed away to escape. Good gods, to think that such a lady, so faithful and sober, has befouled herself so shamefully and disgracefully! I
swear . . . even now I can hardly believe my own eyes about a woman like that.)

The Apuleian character's surprise and disgust are nowhere echoed by Boccaccio's
Pietro, who comments only, "io, temendo per me medesimo la segnoria . . . non
lo lasciai uccidere" (fearing for my own neck should the police get involved, I
jumped up and prevented Ercolano from murdering the man [V, 10, 41]). This
remark revisits Apuleius, where the baker intervenes to prevent the murder of the
lover and even persuades the wife to leave the house until the husband's anger
subsides. Apuleius's baker is motivated by "communi periculo," in contrast to

Boccaccio's isolationist Pietro, concerned for "me medesimo." In Boccaccio's version of the story within the story, the wife flees and the lover is taken away, both to some unknown place.

Given the Apuleian character's vituperative commentary on his friend's wife, it is consistent for him to take revenge for adultery in his own house: reneging on his promise of a threesome, he sodomizes the young lover all night while his wife is locked up elsewhere, then has the man flogged, and later divorces his wife. Unlike his Apuleian antecedent, Pietro relates Ercolano's story without comment. It is precisely this reticence that facilitates the Boccaccian solution. Pietro's tacit refusal to recast in moralistic terms someone else's story allows him to recast in his own terms, and to his own (literal) ends, what turns out to be the prototype of his own story.

In the Apuleian episode, the baker does not berate his own wife, reserving his strictures for the lover who, still "tam mollis ac tener et admodum puer" (soft and tender, . . . a child), should not be cheating male lovers by chasing women and breaking up marriages (IX, 28). Boccaccio's Pietro does vituperate his wife, but not for her adultery. Instead, he attacks her for her typically feminine hypocrisy, for the lack of correlation between her words and deeds:

> "Or tu maladicevi cosí testé la moglie d'Ercolano e dicevi che arder si vorrebbe e che ella era vergogna di tutte voi: come non dicevi di te medesima? . . . [C]ome ti sofferiva l'animo di dir di lei, sentendoti quello medesimo aver fatto che ella fatto avea? Certo niuna altra cosa vi t'induceva se non che voi siete tutte cosí fatte, e con l'altrui colpe guatate di ricoprire i vostri falli." (*Dec.* V, 10, 54)

> (Just a moment ago when you were carrying on, cursing Ercolano's wife in such a fashion and saying that she should be burned and that she was the disgrace of all you women, why didn't you say the same about yourself? . . . [H]ow did you have the nerve to talk about her, when you had done the same thing she did? Certainly nothing made you do it other than the fact that you women are all alike, and you like to cover up your own transgressions with the faults of others [Musa and Bondanella, 375].)

Here, verbal dissimulation, or telling tales (a feminine vice, as Pietro insists), is regarded with a deeper disgust than is adultery. Significantly, having damned all women as hypocrites, Pietro invokes divine—or perhaps Dantean—retribution: "che venir possa fuoco da cielo che tutte v'arda, generazion pessima che voi siete!" (V, 10, 54). (I just wish a fire would descend from Heaven and burn the whole disgusting lot of you up! [Musa and Bondanella, 375])

This is a crucial moment in the tale. The punishment invoked for the wife's false words—fire falling from the heavens—is apparent both in the third *girone* of the seventh circle of Dante's *Inferno*, where violence against God, Nature, or industry is punished, and in the eighth circle, where simple fraud is punished.

The Inquisition had recently adopted the punishment of being burnt alive for "sins against nature," which by Dante's day included the increasingly demonized sin of homosexuality.[20] According to Genesis 19:24, a passage commonly invoked with reference to homosexual behavior, "the Lord rained down burning sulphur on Sodom and Gomorrah—from the Lord out of the heavens."[21] Given Pietro's reference to divine retribution, one might expect the wife in the tale to insist that fire is more likely to descend from heaven to burn her husband and all other sodomites. Instead, she reiterates her husband's words, saying, "Io ne son molto certa che tu vorresti che fuoco venisse da cielo che tutte ci ardesse, sí come colui che se' cosí vago di noi come il can delle mazze; ma alla croce di Dio egli non ti verrà fatto" (V, 10, 55). (I'm sure you'd like fire to descend from Heaven and burn us all up, for you are about as fond of women as a dog is of a whipping;[22] but by God's Holy Cross, you won't see it happen! [Musa and Bondanella, 375].)

It is hardly conceivable within the logic of the tale that the wife would not be familiar with the punishment for a sin that she herself identifies as contrary to both the law and Nature, in contrast with her own adultery, which transgresses only the law (V, 10, 13). Even if we accept that male homosexuality in late medieval Florence was ineradicable (Johansson and Percy, 177), it appears nonetheless that the wife, by repeating Pietro's words without reallocating the punishment, reinforces through repetition the notion that she is the one who deserves to be punished. However, she invokes the cross—the sign of Christ, the Word—in saying that the punishment "will not be done." In the wife's phrase just cited, "non ti verrà fatto" can be read in context as meaning that the punishment will not be done for the husband, but it could also mean that the punishment will not be done to him. In either case, the Word is invoked to preclude the husband's words' becoming *fatti*: thus, in the wife's formulation, the Word refutes its own power to effect the transition from the spoken optative to the real, just as it denies the truth of its own written representation.

In addition to this paradox, nowhere in the novella is the traditional punishment of sodomites associated with the homosexual Pietro di Vinciolo or his friend Ercolano. Vittore Branca (*Dec.* 2:698, n. 8) notes that the name Ercolano—that of the city's martyred saint and former bishop—was diffuse in Perugia; Manlio Pastore Stocchi (352) points out the traditional homosexual stigma immediately summoned up by the narrative opening of the tale: "Fu in Perugia . . ." (IV, 10, 6). The typically Perugian name, to which the narrator apparently draws unnecessary attention, seems to imply underlying homosexuality. This would belie the assertion that Ercolano's wife "ha di lui ciò che ella vuole" (V, 10, 56) (gets what she wants from her husband [Musa and Bondanella, 375]).

Sulphur, fire, and death are associated with Ercolano's wife's lover, who is nearly killed by sulphur fumes,[23] and then with Ercolano's wife, as Pietro's wife declares: "[C]osí fatte femine . . . si vorrebbero uccidere, elle si vorrebbon vive

vive metter nel fuoco e farne cenere!" (V, 10, 45). ([S]uch women deserve to be killed, to be burned alive and reduced to ashes! [Musa and Bondanella, 374].) Finally, in the optative punishment discussed earlier, Pietro's wife is associated with fire and death. Thus, in this novella, the wife's hypocrisy and the husband's homosexuality are at best equally culpable if, in fact, hypocrisy is not considered in a worse light, given both the Dantean position of perpetrators of simple fraud as lower than sinners against God and Nature and the repeated association of the punishment for sodomy with the heterosexual lovers in the tale.

Following the Aristotelian theory of generation, medieval theorists typically connect procreation, writing, and coining. Thus, Alain de Lille and Jean de Meun condemn sodomy as a male refusal to impose form on receptive female material. Whereas Alain de Lille denounces the stamp that leaves no imprint,[24] Jean de Meun's Genius condemns

> [. . .] cil qui des greffes n'escrivent
> Par coi li mortel toz jors vivent,
> Es beles tables precieuses
> —Que nature, . . .
> leur avoit pour ce prestees
> Que tuit i fussent escrivain. (*Roman de la Rose*, II. 19633–39)

> (. . . those who do not write with their styluses, by which mortals live forever, on the beautiful precious tablets that Nature . . . loaned to them in order that everyone might be a writer.)[25]

The idea of procreation is clearly connected with the idea of male authorship as "come l'*uom* s'etterna" (*Inf.* XV, 85, emphasis added). Ronald L. Martinez notes the irony in the claim that Dante's Brunetto leaves his "buona imagine paterna" on his pupil Dante.[26] Hollander observes that Boccaccio's Cepparello is an antithetical version of Dante's Brunetto: both are sodomites and notaries (their profession is connected etymologically and practically with writing) who teach how man makes himself eternal through words ("Boccaccio's Dante," 182). Gloria Allaire has demonstrated that Frate Cipolla, another homosexual famed for his ability to tell stories, gains credibility due also to his talents as a writer (that is, as a scribe).[27] The irony of these homosexual characters is that sodomy as the sterile sin cannot (pro)create or write on the tablet of life and is the sin against the creator, the Word.

Homosexuality was forced into the paradigm of "facts without words," the unmentionable sin that already "in Dante's day . . . dare[d] not speak its name" (Durling and Martinez, 557). Whereas the knight in VI, 1 is a feeble storyteller, Pietro in V, 10 is an able storyteller who nonetheless initiates a progressive movement toward the reticence traditionally intrinsic to the "sin without words." When he becomes the protagonist of the story he has just told, Pietro reformulates the indirection of the prototype story through silence, as his conjunctive solution negates creation and writing. Although he invites the lover to tell him "everything," the lover's discourse is elided as redundant (V, 10, 53). Pietro briefly vituperates his wife for her words, using the verb *dire* or its derivation *maladire* no less than five times in two sentences,[28] and calling for the destruction of women who represent for him (false) words. In an ironic contradiction of the "sin without words," Pietro initially acts only through words: "altro male che di parole fatto non l'avea" (V, 10, 55). (Pietro was going to inflict nothing worse than words upon her [Musa and Bondanella, 375].)

Pietro, concerned ultimately with the action that negates words, "s'avide che le parole non eran per venir meno in tutta notte" (realized that words would not fail her all night long [V, 10, 59; translation mine]). He silences his wife, insisting on the *fare* of dinner, rather than the endless *parlare*! Pietro mentions elliptically that his wife will not have cause to complain, and then initiates the unmentionable solution. By symbolically silencing the narrative of his own story through its resolution, Pietro moreover imposes silence on an uncharacteristically reticent Dioneo, who elides the solution from his narration: "quello che Pietro si divisasse a sodisfacimento di tutti e tre m'è uscito di mente" (V, 10, 63). (What exactly Pietro had thought up to satisfy all three of them after supper now slips my mind [Musa and Bondanella, 376].) Pietro's solution further quiets the *brigata*, who laugh less than usual, "meno per vergogna . . . che per poco diletto" (V, Concl., 1) (more out of modesty than lack of amusement [Musa and Bondanella, 376]). This silencing extends to modern-day critics, who seem to have little to say about Pietro's story.

The storytelling *cavalcare* of the knight in VI, 1 is a verbal gesture that never leads to real sex but only to a formless flow of words, endless stories without resolution, *parole* never leading to the satisfaction of *fatti*. Unlike the sodomites Cepparello and Cipolla—both of whom are adept storytellers—the knight is incapable of imposing verbal form on even the most receptive content; metaphorical and actual sexual power to *cavalcare* are simultaneously denied to him. His title *cavaliere* is as ironic as Cepparello's sainthood and Brunetto's metaphorical generation of Dante in *Inferno* XV. By contrast with this knight, Pietro di Vinciolo, although able to tell a story, reformulates the story he has told through a factual *cavalcare* that can never be expressed in words to the extent that even the riding metaphor seems inapposite, since his action cannot impose physical form on content.

This symmetrically signified double break between the word and the deed, or the deed and the word, precisely at the midpoint of the *Decameron*, seems to call into question the self-proclaimed status of the work as a *Galeotto*, a book in which the *diletto* of words leads directly to the *diletto* of deeds. Moreover, the break between deeds and the Word also seems clear: the Church's prescribed punishment for sodomy and hypocrisy—punishment associated here only with the heterosexuals—is bandied about verbally, but "alla croce di Dio" these verbal threats will not become fact, according to Pietro's wife, the woman guilty of false words (V, 10, 55).

And yet it appears that the wife in V, 10 does turn words into deeds. In the first part of the story, her affairs prosper through the agency of the old woman, the Galeotto figure. However, the wife's eventual downfall is through her own words: in contrast with Pietro's reticence in relating Ercolano's story, the wife's profuse commentary is a negative move from her previous conversion of *utile consiglio* into *diletto*, to "telling tales"; that is, converting factual *diletto* into verbal dissimulation. As with the knight's "horse" in VI, 1, the wife's discourse must be halted by someone else: "le parole non eran per venir meno in tutta notte" (V, 10, 59). In VI, 1 Madonna Oretta silences the knight only momentarily, because as a woman she depends on the agency of words. By contrast, the wife of V, 10 is silenced by her husband's male authority to act. The diametric opposite of her reticent homosexual husband, the wife is unable to impose consistent form on her own story. Ironically, the story's resolution must be therefore be imposed by Pietro, and thus it negates form entirely.

We noted earlier the parallels between Boccaccio's appropriation of artistic authority (VI, 5, 5–6; Concl., 6) and the *vecchia*'s claim in V, 10 to godlike power to re-create and re-mold through language. Certainly the old woman's efforts as a Galeotto seem successful, although even she discards the human material that is so hard as to be the rock, Pietro.[29] As Galeotto and giver of *utile consiglio*, the old woman wields formative power over the tale and, by extension, over the women supposedly comprising Boccaccio's audience. However, she represents a disconcerting rift between word and deed, as she completes endless and apparently meaningless religious gestures (V, 10, 14). Almost everyone considers her a saint on account of her deeds. This suggests that she is a feminine counterpart to Cepparello and Cipolla, all of whom come to be venerated on account of their words. Although Cepparello and Cipolla are associated with speaking and writing, the old woman's authority derives from her claim to a verbal power that essentially re-forms.

If we accept Hollander's connection between Dante's Brunetto and Boccaccio's Cepparello ("Boccaccio's Dante"), we can even see the old woman's useful advice to do rather than to tell tales as teaching how man makes himself eternal. This revision of Dante's use of the phrase is consistent with the antisodomy invective in the *Roman de la Rose*. However, the old woman represents a word-deed contradiction that is inevitable precisely because she is an old woman and thus cannot convert her advice to actual sex, just as Brunetto's metaphors cannot convert to actual "fathering." Similarly, although the *Decameron* refers to old men as sexually vigorous and the author asserts that this is true also for himself (IV, Intro., 33), it is evident that Boccaccio is reduced to telling tales like an old, infertile woman.

It is perhaps symptomatic of the contradictions at the center of the *Decameron* that the figure who most closely represents the agency of Galeotto in V, 10 is the character whose discourse is elided and who makes no claims to authorial power or transcendent truth. The unnamed lover through whom the husband and wife are finally joined might be said to assume the role of literal Galeotto: his success in "uniting" this unlikely couple eclipses the achievements of the *vecchia* as Galeotto. The passivity and silence inherent in his narrative and sexual role question the claims of Boccaccio's tales as Galeotto.

A disjunction in the word-to-deed conversion process is intimated by the intrusion of the two servants into the frame tale between Days Five and Six, ostensibly days of *fatti* and *parole*.[30] In the Introduction to Day Six, Licisca silences her male counterpart and asserts the truth of sexual *fatti* in the lives of young women. On the *parole* side of the division between the days, Licisca swears by faith in Christ the Word to an absolute correlation between her words and fact: "Alla fé di Cristo, ché debbo sapere quello che io mi dico quando io giuro" (VI, Intro., 10). (I swear by the faith of Christ—and I don't swear like that if I don't know what I'm saying [Musa and Bondanella, 381, modified].) In the passage from V, 10, 55 (quoted earlier), Pietro's wife, the dissembler in words in the previous tale, has just sworn by the sign of the cross that there will be no correspondence between Pietro's word and fact; that is, no divine retribution.

Rather like Pietro's wife, who could go on talking all night, Licisca has to be silenced by threats of action. Her interruption follows a parallel episode at the end of Day Five, in which Elissa, the new queen, asks Dioneo to sing a song. Whereas Licisca's discourse asserts its correspondence with *fatti*, Dioneo's almost uncontrollable flood of song suggestions are *ciance*, bawdy idiocies that are symptomatic of the breach between sexual delight and mere stories about delight that the *brigata*, and Dioneo in particular, narrate (V, Concl., 9–15). The entire project of the *Decameron* is threatened by Dioneo's assertion, "Io ne so piú di mille": The thousand or more "empty" songs that Dioneo knows could engulf Boccaccio's mere one hundred tales, overriding the conditions imposed by the queen and confounding not only the symbolic order of the *brigata* but also the Galeotto function of the text.

Dioneo submits to Elissa's repeated attempts to check his verbal flow once she symbolically retracts the imposed rule of the day: "lascia stare il motteggiare" (stop joking around [V, Concl., 14]). The restrained stilnovism of the song he eventually sings seems parodic, contrasted with the thousand or more bawdy *ciance* he would have produced. In the lyrics of this song, Branca (*Dec.* 2:709, n. 7) notes that there are multiple echoes of other poets, including Cino da Pistoia and Dante, whom Boccaccio had earlier cited as authorities to justify the enterprise of writing to please women (IV, Intro., 33). Both the love song Dioneo eventually sings and the endless flow of bawdy songs cannot convert to facts without threatening the enterprise of the larger *Galeotto*: literature must remain literature.

Elissa, who imposes the rule of the *motto* and then has to retract it to restrain Dioneo's discourse, herself represents a combination of femininity with masculinity, words and deeds. In Boccaccio's account, Elissa was the original name of Dido and was renamed because "posita feminea mollicie et firmato in virile robur animo, ex quo postea Didonis nomen meruit, Phenicum lingua sonans quod virago latina" (she cast aside womanly weakness and hardened her spirit to manly strength): "Dido" means "heroic" (*De mulieribus claris*, XLII, 5).[31] In Boccaccio's rewriting, Dido chooses suicide as a last defense of her chastity against a marriage that is the result of a verbal trap. Although Dido founds a city and thus makes herself immortal through (manly) acts, she ultimately silences herself, ending her story as abruptly as Pietro di Vinciolo ends his. Thus, the importance of Elissa's topic for the day, the power of words to escape "perdita o pericolo o scorno" is highlighted by the Elissa/Dido story, in which words constitute both *pericolo* and an insufficient defense against *pericolo*. The only way in which Boccaccio's Dido can remain true to her word (her vow of chastity) is by negating words entirely.

The contradictions at the beginning of Elissa's rule intensify the significance of the Elissa/Dido story. Although the rule of *motti* might appear to assert the power of words, Elissa is unable to silence first Dioneo and then Licisca without the threat of action: her repeated verbal requests have no effect on their discourse (V, Concl., 14; VI, Intro., 11). Similarly, in VI, 1 Madonna Oretta's *motto* is unable to halt the knight's "horse"; the story therefore lacks resolution and can never move from telling tales to the horsemanship that results in procreation. In V, 10, Pietro's story is resolved through a *cavalcare* that can be expressed only through silence. The simultaneity of the *Galeotto* book and its effects as seen in the medieval pictorial tradition of Galeotto on horseback is inherently denied at the very midpoint of the text.

The various forms of Galeotto at the center of the *Decameron* are essentially paradoxical. The old woman in V, 10 claims a male, authorial, godlike power to mold human material through words, yet neither she nor the author can move from the realm of *parole* to that of *fatti*: their useful advice might just as well be *ciance*. Dioneo's poem at the end of Day Five is a defeatist Galeotto that can never lead to actions without threatening the integrity of the book *Galeotto*. The role of literal Galeotto accorded to the passive and silent male lover in V, 10 belies the power of words claimed by the others.

The multiple and often contradictory or suspect claims about words and the Word threaten the very idea of agency through words. The old woman in V, 10 justifies her verbal injunctions to deeds in the name of God, just as Boccaccio justifies his stories in the name of the great writers. The servant Licisca affirms, by faith in the Word, a perfect correspondence between her words and *fatti*. Pietro's wife in V, 10 swears by "God's holy cross" that there is no divine retribution for the dissembler in words or for the sodomites, those who "exchanged the truth of

God for a lie" (Romans 1:25). In this last instance, the sign of the Word is invoked, ironically, to refute the Word's own agency.

The apparent impossibility of establishing a clear relationship between *parola* and *fatti*, to the extent that even God's truth is denied authority, highlights the irony of the *Galeotto* text: *utile consiglio* is really whatever the reader wants it to be. Thus it is not too surprising that the hypothetical continuum from the *cavalcare* of storytelling to the *cavalcare* of sex, posited by the title *Galeotto*, appears reversed by the passage from deeds to words indicated in the rubrics to Days Five and Six. This ironic turning back is highlighted by the impossibility of, first, the deed-to-word conversion in V, 10 and then the word-to-deed conversion in VI, 1. Both eternal silence and endless chatter threaten the enterprise of the *Galeotto* at its center, symptoms of the precariousness of the project and of the profound rift between words and actions, between mere *novellare* and active *cavalcare*.

Notes

An earlier version of this essay was presented at the Thirty-Sixth International Congress on Medieval Studies, Western Michigan University, Kalamazoo, Michigan, May 5, 2001.

1. Guido Almansi, "Lettura della novella di Madonna Oretta," *Paragone. Letteratura* 23.270 (1972): 139–40.
2. Roberta Bruno Pagnamenta, *Il* Decameron: *L'ambiguità come strategia narrativa*, Memoria del tempo, no. 14 (Ravenna: Longo Editore, 1999), 107.
3. Teodolinda Barolini, " 'Le parole son femmine e i fatti sono maschi.' Toward a sexual poetics of the *Decameron (Decameron* II. 10)," *Studi sul Boccaccio* 21 (1993): 175–76; hereafter cited in text as Barolini.
4. All references to the *Decameron* are taken from Vittore Branca's edition, 2 vols., Einaudi Tascabili. Classici, no. 99 (1980; reprint, Turin: Einaudi, 1992); hereafter cited in text as *Decameron.*
5. *The Decameron*, trans. Mark Musa and Peter Bondanella (New York: Penguin Books/New American Library/Mentor, 1982), 3. Except as noted, English quotations from the *Decameron* follow this translation, hereafter cited in text as Musa and Bondanella.
6. "Degli uomini non avvien cosí: essi nascono buoni a mille cose, non pure a questa, . . . ma le femine a niuna altra cosa che a fare questo e figliuoli ci nascono" (V, 10, 18).
7. Robert Hollander, "*Utilità* in Boccaccio's *Decameron*," *Studi sul Boccaccio* 15 (1984): 214–35; hereafter cited in text as "*Utilità*."
8. Fortunato Bellonzi, *Proverbi toscani* (Milan: Aldo Martello Editore, 1968), 9. Regarding possible erotic overtones in the sixteenth-century use of the noun "cat" and female genitalia, see the essay by Domenico Zanrè, chapter 9 in this volume.
9. Aristotle, *Generation of Animals*, trans. A. L. Peck, Loeb Classical Library, no. 366 (1943; rev. ed., London: William Heinemann Ltd, 1963), 185.

10. Robert Hollander, "Boccaccio's Dante: Imitative Distance," *Studi sul Boccaccio* 13 (1982): 194; hereafter cited in text as "Boccaccio's Dante."

11. Maria C. De Matteis, "Aristotele," in *Enciclopedia dantesca*, vol. 1 (Rome: Istituto della Enciclopedia Italiana, 1970), 373.

12. Alan Freedman, "Il cavallo del Boccaccio: fonte, struttura e funzione della metanovella di madonna Oretta," *Studi sul Boccaccio* 9 (1976): 237.

13. Robert M. Durling, "Boccaccio on Interpretation: Guido's Escape (*Decameron* VI.9)," in *Dante, Petrarch, Boccaccio: Studies in the Italian Trecento in Honor of Charles S. Singleton*, ed. Aldo S. Bernardo and Anthony L. Pellegrini, Medieval and Renaissance Texts and Studies, no. 22 (Binghamton, N.Y.: Center for Medieval and Early Renaissance Studies, 1983), 279–80.

14. Franco Fido, "Silenzi e cavalli nell'eros del *Decameron*," *Belfagor* 38 (1983): 82. The equivocal comments that Fido highlights are "forse non [gli] stava meglio la spada allato che 'l novellar nella lingua" (VI, 1, 9), and "a madonna Oretta, udendolo, spesse volte veniva un sudore e uno sfinimento di cuore, come se inferma fosse stata per terminare" (VI, 1, 10).

15. V.A. Kolve, *Chaucer and the Imagery of Narrative: The First Five Canterbury Tales* (Stanford, Calif.: Stanford University Press, 1984), 245.

16. Guillaume de Lorris and Jean de Meun, *Le roman de la rose*, ed. and trans. Armand Strubel, Lettres gothiques, no. 4533 (Paris: Librairie Générale Française, 1992).

17. Daniela Delcorno Branca, *Tristano e Lancilloto in Italia: Studi di letteratura arturiana*, Memoria del tempo, no. 11 (Ravenna: Longo Editore, 1998), 155–64.

18. For a discussion of sources for V, 10, see Manlio Pastore Stocchi, "Un antecedente latino-medievale di Pietro di Vinciolo (*Decameron*, V 10)," *Studi sul Boccaccio* 1 (1963): 349–62; hereafter cited in text as Pastore Stocchi. A second possible source is a twelfth-century Latin *contrasto* in which a wife vitupera her husband for his homosexual habits, insisting that she receive some attention herself. Eventually the two reach a compromise, agreeing to share the husband's lovers. Significantly, Pietro is the only protagonist who arranges for the simultaneous satisfaction of all three parties; Cavicchiolo, the husband in the poem, leaves the house as a young lover approaches. However, Francesco Bruni points out the possibility that this text might postdate the *Decameron* (*Boccaccio: L'invenzione della letteratura mezzana*, Collezione di testi e di studi, Linguistica e critica letteraria [Bologna: Società Editrice il Mulino, 1990], 321, n. 35).

19. Latin and English references are to Apuleius, *Metamorphoses*, ed. and trans. J. Arthur Hanson, 2 vols., Loeb Classical Library, nos. 453–54 (Cambridge, Mass.: Harvard University Press, 1989), 2:166–79.

20. Warren Johansson and William A. Percy, "Homosexuality," in *Handbook of Medieval Sexuality*, ed. Vern L. Bullough and James A. Brundage, Garland Reference Library of the Humanities, no. 1696 (New York: Garland Publishing, Inc., 1996), 169; hereafter cited in text as Johansson and Percy.

21. The Bible. *New International Version*, ed. Kenneth Barker (Grand Rapids, Mich.: Zondervan, 1995).

22. Ironically, her words mark him as guilty of sodomy: The metaphor "as fond of women as a dog is of a whipping" had been used by Boccaccio in Day I, Story 1

to describe the recognized sodomite Cepparello who was "as fond of women as dogs are of a beating with a stick" (Musa and Bondanella, 23). According to Branca, the phrase appears to have been almost proverbial (*Dec.* 1:53–54, n. 7).

23.   The sulphur reference might well merely be a useful reprise from Apuleius, where one would expect the fuller's wife to have clothes distended for bleaching by sulphur. However, it seems less likely that the wife of Ercolano, the "amico" of a rich man, would have garments bleaching under the stairs leading directly from the dining area (V, 10, 34–35). Branca notes the high social and political position of the Vincioli family (*Dec.* 2:694, n. 2). The narrator seems to sense this, insisting on the normalcy of the cupboard under the stairs.

24.   Alan of Lille, *The Plaint of Nature*, ed. and trans. James J. Sheridan, Mediaeval Sources in Translation, no. 26 (Toronto: Pontifical Institute of Mediaeval Studies, 1980), 69.

25.   Guillaume de Lorris and Jean de Meun, *The Romance of the Rose*, trans. Charles Dahlberg (1971; 3rd ed., Princeton, N.J.: Princeton University Press, 1995), 323.

26.   Dante Alighieri, *The Divine Comedy of Dante Alighieri: Inferno*, ed. and trans. Robert M. Durling and Ronald L. Martinez (New York: Oxford University Press, 1996), 558; hereafter cited in text as Durling and Martinez.

27.   Gloria Allaire, "The Written Eloquence of Frate Cipolla (*Decameron* VI, 10)," *Neophilologus* 82 (1998): 398–99.

28.   "Or tu *maladicevi* cosí testé la moglie d'Ercolano e *dicevi* che arder si vorrebbe e che ella era vergogna di tutte voi: come non *dicevi* di te medesima? o se di te *dir* non volevi, come ti sofferiva l'animo di *dir* di lei, sentendoti quello medesimo aver fatto che ella fatto avea?" (V, 10, 54, emphasis added).

29.   The Biblical resonance of the name Pietro with Peter, the "rock" on whom Christ—the Word—founded the Church, adds irony to the idea of immortalization through words.

30.   For an investigation into the role of servants and their relationships with their masters in the *Decameron*, see the following essay by Cormac Ó Cuilleanáin.

31.   Giovanni Boccaccio, *De mulieribus claris*, ed. Vittorio Zaccaria, in *Tutte le opere di Giovanni Boccaccio*, vol. 10, I Classici Mondadori (Milan: Arnoldo Mondadori Editore, 1998), 170; id., *Concerning Famous Women*, trans. Guido A. Guarino (New Brunswick, N.J.: Rutgers University Press, 1963), 87–89.

3

Master and Servant Roles in the *Decameron*

Cormac Ó Cuilleanáin

The *Decameron* offers a composite vision of society in its various forms, with special attention to the social consequences of individual desires.[1] The present essay considers an aspect of characterization central to that social vision. Boccaccio depicts the interaction of individual and society from not only a practical but also a poetic viewpoint, and his treatment of hierarchical relationships, especially the dealings of masters and servants, can be studied from several angles to highlight key issues and values at stake in the Hundred Tales, which are so often concerned with winning and losing, the struggle for power and mastery.

This topic begs some larger questions concerning the weight to be attached to fictional characters and the proper limits of any sympathy a reader might feel for them. Wayne C. Booth, in *The Rhetoric of Fiction*, cites José Ortega y Gasset's ban on fraternizing with characters: "Not only . . . is grieving and rejoicing at such human destinies as a work of art presents or narrates a very different thing from true artistic pleasure, but preoccupation with the human content of the work is in principle incompatible with aesthetic enjoyment proper." Booth goes on to disagree with Ortega:

> If we look closely at our reactions to most great novels, we discover that we feel a strong concern for the characters as people; . . . we are made to admire or detest, to love or hate, or simply to approve or disapprove of at least one central character, and our interest in reading from page to page, like our judgment upon the book after reconsideration, is inseparable from this emotional involvement. . . . Such concerns are not simply a necessary but impure base, as Ortega would have it, to "make contemplation possible." . . . In many first-rate works they are the very core of our experience."[2]

Booth is, of course, speaking of modern fiction, which frequently offers a seemingly organic linkage of character, feeling, and action. Characters in Boccaccio tend to be far less rounded and dimensional; most are given a light, perfunctory, noncomplex characterization far closer to the medieval *exemplum* than to the modern novel, and their motivations can often be represented in a formulaic manner.[3] Yet there are cases in the *Decameron* where, although individual characters are not particularly fleshed out, the relationships between them strike us as powerfully realistic and convincing. In other words, pairs or clusters of characters in Boccaccio might jointly contain the paradox, contradiction, or "dimension" that we routinely demand in modern characters.[4]

Our topic also raises the general status of ancillary figures in fiction, those half-realized, shadowy creatures who may move the action forward, act as intermediaries, or "start a scene or two" without ever springing fully into being.[5] The presence of these choral characters helps the protagonists to stand out from their bas-relief background with contrasting texture and depth. Modern literature offers many characters of the kind that Henry James described as "wheels to the coach" of the main story—not just the obvious featureless bystanders, but also some characters who appear to be capable of stepping into the foreground yet never quite manage it.[6] Medieval literature is likewise rich in lightly sketched secondary characters, some, but not all, of whom are cast as servants.[7] We also find servant characters stepping into the foreground and—like the nurse in *Romeo and Juliet* and her medieval forerunners—voicing important thematic elements of the story.[8]

At this point, it would be helpful to identify some typical conditions for the foregrounding of servant characters in Boccaccio, the most obvious case being the servant who wishes to transcend his or her status or who was never a genuine servant in the first place. We can start with "normal" portrayals of servants in the *Decameron* before considering some deviant cases. Some of the deviant cases are "abnormal" merely in the sense of being indecorous or indecent, but the best examples go far beyond that. Although Boccaccio skillfully uses master-servant interaction as part of his lifelike depiction of the texture of contemporary society and the realities of power, and even more skillfully uses servants for the construction of well-oiled, complex plots, the most effective uses of the master-servant nexus are metaphoric: the notion of love as service, and the use of a symbiotic master-servant duo to convey the mysteries of feeling and motivation, or the ambiguities of individual identity. On the simplest level, the depiction of social reality, servants, and relationships of service play a natural role in rounding out the social picture in the frame story and in many novellas, but the author's active approach to the elements in his stories means that servant characters often transcend this rather inert function.

Two examples will show the logistical importance of servant roles—real and assumed—in gaining desired ends. First, a lady's maid takes pity on the freezing and almost naked Rinaldo, who has been abandoned outside the city walls after being held up by highwaymen (*Dec.* II, 2, 25). Rinaldo just happens to be the sort of man that the maid's lady needs as a bedfellow, and through the maid's agency both Rinaldo and the lady are brought to a state of bliss. In a second example, a servant is commanded to kill the wife of the foolish Bernabò Lomellin of Genova but has the good sense to let her live (II, 9, 41). Later, by dressing as a man and becoming a (pseudomasculine) retainer of the Sultan, the wronged wife wins rehabilitation and revenge.[9] Examples of real or imagined servants playing pivotal roles in the logistical fulfillment of plots can be multiplied throughout the book, but the metaphorical implications of servant roles are even more important. A closer look at these two examples shows that the maid might represent the more basic impulses of the lady, who must incline to this side of her nature in order to realize her latent needs—the relationship between lady and maid representing, in an external, social way, higher and lower manifestations of human instinct— whereas Bernabò's merciful servant might represent the contradictions in his master's desire to effect his wife's murder, with the lower social actor redeeming the cruel folly of the higher. There are other examples where a metaphorical reading of service is the most fruitful way of understanding what is going on, such as the metaphorical relationship between the eloquent fraud Cipolla and his unspeakable servant Guccio, whose adventures with the kitchen-maid (VI, 10, 21–24) threaten to undermine his master's high-flown rhetoric. Some of the most interesting metaphorical explorations take place at the boundary between realism and wish-fulfillment; because, as G. H. McWilliam pointed out, "the conversion of fantasy into the realm of the possible is what constitutes the *Decameron's* peculiar dynamic."[10]

The book provides us not only with normal or unmarked narrative depictions of servants—especially in the frame story or *cornice*—but also with occasional glimpses of the historical or theoretical norms underlying that narrative normality. We gather that servants must always act for the honor and interest of their masters, who are entitled to exact fearsome punishments if they are disobeyed.[11] Serious infractions can mean death, but lesser misdemeanors can also entail violent retaliation: we infer that having a troublesome female servant whipped is a feasible option for the gentle ladies of the *cornice*.[12] There are hints of other historical realities of servant life. There is no mention in the grossly comic tales of servants being fair game for their masters' sexual appetites, but that possibility is played out in an elevated key when, in a respectable London household, a dependant girl (not a real servant, but the daughter of an exiled French aristocrat) is urged to satisfy the desires of her benefactors' son (II, 8, 57–68). Iris Origo has studied the historical realities concerning the sexual exploitation of domestic servants and slaves in medieval Tuscan households: "In these great organisms there was a place not only for wives, but concubines. . . . Many a young bride, arriving in her new home, might find among the maidservants of the house some who were her husband's concubines and others who were his sisters." Origo traces this culture back, in part, to the *patria potestas* of Rome, the traditional power of the head of the family, which had included sexual dominion over the household: "[A]s for slaves . . . it was understood as a matter of course that they were obliged to satisfy their owner's desires."[13]

The position of domestic servants fits into a deeply hierarchical view of society in which identity is linked to allegiance, and the symbolic value of retainers is as great as their practical value. As the individual looks up the chain of social being towards his or her social superiors, the relationship might appear as one of hierarchy rather than of personal service—among ecclesiastical examples, one thinks of a monk and his abbot (I, 4) or a nun and her superior (IX, 2)—but in a feudal society these social relationships will be experienced in strongly personal terms. Looking down the same chain of social being, the most important "meaning" of servants for their masters—more important than the actual work they do—is the social aggrandizement they confer. In antiquity, it had been regarded as infamous for a Roman matron or respectable young boy to be seen on the street without a retinue; a similar ethic and aesthetic of being decorously accompanied can be found in medieval literature.[14] Although the escort is not always provided by servants, those moments where a woman slips away from her servants to be alone or unchaperoned with another person are powerful liminal events in which the social self is stripped away. In the *Decameron*, Ghismonda's first encounter with Guiscardo is set in precisely this context of attendance (IV, 1, 13). By contrast, the decorous Madonna Dianora visits her admirer with a modestly suitable retinue of two serving-men and a chambermaid (X, 5, 17).

It can be argued that the primary role of servants is to provide a decorous texture and consistency to the lives of the great. Montaigne remarked that no man is a hero to his valet; yet a protagonist does need a valet, or other secondary characters, to proclaim his or her preeminence. The service rendered might be the performance of a verbal or nonverbal "precursor" role, announcing the hero's arrival, or it might involve explicit praise and promotion of the employer's status. A striking erotic example of the precursor function comes in Boccaccio's tale of Salabaetto, as the Florentine merchant waits for his first encounter with his new Sicilian mistress:

[E]gli non stette guari che due schiave venner cariche: l'una aveva un materasso di bambagia bello e grande in capo e l'altra un grandissimo paniere pien di cose; e steso questo materasso in una camera del bagno sopra una lettiera, vi miser sú un paio di lenzuola sottilissime listate di seta e poi una coltre di bucherame cipriana bianchissima con due origlieri lavorati a maraviglie; e appresso questo spogliatesi e entrate nel bagno, quello tutto lavarono e spazzarono ottimamente. Né stette guari che la donna con due sue altre schiave appresso al bagno venne; dove ella, come prima ebbe agio, fece a Salabaetto grandissima festa e dopo i maggiori sospiri del mondo, poi che molto e abbracciato e basciato l'ebbe, gli disse: "Non so chi mi si avesse a questo potuto conducere altri che tu; tu m'hai miso lo foco all'arma, toscano acanino." (VIII, 10, 14–15)

(He had not been waiting long before two slave girls came along, laden with gear. One was carrying on her head a fine broad fleecy mattress, while the other was carrying on her head a huge basket full of things. The mattress they set on a bedstead in one of the chambers of the bathing-house and spread on it a pair of very fine sheets, laced with silk, together with a counterpane of snow-white Cyprian buckram and two wonderfully embroidered pillows. Then, taking off their clothes, they entered the bath and swept it all and washed it thoroughly. Nor was it long before the lady herself arrived with two other slave-girls, and greeted Salabaetto with the utmost joy; then, at the first opportunity, after she had both embraced and kissed him copiously, breathing the heaviest sighs in the world, she said to him, "I don't know who could have brought me to this pass, other than you; you've kindled a fire in my vitals, you gorgeous Tuscan!")[15]

A classic case of aggrandizement of the master's standing is Charles Perrault's story of Puss in Boots (which may be traced back to Giovanfrancesco Straparola's *Le piacevoli notti* [1553] and Giambattista Basile's *Pentamerone* [1634]), in which a helpful cat exalts the prospects of a poor young boy to the extent that the king gives the boy his daughter in marriage.[16] In the *Decameron*, we find the inept Guccio Imbratta singularly failing to play this role, all the while claiming for himself the status that a really good servant would confer on his master: Guccio tells the kitchen-maid Nuta "che egli sapeva tante cose fare e dire, che domine pure unquanche" (he was in a position to do and say things that his master could only dream of [VI, 10, 22]), a comment that also ironically points to the servant's broader capacity for transgression.

Taking the foregoing points as a conceptual framework, we can begin to construct a taxonomy of master and servant roles in the *Decameron* with normal or unmarked depictions of servants. The "zero case" from which other examples can be measured is service so unobtrusive as to be almost invisible, where the person providing the service is overlooked or barely mentioned. For example, after his dramatic discovery and retaliation for his wife's unfaithfulness, Arriguccio Berlinghieri "quanto piú tosto poté n'andò alla casa de' fratelli della moglie, e quivi tanto picchiò, che fu sentito e fugli aperto. Li fratelli della donna, che eran tre, e la madre di lei, sentendo che Arriguccio era, tutti si levarono e fatto accendere de' lumi" (went with enormous haste to the house of his wife's brothers and there knocked so long and so loudly that he was heard and the door was opened to him. The lady's three brothers and her mother, hearing that it was Arriguccio, all rose and had their lamps lit [VII, 8, 24]). Those actions (opening the door, lighting the lamps) were obviously performed by somebody, but the agents providing the service are not worth specifying at this fast-moving juncture even though the same story gives a prominent role to the maidservant who helps to trick Arriguccio by taking the beating he had meant for his wife.[17]

Unobtrusive service—sometimes nearly as invisible as the "zero case" just mentioned—is the norm in the *cornice*, that great repository of decorum. When the ten storytellers, accompanied by seven servants, escape to the first of their three villas in the countryside, "tutto spazzato, e nelle camere i letti fatti, e ogni cosa di fiori quali nella stagione si potevano avere piena e di giunchi giuncata la vegnente brigata trovò con suo non poco piacere" (on their arrival the company was delighted to find the place all swept, and the beds made in the bedchambers, and everything covered with such flowers as could be had at that season, and strewn with rushes [I, Intro., 91]). Efficient service is something that the aristocratic storytellers expect and of which they have been tragically deprived during the plague. One of the signs of social collapse in Florence in 1348 had been precisely the aggravation of the servant problem. The scarce, overpaid, and grasping helpers hired by desperate plague victims were "uomini o femine di grosso ingegno, e i piú di tali servigi non usati, li quali quasi di niuna altra cosa servieno che di porgere alcune cose dagl'infermi adomandate o di riguardare quando morieno; e servendo in tal servigio sé molte volte col guadagno perdeano" (I, Intro., 28). (Men and women of low understanding and mostly unused to domestic duties, who served for almost nothing other than fetching things called for by the sick, or taking note when they died. In performing these services, many of the servants perished along with their earnings.) Worse still, sick women were driven to have themselves tended by male nurses, a new and almost unheard-of custom.

Clearly the proprieties of service were immensely important, and it is no surprise that when the ten storytellers elect their first queen, Pampinea, her first action is to summon the three servants of the young men and the four maidservants to appear before her. Showing a remarkable command of household organization, she addresses them as follows:

"Acciò che io prima essemplo dea a tutti voi, per lo quale di bene in meglio procedendo la nostra compagnia con ordine e con piacere e senza alcuna vergogna viva e duri quanto a grado ne fia, io primieramente constituisco Parmeno, famigliare di Dioneo, mio siniscalco, e a lui la cura e la sollecitudine di tutta la nostra famiglia commetto e ciò che al servigio della sala appartiene. Sirisco, famigliar di Panfilo, voglio che di noi sia spenditore e tesoriere e di Parmeno seguiti i comandamenti. Tindaro al servigio di Filostrato e degli altri due attenda nelle camere loro, qualora gli altri, intorno alli loro ufici impediti, attender non vi potessero. Misia, mia fante, e Licisca, di Filomena, nella cucina saranno continue e quelle vivande diligentemente apparecchieranno che per Parmeno loro saranno imposte. Chimera, di Lauretta, e Stratilia, di Fiammetta, al governo delle camere delle donne intente vogliamo che stieno e alla nettezza de' luoghi dove staremo. E ciascun generalmente, per quanto egli avrà cara la nostra grazia, vogliamo e comandiamo che si guardi, dove che egli vada, onde che egli torni, che che egli oda o vegga, niuna novella altra che lieta ci rechi di fuori." (I, Intro., 98–99)[18]

(I want to set you a first example, by which, proceeding from good to better, our company may live and last in order and enjoyment and without reproach so long as it is agreeable to us. Therefore, first of all, I appoint Parmeno, Dioneo's servant, to be my chief steward. I entrust him with the care and ordinance of our entire household and the service of meals. Sirisco, Panfilo's servant, is to be our dispenser of money and our treasurer; he will follow the commands of Parmeno. Tindaro will look to the service of Filostrato and the other two men in their rooms, whenever the others, being taken up with their various duties, cannot attend to them. Misia, my maid, and Filomena's Licisca will stay permanently in the kitchen, where they will diligently prepare such food as Parmeno decides. Lauretta's Chimera and Fiammetta's Stratilia are to occupy themselves with the arrangement of the ladies' chambers and the cleanliness of the places where we spend our time. And it is our will and command that all persons, if they wish to remain in our favor, must be careful, wherever they go to or return from, and whatever they may hear or see, to bring us from the outside world no news other than happy news.)

This concern with practical order is repeated obsessively throughout the frame story as each new ruler takes up office and issues instructions to the chief steward, and it appears in each Conclusion to Days One through Nine. Servants are set up in their own rather rigidly stratified sphere of action and are given another crucially important role connected with decorum: they are to protect their masters from reality.

As the frame story continues, the servants fetch and carry, cook and clean in the background.[19] Only once, at the start of the Sixth Day, do they burst into the scene with a squabble about whether a female acquaintance of theirs was a virgin on her wedding night (VI, Intro., 4–15), an episode that is conducted in crudely comical language. This breakdown of propriety might seem at first glance to threaten the normative decorum of the *cornice*, but the opposite interpretation may be closer to the truth. The depiction of clashing social codes serves to problematize the isolation of the storytellers from all that happens around them; once it has been dealt with, however, the crudity of the lower class, which requires firm repression by their betters, underscores rather than undermines the need for a hierarchical social order. Far from conferring any extra narrative status on the servants, being foregrounded "in character," that is, behaving according to one's social stereotype, hardly amounts to being foregrounded at all. Yet at the end of the same day, when the intrusion has been repressed and almost forgotten, Dioneo proposes to the ladies and gentlemen of the *cornice* that they should adopt the theme adumbrated by the servant Licisca as their topic for the next day's stories: "[V]oglio che domane si dica, poi che donna Licisca data ce n'ha cagione, delle beffe le quali o per amore o per salvamento di loro le donne hanno già fatte a' lor mariti, senza essersene essi o avveduti o no" (VI, Concl., 6). (I determine and ordain that, since Licisca has given us occasion for it, our conversation tomorrow will be about the tricks which, either for love or for their own preservation, women have played on their husbands, with or without the husbands realizing what has been done to them.) Balance is restored; the previously rejected element of servant humor is now happily incorporated, as the aristocratic storytellers embark on ten tales of marital infidelity so crude that even servants would enjoy them if they weren't confined to the kitchen.[20] Nevertheless, their narrative is conducted in the best possible taste, and their ability to handle indecorous topics without descending into indecorous behavior demonstrates to us just how very decorous they really are. After this episode, the servants in the frame story recede once again into quasi-invisibility, as good servants should.

The *cornice* clearly represents a social norm in this as in other matters. We may now proceed to an examination of servant roles throughout the *Centonovelle*, developing this theme from the decorous to the logistical and often indecorous aspects of the master-servant relationship, and then on toward the metaphorical. In exploring the notion of decorum, one must realize that it can sometimes include negative conduct appropriate to a particular class of character. Domestic servants are allowed to twit their masters, although always within certain closely defined parameters. They tread a fine line between amusement and punishment; although they will be beaten if they go too far, a touch of well-judged insolence may be to their advantage.[21]

A famous example of harmless contention concerns the cook Chichibio and his master Currado Gianfigliazzi, a rich Florentine (VI, 4). When roasting a crane killed by Currado's falcon, Chichibio steals one of the legs and gives it to his girlfriend. In front of his dinner guests, Currado challenges Chichibio to explain what has become of the missing leg. Chichibio protests that cranes have got only one leg and offers to prove it by showing Currado some live cranes. The next day in the country, Chichibio does indeed show his master the cranes, each resting on one leg, but his master gives a shout whereupon the cranes lower their other legs and fly away. Chichibio protests that he had not shouted at the roasted crane the night before, which was why it had failed to put down its second leg. "A Currado piacque tanto questa risposta, che tutta la sua ira si convertí in festa e riso, e disse: 'Chichibio, tu hai ragione: ben lo doveva fare.' Cosí adunque con la sua pronta e sollazzevol risposta Chichibio cessò la mala ventura e paceficossi col suo signore" (VI, 4, 19–20). (This reply so pleased Currado that all his wrath was instantly changed into amusement and laughter, and he said, "Chichibio, you're absolutely right; indeed that's what I should have done." And so, with his prompt and comical answer, Chichibio staved off bad luck and made peace with his master.)

The story of Chichibio conveys the social meaning that a witty retort requires not only a clever person to utter it, but also an equally clever recipent to understand it. The social conflict between master and servant that had threatened to lead to brutal retaliation dissolves into lighthearted mutual toleration. The social norm, by being lightly tested through episodes such as this, is not weakened but confirmed.

A more complex and many-sided version of normal hierarchical relations is provided by the story of Cisti the baker, a serviceable citizen who is happy to oblige the prominent Florentine citizen Geri Spina and his guests with free supplies of cool white wine, but who indulges in sharp rudeness to Geri's servants, perhaps because their status is a little too close to his own (VI, 2). The relationship of social status to freedom and servitude is nicely problematized by this tale.

The normal decorum of master-servant symbiosis, even when lightly tested by being narrated in a comic mode, remains one of the simplest versions of this paradigm. Far more dynamic results are obtained in other versions of the master-servant relationship, such as the logistical function. Servants in the *Decameron* often act as helpers or accomplices in the attainment of desirable but indecorous or even completely inadmissible ends. Social normality is considerably stretched in the testing-ground of fiction. At one level, these accomplice roles are merely criminal, as when a small boy casually sends Andreuccio to almost certain death with the banal direction "Andate là entro" (Go in there [II, 5, 37]). Far more complex in social, psychological, and narrative terms are the tales of maidservants acting as replacements for their mistresses in an erotic setting. The most striking case is when Monna Piccarda (VIII, 4), a respectable widow courted by the repulsive rector of Fiesole, persuades her ugly servant-maid Ciutazza to take her place in an amorous encounter with the elderly churchman. The bishop of Fiesole, called as a witness to surprise the rector in bed with Ciutazza, commends the widow's action in disgracing him in a nonviolent manner; however, the servant's moral and social being is entirely expendable in this happy resolution. (A benign inversion of this social contrast occurs in Day III, Story 9, when the Countess of Roussillon replaces a poor but honorable girl in a sexual encounter with the Countess's own unwilling husband.) Apart from the questionable moral nature of Monna Piccarda's action, the substitution of Ciutazza raises an interesting psychological point: on the basic, physical level, one woman is very much like another; all are "sisters under the skin." Ugliness and beauty lose their specific character, and intimacy is something entirely impersonal.

A less direct substitution function is performed by Monna Sismonda's maid, who is beaten and shorn by Sismonda's husband, Arriguccio, in place of his errant wife (VII, 8). Like Ciutazza, Sismonda's maid will be rewarded in material terms, but this time there is no suggestion that her ordeal is enjoyable. A third case of substitution involves both verbal and physical action when a maid sacrifices her honor to save her mistress from discovery: she happily "confesses" to her mistress's husband that she, and not her mistress, was entertaining her mistress's lover, who has been arrested in suspicious circumstances (IV, 10). That substitution was a pure fabrication, but she then proves her loyalty in physical terms by having sex with the judge in order to smooth the resolution of the case. Conflicting messages can be taken from this tale: the maid is a forceful and instinctual character, yet her life is bound up in her mistress's fate. She may be a free spirit, but she is not a free agent.

The almost symbiotic comradeship of mistress and maid is developed in many ways. For example, the handsome young Rinaldo of Siena, in love with his neighbor's wife, first becomes the godfather of her child and then becomes a friar so as to facilitate her eventual seduction. The crisis in the story arises one day when Rinaldo, accompanied by another friar as was the custom, has called at the lady's house "e vedendo quivi niuna persona essere altri che una fanticella della donna, assai bella e piacevoletta, mandato il compagno suo con essolei nel palco de' colombi ad insegnarle il paternostro, egli colla donna, che il fanciullin suo avea per mano, se n'entrarono nella camera" (VII, 3, 23) (and finding nobody with her but a little maid of hers, who was very pretty and agreeable, he sent his companion up to the pigeon-loft with the little maid, to teach her the Paternoster, and went with the lady, who had her child by the hand, into her bedroom).

Her husband returns unexpectedly, but the lady convinces him that their friend the friar has merely been casting a spell on their little son who is suffering from worms. If the lady's needs are served by the friar, those of her maid are even more amply met by his companion who "non un paternostro ma forse piú di quatro [*sic*] n'aveva insegnati alla fanticella" (VII, 3, 39). (He had by this time taught the serving-wench not one, but maybe more than four Paternosters.) The second friar's status as a shadow-character is nicely matched with the lady's maid whose sole function is to replicate her mistress's instincts in a simpler and more energetic form. Although Rinaldo had to seduce his lady by elaborate syllogisms, no such persuasion is necessary for these ancillary characters.

A less benign form of complicity between mistress and maid occurs in Day VIII, Story 7. The two women combine forces to torment Rinieri, the mistress's admirer, and he wreaks savage retribution on them both. A close reading of the tale reveals the escalating stages of the maid's complicity. She helps her mistress to entice and deceive Rinieri, keeping him shivering in the snow one winter night as her mistress entertains another man in her house.[22] She later asks Rinieri to bring back her mistress's lost lover. Seizing this opportunity and abetted by his own manservant, Rinieri tricks the mistress into climbing a tower stark naked on a summer night, trapping her there throughout the following day, where she is "dal caldo inestimabile, dal sole, dalle mosche e da' tafani, e ancor dalla fame ma molto piú dalla sete e per aggiunta da mille noiosi pensieri angosciata e stimolata e trafitta" (tortured and stung and pierced to the quick by the inexpressible heat of the sun, by the horseflies and mosquitoes, and also by hunger, but much more by thirst and by a thousand irksome thoughts [VIII, 7, 117]). At the end of the day he goes to her house with her clothes, threatens the maid with retribution, and tells her where her mistress is. The lady's maid takes the clothes to the tower for her mistress, who greets her as "my sister." But as the maid climbs down from the tower, she also meets her nemesis: "La fante cattivella, che di dietro era rimasa, scendendo meno avvedutamente, smucciandole il piede, cadde della scala in terra e ruppesi la coscia, e per lo dolor sentito cominciò a mugghiar che pareva un leone" (VIII, 7, 142). (The unlucky maid, who had remained behind, descending less circumspectly, made a slip of the foot and falling from the ladder to the ground, broke her thigh, whereupon she started roaring with pain like a lion.) The seemingly fortuitous punishment of the maid once again shows to what extent the lives of shadow characters are shaped by those of the protagonists.

Maids and mistresses might be complicit in matters of love; the complicity between male servants and masters extends also to murder. It is not only in the criminal world, as in the case of Andreuccio (II, 5, 37), that such behavior is required. There is a repeated motif of the faithful servant ordered to kill members of the family circle—a wife (II, 9, 38), children (V, 7, 45; X, 10, 30–31), a daughter's lover (IV, 1, 46)—or even to serve them as food (IV, 9, 16).[23] Even when the order is a pretense, or the outcome is benign, these cases are presented as fortunate deviations from a grim norm.

Space does not permit a full reading of these examples, but the case of the Genoese merchant Bernabò Lomellin (II, 9), who orders his servant to kill his wife, is especially pertinent. Bernabò has been tricked by a fellow merchant, Ambruogiuolo, into believing that Ambruogiuolo has seduced his virtuous wife while Bernabò was away in Paris, a trick carried out with the aid of a humble intermediary: "una povera femina che molto nella casa usava e a cui la donna voleva gran bene" (a poor woman, who frequently visited Bernabò's house, and who was held in great affection by the lady [II, 9, 25]).[24] Obviously, the "correct" reaction by a self-respecting family head would be to kill his wife. Bernabò, however, decides to delegate this duty, instructing a trusted servant to kill her. The faithful servant leads her to a lonely wooded valley, pulls out his knife, and announces his intentions. She asks what offense she has done him.

"Madonna," disse il famigliare, "me non avete offeso d'alcuna cosa: ma di che voi offeso abbiate il vostro marito io nol so, se non che egli mi comandò che senza alcuna misericordia aver di voi io in questo cammin v'uccidessi; e se io nol facessi mi minacciò di farmi impiccar per la gola. Voi sapete bene quanto io gli son tenuto e come io di cosa che egli m'imponga possa dir di no: sallo Idio che di voi m'incresce ma io non posso altro." (II, 9, 38)

("Madam," answered the man, "I have suffered no offense from you; but how you have offended your husband I do not know, except that he has commanded me to slay you on the road, without having any pity upon you, threatening that if I did not do it he would have me hanged by the neck. You know well the duty I have to him, and how I cannot refuse him anything that he may impose upon me. God knows I am sorry for your sake, but I cannot disobey.")

Nevertheless, he does disobey his master, despite the threat of being hanged, and even gives her some of his clothes and money, thereby allowing her to emigrate dressed as a man. The advantage of Bernabò's decision to delegate his dirty work to the servant now becomes clear: servants can protect their masters by carrying out their darkest wishes, but they can sometimes do even better by correctly interpreting the conflict between the stated wishes and subconscious needs of the masters.

The logistical usefulness of servants in attaining indecorous or inadmissible ends is most obviously embodied in their functions as go-betweens in love-affairs.[25] The *Decameron* gives a prominent place to go-betweens in general and is even subtitled "Prencipe Galeotto" in honor of the go-between who brought Lancelot and Guinevere together and whom Dante condemned in the shape of the guilty book (*Inferno*, V, 137). The servants' go-between role can be a crude and simple matter; in a few cases, however, it reaches interesting levels of psychological complexity, as in the intriguing approach used by Ghismonda, daughter of the Prince of Salerno, to make an arrangement with her father's retainer, Guiscardo:

> [N]iuna altra cosa tanto disiderando la giovane quanto di ritrovarsi con lui, né vogliendosi di questo amore in alcuna persona fidare, a dovergli significare il modo seco pensò una nuova malizia. Essa scrisse una lettera, e in quella ciò che a fare il dí seguente per esser con lei gli mostrò; e poi quella messa in un bucciuolo di canna, sollazzando la diede a Guiscardo e dicendo: "Fara'ne questa sera un soffione alla tua servente, col quale ella raccenda il fuoco." Guiscardo il prese, e avvisando costei non senza cagione dovergliele aver donato e cosí detto, partitosi, con esso se ne tornò alla sua casa: e guardando la canna e quella vedendo fessa, l'aperse, e dentro trovata la lettera di lei e lettala e ben compreso ciò che a fare avea, il piú contento uom fu che fosse già mai e diedesi a dare opera di dovere a lei andare secondo il modo da lei dimostratogli. (IV, 1, 7–8)

> (The young lady, who desired nothing so much as to be together with him, but was unwilling to make anyone a confidant of her passion, thought up a rare trick to let him know how this could be arranged: she wrote him a letter, in which she told him what he should do to meet with her on the following day. Placing the letter in the hollow of a cane, she handed the cane jestingly to Guiscardo, saying, "You can make a bellows of it for your serving-maid, so she can blow up your fire tonight." Guiscardo took the cane, and thinking that she would not have given it to him or spoken like that without some reason, took his leave and returned with it to his lodging. There he examined the cane and seeing it to be cleft, he opened it and found the letter inside.)

This inflammatory reference to an imaginary or real maid suggests among other things Ghismonda's keen awareness of hierarchies of service: Guiscardo is subject to her father, but she wishes to "alter services with him."[26]

A more concrete example of the servant as go-between, also with psychological overtones, is contained in Day II, Story 2. Rinaldo d'Asti is set upon by a group of highwaymen and left standing by a river bank in the midst of winter in nothing but his shirt. Rinaldo, like any respectable man, had been accompanied on his journey by a servant, but "veggendolo assalire, come cattivo, niuna cosa al suo aiuto adoperò, ma volto il cavallo sopra il quale era non si ritenne di correre sí fu a Castel Guiglielmo, e in quello, essendo già sera, entrato, senza darsi altro impaccio albergò" (II, 2, 14). (Like the coward he was, seeing him attacked, did nothing to help him, but turned his horse's head and bolted off without stopping until he came to Castel Guglielmo, and entering the town, he took lodging there, without worrying any more about his master.)

Happily, that bad image of service is soon superseded. A lady's maid in Castel Guglielmo discovers Rinaldo shivering outside the walls of the town and, with her mistress's permission, invites him in. He soon progresses to the lady's bath and then to her bed. Considerable psychological and metaphorical interest attaches to the gradual stages by which Rinaldo is brought from misery to joy and to the complicity between the two women—mistress and maid—in gradually embarking on this course of action. The mistress might never have ventured so far on her own. It is the maid who sees Rinaldo first and who praises him to her mistress. Like any good servant, she discreetly anticipates her employer's unstated needs. Metaphorically, the lower side of instinctual nature is represented by the servant character; the higher nature of her mistress would be the poorer without it. Together they make up a fully dimensional composite "character."[27]

The metaphorical implications of servant roles in the *Decameron* are even more important than their practical or logistical effects. This is particularly clear when one considers fake or ambitious servants, whose changeable identity is self-consciously problematized as they change their state and transcend their allotted realm. The story of Lodovico (VII, 7) offers a particularly fruitful blend of logistics and metaphor. Lodovico, the son of an impoverished Florentine nobleman reduced to a life of trade, has been trained in the rituals of service at the French court in Paris. Listening one day to some knights returning from a pilgrimage and talking about the beautiful women of different countries, he hears that the most beautiful woman ever seen is Beatrice, wife of Egano de' Galuzzi in Bologna. Lodovico promptly changes his name to Anichino, goes to Bologna, sees the lady, finds she is even lovelier than he had thought, sells his horses, tells his servants to pretend not to know him, pays his account at the inn, and gets a job through the innkeeper as a servant of the unfortunate Egano, who likes good-looking servants. He quickly maneuvers his way into a position of trust in the household and wins his lady's heart over a game of chess, but when he comes to her bedroom she seizes him by the hand and tells her husband that Anichino is trying to seduce her. She says she has agreed to meet Anichino that very night down in the orchard and advises her husband to dress up in one of her cloaks and go down there so that he can unmask this wicked servant. The husband goes off, and the lovers get into bed together. After a suitable interval Anichino goes to the garden and, in the guise of a loyal servant, beats up his master while affecting to think he is punishing his faithless mistress. Thus the false servant—false in every sense—both enjoys his lady's favors and punishes her innocent husband, who ever afterwards believes that he is blessed with the most faithful wife and the most loyal servant that any nobleman ever had.[28] The story not only relates a cruel *beffa* that rewards deceit and punishes credulity, but it also enacts two fine courtly images: the lover who falls in love with an unseen lady purely on the basis of her reputation, and the servant of love whose metaphorical service of his lady is expressed in literal terms of domestic employment. In this tale, low comedy supports a higher, idealized realm.

By contrast, the fine image of love as service yields to a horribly perverse image of marriage as abject domestic service in the last story of the *Decameron*, which tests to the limits of destruction the possibilities of a master-servant relationship within a marriage. Gualtieri, Marquis of Saluzzo, is forced to take a wife and selects Griselda, the daughter of a poor man. He has her stripped naked in public, then dressed in fine robes and brought to court. They have a son and a daughter. Gualtieri's restless and bizarre nature leaves him unsure whether his wife really loves him, so he decides to test her. He has a trusted servant take the children away, pretending that they are to be killed. Griselda acquiesces in this, as she does when Gualtieri pretends to divorce her. She is finally reduced to the status of "wedding planner" at her husband's remarriage:

> [M]andò per la Griselda che a lui venisse; alla quale venuta disse: "Io meno questa donna la quale io ho nuovamente tolta e intendo in questa sua prima venuta d'ono-rarla; e tu sai che io non ho in casa donne che mi sappiano acconciar le camere né fare molte cose che a cosí fatta festa si richeggiono: e per ciò tu, che meglio che altra persona queste cose di casa sai, metti in ordine quello che da far ci è, e quelle donne fa invitar che ti pare e ricevile come se donna di qui fossi: poi, fatte le nozze, te ne potrai a casa tua tornare. (X, 10, 49–50)

> (He sent for Griselda to come to him, and said to her, "I am about to welcome this lady, whom I have recently chosen as my wife, and I mean to receive her honorably at her first arrival. Now you know I have no women here who know how to decorate my rooms or do the many things required for such a celebration; and so I want you, who are better versed in these household matters than anyone else, to arrange what is to be done here, and send out invitations to such ladies as you consider appropriate, and receive them as if you were the mistress of the house; then, when the wedding-feast is ended, you can be off home again to your own house.")

She accepts his outrageous commission. At the wedding, however, Gualtieri reveals that the alleged bride is in fact her long-lost daughter. He then settles down with Griselda and they live happily ever after. This monstrous story marks the limits of service by exceeding them, just as it negates many other values expressed in the book.

The roles of master and servant as metaphors of higher and lower nature can be seen with particular clarity in the wonderfully comic story of Frate Cipolla

(VI, 10), who comes to a small town in Tuscany to mesmerize the local people with his eloquence and to show them a fake relic: a parrot feather allegedly fallen from the wing of the Angel Gabriel. The friar arrives in Certaldo flanked by his coarse and vulgar servant, variously known as Guccio the Whale, Guccio the Mess, and Guccio the Pig. It is the servant's absence from the friar's room at the inn that allows two young men to break in and steal the preacher's feather. We might plausibly read the figures of Frate Cipolla and his servant Guccio as allegorical representations of pretension and reality, the friar's angelic eloquence being contrasted with the animal stupidity of his frightful servant, whose faults he memorably enumerates:

> "[E]gli è tardo, sugliardo e bugiardo; negligente, disubidente e maldicente; trascutato, smemorato e scostumato; senza che egli ha alcune altre teccherelle con queste, che si taccion per lo migliore. E quel che sommamente è da rider de' fatti suoi è che egli in ogni luogo vuol pigliar moglie e tor casa a pigione; e avendo la barba grande e nera e unta, gli par sí forte esser bello e piacevole, che egli s'avisa che quante femine il veggan tutte di lui s'innamorino, e essendo lasciato, a tutte andrebbe dietro perdendo la coreggia." (VI, 10, 17–18)

> (He's a mess maker, a loafer, a liar; he's lawless, uncouth, and obscene; he's gawky and awkward and rude; besides which he has a few other peccadilloes that I wouldn't care to mention. But what's most ridiculous about him is that wherever he goes he's always fixing to marry a wife and rent him a house, for despite his big black greasy beard, he thinks he's so desperately handsome and winning that he's convinced any female who sees him must instantly fall in love with him. If you let him, he'd run after them all till he lost track of his trousers.)

Guccio is the alter ego of his master: the animal truth underlying the angelic falsehood. Being a servant, he becomes appropriately involved with another servant in the comic episode of the stealing of the father. He has been left at the inn to guard the "relic" while Cipolla goes out to lunch in the citadel of Certaldo, but he abandons his post and goes downstairs to pay court to Nuta the cook, a greasy gargoyle like himself. In keeping with the story's feathery theme, their encounter is introduced with bird imagery:

> Ma Guccio Imbratta, il quale era piú vago di stare in cucina che sopra i verdi rami l'usignuolo, e massimamente se fante vi sentiva niuna, avendone in quella dell'oste una veduta, grassa e grossa e piccola e mal fatta, con un paio di poppe che parean due ceston da letame e con un viso che parea de' Baronci, tutta sudata, unta e affumicata, non altramenti che si gitti l'avoltoio alla carogna, lasciata la camera di frate Cipolla aperta e tutte le sue cose in abbandono, là si calò. (VI, 10, 21)

> (But Guccio loved being in kitchens more than nightingales love perching on green boughs—especially if he knew there was some serving-wench there, and he had seen in the kitchen of the inn a gross, fat kitchen-maid, low-sized and shapeless, with a pair of tits like two baskets of manure and a face like one of the Baronci clan,

all sweaty and greasy and smoky. So he left Fra Cipolla's chamber and all his gear
to look after themselves, and swooped down on the kitchen like a vulture landing on
a fresh carcass.)

Cipolla and the two young men who steal his feather represent (however falsely)
higher rational aspects of humanity, while the servants Guccio and Nuta embody
lower irrational or animal aspects. Taken together, they offer a composite
metaphor for human nature in all its alarming variety.[29]

    This is not the place to draw broad conclusions about possible meanings of
masters and servants in literature, although it is clear that the mutual necessity of
the two categories and the range of their practical and metaphorical interactions
extend well beyond the *Decameron*. Whatever the historical changes in social
structures, one may guess that the analogy between the master-servant relationship and the reader-writer relationship also remains valid across different epochs.
The reader demands to be amused by the antics of the writer whose efforts he
condescends to survey. The writer is not a body servant, although he may think of
himself as the freest of men. Yet as an entertainer he depends upon the goodwill
of his patrons almost as much as a slave, freedman, or domestic servant depends
upon the goodwill of his master. The creation or performance of cultural entertainment can even be seen as a parasitic activity, dependent for its very being on
the consumer who judges it. In *De institutione musica*, Boethius argued that performing artists, for all their skill, act merely as slaves without making use of reason. Even the poets who make songs are impelled by instinct rather than reason.
Only those who acquire an ability for judging, one that "is totally grounded in
reason and thought, will rightly be esteemed as musical. That person is a musi-
cian who exhibits the faculty of forming judgments according to speculation or
reason."[30] This apotheosis of the critic marks not the death of the author but the
reduction of artistry to the level of a servile skill. The creative artist is relegated at
best to the status of a half-free spirit: not only is he economically bound to the
service of patrons, aristocratic or otherwise, but he becomes their artistic as well
as their social inferior. The writer may be puppet-master to his characters, but he
can only aspire to be a humble servant contributing to the higher cultural creativity of his discerning readers. The figure of the writer as entertainer[31] has much in
common with Feste the clown in Shakespeare's *Twelfth-Night*. Feste may be a
disrespectful sponger on the Lady Olivia's hospitality, but he has to work hard to
entertain her household and humbly offers a similar pledge to the theatrical audience in the play's last line: "we'll strive to please you every day."

Notes

1.   Vittore Branca deems it the first book whose protagonist was contemporary soci-
    ety: "Per una grande e organica rappresentazione narrativa è stata scelta per la
    prima volta nel *Decameron*, quale protagonista, la società contemporanea" ("Una

chiave di lettura per il *Decameron*: Contemporaneizzazione narrativa ed espressivismo linguistico," in Giovanni Boccaccio, *Decameron*, ed. V. Branca, 2 vols., Einaudi Tascabili. Classici, no. 99 [1980; reprint, Turin: Einaudi, 1992], 1:vii); hereafter cited in text as *Decameron*. I have also benefitted from consulting Branca's edition as found on the Decameron Web site: www.brown.edu/ Departments/Italian_Studies/dweb/dweb.shtml. On the relationship between the needs of society and those of the individual, see Thomas M. Greene, "Forms of Accommodation in the *Decameron*," *Italica* 45 (1968): 297–313.

2. Wayne C. Booth, *The Rhetoric of Fiction* (Chicago: The University of Chicago Press, 1961), 119, 129–30.

3. See the essay by Maria Bendinelli Predelli, chapter 6 in this volume. According to Guido Almansi, the majority of characters in the *Decameron* are "voyageurs sans bagages" (*The Writer as Liar: Narrative Technique in the* Decameron [London: Routledge and Kegan Paul, 1975], 33). On "rounded" characters, see E. M. Forster's distinction between "flat" characters constructed around a single idea or quality, and "round" characters sufficiently developed to be "capable of surprising in a convincing way" (*Aspects of the Novel, and Related Writings*, the Abinger Edition of E. M. Forster, no. 12 [1927; reprint, London: Edward Arnold, 1974], 46–54.)

4. In speaking of characters in cinema, Robert McKee has noted: "Dimensions fascinate; contradictions in nature or behavior rivet the audience's concentration. Therefore, the protagonist must be the most dimensional character in the cast to focus empathy on the star role" (*Story: Substance, Structure, Style and Principles of Screenwriting* [New York: ReganBooks, 1997], 378). According to Leonard Tourney, "characters are more interesting if they are made of mixed stuff, if they contain warring elements" (quoted in Linda Seger, *Creating Unforgettable Characters*, An "Owl" Book [New York: Henry Holt and Company, 1990], 33).

5. T. S. Eliot, "The Love Song of J. Alfred Prufrock," in *The Waste Land and Other Poems* (London: Faber and Faber, 1940), line 113. Significantly, "Prufrock" places the ancillary, the unrealized, in the central "protagonist's" position.

6. See the remarks on Henrietta Stackpole and Maria Gostrey in James, *The Portrait of a Lady*, intro. and notes Nicola Bradbury, World's Classics (Oxford: Oxford University Press, 1995), 15–16.

7. Consider the minor partners in Dante's infernal diptychs: Paolo (*Inferno* V), Cavalcante (X), Diomed (XXVI), and Archbishop Ruggieri (XXXIII). Actual servants or retainers include Pier delle Vigne (*Inf.* XIII), Ciampolo (*Inf.* XXII, 49–52), and Romieu of Villeneuve (*Par.* VI, 127–42). See *La Divina Commedia*, ed. C. H. Grandgent, revised by Charles S. Singleton (Cambridge, Mass.: Harvard University Press, 1972).

8. Nicole Prunster, *Romeo and Juliet before Shakespeare: Four Early Stories of Star-Crossed Love, by Masuccio Salernitano, Luigi da Porto, Matteo Bandello, and Pierre Boaistuau*, Renaissance and Reformation Texts in Translation, no. 8 (Toronto: Centre for Reformation and Renaissance Studies, 2000), 40–41, 73, 95–98, 101–02, 113. See also *Dec.* IV, 6, 24–25 for the depressingly realistic advice of Andreuola's maid.

9. On the topos of female characters disguised as men, see the essay by Christopher Nissen, chapter 11 in this volume.

10. Giovanni Boccaccio, *The Decameron*, trans., intro., and notes by G. H. McWilliam (Harmondsworth, U.K.: Penguin Books, 1995), xcii.

11. " '[T]u sai quanta e quale sia la 'ngiuria la quale tu m'hai fatta nella mia propia figliuola, là dove, trattandoti io bene e amichevolemente, secondo che servidor si dee fare, tu dovevi il mio onore e delle mie cose sempre e cercare e operare; e molti sarebbero stati quegli, a' quali se tu quello avessi fatto che a me facesti, che vituperosamente t'avrebbero fatto morire: il che la mia pietà non sofferse' " (II, 6, 49).

12. "[S]e non fosse che la reina con un mal viso le 'mpose silenzio e comandolle che piú parola né romor facesse se esser non volesse scopata e lei e Tindaro mandò via, niuna altra cosa avrebbero avuta a fare in tutto quel giorno che attendere a lei" (VI, Intro., 15).

13. Iris Origo, "The Domestic Enemy: The Eastern Slaves in Tuscany in the Fourteenth and Fifteenth Centuries," *Speculum* 30 (1955): 340, 218.

14. "Like respectable women, respectable boys in Rome were not allowed to go out on their own: they had to be accompanied by their *comites*" (Eva Cantarella, *Bisexuality in the Ancient World*, trans. Cormac Ó Cuilleanáin [New Haven, Conn.: Yale University Press, 1992], 116). For medieval examples, see *Troilus and Criseyde* in *The Works of Geoffrey Chaucer*, ed. F. N. Robinson, 2nd ed. (1957; reprint, Oxford: Oxford University Press, 1974), II, 131, 160, 168; III, 86, 95, 96, 98, 99; IV, 32; V, 76, 99.

15. All translations from the *Decameron* are taken from my forthcoming translation (Wordsworth Classics of World Literature [Ware, U.K.: Wordsworth Editions]), a new version based on John Payne's 1886 version.

16. For Perrault's 1697 version of the tale, translated by Robert Samber in 1729, see Iona Opie and Peter Opie, *The Classic Fairy Tales* (London: Oxford University Press, 1974), 110–16.

17. Other examples of anonymous or unobtrusive service include *Dec.* VIII, 1, 6, in which the German mercenary soldier Gulfardo sends to his beloved lady to ask for her favors; IX, 9, 32–33, in which the beaten wife has everything done (but not by herself) to serve her masterful husband just as he requires; and X, 9, 20, in which Torello's wife has a great banquet prepared to welcome Saladin.

18. The names of the seven servants in the *cornice* are taken from Hellenistic comedy and contrast with the everyday realistic names that abound in the *novelle*, as Branca points out: "contribuiscono cosí anch'essi a dare al mondo della 'cornice' una patina di sopramondo" (*Dec.*, 1:44, n. 3).

19. David Wallace points out women have more menial tasks than men in this "shadow-*brigata*" and notes that there is no "democratic" rotation of office as in the storytellers' group (*Boccaccio*: Decameron, Landmarks of World Literature [Cambridge: Cambridge University Press, 1991], 24–25).

20. Pier Massimo Forni illuminates the social and narrative meaning of Licisca's raucous challenge to the queen's prerogative of speech and topic selection by noting an intertext from Juvenal's sixth *Satire*, where the Empress Messalina tries to satisfy her sexual cravings by working in a brothel under the pseudonym of Lycisca (*Adventures in Speech*: *Rhetoric and Narration in Boccaccio's* Decameron, Middle Ages Series [Philadelphia: University of Pennsylvania Press, 1996], 11–15).

21. Anna Fontes has observed that the *motto* (a witty saying or retort) often serves to bridge a social gap when a person of lower status is mocking a superior, for instance; whereas the *beffa* (a practical joke often involving serious damage or physical cruelty) is usually played between people of similar social standing. See "Le thème de la 'beffa' dans le *Décaméron*," in *Formes et significations de la 'beffa' dans la littérature italienne de la Renaissance . . .*, ed. André Rochon (Paris: Université de la Sorbonne Nouvelle, 1972), 35. Thus the *motto* is suitable for judicious use by servants.

22. This motif of sexual frustration and near-death by freezing is in direct contrast to the kindly lady and her maid who rescue Rinaldo d'Asti from the snow (*Dec.* II, 2), discussed later.

23. Two variants on the food-preparation motif: Ghismonda is supplied with the raw heart of her lover in a golden chalice, a metaphor of Holy Communion (*Dec.* IV, 1, 47); and Federigo kills his beloved falcon and has his maid roast it before serving it to his lady, a parody of Communion (V, 9, 26). See my *Religion and the Clergy in Boccaccio's* Decameron, Letture di pensiero e d'arte (Rome: Edizioni di Storia e Letteratura, 1984), 138–39; hereafter cited in text as *Religion and the Clergy.*

24. Such ancillary characters are not servants but stand in a relationship of intimacy and dangerous wish-fulfillment via-à-vis the main characters; for example, the old Greek woman in IV, 3, 23, and the old procuress in V, 10, 14–23.

25. Other examples of the servant as go-between include V, 5, 9–12; V, 8, 41; VII, 1, 6; and VIII, 10, 11.

26. Shakespeare's *Twelfth-Night, or What You Will,* in *The Complete Works of Shakespeare,* ed. W. J. Craig (1914; reprint, London: Oxford University Press, 1968), Act II, Scene 5. Here, the steward Malvolio is deceived by a love-letter from his employer, the Countess Olivia (but actually forged by her housekeeper Maria), which reminds him, "I may command where I adore." The letter is signed: "She that would alter services with thee."

27. In *Phaedrus,* par. 246, Plato describes the composite nature of the soul as being like a chariot with two winged horses, one noble and one ignoble, needing to be driven in tandem by a single charioteer (*The Dialogues of Plato,* trans. B[enjamin] Jowett, 2 vols. [1892; New York: Random House, 1937], 1:250–51). For a detailed analysis of *Dec.* II, 2, see *Religion and the Clergy,* 217–21.

28. The category of "fake servants" or "servants by mistake" includes Teodoro, a slave from the East later discovered to be the son of an Armenian prince, who is saved from being burned at the stake for seducing his master's daughter (V, 7); and Cecco Angiolieri, who unwillingly exchanges his master-servant status with his rascally namesake Cecco Fortarrigo (IX, 4).

29. See my analysis of this tale in *Religion and the Clergy,* 188–208.

30. Anicius Manlius Severinus Boethius, *Fundamentals of Music,* trans. Calvin M. Bower, ed. Claude V. Palisca, Music Theory Translation Series (New Haven, Conn.: Yale University Press, 1989), 51. I wish to thank Fr Tom O'Loughlin for bringing this passage to my attention.

31. Entertainer figures in the *Decameron,* who might, to some extent, stand as figures of the author, include Bergamino and Primasso (I, 7), Guglielmo Borsiere (I, 8), and Martellino (II, 1).

4

Telling Lies, Telling Lives: Giovanni Sercambi between *Cronaca* and *Novella*

Myriam Swennen Ruthenberg

When faced with the work of Giovanni Sercambi (1348–1424), author of *Le Croniche di Luccha* and the 155 novellas in his incomplete *Il Novelliere*, any attempt to methodologically establish boundaries between different kinds of autobiography as made by Philippe Lejeune becomes problematic.[1] The quandary of approaching these two narratives as in part autobiographical is no different from that which Paul John Eakin contends with, though in a different context: "The endless debate among critics today about the definition of autobiography and the boundaries of fact and fiction reflects a fundamental uncertainty about the relationship between autobiographical *narrative* and the life it claims to *record*" (emphasis added).[2] It is precisely this relationship between autobiographical narrative and the life that asks to be recorded that haunts Giovanni Sercambi. At a time when the very notion of genre is only in an embryonic stage, the merchant-politician-chronicler-*novellatore* explores how narrative works to express autobiographical truth that for personal and political reasons cannot be recorded through the medium considered suitable for that purpose, the chronicle. Instead, he deems the cloak of fiction of the novella format more appropriate to expose the self that yearns to be expressed and recognized.

In the pages that follow, I shall demonstrate how a unique first-person autobiographical fragment inserted toward the end of *Le Croniche* is reflected in *Il Novelliere* through an intricate game of author-narrator-subject identity hide-and-seek, culminating in the insertion into *Il Novelliere* of one metanovella in chronicle format. This novella, or "exemplo," as Sercambi calls his tales—he uses the terms interchangeably, although in the *cornice* he refers to them as "novelle"—is told by the narrator-author about himself in the third person and dramatizes Sercambi's manipulation of two symbolic systems: the chronicle and the novella.

This point is valid only with the understanding that a "novella" for Sercambi is indeed a short, fictional tale that might still contain the connotations of "novelty," "news," and/or "oddity." Walter Pabst informs us that from the first time the word was used by Bonvesin della Riva in the mid-thirteenth century, "novella" contained strong connotations of fictionality in content and was therefore associated with deception. According to Pabst, the term has to do with the "novelty" of combining the truth of a religious subject, such as the annunciation, with deception of the listener who receives a contorted version of the religious story.[3] Its meaning and use were rooted in historical truth or what was perceived as such, including the Bible, hagiography, and mythology, but presented as fiction, a "truth that has the face of a lie" with either an exemplary or diverting purpose.[4] First, the choice of the Italianized term *exemplo* and its plural *exempli*—rather than the Latin *exemplum, exempla*—alongside that of "novella" simultaneously underlines the didactic purpose of Sercambi's tales, betraying his need, perhaps, for exemplary writing. Second, it must be acknowledged that the term *entrare in novelle* is a deliberate wordplay employed by Sercambi connoting both "starting to talk" and "starting to tell stories." Alternatives can be found in Boccaccio's *Decameron*, where the expressions "entrare in ragionamenti" (IX, 9, 11) or "entrata in parole" (II, 9, 43) mean "to talk."[5] "Entrare in novelle" might well be a deliberate choice by Sercambi as one who is conscious of the power of fiction. The term is employed only once in *Il Novelliere*, specifically in *Exemplo* 79; in addition, it must be recognized that the term denotes a way of "narrare," a verb Sercambi frequently uses in juxtaposition to "notare," a term grounded in fact. The verb "notare" is often encountered in fourteenth-century chronicles as authenticating events as true, indeed as the activity of, for instance, a "notaio." Finally, it should be understood that it is not my intention to study the notion of *cronaca* in the larger framework of historiography. I do, however, use the term *cronaca* in opposition to *novella*: the former as a discourse of the real, the latter as a discourse of the ideal.

Having made these parenthetic statements, this essay will focus on *Exemplo* 79, via a detour through relevant chapters from *Le Croniche*. This tale is symptomatic of Sercambi's awareness of the possibilities offered by the novella format and the limits of chronicle writing, two modes of expression that create a tension that constitute the dynamics of Sercambi's fascinating work. It is noteworthy that, unlike the rest of *Il Novelliere*, *Exemplo* 79 was written like a chronicle but inserted into a body of novellas, and it performs the oscillating movement between storytelling and chronicle writing.

Le Croniche di Luccha, which Giovanni Sercambi started writing in about 1368 at age twenty and which was suddenly interrupted in 1424 when its author was struck down by the plague, presents an unusual structure. It was written in two parts differing from each other in purpose, form, and content. The second part is especially interesting because it contains a nucleus of angry autobiographical chapters that find their reflection in novella format in Sercambi's other work, *Il*

Novelliere, an incomplete collection of 155 novellas.[6] I will briefly dwell on this second part in order to demonstrate why Sercambi might prefer the format of the "ideal" through storytelling: I will use the term *novellare* in preference to that of the "real," that is, chronicle writing as a vehicle for autobiographical truth.

What was the terrible truth that Giovanni Sercambi needed to express? On the surface, Sercambi was a respectable citizen of the city of Lucca, a merchant-politician, a *speziale* (apothecary) who had gained the favor of Francesco and Lazzaro Guinigi, the rulers of Lucca between 1348 and 1400. Under their reign, Sercambi had earned respect and recognition for his unconditional loyalty, advisory capacities, and foresight. However, when Lazzaro Guinigi was assassinated in 1400 in a conspiracy by one of his brothers and his brother-in-law, Sercambi played a crucial part not only in bringing the murderers to justice, but also in installing into power Paolo Guinigi, Lazzaro's younger brother, a decision that Sercambi would soon regret. In fact, in 1400 Sercambi quite unexpectedly added a sequel to *Le Croniche*.

The title of the first chapter of the second part of Lucca's chronicles clearly indicates Sercambi's real concern: "Croniche del secondo libro di Lucha et del signore Paolo Guinigi di Luccha e d'altri paezi, come chiaramente apparirà per ordine" (Chronicles of the Second Book of Lucca and of his Lord Paolo Guinigi of Lucca and of other cities, as will be evident from the order of events [3:3]). In this chapter, he further explains: "pur l'amore della patria e le cose occorrenti, m'inducono a *narrare* et *dovere scrivere* alquante cose delle molte che segueno" (the love for my city and the current events lead me to *tell* [*narrare*] and *force me to write* [*dovere scrivere*] some of the many things that follow [3:3, emphasis mine]). Sercambi explicitly states that his writing is propelled by necessity ("m'inducono a narrare") and that he will proceed selectively ("alquante cose delle molte"). Furthermore, what Sercambi writes in his chronicles had been articulated as an act of *notare* from the moment he established his own authority over the text in *Le Croniche* part I, chapter 118. Here Sercambi distinguishes three categories of writers: "religiosi" (clergymen who are responsible for books on matters of theology); "gran maestri e poeti . . . in scienzia experti" (great masters and poets . . . who are experts in learning), whose task is to write about civil and moral law, philosophy, medicine, and "le .vii. scienzie" (the seven liberal arts); and finally, "homini senza scienzia aquisita, ma segondo l'uzo della natura experti e savi" (men who have not acquired any [formal] knowledge, but who have gained expertise and wisdom from experience [1:64]). Their writings are aimed at providing "dilecto alli homini simplici et materiali, e alcuna volta di *notare* alcune cose che appaiono in ne' paezi, segondo quello che può comprendere" (entertainment to the simple and material man, and occasionally to *record* a few things that happen in our land, in such a way that they can be understood [1:64, emphasis mine]). Sercambi places himself in the latter category, not only as one who has learned from experience but also as one who wants both to provide "dilecto," an activity usually associated with *novellare*,[7] and to record events, the principal activity of the chronicler. Sercambi thus seems to reveal his double nature as storyteller and chronicler repeatedly in the lexicon of his *Croniche*: *narrare* and *notare*, "to tell" and "to record." As Alberto Dinucci once observed, fewer events are recorded in the second book, but more narrative space is given to them.[8] In addition, a considerable amount of "cronaca" is dedicated to sixteen exemplary novellas about both good and bad government, fourteen of which find their echo in *Il Novelliere*. Hence certain areas of this second book read like a *speculum principis*.

These chronicles cover a period of twenty-four years, beginning with an account of the events that led to the installation of Paolo Guinigi. After this opening, however, Paolo Guinigi is scarcely mentioned until we reach the last few pages of *Le Croniche di Luccha*, in particular chapter 374, which is significantly entitled: "Del danno che Iohanni Sercambi di Lucha à ricevuto per esser stato amico della casa de' Guinigi e del signore Paulo Guinigi" (Of the harm that Giovanni Sercambi suffered for having been a friend of the house of Guinigi and of the Lord Paolo Guinigi [3:333]). He subsequently lists eight different incidents that happened over the previous twenty-four years that led to his financial distress and to the loss of his honor. They range from an attack on his life to the burning down of his apothecary shop, and from legal hassles with an inept judicial system to the loss of several hundred florins. Although it is not my purpose to demonstrate how the concerns expressed in these crucial chapters are reflected in the introduction to *Il Novelliere*, the frame story, and several key novellas (1, 4, and 131), it is highly relevant that apparently for a quarter of a century Sercambi had been filtering autobiographical data through the fictional filter of the novella format.[9] It is also worth noting that Sercambi waited until the last few months, perhaps even days, of his life to vent, in straightforward, unequivocal prose, his frustration with the Guinigi government that he had helped install. Furthermore, only in the second part of his chronicles does Sercambi resort to exemplary storytelling. Hence the presence of sixteen novellas nested within the chronicles underscores the need to play out both forms of literary expression against each other, as the juxtaposition of "narrare" and "notare" indicates.[10] Luciano Rossi appears correct when he asserts, "Narratore e cronista, il Sercambi ha bisogno di integrare continuamente questi due tipi di attività letteraria, arricchendo in tal modo sia la materia dell'opera storica che quella del novelliere." (As both narrator and chronicler, Sercambi feels the need to continuously integrate both forms of literary activity, thus enriching both the matter of his historical writings and that of his work as writer of tales [*Novelliere*, 1:xxxiv].) In other words, a close comparison of Sercambi's two major literary endeavors, *Le Croniche di Luccha*—especially the second part—and *Il Novelliere*, demonstrates his remarkable ability to function simultaneously as chronicler within a novella collection and as *novellatore* within the textual confines of *cronaca*.[11] In both cases, however, the subject is "Io, Iohanni Sercambi."

Further examination of these dual roles shows how Sercambi's ambiguous artistic nature takes on the form of fiction, and how the interplay between both *cronaca* and *novellistica* is a deliberate and conscious act on the part of one for whom *novellistica* is an alternate vehicle for revealing autobiographical truth. This is demonstrated by one of *Il Novelliere*'s *exempli*, in which the possibilities and limits of both *cronaca* and *novella* are in themselves the subject that Sercambi self-consciously treats from within the framework of the "ideal."[12] The text in question is *Exemplo* 79, entitled "De bona providentia contra homicidam" (2:103–106). Although this tale usually captures critical attention as an oddity in the corpus of Sercambi's tale collection, it has remained just that: a surprising autobiographical tale about an adventure that happened to the author outside Lucca's city walls.

On Tuesday before Carnival the *altore* (author), his uncle, and a young man from Prato who has made Lucca his home are traveling from Lucca to Florence in order to buy some merchandise. Approximately one mile outside Lucca, near the Casa delli Aranci, they are approached by a poorly equipped youth, carrying only a lance and a knife ("un fante assai male in arnese, con una lancia e con un coltello"). He pretends he does not know the road to Pistoia and invites himself along. The four travelers reach Colli delle Donne, described as a notoriously dark and dangerous road ("là u' mal passo e scuro è sempre stato"). Here the youth suddenly becomes very talkative. The author, whose suspicions are aroused by the young man's sudden loquacity and the darkness of the path, grabs him by the collar and orders his uncle and the Pratese to remove their young companion's weapons. From here on, the fearful lad walks in front of them in silence ("non faccendo motto") until the small *brigata* reaches San Gennaio, where they spend the night. At the next stop, Borgo a Bugiano, the lad, who is recognized by an innkeeper as being of "cattiva condisione," leaves the Luccan travelers. When they reach Florence that night, the trio learns that several murderers were caught in the Pistoia area and that their young ex-companion is one of them. Upon their return to Lucca, on the Sunday of Carnival, the three travelers stop at the same inn at Borgo a Bugiano; the innkeeper confirms the news and adds that the murderers have since been hanged. He then relates to the wayfarers how the assassins used to roam the Luccan countryside, join unsuspecting travelers, and wait for a dark place on the road to kill and subsequently rob them. The author concludes this tale with the lesson that "d'alora in qua mai con straino in camino (*sic*) non preseno compagnia" (from then on they never traveled in the company of strangers).

From a purely formal perspective, even the casual reader is struck not only by the nearly central position of this novella in the collection, but also by its singular structure and unusual characteristics. The positioning of this novella suggests that it was intended to be centrally located and function as a metanovella, as did Boccaccio's novella of Madonna Oretta (*Dec.* VI, 1).[13] It is generally accepted that the manuscript of the *Novelliere*, mutilated at *Exemplo* 155, would most likely not have gone far beyond the number 155, given that the *brigata* is in Luni, which is close to Lucca, where the trip and hence the storytelling would most likely end. Bartolomeo Gamba pointed this out as early as 1816 in his partial edition of Sercambi's novellas: "A questo passo il codice manca, ma da Savona a Lucca, essendo breve il tragitto, pare che non possano desiderarsi se non che due o tre novelle a compimento dell'opera, e a vedere restituita la sollazzevole brigata alla città che dee reputarsi patria del Novellatore."[14] (At this point the manuscript ends, but from Savona to Lucca, which are in each other's vicinity, it seems plausible not to expect more than two or three novellas to finish the work and to have the brigata return to their city of departure, home of the narrator.)

Foremost among the unusual features that give *Exemplo* 79 a special place among the 155 novellas is the tale's autobiographical nature. The second atypical feature that obviously and purposefully distinguishes this story is its extreme attention to both chronological and geographical detail, which gives it the appearance of *cronaca*. The energy released by the dialectic interplay of these two characteristics inside their novellistic setting generates the dynamics of this particular tale.

At the outset of this novella, the reader is met by a surprising cameo appearance of the author himself: for the first and only time in these novellas, the *altore* narrates his persona by using the third person singular. By so doing, he introduces an autobiographical factor that follows the definition articulated by Eakin as borrowed from Philippe Lejeune's *Le pacte autobiographique*: "the identity of the proper name as shared by author, narrator, and protagonist" (24). The author's remarkable emergence as protagonist in the third person marks this *exemplo* as more than "[un] semplice resoconto d'un'avventura di viaggio occorsa all'autore nel periodo della sua giovinezza" (a simple account of an adventure that happened to the author during his youth [*Novelliere* 2:103, n. 5]). Moreover, this is the only time in *Il Novelliere* where the *altore* reconfirms his authority as maker of the book: "L'autore di questo libro fu con uno suo sio" (The author of this book was with his uncle [2:104]).

Sercambi-*altore* is here echoing his awareness of his role as author of the book as he had formulated it in *Il Novelliere*'s introduction in the form of an acrostic spelling of his name. About this peculiar acrostic, Sercambi wrote that "colui che vi si trovò per nome e sopranome, sens'altro dire comprese che li doveva essere *autore di questo libro*" (he who recognized his first and last name, without saying anything else, understood that he had to be *the author of this book* [emphasis added]). The repetition of this narcissistic game at the novella's outset coincides with the addition of a new rule for the *brigata* to abide by: "disse a l'altore che cominciasse qualche moralità e poi una novella dica . . . e se 'l camino fusse magiore che per uno díe, se ne faccia du', come è stato fatto fine a qui" (he told the author to start with a moral and to then tell a tale . . . and if the road was longer than the distance of one day, to tell two tales, as has been done until now [2:103]). A change in the formal presentation of the novella thus sets it apart from the previous tales.

A close look at *Exemplo* 79 reveals such a remarkable amount of detail that it actually nourishes our sense of "cronaca vissuta" and momentarily removes us from the formality of the novella. Sercambi describes with precision the chronological parameters of the trip: "il martedì innanti il carnelevare" (the Tuesday before Carnival [2:104]) for the beginning of the journey and "la domenica di carnolovare" (Carnival Sunday [2:106]) for the return to Lucca. We also know that the execution of the young boy and his companions takes place on a Saturday. Moreover, the year is 1369, a time when "Lucca fu dalla tirannica servitú de' pisani libera, di poghi mesi apresso" (Lucca had only for a few months been free of the tyrannical yoke of Pisa [2:104]). Geographical detail is no less evident. The journey proceeds along a logical succession of places: from Lucca to the Casa delli Aranci outside Lucca, via Colli delle Donne, San Gennaio, Pescia, and Borgo a Bugiano to Florence. The formal features of this unexpected *exemplo* are thus reminiscent of straightforward *cronaca*.

If the chronological and geographical precision of *Exemplo* 79 alert the reader to the tale as *cronaca*, it is remarkable that precisely within the boundaries of *cronaca* Sercambi has incorporated a discourse about the nature of *novellare*:

> E mossi insieme, andaron tanto che a' Colli delle Donne [giunseno], là u' mal passo e scuro è sempre stato. E come quine presso funno arivati, quello fante *intrò in novelle*, e sensa che neuno se n'acorgesse l'ebbe conduti in uno pratello intorniato di boschi dubievoli. Di che l'altore, ciò vedendo, pensando quel fante doverli tradire, subito la mano le misse al collaretto; e lla punta della lancia messoli al petto dicendo a lo ssio e al pratese che lla lancia e 'l coltello del fante prendessero, coloro cosí fenno. (emphasis added [2:104–105])

> (And together they walked until they reached Colli delle donne, where the path had always been dark and treacherous. As they arrived there, the young lad *started to tell stories*, and without anyone noticing he had led them into a small grassy area that was surrounded by suspicious woods. As soon as the author saw this, and, thinking that this youngster had plans to betray them, he grabbed him by the collar; and while pointing his lance against the lad's chest, he instructed his uncle and the Pratese to remove the young man's weapons. And so they did.)

The young man's conventional weapons are obviously not as powerful as his tongue. It is precisely because of his seductive "entrare in novelle" that he is able to lure the three travelers, unaware of imminent danger ("sensa che neuno se n'accorgesse"), into a dark and perilous area. Only at this point does the *altore* become suspicious of the young man and overpowers him. His premonitions are correct, as the rest of the story reveals. The *altore* has foreseen danger; he has been the able interpreter of both physical signs (we remember that the young lad is first described as "poorly equipped . . . carrying only a lance and a knife") and linguistic signs (his sudden loquacity). He has seen through the youth's use of *novellare* as a weapon of deception, indeed as a way of lulling his companions into a false sense of security. In other words, he meets the requirements expected of true leadership, both as commander of the mini-brigata and as author of the book: as leader, he has displayed the foresight to disarm a traitor before he can strike; as author of the book, he shares those same skills that enable him to penetrate the deception and resist the temptation of the text. He thus provides the "rimedio," that is, the ability to avert betrayal. As such, "rimedio" is defined by the narrative voice at the beginning of the next novella: "Lo preposto udito lo subito *rimedio* che l'altore prese di quel malandrino *traditore*, parlando alla brigata che prendano exemplo dalla dilettevole *novella*." (When the leader heard the swift action [literally, "remedy"] taken by the author on this evildoer and *traitor*, he told his brigata to take this pleasant *novella* as an example [emphasis added].) "Entrare in novelle" (starting to tell stories) is a means of betrayal ("pensando quel fante doverli tradire"): it can deceive the listener. As *altore* of the tales of *Il Novelliere*, Sercambi issues a warning against the seduction of his own novellas, which, as such, might deceive the listener or reader, including this metanovella about *novellare* as untruth.

Can this seventy-ninth novella possibly constitute a kind of dark metanovella (or should we call it meta-*cronaca*)? To support this claim, it is relevant that one of the conventional ingredients of *novellistica*, namely, the telling of tales in a *locus amoenus*, is here reversed. The "pratello" (small grassy area) where an act of betrayal is imminent is not colored green but is surrounded by "boschi dubievoli" (suspicious woods). The treacherous nature of the place is further enhanced by other images of darkness: the three travelers are led into a "mal passo e scuro" (a dark and treacherous path), and darkness prevails the entire time that the betrayer is in their presence; it is nighttime when they reach San Gennaio; it is night when they reach Florence. The place of deceptive *novellare* is thus situated in an anti–*locus amoenus*, an actual place called Colli delle Donne, which provides a neat contrast to that *locus amoenus* "per eccellenza" of Sercambi's great precursor: the Valle delle Donne of Boccaccio's *Decameron*.[15] Sercambi's play with so-called real *cronaca* and so-called fictional novella should make us both skeptical of, and receptive to, this detail. In anticipation of such an anti–*locus amoenus*, outside the novella, the frame story contains an identical thematic configuration: the *altore* tells this novella while the *brigata* traverses a "paese di malandrini e malfattori" (a town of bad folk and evildoers) and just after having spent some time in a pleasant garden where the previous two tales were related. The conventional notion of storytelling as a restorative activity is also inverted. The young man entertains the *brigata* of Luccan merchants intending an effect quite the opposite of restorative. Once the suspected betrayer has been deprived of his weapons, however, he also loses his speech, and the remainder of the itinerary is traversed in silence, "non faccendo motto" (not saying a word). Moreover, if deception through speech lies at the core of this novella, it should not surprise us that the temporal perimeters are marked by the days of Carnival: Sercambi has a masquerade of words performed during a time when masquerading is expected.

If *novellare* constitutes deception, its very nature paradoxically confirms the superiority of the "ideal" over the "real" medium. The *cronaca* mold into which Sercambi pours this tale of deception brings the discourse on *novellare* back into a "real" context, that is, into the conventionally accepted formal boundaries for relating true events. By presenting *Exemplo* 79 with the external features of the vehicle for truth telling, namely *cronaca*, Sercambi signals to the reader that *novellare* inside such a context constitutes deception. This also explains the various antinovellistic features that are at play within this unusual tale. By the same token, Sercambi sets his tale of deceptive storytelling in *cronaca* format within the larger framework of *Il Novelliere*. As an isolated instance of *cronaca*, it is textually overshadowed by the novellas that surround it, that is by the forms conventionally associated with fiction. Although this unusual tale presents itself externally as fact, as "truth," it is hidden behind the veil of fiction. As a novella that presents itself as *cronaca* and as such makes assertions about the deceptive nature of *novellare*, *Exemplo* 79 in fact proclaims itself as fiction and "untrue," informing us that *novellare* is deceptive. In other words, Sercambi makes a point of writing about the power of *novellare* by contradictorily curtailing that power through this tale written in chronicle format. In this format, *novellare* is fallible and susceptible to misinterpretation. Only in the extended context of *novellistica*, that is, in a reality-transcending medium where the novellistic message is open to interpretation, can the power of fiction prevail over truth.[16]

Sercambi dramatizes the problem identified by modern critics such as Hayden V. White, namely that "narrative becomes a 'problem' only when we want to give to 'real' events the 'form' of story. It is because real events do not offer themselves as stories that their narrativization is difficult" (4). Sercambi offers a real event in the form of story disguised as *cronaca* about the impossibility of relating real, autobiographical events in the context of *cronaca*, that is, in a context that claims to be "real." Our author invests the problem of "narrativization" of real events with the narrative form that brings that very problem into the realm of the real (*cronaca*), hiding it under the cloak of the ideal (*novella*). Since writing is a "discourse of separation,"[17] expressing oneself by calling upon a medium that has no pretensions to being "real" might paradoxically be more truthful. Writing (narrating) about a real event in the traditional format and presenting it as transcending reality, namely as *novella*, can be more true than straightforward chronicle writing. What White says about historiography—that it is "an especially good ground on which to consider the nature of narration and narrativity because it is here that our desire for the imaginary, the possible must contest with the real, the actual" (4)—Sercambi dramatizes through this intriguing instance of novella-writing in *cronaca* form.

Notes

A shorter version of this essay was read at the Thirty-Fifth International Congress on Medieval Studies, Western Michigan University, Kalamazoo, Michigan, May 6, 2000.

1. Giovanni Sercambi, *Le* Croniche *di Giovanni Sercambi, Lucchese, pubblicate sui manoscritti originali*, ed. Salvatore Bongi, 3 vols., Fonti per la storia d'Italia pubblicate dall'Istituto storico italiano. Scrittori, secc. XIV–XV, nos. 19–21 (Lucca: Tipografia Giusti, 1892); hereafter cited in text as *Croniche*.

    Lejeune distinguishes different types of "literature that speaks of oneself": memoirs, biographies, autobiographical novels, and the journal or diary. Whereas the notion of autobiography is present in all cultures, Lejeune admits that its definition as a genre is as impossible to define as that of the term "baroque" and that, for France, it dates back only about two centuries (*L'autobiographie en France* [Paris: Librairie Armand Colin, 1971], 5 and 12).

2. Paul John Eakin, *Touching the World: Reference in Autobiography* (Princeton, N.J.: Princeton University Press, 1992), 130. Eakin relates this problem to Jean-Paul Sartre's *Les Mots*.

3. Walter Pabst, *Novellentheorie und Novellendichtung. Zur Geschichte ihrer Antinomie in den romanischen Literaturen*, Hamburg Universität. Abhandlungen aus dem Gebiet der Auslandkunde, no. 58 (Hamburg: Cram, De Gruyter, and Co., 1953), 21–23; hereafter cited in text as Pabst. Pabst's work traces the development of the genre from Provençal *vidas* and *razos* and addresses issues of verisimilitude and fiction in the short prose tradition in medieval and Renaissance Italy. Bonvesin used the term *novella* to define his *De peccatore cum virgine*, a novella that, in spite of the Latin title, included dialogue written in Milanese dialect for the purpose of providing *diletto*. For other attempts to define the term *novella*, see Joseph Gibaldi, "Towards a Definition of the Novella," *Studies in Short Fiction* 12.2 (1975): 91–97; and Gerald Gillespie, "Novella, Nouvelle, Novella, Short Novel? A Review of Terms," *Neophilologus* 51 (1967): 117–27 and 225–30.

4. See Dante's description of the monster Geryon as "Quel ver c'ha faccia di menzogna" in *Inferno* XVI, 124.

5. References in text are to Boccaccio's *Decameron*, ed. Vittore Branca, 2 vols., Einaudi Tascabili. Classici, no. 99 (1980; reprint, Turin: Einaudi, 1992).

6. All references are to Giovanni Sercambi, *Il Novelliere*, ed. Luciano Rossi, 3 vols., I Novellieri italiani, no. 9 (Rome: Salerno Editrice, 1974); hereafter cited in text as *Novelliere*. All translations from Italian are mine.

7. Robert John Clements and Joseph Gibaldi, *Anatomy of the Novella: The European Tale Collection from Boccaccio and Chaucer to Cervantes*, The Gotham

Library of the New York University Press (New York: New York University Press, 1977), 8–12.

8. Alberto Guglielmo Dinucci, "Le novelle nelle Cronache di Giovanni Sercambi," in *Miscellanea lucchese di Studi Storici e letterari in memoria di Salvatore Bongi* (Lucca: Scuola Tipografia Artigianelli, 1931), 11; hereafter cited in text as Dinucci.

9. For an autobiographical reading of these novellas, see my "The Revenge of the Text: The Real-Ideal Relationship between Giovanni Sercambi's *Croniche* and *Novelliere*," Ph.D. diss., New York University, 1994.

10. All but two of *Le Croniche*'s sixteen novellas—the one to the Pisans (part II, chapter 89) and the one addressed to Pope Martin V (part II, chapter 280)—find their echo in *Il Novelliere*. Following the order in which the novellas appear in the Trivulziano MS 193, these correspondences are:

Exemplo 48	"De recto amore et giusta vendetta"	cfr. *Croniche* Part II, chap. 301
Exemplo 54	"De falsitate et tradimento"	cfr. *Croniche* Part II, chap. 60
Exemplo 60	"De superbia contra remm sacratam"	cfr. *Croniche* Part II, chap. 115
Exemplo 73	"De amicisia provata"	cfr. *Croniche* Part II, chap. 11
Exemplo 115	"De pigritia" (four novellas in one)	cfr. *Croniche* Part II, chap. 64
Exemplo 117	"De nemico reconciliato ne confidentur"	cfr. *Croniche* Part II, chap. 81
Exemplo 123	"De disperato dominio"	cfr. *Croniche* Part II, chap. 84
Exemplo 133	"De perfetta societate"	cfr. *Croniche* Part II, chap. 14
Exemplo 135	"De tiranno ingrato"	cfr. *Croniche* Part II, chap. 260
Exemplo 136	"De summa ingratitudine"	cfr. *Croniche* Part II, chap. 22
Exemplo 138	"De summa et iusta vendetta de ingrato"	cfr. *Croniche* Part II, chap. 29
Exemplo 152	"De muliere constante"	cfr. *Croniche* Part II, chap. 255

For a comparison of these novellas in their respective historical and novellistic surroundings, see Dinucci; see also *Il Novelliere*, ed. Rossi, vol. 3, "Apparato 2." On the role of chronicles and annals as forms of historiographic representation, see Hayden V. White, "The Value of Narrativity in the Representation of Reality," in *The Content of the Form: Narrative Discourse and Historical Representation* (Baltimore: The Johns Hopkins University Press, 1987); hereafter cited in text as White.

11. Giorgio Petrocchi, "Il novelliere medievale di Giovanni Sercambi," *Convivium* 1 (1949): 83.

12. Piotr Salwa dedicated his study *Narrazione, persuasione, ideologia: una lettura del* Novelliere *di Giovanni Sercambi, lucchese*, L'unicorno, no. 7 (Lucca: Maria Paccini Fazzi Editore, 1991) to the relationship between fiction and reality in *Le Croniche* and *Il Novelliere*. He argues that this relationship is true on several levels of meaning and involves various structures of the text and various aspects of the communicative process in literature.

13. See Pamela Stewart, "La novella di Madonna Oretta e le due parti del *Decameron,*" *Yearbook of Italian Studies* 3 (1973–1975): 27–40.

14. *Novelle di Giovanni Sercambi lucchese ora per la prima volta pubblicate,* ed. Bartolomeo Gamba (Venice: Alvisopoli, 1816), vii.

15. I wish to thank Teodolinda Barolini for pointing out this contrast.

16. Hermann H. Wetzel, "Novelle und Zentralperspektive. Der Habitus als Grundlage von Strukturellen Veränderungen in verschiedenen symbolischen Systemen," *Romanistische Zeitschrift für Literaturgeschichte* 4 (1985): 398.

17. Michel de Certeau, *The Writing of History,* trans. Tom Conley, European Perspectives (New York: Columbia University Press, 1988), 2.

5

Sercambi's *Novelliere* and *Croniche* as Evidence for Musical Entertainment in the Fourteenth Century

Cathy Ann Elias

Questions that continually vex performers and musicologists when performing early music are the most basic ones: How was the music performed? Who performed the various genres and in what context? What was the role of instruments in vocal performances? Surviving manuscripts preserve the musical repertoire but typically offer little information concerning performance practice. Specific instrumentation rarely was indicated, leaving us with only a blueprint of the music that surely had a lively and varied performance history. To understand the performance practice of early works, one must return to the place of origin and survey the cultural landscape. Documents available to modern musicians include accounts of historical events, payment records from institutions, treatises and instruction books, re-creations of social occasions in the form of dialogues, pictorial evidence, and works of imaginative literature. To create a more complete picture of musical entertainment in fourteenth-century Tuscany, I will discuss evidence found in two texts by Giovanni Sercambi, *Il Novelliere*, a narrative work modeled on Boccaccio's *Decameron*, and *Le Croniche*, an historical account of events in and around Lucca. In particular, I will focus on activities and entertainments described in the *cornice* of Sercambi's *Il Novelliere*.[1]

In any discussion of medieval Italy, one must remember that it was not a single unified place but only a geographic expression composed of many different city-states, duchies, republics, and so on. The social, cultural, and political situation in Lucca, for example, differed from that of Florence. Local practices are also reflected in musical repertories, but a glance at the major Florentine musical sources indicates that a shared musical tradition existed.

In his *Novelliere*, Giovanni Sercambi, a merchant, statesman, chronicler, and *novella* writer from Lucca, includes texts of songs, most of which had been set to music by Florentine composers, as well as brief discussions on how they were performed. He does not mention composers' names, nor does he include any music in his book. Unlike the situation for Boccaccio, however, the music for texts indicated by Sercambi is extant. Musical settings for all the texts he mentions appear in Florence, Biblioteca Medicea Laurenziana, Med. Pal. MS 87 (*Sq*), commonly known as the Squarcialupi Codex.[2] Several pieces mentioned by Sercambi also appear in three other important manuscripts: Florence, Biblioteca Nazionale Centrale, Panciatichiano MS 26 (*Fp*); London, British Library, Add. MS 29987 (*Lo*); and Paris, Bibliothèque Nationale, it. MS 568 (*Pit*). These manuscripts were compiled at the end of the fourteenth and the beginning of the fifteenth centuries and include works by composers working mostly in and around Florence.[3] The majority of pieces in these sources are secular. Whatever political differences existed between these cities, it is clear that Florentine composers were well known, and their music performed, throughout Tuscany. Musical manuscript sources and Sercambi's *Il Novelliere* support this notion.

We know little about the early life of Giovanni Sercambi (1348–1424), the son of a *speziale*, an apothecary. He married into an affluent merchant family of Lucca, and by 1372 he was a member of the *Consiglio generale della Repubblica* (the General Council of the Republic) where he served until 1397. In 1381 he held a seat in the *Consiglio dei Trentasei* (the Council of Thirty-Six). Distinguishing himself as a diplomat, he became entrenched in the intricate politics surrounding the powerful Guinigi family of Lucca.[4]

One might expect Sercambi's *Croniche*, a narrative history, to provide more accurate information than his *Novelliere*, a work of fiction, but this is not the case: a unique relationship exists between them.[5] When the political situation became personally unbearable under the rule of Paolo Guinigi, the *signore* of Lucca, Sercambi used the novella as an outlet to write about the failing government and moral decline under Guinigi's rule. Sercambi could "avenge with fiction (*novella*) what was impossible to express with non-fiction (*cronaca*)" (Ruthenberg, 6). A close reading of these two works reveals the overlap and reuse of material, blurring the lines between the two genres: "The *Croniche-Novelliere* interdependency is either explicit, because of identical or near-identical *novelle* present in both works—14 of them—or implicit, because many *novelle* conceal a truth that can only be expressed through a medium that allows the author to conceal *sub velum*" (Ruthenberg, 5). Sercambi also intertwines fact and fiction in other ways. Ruthenberg points out that "crucial pages of the *Croniche* are mirrored in ideal format in four places in the *Novelliere*: the 'Introduzione' and *novelle* 1, 4, and 131" (Ruthenberg, 4). Furthermore, historiography and fiction are conflated with autobiography. In Book Two of *Le Croniche*, Sercambi shifts into the first person to express his unhappiness under Paolo Guinigi (Ruthenberg, 4–5). Similarly, in *Il Novelliere*, Sercambi writes himself into the opening of the *cornice*. The leader of the group, called the *preposto*—alternately written *proposto*—selects an *autore* (storyteller) in the form of an acrostic, which outlines his name, "Giovanni Sercambi" (*Novelliere*, 1:10–11).

Beyond one early study by Howard Mayer Brown, references in Trecento literature to music and its performance have been generally ignored by music historians. Brown studied the musical descriptions that Boccaccio provides in the *Decameron* and drew conclusions about the musical repertoire that was performed and enjoyed by well-to-do Florentines throughout the first half of the fourteenth century.[6] Boccaccio includes the texts of the songs the group sang: without exception, all are ballatas. Neither musical settings nor references to possible musical performance for these pieces have ever been discovered. Since Boccaccio wrote these ballatas for the *Decameron*, no one would have had a chance to set his texts to music earlier than 1348–1352, the estimated dates of its composition.[7]

The ballata, originally monophonic, derives its name from *ballare*, to dance. The texts center on love and virtue, fitting topics for well-to-do Tuscans. Typically, the music is in two parts: the verses alternate with a refrain, creating the *AbbaA* structure outlined in Table 5.1.[8] With some deviations, Trecento composers followed the scheme shown in the table.

In the *Decameron*, at the end of seven of the ten evenings, a single person sings a ballata. Brown concludes that evidence in "the *Decameron* would seem to suggest that monophonic ballate were far and away the principal—indeed, the only—poetic form set to music and performed by and for the upper classes in the first half of the 14th century" (Brown, 327). Brown observes that this conclusion is at odds with the evidence provided by the musical sources. He points out that monophonic ballatas account for only 15 of the 176 pieces composed by the first generation of Italians writing polyphonic music, suggesting that the "surviving sources of [T]recento music reflect very badly the true situation in the first years of the century" (Brown, 327). To illustrate what the music sung by Boccaccio's brigade might have sounded like, Brown provides a musical setting of a ballata contemporary with the *Decameron*, "I' vo' bene a chi." The text, by Niccolò Soldanieri, was set to music by Gherardello da Firenze (see Appendix One, Example One).[9]

Despite such musical evidence, Brown is not convinced that Boccaccio's *brigata* performed ballatas such as this one because he feels the florid melodies, with their elaborate rhythms and irregular phrasings, were difficult to sing. Brown suggests instead that the group might have sung simpler settings of short poems with one-line refrains and one-line *piedi*, such as those in the Rossi Codex (Vatican

Table 5.1. Formal Structure of a Ballata

Poetic Form	Ripresa	Stanza (2 Piedi + Volta)			Ripresa
Poetic lines:	1 2 3	4 5	6 7	8 9 10	1 2 3
Music:	A	b	b	a	A

City, Biblioteca Apostolica Vaticana, Rossi MS 215), which preserves the earliest examples of Trecento music (dated c. 1325–1355). He suggests that they would have sung ballatas like these, but he points out that the manuscript contains pieces more elaborate in style (Brown, 327). The situation is different from the one that Brown describes, however, as even a visual inspection of the music shows: the actual style of the music in the Rossi Codex is not simpler. Several of the ballatas that Brown mentions are shorter and thus could be learned more quickly, but that has little to do with someone's musical skill (see Appendix One, Example Two). A performer would have had to possess the same musical abilities to sing the ballatas in both examples (see Appendix One, Examples One and Two). Nino Pirrotta suggests that the monophonic ballata was the most frequently sung poetic form, but one that must have been transmitted orally, which would explain why so few survive in manuscript sources.[10] Why were only five monophonic ballatas preserved in the Rossi Codex alongside some thirty madrigals for two voices? Before answering this question, one should remember that a large portion of this manuscript is missing, and no peripheral evidence allows us to hypothesize what it may have contained.

It would seem more likely that ballatas, along with other poetic texts, were performed both as quasi-improvised pieces and as more learned, and even notated, songs. Perhaps many of these settings began as simple songs, became embellished through improvised performances, and eventually were written out in more extended forms. The more elaborate versions would have to be written down to be learned and remembered. For instance, a madrigal for two voices in the Rossi Codex by Maestro Piero, "Quando l'aire (*sic*) comença," also appears in Panciatichiano MS 26. The significant differences between the two versions support the evolutionary scheme outlined: the version in the Rossi Codex lacks most of the ornamentation found in the Panciatichiano version (Appendix One, Example Three).

Brown suggests that the early ballatas were similar to laude and confirms that laude were sung by the upper classes, not just the lower classes, as other authors have proposed (Brown, 329). Lauda melodies survive in two manuscripts: the thirteenth-century *laudario*, Cortona, Biblioteca del Comune, MS 91, and the fourteenth-century *laudario*, Florence, Biblioteca Nazionale Centrale, Magliabechiano MS II.I.122 (*Banco Rari* MS 8).[11] The pieces in the Florentine manuscript are simpler and easier to sing, consisting of stanza(s) and a refrain. The musical form that best describes this repertory is *lauda-ballata*. Brown suggests that Boccaccio's well-to-do brigade members sang songs more closely related to laude that were similar to the simple ballatas found in the Rossi Codex rather than the ones in the florid style of Gherardello da Firenze and his contemporaries (Brown, 329). Unfortunately, none of the five ballatas in the Rossi Codex approach the simplicity of these laude. For instance, the ballata "Non formò Cristi" (Appendix One, Example Four) is longer and more complex than Gherardello da Firenze's "I' vo' bene a chi." This does not rule out the possibility that simple ballatas, similar to laude, were sung in an improvised fashion.

We also know that lauda texts often were sung to existing secular music, both monophonic and polyphonic. Gherardello da Firenze, who was for several years a member of the laude Company of San Zenobi, is thought to have composed pieces for them or at the very least, set lauda texts to his monophonic ballatas (Barr, 22). Since the majority of Gherardello's output is polyphonic, he most likely set lauda texts to polyphonic secular pieces as well. It would also not have been unusual for others to set new texts to his music. For instance, the music for "I' vo' bene a chi" that Brown mentions was used in a setting of the lauda text "Chi ama, in veritá prima a dia sè" by Neri Pagliaresi (c. 1350–1406), secretary and confidante to St. Catherine of Siena, and a contemporary of Sercambi. Several lauda texts were set to the music of the ballata for two voices "Ciascun faccia per se" (*Sq*, fol. 90r) mentioned by Sercambi in *Il Novelliere* by his contemporary Niccolò da Perugia. By the late Quattrocento, setting lauda texts to polyphonic ballatas was common practice.

The monophonic ballata by Gherardello, "I' vo' bene a chi," is noteworthy because Sercambi, writing in the next decades, includes this text in the *cornice* of his *Novelliere*. Music survives for eleven of the texts in Sercambi's *Il Novelliere*, but only this one is a monophonic setting; the rest are polyphonic (see Appendix Two). Among the composers of texts cited by Sercambi who were contemporary with the *Decameron* are Gherardello da Firenze, Lorenzo Masini, Donato da Cascia, and Niccolò da Perugia. Two younger composers whose texts are present in *Il Novelliere* are Bartolino da Padova and Francesco Landini. Biographical information for these composers is sketchy at best.

Gherardello da Firenze was born between 1320 and 1325 and died in Florence in 1362 or 1363. We know that in 1343 he was a clerk at Santa Reparata, the Cathedral of Florence. Two years later, he was ordained and became chaplain. In around 1351 he is identified as Ser Gherardello, upon his entry into the order of the Vallombrosa. Later he is associated with the Church of San Remigio in Florence (*New Grove II*, 9:808). Frank A. D'Accone indicates that between 1360 and 1363, Ser Gherardello was a frequent guest at the monastery there, which belonged to the Vallombrosa order, where on at least one occasion he was joined by Niccolò da Perugia.[12] Although he was known throughout his lifetime for his liturgical compositions, only two Mass movements have survived. His *Agnus Dei* for two voices is noteworthy because the style is similar to his madrigal settings.

We have even less information about several other composers who did musical settings of texts mentioned in Sercambi's *Il Novelliere*. Donato da Cascia was an Italian composer who lived in Florence during the second half of the fourteenth century. The placement of his works in the Squarcialupi Codex—composers are arranged by age—indicates that he is younger than Lorenzo and probably older than Landini (*New Grove II*, 7:459–60). Bartolino da Padova was active in Padua and most likely in Florence from 1365 to 1405. His inclusion in the Squarcialupi Codex and Sercambi's mention of him in both *Il Novelliere* and *Le Croniche* indicate that he was well known in Tuscany (*New Grove II*, 2:820–21). Niccolò da Perugia was active in Florence during the second half of the fourteenth century. Given that he set some texts by Sacchetti, he might have composed the pieces in Florence between 1354 and 1373. We also know that he and Gherardello da Firenze visited the Florentine monastery of Santa Trinita in 1362. All of his surviving works are found in Tuscan manuscripts. Thirty-six pieces, twenty-three *unica*, are found in *Sq* (*New Grove II*, 17:861–62). Lorenzo Masini was a member of the second generation of Trecento composers, a *canonicus* at San Lorenzo, Florence, from 1348 until his death in December 1372 or January 1373. His music is preserved only in Tuscan sources (*New Grove II*, 15:189).

There is no record of the birth of Francesco Landini, one of the greatest and most prolific Trecento composers. He was most likely born in Fiesole in around 1325 or 1335. He was the son of the painter Jacopo del Casentino, who belonged to the school of Giotto and who cofounded the Florentine painters' guild in 1339. Unfortunately, Francesco lost his sight from smallpox as a child. He apparently served as organist at the monastery of Santa Trinita in 1361 and as *cappellanus* at the church of San Lorenzo from 1365 until his death at the end of the century. The largest collection of his works, 145 pieces, survives in the Squarcialupi Codex (*New Grove II*, 14:212–13).

Did the situation change drastically from one generation to the next—predominately monophonic to polyphonic singing—within the same social milieu even though much of the same music would have been most likely available to both Boccaccio's and Sercambi's generations? To answer this question, we must examine *Il Novelliere* of Sercambi, who consciously imitates the *Decameron*. A copy of it was at his disposal in the Guinigi Library (Rossi, 1:xv). In reenvisioning the *Decameron*, Sercambi begins his *cornice* as follows: In 1374, a group of laymen, as well as children and clergy, meet and decide to leave Lucca to escape the current plague. In creating the *cornice*, Sercambi reinterprets parts of the *Bianchi* movement—to which he was an eyewitness—making it a civil rather than a religious event. The group travels from city to city throughout Tuscany, and later all over the peninsula.[13] Unlike the austere *Bianchi*, however, they eat wonderful meals, tell stories, sing, dance, and recite *moralità*.

Before they begin their travels, the *preposto* provides guidelines for the trip, including musical entertainment. He suggests that those who entertain the men at lunch and dinner should sing and tell tales of jousts and morality, using instruments and sometimes swords used in fencing. Others should perform songs of love and honesty to the women with lutes and pleasant instruments, in soft, low, and youthful voices (*Novelliere*, 1:9). Besides well-to-do young men and women, the group includes clergy as well as children, who are asked to perform on occasion: "Ordinò alcuni pargoletti saccenti col salterio sonare un salmo e una gloria, e quando s'udiva la messa e al levare del Nostro Signore uno *Sanctus sanctus, Deus*" (*Novelliere*, 1:9–10). (He ordered several children who knew how to play the psaltery, to play a psalm and a *Gloria*, and at Mass at the elevation of our Lord, play a *Sanctus, sanctus, Deus.*)[14] Citing descriptions from Luca Dominici's *Cronaca della venuta dei Bianchi e della moria*, Daniel E. Bornstein confirms that children were grouped together and performed music: "other groups were age-specific, like the children who dressed like their elders in white and went from church to church singing piously."[15]

Eight of the eleven texts in Sercambi's *Il Novelliere*, for which there is extant music, are by Niccolò Soldanieri (d. 1385), a prosperous and educated man from Florence. These texts—ballatas, and madrigals with extant music—are not intellectually, formally, or linguistically on par with the poetry of the high cultural register and obviously did not originate in a university or ecclesiastical milieu. They were intended for upper-class entertainment, to be accompanied by music or dance. Since these texts with polyphonic musical settings were written for the upper class, very likely they were performed by upper-class amateur musicians as well.

If these poems are for accompaniment to music and dance, one might ask, where is the music? Was it still being transmitted orally for the most part, as Pirrotta suggested? The answer is unclear, but the evidence of *Il Libro delle rime* of the Florentine poet and businessman Franco Sacchetti suggests that a large portion of the musical sources has been lost; therefore arguments based on the practice of polyphonic versus monophonic music in extant sources are not necessarily reliable. In Sacchetti's compilation of verses dating from 1354 to 1380, which he prepared himself, he lists the names of composers who set thirty-four of his texts. These are in various forms: *madrigale, ballata, caccia,* and *canzonetta.* Unfortunately, only twelve of the musical settings he mentions have survived. Composers he mentions include Lorenzo, Gherardello da Firenze, and Donato.[16] This would suggest that many musical sources have been lost because this repertory was well known and circulated widely at the time.

A closer look at selected descriptions of texts in Sercambi's *Il Novelliere*, compared with extant music, reveals seven two-voice madrigals, three two-voice ballatas, and one monophonic ballata. The music for all of these appears in the Squarcialupi Codex. This is noteworthy because six of them are only known to exist in this manuscript, which postdates Boccaccio and most likely Sercambi as well (*New Grove* II, 23:891). There are many textual variants, suggesting that Sercambi's source for the texts was not the Squarcialupi Codex or sources used in its compilation; as a writer, he might himself have introduced variants into the texts. Perhaps manuscripts containing these pieces were part of the Guinigi family library, to which we know Sercambi had access. In any case, clearly other sources for these pieces must have circulated outside Florence. The beautiful illumination of the Squarcialupi Codex suggests that it was not produced as a copy for use in performance but as a presentation copy.

Sercambi indicates that these pieces are to be sung by several people, not just one as in the *Decameron*. For example, the *preposto* or leader of the group indicates that both men and women are to sing together "Come da lupo pecorella presa," a madrigal for two voices by Donato: "La brigata e 'l preposto udita la dilettevole novella, e' cantatori e le cantarelle comincionno a cantare cansonette piacevoli e oneste in questo modo" (*Novelliere*, 1:326). (The brigade and the leader having listened to the delightful tale, and men and women singers started to sing pleasing and respectable songs in this fashion.) Another time the *preposto* asks only the men to perform "Un bel giffalco scese alle miei grida," also a madrigal for two voices by Donato: "Venuta l'ora della cena, prendendosi li cantatori per mano, con una cansonetta, dicendo in questo modo" (*Novelliere*, 2:84). (Dinner hour having arrived, the men singers, taking each other's hands, began singing a little song in this way.)

Elsewhere, the leader asks only the women to sing: "[E] perché l'ora della cena non era, lo proposto comandò che qualche rittimo per le cantarelle si dica, alto sí che ciascuno lo 'ntenda" (*Novelliere*, 3:203). ([A]nd because it was not yet dinnertime, the leader ordered that some rhymes be sung by the women with high and clear voices so all could hear.) Before dinner that evening, for example, the women sing "La fiera biscia che d'uman si ciba."[17] Afterwards, the leader points out how delightfully the women had sung:

La divisa cansonetta cantata per le cantarelle dié molto diletto alla brigata; e il proposto, molto contento che la sua brigata per lo caminare agiatamente avea imparato gramatica, lingua tedesca, franciosa e altre lingue. . . . (*Novelliere*, 3:204)

(The little song for two voices sung by the women singers brought much delight to the brigade; and the leader, very happy that his brigade through their walk had nimbly learned Latin, German, French, and other languages. . . .)

The one monophonic ballata, "I' vo' ben a chi" by Gherardello, is also sung here by singers who are clearly indicated as boys and girls:

[I]l quale proposto comandò a' dansatori che una dansa facesseno, e fatta, li cantatori una cansonetta cantassero, e ditta, la brigata a cenare andasse. E fatto il comandamento, le danse prese, li stromenti sonando tanto che le danse restarono, e restate, i cantarelli e cantarelle con voci puerili cantarono in questo modo una cansona . . . . (*Novelliere*, 2:355)

([T]he leader commanded the dancers to dance, having done it, that the singers sing a little song; and after that, the brigade should go to dinner. And, having given the order, the dances began; the instruments continued to sound until the dances stopped, and having stopped, the boys and girls sang in this way a song. . . .)

It is interesting that children—"i cantarelli e cantarelle con voci puerili"—sing the only monophonic ballata mentioned by Sercambi for which there is extant music. Was this because it would be easier for children to sing in unison? This also might suggest that monophonic ballatas were considered at the time not so very difficult to sing.

Sercambi rarely indicates that instruments should accompany singers. He tells us that they should be played while the group has lunch or dinner: "con una cansonetta spettaro la cena, dicendo: 'Virtú luogo non ha perché genti- le....' ... Ditta, messe le vivande in taula, tutti asettati, li stormenti sonando, cenarono con molto diletto" (*Novelliere*, 2:57). ([W]hile waiting for dinner, they sang a little song: "Virtú luogo non ha perché gentile." ... [H]aving sung it, with food on the table, and everyone seated, while the instruments played, they ate with much delight.) Although we have little information concerning the use of instruments to accompany vocal performances, one would assume that this was not unusual. Sercambi offers evidence to support this when he describes how "il preposto comandò che li stormenti sonassero e i cantatori cantassero. Li quali cantaron in questo modo: 'Vita non è piú misera e piú ria...'" (*Novelliere*, 2:201). (The leader ordered that they play instruments and that the singers sing. They sang thus: "Vita non è piú misera e piú ria....")

When the brigade enters Cremona, *i religiosi* sing some verses with sweet melodies, suggesting some type of quasi-improvised performance using stock melodies. The leader thanks them for singing something of serious substance. After that, " 'per dare a' grossi alcuno piacer comando che i cantatori dicano qualche cansonetta.' Loro presti dissero: 'Ciascun faccia per sé...'" (*Novelliere*, 3:64). (To give pleasure to the commoners, I order the singers to sing some little songs. They quickly sang: "Ciascun faccia per sé....") Here Sercambi suggests a distinction between types of music and social classes, but he is quick to point out that "la *notabile cansonetta de' cantatori*, non meno piaciuta che quella de' religiosi" (*Novelliere*, 3:65, emphasis added). ([T]he *notable little song of the singers* was no less pleasing than that of the *religiosi.*) As mentioned above, Rossi indicates that the music for this ballata was also used for singing lauda texts. In one manuscript exemplar, there is an incipit referring to this text with the direc- tion "cantasi come" (sing like ["Ciascun faccia per sé"]) (*Novelliere*, 3:64, n. 4).

One ballata text from Sercambi's *Novelliere* is particularly interesting because it also appears in his *Croniche*: "Coloro presti cominciaron a cantare in questo modo: 'Ama chi t'ama...'" (*Novelliere*, 3:35–36). (They quickly began to sing thus: "Ama chi t'ama...") There are several striking differences between the version of the poem, "Ama chi t'ama" found in *Il Novelliere* and the one found in *Le Croniche*. In *Il Novelliere*, Sercambi presents the poem without any repeated lines, but in *Le Croniche* he repeats the *ripresa*—sometimes all of it, sometimes just the first line—suggesting that he was writing down the lyrics to a song as it had been performed, in this case a ballata. Because Sercambi repeats

Table 5.2. First Stanza of the Ballata Text from *Le Croniche*

Text	Musical Form
Ama chi t'ama e sempre a buona fè;	A
serve qualumqua e non guardar perchè.	
Ama chi t'ama.	
Così faccendo pur tempo verrà,	b
La fama è cosa che va qua e chulì,	
Che un solo per tucti ti meriterà,	b
E per un cento farà quello a ti;	
Cosa non è che amor più tiri a sì	a
Com a servir sensa sperar merciè.	
Ama chi t'ama.	A
(*Croniche*, 2:242)	

the *ripresa*, one could infer that he knew this song and simply wrote down the lyrics from memory. When Bartolino da Padova sets the first strophe to music (see Table 5.2), he does not repeat "Ama chi t'ama" at the end of the first *ripresa*. It would be safe to assume that Sercambi simply did not write out the entire *ripresa* in the middle because it would have been obvious.

This ballata text appears at the end of the chapter "Come Guccio Signore di Cortona con Madonna Tancia sua moglie vennero a Luccha e a loro fu facto Grande Honore." After recounting the events, Sercambi inserts the poem to comment on the passage in an elegant fashion. This is an example of the "author" adding a verse insertion to the historical narrative to make it more literary in nature: "Racordando a te, Luccha, quello che li 'mfrascripti versi dicono, cioè: 'Ama chi t'ama' " (*Croniche*, 2:241–42). (Reminding you, Lucca, of that which the verses say, that is: "Ama chi t'ama.")

The descriptions of the last two texts with known extant music are important because they further illustrate the preference of performing vocal pieces without instrumental accompaniment:

e' cantatori dissero una cansona in questo modo: "Dà, dà a chi avansa pur per sé . . ."[18] (*Novelliere*, 2:224)

(and the singers sang a song in this way: "Dà, dà a chi avansa pur per sé . . .")

li cantatori comincionno alcuna cansonetta in questo modo, cioè: "L'aguila bella nera pellegrina . . ." (*Novelliere*, 2:91)

(the singers began to sing some little songs in this way, that is to say [like]: "L'aguila bella nera pellegrina . . .")

A survey of Sercambi's descriptions of verses for which there is extant music indicates that polyphonic music was the norm; the brigade performed all of them, including the monophonic one, with several singers to a part. The evidence in Sercambi suggests that all of these performances except one were performed *a cappella*. Instruments are mostly associated with dancing and usually come to a rest when the singing begins.

What can we glean from a survey of the texts Sercambi refers to but for which there is no extant music? Sercambi divides his brigade into two main groups: *li cantatori* (*le cantarelle*) and *li religiosi*. On occasion, children's voices are explicitly indicated. For the most part, *li cantatori*, as one might expect, sing songs. Almost without exception, Sercambi describes several people singing together. Two of his descriptions of ballata performances without known extant music are remarkable because they provide valuable insights into improvisatory-type performance practices. Both texts are by Soldanieri.

> [I]l proposto comandò che una cansonetta si dica con quelle melodie che siano piacevoli alla brigata, e ditta, si prenda una dansa e cosí apresso alla cena se ne vada. *Le cantarelle*, udendo la volontà del proposto, comincionno a cantare in questo modo, cioè: "Tu, che biasmi altrui, guarda in te prima. . . ." (*Novelliere*, 2:338, emphasis added)

> ([T]he leader ordered that a little song be sung with those melodies that would be pleasing to the brigade and, having sung it, one should dance, and afterward, one should go to dinner. The female singers upon hearing the leader's wishes, began to sing in this fashion, "Tu che biasmi altrui, guarda in te prima. . . .")

This passage suggests that some ballatas were sung to preexisting melodies, indicating that a form of quasi-improvisatory performance using well-known melodies was part of this group's agenda. Once again, several women sing together. The tradition of women singing without men was common. In the next example, Sercambi describes the following performance by either male singers or males and females together (*cantarelli*):

> Ma perché non era l'ora della cena, il proposto, volendo alquanto da' cantarelli piacere, comandò loro che una cansonetta dicessero con bello tinore . . . "I' servo e non mi pento, ben che a 'ngrato. . . ." (*Novelliere*, 3:118)

> (But because it was not yet dinnertime, the leader, wanting something pleasant from the singers, commanded them to sing a little song with a beautiful tenor . . . "I' servo e non mi pento, ben che a 'ngrato. . . .")

In this instance, they sing a melody above a "tenor" (possibly a drone), illustrating a quasi-improvisatory polyphonic piece. Perhaps they added a tenor to a well-known melody or they improvised a melody to a preexisting tenor?

The other group, the clerics, mostly performs *moralità*—didactic songs—usually one verse without mention of music, but there are notable exceptions. In one instance, Sercambi indicates that these texts are to be sung to the "beautiful melodies" in unison by the *religiosi*. For example, the leader commands the following: "[V]oi *religiosi* dite qualche *moralità* in canto soave" (emphasis added; *Novelliere*, 3:165). ([Y]ou *religiosi*, declaim some *moralità* in gentle song"). The text they sing, "Roma fu già del secol la colonna," is also by Soldanieri. Referring once again to songs sung by the clerics, Sercambi writes how

> li religiosi comincionno a dire, con quelle melodie in canto che si richiede, in questo modo: "Tu, ignorante, segui le ricchesse. . . ." Lo proposto udite le dolce melodie, essendo l'ora della cena. . . . (*Novelliere*, 2:362–63)

> ([T]he *religiosi* began to sing, with those melodies in song that were requested, in this way: "Tu, ignorante, segui le ricchesse. . . ." The leader, having heard the sweet melodies, being the time for dinner. . . .)

This text by Soldanieri is the second stanza of a *canzone morale* that also appears in Sercambi's *Le Croniche* (2:372–75). In describing the *Bianchi*'s visit to Lucca, Sercambi lists several laude that they sang followed by a complete version of this devotional piece. The first and fourth stanzas of this *moralità* are also sung by the *religiosi* in *Il Novelliere*. The following is the reference to the first stanza:

> prima che si cenasse i religiosi dicessero qualche buona cosa. E pregati, rispuoseno esser presti e con dolce melodie disseno: "Cosí del mondo e stato alcun ti fida. . . ." (*Novelliere*, 3:64)

> (before dinner the *religiosi* should sing something good. And, having been asked, they responded that they were ready, and with sweet melodies sang: "Cosi del mondo e stato alcun ti fida. . . .")

On another occasion, they sing the fourth stanza:

> [L]o proposto . . . disse a' religiosi che una moralità dicesseno acciò che lo spettare non faccia rincrescimento alla brigata. Loro presti a ubidire con canti, suoni, dissero: "Colui pover non è che di' c'ha pogo. . . ." (*Novelliere*, 3:158)

> ([T]he leader . . . told the *religiosi* to sing a *moralità* so that the wait would not trouble the brigade. They were quick to obey with songs and instruments, playing: "Colui pover non è che di' c'ha pogo. . . .")

The generally accepted notion that the *Bianchi* sang only simple songs of praise needs to be revisited. Descriptions in Dominici's *Cronaca* indicate that the second wave of *Bianchi* moved initially in distinct groups corresponding to precise social classes, the elite class being very small. "The ordinary folk followed the bishop in the morning; but in the afternoon, the members of an elite group went like us where we did this morning" (Bornstein, 113). This notion that didactic chansons were sung by an elite group is borne out by Sercambi's references in his *Novelliere*. Similarly, in his *Croniche* Sercambi suggests that more than one class traveled together; the ones in front, perhaps more learned, led the group singing laude in Latin, and the others who followed mimicked them:

> E quelli che vanno dinanti, denno cantare una delle lalde dicendo:
>> Stabat mater dolorosa
>> Iuxta crucem lacrimosa
>> Dum pendebat filius;
> e questo verso denno tucti i Bianchi rispondere. (*Croniche*, 2:321)

> (And those who go in front must sing one of the laude, saying:
>> Stabat mater dolorosa
>> Iuxta crucem lacrimosa
>> Dum pendebat filius;
> and all the *Bianchi* must respond with this verse.)

The laude that follow in *Le Croniche* are in Italian, suggesting a mixture of clergy and laymen singing together.

The one time that no one sings or plays instruments is on Friday: "E perché non era l'ora della cena, [né] di stromenti [il proposto] volse che li religiosi dicesseno sensa canto qualche cosa morale: '*Quotiescunque claudicat Justitia / per l'universo pondo della terra. . . .* ' " (*Novelliere*, 3:87). (And because it was not the time for dinner or [to play] instruments, he wanted the *religiosi* to say without song something devotional: "*Quotiescunque claudicat Justitia* / per l'universo pondo della terra . . ."). The passage in Sercambi suggests that these *religiosi* sang mostly monophonic melodies in unison, perhaps stock ones to these more complicated texts, and instruments are rarely mentioned.

This brigade provided still other types of entertainment for each other. Several times throughout *Il Novelliere*, Sercambi indicates that they performed some *bisticci*, apparently a type of improvised call and response. For instance, one day in the garden of an inn, Sercambi writes:

> E dapoi, restato la dansa, comandò che qualche bisticcio per li cantarelli e canterelle si dicesse. E trattosi da parte li cantarelli et alla incontra le canterel[le], con voci alte e squillanti dissero l'uno a l'altro in questo modo:

>> "Ami tu, donna, me come dimostri?"
>> "Cosí non t'amasse io!"
>> "E io piú te che 'l cuor del corpo mio!"
>>> "I' temo, donna, che tu non m'inganni."

"I' non t'inganno, ma tu inganni me."
"Tu sai ch'i' porto per te tanti affanni?"
"Oh, tu che sai ch'i' porto per te?"
"Poss'io credere che piú non m'inganni?"
"No, se m'aiuti Idio."
"E io piú te non metterò in oblio."
    "Io son Ballata e vegno a voi, madonna,
ringrasiando e sempre ringrasierò,
dapoi che d'ancilla sete colonna
di questo servo lo qual ditto v'ho."
    "A te, Ballata, si risponderò
secondo il parer mio
che tu stii fermo, e me contenti io." (*Novelliere*, 3:169–70)

(And after the dance ended, he ordered the male and female singers to say some *bisticci*. After the male and female singers positioned themselves in two groups, one facing the other, they sang to each other with loud and shrill voices thus:

    "Do you love me, Lady, as you show?"
"As if I wouldn't love you so!"
"And I love you more than the heart of my body!"
    "I am afraid, lady, that you deceive me."
"I do not deceive you, but you deceive me."
"You know that I suffer so much anxiety because of you."
"Oh, you know that I suffer so for you?"
"Can I believe that you no longer deceive me?"
"I do not, so help me God."
"And I shall no longer forget you."
    "I'm a Ballata, and come to you, my lady,
thanking [you], and I shall become ever more grateful,
since you are the main support
of this servant of whom I spoke to you."
    "To you, Ballata, I shall reply,
according to my opinion
that you are steadfast, and this makes me content."

Were the members of the brigade supposed to improvise these verses as they went along, and perhaps sing them to a simple tune? I suggest that this is the case.

To conclude, if Boccaccio's brigade were familiar with the monophonic works of composers such as Lorenzo, Donato, and Gherardello, as Brown suggests, then they must have known of the polyphonic works of these composers as well. The evidence exists in Sercambi's works. Although Sercambi was born a generation later, the productive period of these composers spans the lives of both writers. Did well-to-do Tuscans over the quarter century between the completion of the *Decameron* and the initiation of Sercambi's writings become much better musicians and favor, almost to exclusion, secular polyphonic works? I believe the practices of Sercambi's brigade were not an anomaly, and perhaps Boccaccio's descriptions are more connected with enhancing the literary work than with representing the comprehensive musical practices of the time. As far as can be ascertained, Boccaccio wrote these ballatas for the *Decameron*. Whether he wrote them contemporaneously with the text or immediately afterward and then inserted them into appropriate places is still a point of debate (Beck, 46–50). For our purposes, it does not matter, because these texts had not yet been set to music at the time Boccaccio was writing the *Decameron* and thus he was not recalling any specific musical composition. On the other hand, Sercambi continually refers to texts with well-known musical settings in and around Lucca and Florence.

It would appear that the sharp division between the monophonic and polyphonic singing of upper-class Tuscans one generation apart should be blurred, suggesting a possible shift in emphasis between the two styles—monophonic and polyphonic—of singing, not a break from one to the other. After all, Sercambi's brigade sang ballatas to "well-known melodies." If this quasi-improvisatory method of performing ballatas was common also, Boccaccio would not have needed to place much emphasis on the aspects of musical performance.

In reflecting on the performance practice of his day, Francesco Landini's madrigal, "Musica son / Già furon / Chi vuol," sheds valuable light on the musical situation just described. The text expresses sadness at the decline of taste and dismay at the rise of the *frottola*. Landini complains that too many unskilled musicians have the audacity to write madrigals, *cacce*, and ballatas before developing the skill necessary to create excellent music:

> Ciascun vuole innarrar musical note,
> [E] compor madrial, cacce, ballate,
> Tenendo ognum le sue autenticate.
> Chi vuol d'una virtù venire in lloda
> Conviengli prima giugner alla proda. . . . [19]

> (Everyone wants to write musical notes
> And to compose madrigals, *cacce*, and ballatas,
> Each one regarding his own as authentic.
> He who wants to be praised for his efforts,
> Must first arrive at the shore. . . .)

Landini's verses suggest that too many people were composing these pieces with little skill. If so many people were composing polyphonic music, surely they were capable of singing it, too!

APPENDIX ONE

Example One: Gherardello da Firenze's setting of "I' vo' bene a chi" by Soldanieri. Florence, Biblioteca Medicea Laurenziana, Med. Pal. MS 87 (*Sq*), fol. 29r.

Example Two: "Per tropo [*sic*] fede." Vatican City, Biblioteca Apostolica Vaticana, Rossi MS 215 (*Rs*), fol. 19r.

Example Three: Two versions of Maestro Piero's "Quando l'aire [*sic*] comença," measures 1–11.

a. Vatican City, Biblioteca Apostolica Vaticana, Rossi MS 215 (Rs), fol. 7r.

b. Florence, Biblioteca Nazionale Centrale, Panciatichiano MS 26 (FP), fols. 57v–58r.

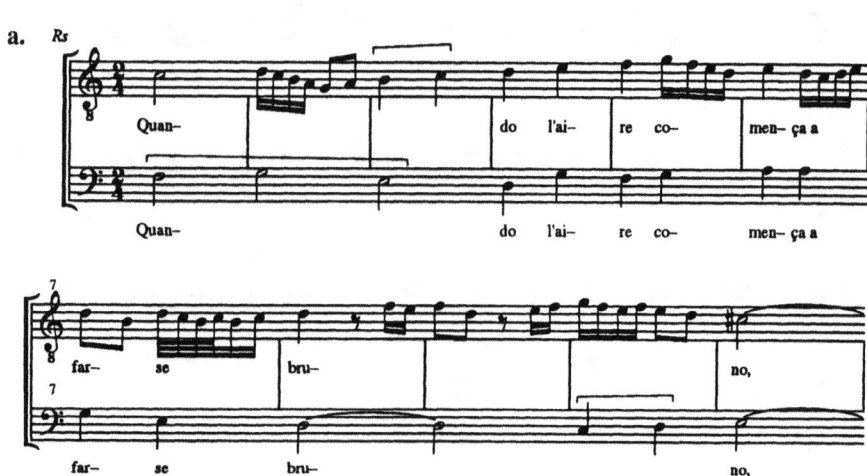

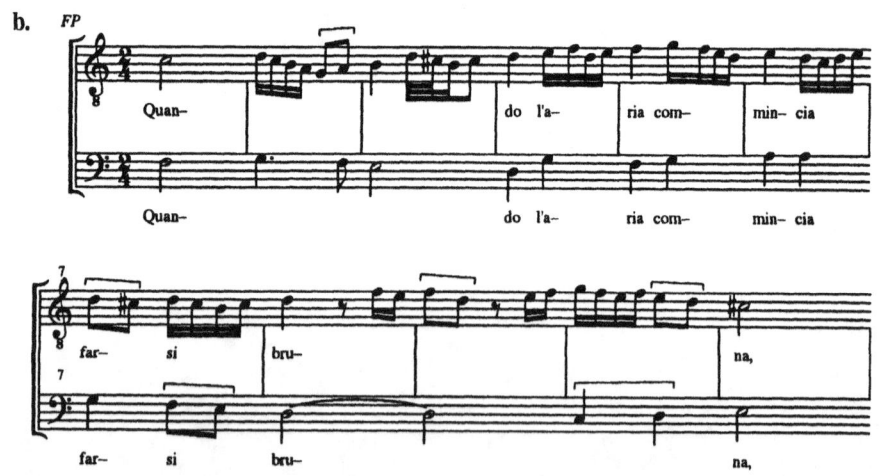

Example Four: "Non formò Cristi." Vatican City, Biblioteca Apostolica Vaticana, Rossi MS 215 (*Rs*), fol. 23v.

APPENDIX TWO

Texts mentioned in Giovanni Sercambi's *Il Novelliere* and their extant musical sources.

Music	Composer	Text	Form	MS Music	Novella	Vol./Page
Come da lupo	Donato da Cascia	Soldanieri	M à2	*Sq*	LVII	1:326
Virtù lungo, non ha	Niccolò da Perugia	Soldanieri	M à2	*Sq*	LXIX	2:57
Un bel giffalco	Donato da Cascia	Soldanieri	M à2	*Sq, Pit, Sl*	LXXV	2:84
L'aguila bella	Gherardello	Soldanieri	M à2	*Sq*	LXXVI	2:91
Io fui già ruzignolo	Donato da Cascia	Soldanieri	M à2	*Sq, Pit, Sl*	LXXVIII	2:99
Vita non è più misera	Francesco Landini	Landini (?)	B à2	*Sq, Fp, Pit, Sl, R*	LXXXVII	2:201
Dà, dà a chi	Lorenzo Masini	Soldanieri	M à2	*Sq*	CI	2:224
I' vo' ben a chi	Gherardello	Soldanieri	B à1	*Sq*	CXXIIII	2:355
Ama chi t'ama	Bartolino da Padova	(?)	B à2	*Sq, R*	CXXXI	3:36
Ciascun faccia per sè	Niccolò da Perugia	Soldanieri	B à2	*Sq, Lo, Pit*	CXXXV	3:64–65
La fiera biscia	Bartolino da Padova	(?)	M à2	*Sq, Pit, Sl*	CLI	3:203–4
	Niccolò da Perugia	(?)	C à3	*Sq*	CLI	3:203–4

M = madrigal, B = ballata, C = caccia

Notes

A shorter version of this essay was read at the Thirty-Third International Congress on Medieval Studies, Western Michigan University, Kalamazoo, Michigan, May 7, 1998. I would like to thank Bonnie J. Blackburn for her helpful suggestions and thoughtful comments on this revision.

1. The principal sources for Giovanni Sercambi's writings are the following: *Le Croniche di Giovanni Sercambi, Lucchese, pubblicate sui manoscritti originali*, ed. Salvatore Bongi, 3 vols., Fonti per la storia d'Italia pubblicate dall'Istituto storico italiano. Scrittori, secc. XIV–XV, nos. 19–21 (Lucca: Tipografia Giusti, 1892); hereafter cited in text as *Croniche*; and id., *Il Novelliere*, ed. Luciano Rossi, 3 vols., I Novellieri italiani, no. 9 (Rome: Salerno Editrice, 1974); hereafter cited in text as *Novelliere*.

2. See *Il Codice Squarcialupi: MS. Mediceo Palatino 87, Biblioteca Medicea Laurenziana di Firenze*, ed. F. Alberto Gallo (Florence: Giunti Barbèra, 1992).

3. See *Il Codice Musicale Panciatichi 26 della Biblioteca Nazionale di Firenze: riproduzione in facsimile*, ed. Gallo, Studi e testi per la storia della musica, no. 3 (Florence: Leo S. Olschki, 1981). The music in *Fp* dates from 1340 to 1440/1450, and contains 185 pieces: madrigals (59), *cacce* (15), ballatas (85), French *ballades* (15), *rondeaux* (9), and *virelais* (2). Composers represented include Francesco Landini (86), Jacopo da Bologna (22), Giovanni da Cascia (18), Maestro Piero (8–9), Donato da Cascia (5), Gherardello da Firenze (5), Lorenzo da Firenze (5), and Guillaume de Machaut (5).

    All the music in *Lo* with the exception of one piece dates from 1340 to 1400; no. 118 is much later. There are 119 pieces: madrigals (35–36), *cacce* (8), ballatas (45), *estampies* (15), *virelais* (3), liturgical works (7), and other pieces. Composers include Landini (29), Niccolò da Perugia (12 or 13), Jacopo da Bologna (7), Bartolino da Padova (5), and Giovanni da Cascia (50).

    Pit contains 199 pieces dating from 1340 to c. 1410. There are madrigals (45), *cacce* (5), ballatas (113), *ballades* (10), *rondeaux* (13), *virelais* (8), and polyphonic settings of five movements from the Ordinary of the Mass. Composers include Landini (61), Paolo da Firenze (32), Niccolò da Perugia (6), Jacopo da Bologna (11), Bartolino da Padova (5), Gherardello da Firenze (5), and Donato da Cascia (5).

    Sq, the most important source, contains 353 different pieces (150 *unic*) dating from c. 1410/1415, most likely originating from the Florentine monastery of Santa Maria degli Angeli whence it passed into the hands of Antonio Squarcialupi, who was organist at Santa Maria del Fiore. The music—madrigals (115), ballatas (227), and *cacce* (12)—dates from 1340 to 1415 and is arranged in chronological order by composer. Each section opens with a portrait of the composer, beginning with Giovanni da Cascia (12). Next follow works by, among others: Jacopo da Bologna (28), Gherardello da Firenze (16), Vincenzo da Rimini (6), Lorenzo da Firenze (17), Donato da Cascia (15), Niccolò da Perugia (36), Bartolino da Padova (37), Landini (146), Egidio and Guiglielmo di Francia (5), Zaccaria da Teramo (7), and Andrea da Firenze (29). This information is based on

The New Grove Dictionary of Music and Musicians, ed. Stanley Sadie, 2nd ed., 29 vols. (London: Macmillan Reference, 2001), 23:888–91; hereafter cited in text as *New Grove II*.

4. For a detailed account of Sercambi's life, see the chapter "Problems and Contra-dictions Surrounding Sercambi's Life and Work," in Myriam Swennen Ruthen-berg, "The Revenge of the Text: The Real-Ideal Relationship between Giovanni Sercambi's *Croniche* and *Novelliere*" (Ph.D. diss., New York University, 1994), in particular 44–45; hereafter cited in text as Ruthenberg.

5. See, in addition, the essay by Swennen Ruthenberg, Chapter 4 in this collec-tion.

6. Howard Mayer Brown, "Fantasia on a Theme by Boccaccio," *Early Music* 5 (1977): 324–39; hereafter cited in text as Brown.

7. For an interesting, but inconclusive, discussion on the topic of when Boccaccio added the ballatas to the *Decameron*, see Eleonora M. Beck, *Singing in the Gar-den: Music and Culture in the Tuscan Trecento*, Bibliotheca musicologica Univer-sität Innsbruck, no. 3 (Lucca: LIM Editrice, 1998), 46–50; hereafter cited in text as Beck.

8. An upper-case letter indicates that both the text and the music repeat; a lower-case letter indicates that only the music repeats.

9. All musical examples may be found in Appendix One. The musical transcriptions are my own. I have benefited from *The Music of Fourteenth Century Italy*, ed. Nino Pirrotta, 5 vols., Corpus mensurabilis musicae, no. 8 ([n.p.]: American Institute of Musicology, 1954–1964), 1:79, 2:2–4, 36, 45; and *Italian Secular Music*, ed. W. Thomas Marrocco, Polyphonic Music of the Fourteenth Century, nos. 6–11 (Monaco: Éditions de l'Oiseau-Lyre, 1967–1978), 6:14–17; 7:92; and 11: 1999, 119.

10. *Il Codice Rossi 215/The Rossi Codex 215*, facsimile ed. Pirrotta, Ars nova, no. 2 (Lucca: Libreria musicale italiana editrice, 1992), 96.

11. Cyrilla Barr, *The Monophonic Lauda and the Lay Religious Confraternities of Tuscany and Umbria in the Late Middle Ages*, Early Drama, Art, and Music Monograph Series, no. 10 (Kalamazoo, Mich.: Medieval Institute Publications, Western Michigan University, 1988), 61; hereafter cited in text as Barr.

12. Frank A. D'Accone, "Music and Musicians at the Florentine Monastery of Santa Trinita, 1360–1363," *Quadrivium* 12 (1971): 145.

13. For details, see Giovanni Sercambi, *Novelle*, ed. Giovanni Sinicropi, 2 vols., Filologia. Testi e studi, no. 5 (Florence: Casa Editrice Le Lettere, 1995), 1:9–10.

14. Unless otherwise noted, all translations are my own.

15. Daniel E. Bornstein, *The Bianchi of 1399: Popular Devotion in Late Medieval Italy* (Ithaca, N.Y.: Cornell University Press, 1993), 113; hereafter cited in text as Bornstein.

16. F. Alberto Gallo, *Music of the Middle Ages II*, trans. Karen Eales (Cambridge: Cambridge University Press, 1985), 65.

17. This text was set as a ballata à2 by Bartolino da Padova and as a madrigal à3 by Niccolò da Perugia. These settings are found in *Sq*, fols. 104v–105r and 95v, with the variant incipit: "La fiera testa che d'uman si ciba."

18. Medieval and Renaissance Italian writers frequently used the verb *dire* to refer to singing. See my "Musical Performance in 16th-century Italian Literature: Straparola's *Le piacevoli notti*," *Early Music* 17 (1989): 50, n. 173.

19. *Poesie musicali del Trecento*, ed. Giuseppe Corsi, Collezione di opere inedite o rare pubblicate dalla Commissione per i Testi di Lingua, no. 131 (Bologna: Commissione per i Testi di Lingua, 1970), 129–30, corrected with reference to the *Sq* facsimile, ed. Gallo, fols. 121v–122r.

6

The Lover Praised by the Husband: A Courtly Tale between *Exemplum* and Novella

Maria Bendinelli Predelli

Manuscript C43 (former 160) of the Biblioteca Augusta in Perugia is an interesting collection of early Italian poetry and rhymed tales that has not attracted much critical attention, probably because of the heavy dialectal patina that the scribe imposed on the texts he was transcribing. Although it was copied in the mid-fifteenth century, it preserves some examples of archaic material.[1] On folios 113r–117v, the manuscript contains a "story," or tale, in *sestine* (stanzas of six hendecasyllables) that represents one more version of a tale that had limited circulation between the Middle Ages and the Renaissance.[2] The story goes as follows: A knight has been in love with a married woman for a long time, but she has always rejected his advances. One day, after her husband had extolled the virtues of that knight with high praises in her presence, the woman is moved to grant him her favors. She summons him and he gladly comes to her, but while they prepare to consummate their love the woman reveals to him that her sudden change of heart is due to her husband's favorable comments concerning him. The knight then suddenly withdraws from their embrace, declaring that he will never be discourteous toward a man who has such great affection for him. He leaves the woman in spite of her protests and puts an end to his wooing.

To my knowledge the version of the cantare conserved in Manuscript C43 has never been considered in studies of this tale and its transmission, yet this version is important enough to justify a reexamination of the background of the tale in order to understand the process of modification the story underwent in the course of the centuries and across cultures.

The known versions of the story are as follows:

1. Walter Map's *De nugis curialium*, written between 1182 and 1189. The story under investigation, here entitled *De Rollone et eius uxore*, is the last and the shortest of the four tales comprising the third "Distinction."[3]

2. Giraldus Cambrensis's *Gemma ecclesiastica*, a manual for the Welsh clergy, written between 1196 and 1199, which presents the story as an *exemplum* of *continentia*.[4]

3. Ser Giovanni Fiorentino's *Il Pecorone*, traditionally dated to the late fourteenth century, in which our story is the first novella of the First Day.[5]

4. Tommaso Guardati's (better known as Masuccio Salernitano) *Il Novellino*, which was begun in 1450.[6] The story, Novella 21, opens the third part in which, according to the author, "il defettivo muliebre sesso será in parte crociato" (the female sex, so full of failings, will be handled somewhat cruelly).[7]

Broadly speaking, the story was redacted in two *exempla* (Walter Map, Giraldus Cambrensis) and two novellas (Ser Giovanni Fiorentino, Masuccio Salernitano). By contrast, the manuscript C43 version can be attributed to the genre of *cantari*, the narrative poems in either *sestine* or *ottave* sung by *canterini* (jongleurs) in piazzas for the entertainment of the general public. It belongs therefore to the realm of "popular literature." This poem has even less literary merit than some other, better-known *cantari*, but contributes evidence to clarify the problem of the transmission of the story, and thus invites the critic to revisit the question of the relationships among the various versions and provides valuable evidence regarding problems in the transmission of a story. In fact, it is still unclear by which chain of transmission the tale, originally narrated by two high-ranking clerics who were connected with the Anglo-Norman court of Henry II, found its way into Italy and resurfaced there in written form two centuries later. The question is all the more interesting considering that the Latin texts of the two British clerics were not well known in the Middle Ages. There is only one extant manuscript of *De nugis curialium* (Oxford, Bodleian Library, Bodley MS 851), and it appears that the section containing the tale had no circulation at all.[8] Similarly, only one manuscript of the *Gemma ecclesiastica* has come down to us,[9] in spite of Giraldus's report that, when presented with his works, Pope Innocent III cherished the *Gemma* over all other works to the point that he refused to lend it to anyone.[10] Letterio Di Francia, discussing the four above-mentioned versions, attributed the survival of the story to oral tradition.[11] James Hinton thought instead that the source, more or less direct, of the Italian novellas was Giraldus's *Gemma*: "We need not imagine . . . that Innocent's successors were all equally fond of the Welshman's work, and we may safely assume that, in the course of time, the book was accessible to Italian clerks. . . . If the story of Reginald de Pumpuna were not more like the two *novelle* than it is the story of Resus, it would still be a more likely source for them, for we can account for its presence in Italy."[12]

In this essay, however, I should like to set aside the strictly philological issues in order to focus on the modification of the story from the point of view of literary history. Here we have a story spanning three centuries and reappearing in basically the same terms across cultures, languages, and chronological periods. If the plot remains the same, does the meaning of the story also remain the same? How can the same plot appear congenial to different milieus and apt to convey different cultural concerns? How can we recognize the worldview a literary artifact conveys when this artifact is handed down from a far distant past? A circumscribed cycle with a limited number of occurrences such as the one we are considering offers a unique opportunity to study such issues. After a quick review of the main points that differentiate the known versions of the tale, I shall first examine the relative "sameness" of the narrative structures, a sameness that persists in spite of superficial changes in content. I shall then try to assess the different meanings that the versions of the story assumed according to their genres and cultural milieus. For brevity's sake, I shall concentrate on the first and last occurrences of the story.

In terms of plot, the five versions diverge considerably in the circumstances that lead the husband to praise the lover. In *De nugis*, the praise occurs after a casual encounter with the lover while husband and wife are on a journey ("iter facienti"); in the *Gemma*, instead, it is given after a tournament while the husband discusses with his men the feats of valor that had been performed (the situation is a *topos* that frequently occurs in the literature at the turn of the twelfth century). The Italian *cantare*, conservative as popular works often are, maintains the *topos* of a *çiostra* but has the lover awarded the prize of the tournament by the *podestade* and the *signoria*, the two clearly recognizable authorities of medieval Italian city government. The husband disappears from this passage, with the odd consequence that the reader or the audience of the *cantare* knows nothing about the praises of the woman's husband until she reveals them to her lover. It is obvious that the writer of the *sestine* has ineptly reworked a previous text, presumably close to the version of the *Gemma*. Masuccio's solution is an interesting one: In his version, the tournament is replaced by a scene in which messer Corrado, his wife, and their followers are out bird hunting. When they see a falcon that disperses a group of starlings, the husband comments that

> gli parea aver visto a la similitudine del falcone misser Bertramo suo capitano ne la battaglia cacciando ed effugando gli inimici, e per modo tale che, ove lui apparea con la lanza e con la spada, niuno de' soi avversarii ardeva d'aspettarlo. (*Novellino*, 184)

> ([The falcon] reminded him of his captain messer Bertramo who chased his enemies in battle and put them to flight in such a way that none of them dared to stand up to him when he appeared with his spear and sword.)

This is the same simile that the husband uses in the *Gemma* when he comments on the feats of the knight:

> "sicut enim ante falconis faciem columbae fugiunt seu monedulae, sic ante Reginaldum milites cuncti, nec impetum ejus aut ictum quisquam ausus est expectare." (*Gemma*, 227)

> (in fact, just as doves or sparrows fly at the sight of a hawk, so all knights [flew] before Reginald, and nobody dared to wait for his assault or his thrust.)

The close concordance between Masuccio's and Giraldus's passages points to the presence in Italy of a version that had maintained a simile found in Giraldus's story. Perhaps the simile itself had suggested the modifications of a tournament into an actual bird-hunting party, since the motif also appears in *Il Pecorone*, where it is attributed to the lover himself. While messere Stricca and his wife happen to be in one of their properties outside the city,

> e 'l detto Galgano passando per la contrada con uno sparviere in pugno e faccendo vista d'andare uccellando, solo per vedere questa donna, e passando presso alla casa dov'ella era. . . . (*Pecorone*, 12)

> (and the aforementioned Galgano, happening to be in those parts with a falcon on his fist and pretending to go bird hunting, only for the sake of seeing this lady, and passing by the house where she was. . . .)

Again in *Il Pecorone*, the husband's comments take the form of a comparison between the brave behavior of a hawk and that of Galgano. Noticeable in Ser Giovanni Fiorentino's retelling of the story is the innovation that transforms the courtly pastimes of the other versions into an extremely bourgeois invitation to dinner:

> [M]essere iStricca il vide e cognobbe, e subito si li fece incontro e dimesticamente il prese per mano, pregandolo che li piacessi d'andare a cena co lui e co la donna sua. Di che il detto Galgano il ringraziò e disse che grandissima merzè, che gli piacesse d'averlo per riscusato, conciosiacosach'egli andava inn-u certo luogo di bisogno. (*Pecorone*, 12)

> (Sir Stricca, having seen and recognized him, went out to meet him and took him by the hand with great familiarity, inviting him to have supper with himself and his wife. At that, the aforementioned Galgano thanked him warmly and said that he was very grateful, but asked to be excused because he had to go to a certain place.)

Furthermore, to add to the bourgeois realism of the scene, Ser Giovanni elaborates on the details of the encounter:

Di che messer Stricca li disse: "Passa almeno a bere." Di che il giovane rispose: "Io non voglio, gran merzè, fatevi con Dio, ch'io ho fretta." Di che messer Stricca, veggendo la volontà sua, il lasciò andare. (*Pecorone*, 13)

(Then Sir Stricca told him: "At least come in for a drink." To which the young man answered: "No, thank you, God bless you, I am in a hurry." Then Sir Stricca, hearing that such was his will, let him go.)

After this double renunciation, the reader himself, along with the lover, is left wondering: "Doh, tristo me, ché non accitta' io? Che almeno arei veduto colei a cui io vo' meglio che a tutto il mondo" (*Pecorone*, 13). (Ah, poor me, why didn't I accept? At least I would have seen the woman I love more than anything in the world.)

It seems likely, therefore, that a motif evoking bird hunting was in the tale from the very beginning, and that subsequent redactions turned it into, or accompanied it with, the aftermath of a tournament or an invitation to dinner. The story was thus adapted to different social contexts. Nevertheless, these changes affected only the details, not the passages that are crucial to the story's plot. The basic narrative structure is the same: the lady's long-lasting rejection of her suitor turns into love when she hears her husband uttering high praises for him, but the suitor overcomes his lust and in turn rejects the woman when he learns that her husband has such a high opinion of him. Each time the climax of the story resides in the words pronounced by the lover to justify his decision, a climax underlined by rhetorical effects. Most versions also convey a negative judgment of the wife's behavior and a misogynistic attitude that belittles the woman's feelings. For example, at the outcome of the failed rendezvous, Walter Map states (not without a touch of sadism):

hec autem in ipso suo fervore libidinis, in ianua Dyones, in precipicio prompte ruine, in desperacione continencie. (*De nugis*, 276)

(yet she remained in the fire of her own lust, at the threshold of Dione, on the very brink of a sheer fall, ready to give up her purity. [*De nugis*, 277])

Giraldus is even more explicit, earlier in the story:

Mulier autem his auditis a mulieri natura non degenerans, licet hactenus invicta, quia "varium et mutabile semper foemina" . . . pravae cupidini victa succubuit, dicens secum et cogitans: "Forsitan huic uni poteram succumbere culpae." (*Gemma*, 227)

(Having heard these words the woman, true to her feminine nature, since "a female is fickle and ever-changing," although unconquered up to that point . . . was conquered and gave in to her wicked desire. Having thought it over she said to herself: "Perhaps just this time I could give in to sin.")

Masuccio elaborates at length the passage found in the *Gemma* about the nature of the female gender and insists at the end of the story,

> Si la donna restasse confusa e schernita, facilmente se pò considerare; pur, tirata da loro innata avarizia, strengendo a sé le carissime gioie, a casa se ne retornò. (*Novellino*, 189)

> (One can easily understand how confused and ashamed the woman was. Nevertheless, moved by the innate greed common to all women, she grabbed the precious jewels and went back to her home.)

In contrast, the decision of the lover appears to lean on values that evidently put male companionship and loyalty above the allure of an amorous relationship with a woman. The joys of love are considered a weakness in a male, and overcoming such a weakness is exalted as a deed worthy of a man.

Remarkably, all the redactors explicitly attribute the same meaning to the story. In spite of the difference in genre, not only the *exempla* but also the novellas and the *cantare* append a moralizing conclusion to the tale that emphasizes in admiring terms the strength of the knight in overcoming desire. The words and phrases that define the virtue of the knight are "continentia, pudicitia" (*Gemma*); "victoria . . . forti parta vigilancia" (*De nugis*); "fermezza" (*Pecorone*); and "singolare vertù e magnificentia" (*Novellino*). The *cantare* calls him "costante." Thus not only the narrative structure of the tale but also the implicit and explicit scale of values conveyed by it remain the same throughout the centuries. It is difficult to discern any development in the meaning when we compare the various versions of the story, yet it is normally assumed that a literary artifact is deeply rooted in the historical moment that originated it and is always linked to the cultural milieu for which it was produced. A theory that has gained favor in recent times places great emphasis on the way the same work is received, or perceived by different milieus, shifting the historicity of literature from the work itself to the societal "orizzonti d'attesa" (range of expectations).[13] It seems to me, however, that when we are faced with different reworkings of the same story, that is, different literary artifacts, the historical correspondence between the work and its milieu should be revealed by the text itself. This is a further level of interpretation that is not limited to, but presupposes the ascertaining of, the elements that remained unchanged across the textual tradition. To search for this deeper layer of meaning, it is essential that we consider each reworking against the background and in the light of similar works of the same period. In other words, we should try to integrate each piece into a network of works that are analogous by either theme or genre. The operation is easier, of course, at the extremes of the chronological span.

If we take Walter Map's tale, we notice that, in spite of its inclusion in a chapter where the author purports to collect *exempla*, the long, moralizing conclusion sounds somewhat artificial and far-fetched on account of its insistence on rhetorical expressions. Giraldus Cambrensis in his version states that the event had happened "in Francia nostris diebus" (in France, in our own days [*Gemma*, 226]). Therefore, the story did not belong to the common stock from which preachers and writers of moral treatises used to derive their *exempla*.[14] Rather, it appears related to the discussions about proper behavior in amorous relationships and the nature of amorous versus conjugal relations that were taking place in courtly circles at the end of the twelfth century. A related text can be found in a *tenzo* written by Gaucelm Faidit, in which the troubadour disputes with En Rembaut (presumably Raimbaut III d'Orange)[15] whether a woman should choose as lover a friend or an enemy of her husband:

Ara-m digatz, Gaucelm Faidit,
Cals val a bona domna mais,
Quan ha marit q'es pros e gais,
E vol de drut penre chauzit;
E dui cavalier pro e gen
An en lieis lor entendimen,
E l'us es enemics mortals
Del marit, l'autr'amics corals?
Chascus fai per lei son poder—
Chauzetz qal deu miels retener. (Mouzat, 172, I, 1–10)

(Now tell me, Gaucelm Faidit, what is best for a gentlewoman, when she has a worthy and merry husband, and she wants to choose a lover; and two worthy knights are very fond of her; and one is a mortal enemy of her husband, the other an intimate friend? Each of the two does his best for her: you choose with which one of them she should form a liaison.)

Gaucelm, who, according to Jean Mouzat (29) "expose constamment les théories les plus courtoises . . . et dans les partimens [soutient] toujours les solutions les plus élevées" (regularly presents the most courtly theories . . . and in literary contests always supports the most refined solutions), supports in this *tenzo* the thesis that the woman should choose the enemy rather than the friend of the husband:

En Raimbaut, anc no m'abeillit
Que vers bona domna s'eslais,
Per jazer, aitals drutz savais,
Q'aissi a son amic traït;
E la domna lui eissamen
Traït, si tracia-l consen. (Mouzat, 173, VI, 1–6)

(Sir Raimbaut, I do not approve that such an uncouth lover should throw himself at a noble woman for the purpose of lying with her. Thus he betrays his friend, and the woman too, if he goes against the accepted conventions.)

The contiguity of the theme with the content of Walter Map's story is poignant. In the course of his many travels, our troubadour had become familiar with lords who were related to the Plantagenet court. As early as 1186, he had frequented in Brittany the court of Henri II's son Geoffrey II, with whom he exchanged a *partimen*, and perhaps also the court of Marguerite, the widow of Henri the Young King. It is therefore quite possible that Gaucelm's poems and/or the issues that he debated reached the Plantagenet court in Great Britain and became known to both Walter Map and Giraldus Cambrensis.

Walter Map's story can very well be read against the subtext of Andreas Capellanus's *De amore*.[16] The reflections of the lover himself are reminiscent of Andreas's attitudes, according to which a lady should bestow her love upon a lover on the basis of careful consideration of his virtues and not on account of any instinctive attraction. Walter Map asserts:

> Rollonem tandem respicit, militem serenissime fame, se vero puerum intra septa cunarum adhuc morantem nichil egisse, nichil egregium gessisse; iam se merito spretum dicit, et nisi prevaluerit non debere preponi. Suam ait iniustam peticionem, illius iustissimam negacionem. (*De nugis*, 270–72)

> (At last he considered Rollo, a knight of the brightest renown, and himself, who, a boy still lingering within his cradle's bounds, had done nothing, achieved no distinction. "I am rightly scorned," said he, "and unless I do better than Rollo, I do not deserve to be preferred to him. My own suit is unjustified, her refusal is most righteous." [*De nugis*, 271–73])

An appropriately corresponding passage from Andreas's *De amore* can be found, for example, in Queen Eleanor's judgment on whether a woman should choose a "Iuvenis . . . nulla probitate decorus" (a young man adorned with no honesty of character [*On Love*, 254–55]) or a "miles adultus omni probitate iucundus" (a mature knight pleasantly endowed with every moral attribute [*On Love*, 254–55]). This is Queen Eleanor's advice:

> Licet probet iunior ab amoris perceptione se ad morum posse ascendere probitatem, minus provide agit mulier, si improbitatem praeeligat amare, maxime quum vir bonus ac morum cultura refulgens ab ea petit amorem. (*On Love*, 256)

> (Even if the younger man proves that he can rise to honesty of manners because of the love he has experienced, the woman would be imprudent to choose to love an unworthy character, especially when a good man, radiant with cultivated manners, seeks her love. [*On Love*, 257])

In addition, the motif of self-restraint and control of the flesh was very much present in the discourse of courtly love. Andreas proposes an odd dilemma: Which of the two is preferable, the enjoyment of the upper part or the lower part of the woman's body? Declaring that the upper part is to be preferred to the lower, he adds the listener's explicit reaction:

> Miror enim si in quoquam tanta sit abstinentia carnis inventa, ut unquam voluptatis promeruerit impetum refrenare et corporis motibus obviare. Monstrosum namque iudicatur a cunctis, si quis in igne positus non uratur. Si quis tamen in hac fide quam dicitis fuerit amoris puritate repertus et in praefata quam dixistis continentia carnis, huius laudo et plenius confirmo propositum et ipsum censeo omni honore dignissimum. (*On Love*, 180–82)

> (I am startled that in any person such abstinence of the flesh has been observed that a man was ever able to curb the onset of pleasure, and repress the motions of his body. Everyone accounts it a prodigy if a man is placed on a fire and does not burn. But if a man were found to practice chaste love with the good faith which you mention and with the restraint of the flesh which you described, I praise and support his proposal to a greater degree, and account him most worthy of every distinction. [*On Love*, 181–83])

Further common motifs from courtly literature that are found in the first part of the tale of Rollo are those of valor induced by love, participation in military activities so as to be noticed by a loved woman, the importance of seeing the beloved, and Love as the lord of the lover.[17] In short, this chapter, more than any other tale by Walter Map, is pervaded by themes typical of the courtly love discourse.

It is therefore my contention that Walter Map overlaid a moralizing purpose onto a story that circulated in secular circles concerned with the issues of courtly love, and presumably one involving the question of love with a husband's friend. It can be argued that such debates, too, had a "moralizing" purpose, insofar as they aimed at establishing directions for proper courtly behavior and at passing judgment on gestures pertaining to amorous relations. In fact, troubadour poetry and courtly romances were in the process of elaborating and defining a set of moral values that distinguished the nobility from the rest of society, as is apparent among other examples in Gaucelm Faidit's discussion. Seen against this background, the story might already have had an exemplary meaning—but in light of a mundane code of conduct and in the name of aristocratic values rather than the spiritual morality Walter Map sought. Hence the importance of the underlying concepts of honor, loyalty, and knightly companionship. When the story was subsumed into the ecclesiastical setting of the *exemplum*, even more pronounced in Giraldus's *Gemma* than in Map's version, its original meaning was distorted both to exemplify the virtue of continence from a religious viewpoint and to generalize its significance insofar as it was proposed as a model for every good Christian and not specifically for the aristocracy. To judge by the moralizing conclusions regularly appended to each retelling, the story must have been preserved and must have reached Italy in the form of an *exemplum*. Nevertheless, its secular origin and whatever mundane flavor was left in its very setting may have facilitated its shifting into the genres of novella and *cantare*.

At the other end of the trajectory, Masuccio's novella too carries its own moral. However, one notices a slight shift in the definition of the virtue for which the protagonist is extolled: not so much for his chastity this time as for his *magnificentia*. The feudal notion of loyalty associated with that of knightly companionship, so pervasive in medieval thought, is not the key issue here. In lieu of the sudden change of heart found in the medieval versions, the protagonist needs to elaborate at length on the perfection of the husband's friendship to finally reach his decision. In fact, Masuccio's version stresses the extreme courtesy of the husband, which calls for an equivalent reciprocal gesture: failing to do so would be *villania*. The lover, talking to himself, says:

> E che questo te sia perfettissimo amico, ultre ogni altra passata esperienzia, tu lo hai da lei medesma sentito apertamente, ché, non per altro che per amore che suo marito te porta, si è qui condutta a donarte il suo amore; quale tu pigliandolo, che digno merito averá [sic] del suo verso de te ben volere, e del sommamente lodarte in assenzia, come negli veri amici se rechiede? Or non piazza a Dio che in cavaliero d'Aquino tal villania casche giá mai! (*Novellino*, 189)

> (Apart from any past proofs of friendship you may have had, she herself openly told you that he is a perfect friend to you. In fact, she came here to give you her love for no other reason than because her husband loves you. If you take her, will you really be worthy of his benevolence and of his high praises of you in your absence, as true friends ought to do? God forbid that such baseness be ever found in a gentleman of the Aquino lineage!)

To understand the shift that took place in this passage, Masuccio's retelling should be measured against other works belonging to the same genre—novella— and dealing with a similar theme by which the author was inspired. In fact, Boccaccio's *Decameron* provides appropriate points of reference. For example, in the novella of Madonna Dianora (*Decameron* X, 5, but anticipated in *Il Filocolo*), Messer Ansaldo and Madonna Dianora find themselves in a situation not dissimilar from that of the lover and the woman at the end of Walter Map's tale. The circumstances and the meaning of Boccaccio's story are totally different, however. The novella's rubric summarizes the situation:

> Madonna Dianora domanda a messer Ansaldo un giardino di gennaio bello come di maggio; messere Ansaldo con l'obligarsi ad uno nigromante gliele dà; il marito le

concede che ella faccia il piacere di messere Ansaldo, il quale, udita la liberalità del marito, l'assolve della promessa, ed il nigromante, senza volere alcuna cosa del suo, assolve messere Ansaldo. (*Dec*. X, 5, 1)[18]

(Madonna Dianora asks Messer Ansaldo to give her a garden that would be as beautiful in January as in May; by hiring a magician, Messer Ansaldo manages to grant her wish; her husband agrees that she must fulfill Messer Ansaldo's desires, but when Messer Ansaldo hears of her husband's generosity, he frees her from her promise, and the magician, refusing to accept anything from him, also frees Messer Ansaldo from his.)[19]

In the same Tenth Day, Boccaccio also tells the tales of Gentile de' Carisendi, who rescues from the tomb the woman he loves, heals her, and returns her untouched to her husband; of Tito and Gisippo; and of Torello and the Saladdin. In all of these, the main theme is the emulation in magnanimity among men. The influence of Boccaccio's novellas was deep and long lasting, far beyond the first half of the fifteenth century. A similar competition in magnanimity is found again, for example, in Gentile Sermini's *Novelliere* (Novella 14) and in the story of Iroldo and Prasildo in Boiardo's *Orlando Innamorato*.[20] It is not therefore inappropriate to surmise that Masuccio kept in mind the Boccaccian model when he reworked the old *exemplum*. Bertramo overcomes his lust not simply by knightly loyalty or by his own virtuous continence, but because he does not want to prove inferior to the perceived magnanimity of the husband. Hence the lengthening and belaboring of the lover's praises on the part of the husband and the insistence of the lover in wanting to know whether those were the only reasons for the woman's capitulation. The moralizing conclusion reads, appropriately:

dove fu dato avanto a misser Bertramo, come era soprano ne l'arme, animoso, discreto e proveduto, cosí de magnificenzie, liberalitá e somme virtú avanzare ogni altro cavaliero, che dentro e fuori Italia ne la sua etá fusse stato giá mai. (*Novellino*, 189)

(whereupon it was proclaimed in praise of Messer Bertramo that, just as he was superior in arms, courage, discretion, and foresig.ht, so also in magnificence, liberality, and every lofty virtue he was superior to any knight that ever lived in his times, in Italy and abroad.)

The surprisingly close textual and lexical relations that link Boccaccio's novella with the *cantare* and with Masuccio's novella confirm this hypothesis:

"Madonna, *unque a Dio non piaccia*, poscia che cosí è come voi dite, che io sia *guastatore dello onore* . . . ; e per ciò l'esser qui sarà, quanto vi piacerà, non altramente che se mia *sorella* foste . . . al vostro marito di tanta cortesia quanto la sua è stata, quelle grazie renderete che convenevoli crederete, me sempre per lo tempo avvenire avendo per *fratello* e per servitore." (*Dec.* X, 5, 22, emphasis added)

(My lady, since things are as you say, *God forbid* that I should *soil the honor* . . . , and so, as long as you wish to stay here, you will be treated just as if you were my *sister*, . . . provided that you give your husband such thanks as you deem befitting such courtesy as his, and that henceforth you always consider me as a *brother* and your servant. [Musa and Bondanella, 626])[21]

"*Or non piazza a Dio* che in cavaliero d'Aquino tal villania casche giá mai!" . . . "Cara madonna, toglialo Dio che . . . in *disonore* li possano né poco né multo retornare; anzi sempre da qui davanti ponerò per lui la persona e le facultá, come per proprio *fratello* e lialissimo amico se deveno ponere e te averò de continuo per *sorella*." (*Novellino*, 189, emphasis added)

(*God forbid* that such baseness be ever found in a gentleman of the Aquino lineage! . . . Dear lady, may God prevent [me from committing any deed] that might turn to his *dishonor* in either great or small measure. On the contrary, from this time on I shall put my estate and myself at his disposal as is it ought to be done for a *brother* and an extremely loyal friend. And you shall always be a *sister* to me.)

non è rason ch'io li faça *dexnore*
. . .
Ma, per la fé ch'io son bom cavaliero,
amare i' 'ntendo lui como *fradelo*.
. . .
E finalmente ti come *sorela*
trattarò sempremai per lo suo amore.
(*Storia della dama*, 41.5–43.2, emphasis added)

(It is not fitting that I should *dishonor* him, . . . But as it is true that I am a worthy knight I will love him as a *brother*. . . . And finally, for his sake, I will always hold you as my *sister*.)

Boccaccio's influence, therefore, infused a new meaning into the old story and helped to transform it into a humanist novella, fitting into the culture that exalted the virtues of men, again in a secular but also in a general sense. In conclusion, I must stress the idea that no literary work can be properly understood if studied in isolation. To borrow a concept from physics, each composition is like a region traversed by lines of force, a sort of meeting place of forms, notions, values coming from far-reaching traditions as well as from closer and contemporary influences. It is important to trace the development of a form, a motif, or a story from a chronological point of view in order to grasp the continuity of certain values. It is equally important to explore the horizontally oriented synchrony of themes and cultural interests that more immediately surround the text. Only such a comprehensive perspective will give depth and persuasiveness to our critical interpretation.

Notes

This topic was first presented at the Thirty-Fifth International Congress on Medieval Studies, Western Michigan University, Kalamazoo, Michigan, on May 6, 2000.

1. For example, the second redaction of the *Cantare di Madonna Elena.* See my "Il *Cantare di Madonna Elena* e l'elaborazione del poemetto cavalleresco in Italia," *Yearbook of Italian Studies* 10 (1991): 53–107; and *Cantare di madonna Elena,* ed. Giovanni Fontana (Florence: Accademia della Crusca, 1992).

2. For the complete text of this tale, with a discussion of its linguistic features, see my "*Storia della dama bolognese che s'innamora sentendo lodare un cavaliere dal marito.* Cantare inedito del Quattrocento," *Letteratura italiana antica* 3 (2002): 19–40; hereafter cited in text as *Storia della dama.*

3. Walter Map, *De nugis curialium. Courtiers' Trifles,* ed. and trans. Montague Rhodes James, rev. ed. Christopher Nugent Lawrence Brooke and Roger Aubrey Baskerville Mynors, Oxford Medieval Texts (Oxford: Clarendon Press, 1983); hereafter cited in text as *De nugis.* In this work, Walter Map purports to write "exempla quibus vel iocunditas excitetur vel edificetur ethica" (examples . . . such as may serve either to excite merriment or edify morals [*De nugis,* 210–11]). For the date of composition, see Brooke and Mynors, Introduction to *De nugis,* xxiv–xxxii, as well as Jean-Thiébaut Welter, *L'exemplum dans la littérature religieuse et didactique du Moyen Âge. La Tabula exemplorum secundum ordinem alphabeti* (1927; reprint, Geneva: Slatkine Reprints, 1973), 49; hereafter cited in text as Welter.

4. Giraldus Cambrensis, *Gemma ecclesiastica,* in *Giraldi Cambrensis opera,* ed. John Sherren Brewer, vol. 2, Rerum Britannicarum Medii Aevi Scriptores, no. 21 (London: Longman and Co., 1862), 2:226–28; hereafter cited in text as *Gemma.* For the date of composition, see Welter, 53.

5. Ser Giovanni Fiorentino, *Il Pecorone,* ed. Enzo Esposito, Classici italiani minori (Ravenna: Longo Editore, 1974); hereafter cited in text as *Pecorone.*

6. Masuccio Salernitano, *Il Novellino,* ed. Alfredo Mauro, rev. ed. Salvatore S. Nigro, Universale Laterza, no. 530 (1940; Bari: Editori Laterza, 1979); hereafter cited in text as *Novellino.* Giorgio Petrocchi found an earlier manuscript version of the novella and argued that the modifications that appear in the printed version must have been created after 1452, when the countess Antonella d'Aquino, to whom the novella is dedicated, married the chamberlain (*camarlingo*) Inico d'Avalos ("La prima redazione del *Novellino* di Masuccio," *Giornale storico della letteratura italiana* 129 [1952]: 266–317).

7. *Novellino,* 177. Translations are mine except as indicated.

8. See Brooke and Mynors, Introduction to *De nugis,* xxxi. The *De nugis* is obvi-

ously an unfinished work and was presumably put together by a friend of Walter Map after his death. See James Hinton, "Walter Map's *De nugis curialium*: Its Plan and Composition," PMLA 32 (1917): 81–132.

9. Manuscript Lambeth, property of the archbishop of Canterbury (see Brewer, Introduction to *Gemma*, x).

10. Brewer, Introduction to *Gemma*, ix–x.

11. Letterio Di Francia, *Novellistica*, vol. 1: *Dalle origini al Bandello*, Storia dei generi letterari italiani (Milan: Casa Editrice Dr. Francesco Vallardi, 1921), 458.

12. James Hinton, "Walter Map and Ser Giovanni," *Modern Philology* 15 (1917): 208–9.

13. The expression is from Hans Robert Jauss, *Perché la storia della letteratura?* trans. Alberto Varvaro (1967; Naples: Guida, 1969), 57.

14. Welter has systematically provided the provenance of the *exempla* found in the *De nugis* (50) and *Gemma* (55–56).

15. An alternative hypothesis identifies the "En Rembaut" of the *tenzo* as Raimbaut de Vaqueyras. See Jean Mouzat, *Les poëmes de Gaucelm Faidit, troubadour du XII siècle* (Paris: A. G. Nizet, 1965), 32 and 174–76; hereafter cited in text as Mouzat.

16. Andreas Capellanus, *On Love*, ed. with English trans. by Patrick Gerard Walsh, Duckworth Classical, Medieval and Renaissance Editions (London: Duckworth, 1982); hereafter cited in text as *On Love*.

17. "Et si nonnisi tantum eam videre debeat, idem fecerit" (He would have done the same had the prize been the mere sight of her [*De nugis*, 272, 273]); "Exit igitur quocumque ipsum magister amor evocat" (He went forth whithersoever Love his lord called him [*De nugis*, 272, 273]). Love is, of course, the Lord of the lover, as made clear by the epitome of courtly love theory and practice, the *Roman de la rose*.

18. Giovanni Boccaccio, *Decameron*, ed. Vittore Branca, 2 vols., Einaudi Tascabili. Classici, no. 99 (1980; reprint, Turin: Einaudi, 1992); hereafter cited in text as *Decameron*.

19. Giovanni Boccaccio, *The Decameron*, trans. Mark Musa and Peter Bondanella (New York: Penguin Books/New American Library/Mentor, 1982), 623; hereafter cited in text as Musa and Bondanella.

20. Gentile Sermini, *Novelle*, ed. Giuseppe Vettori, 2 vols., Classici per tutti, nos. 83–84 (Rome: Avanzini e Torraca, 1968); Matteo Maria Boiardo, *L'innamoramento di Orlando*, in *Opere*, eds. Antonia Tissoni Benvenuti and Cristina Montagnani, La letteratura italiana. Storia e testi, no. 18 (Milan: Riccardo Ricciardi, 1999).

21. The English translation somewhat inaccurately declares that the lover unequivocally intends to propose himself as brother to the lady. The original Italian leaves open the interpretation that the brotherly relationship proposed by the lover include the lady's husband.

7

Masuccio Salernitano's *Gusto dell'orrido*

Michael Papio

In Erich Auerbach's opinion, Masuccio was "ein unübertrefflicher Psycholog des Perversen" (an unsurpassable psychologist of the perverse).[1] Although this might not seem at first blush to be a particularly flattering assessment of the author's literary talents, it is an extremely useful point of departure for anyone concerned with the development of the novella tradition at large, a tradition that emerged from the relatively innocent anecdote or *beffa* and that later developed in numerous directions in the Cinquecento, including the nascent horror tale so important to Elizabethan drama. Within the pages of Masuccio's *Il Novellino* (composed between 1450 and 1475), there exists an assortment of "perverted" characters, among whom can be found abhorrent Moors, profligate wives, lecherous clergymen, lepers, and whores. These all act out their parts, often in surprisingly repulsive fashion, as recorded by an apparently veracious narrator. Since the 1930s critics have compared these characters to carnival masks, personifications of the monstrous, the grotesque, or the harlequin.[2] The fictional world of Masuccio at large has even been described as "un universo dimensionalmente abnorme" (a dimensionally abnormal universe).[3] As one might imagine, however, not all such comparisons were made by scholars who were especially fond of this type of short story.

In order to understand Masuccio's aesthetic contribution to the evolution of the novella genre, it is helpful to consider the roots of *Il Novellino*'s rather ambivalent modern critical reception. Not long after the publication of Alfredo Mauro's 1940 edition of the work, Ferdinando Neri praised the collection in general and singled out two novellas in particular for their exceptional literary value: Novella 33—considered by many to be the remote source of Shakespeare's *Romeo and Juliet*—and Novella 31. The latter tells the tragic story of Martina and

Loisi, two young lovers who attempt to elope in the dark of night only to find
themselves separated from their entourage by a sudden thunderstorm and lost in
the woods. The unlucky couple spots a lantern in the window of a small building
not far off and rushes there, seeking shelter. Their adventure soon assumes nightmarish overtones as the lovers realize they have stumbled into a leper hospital,
inhabited by diabolically deformed creatures. Neri credited Masuccio with a literary success based specifically upon this dark, fatalistic view of the world, upon a
hostile imagination and an ability to communicate moments of unexpected terror:

> In quel suo stile tortuoso, togato e paludato, Masuccio dischiude ai nostri occhi scene
> di una squallida ferocia, che dànno la sensazione, e l'ansia, di un incubo: scene come
> si trovano, a tutt'altro capo del tempo, e della poesia, nelle pagine di Edgar Poe.[4]

> (In that tortuous, solemn, and pompous style of his, Masuccio presents to our
> mind's eye scenes of squalid ferocity which inspire the feeling, and the anxiety, of a
> nightmare: scenes like those that can be found, at the other end of the chronological
> and poetic spectrum, in the works of Edgar Allan Poe.)

What makes his observation particularly interesting is the fact that he singles
out Masuccio's "squallida ferocia" as his aesthetic strong suit during a period in
which Crocean discussions of "poetry" and "non-poetry" were commonplace.
Masuccio's ability to reveal to the reader the darker side of human experience was
not much appreciated by Mario Fubini, who argued that Neri's identification of a
"pallida ferocia" (pallid ferocity), a telling misquotation in itself, was not enough
to persuade him of *Il Novellino*'s overall literary worth.[5] With regard to Novella
31, Fubini writes: "né una sola parola artisticamente viva lo scrittore sa trovare
per dirci lo strazio della giovinetta quando apprende l'uccisione dell'amato e si
vede in balìa dei turpi assassini" (the writer is unable to find even a single artisti-
cally vivid word to describe to us the agony of the young girl when she learns of
her lover's murder and finds herself at the mercy of the vile killers [48]). In
Fubini's opinion, whatever "poetry" was to be found in the tale of Martina and
Loisi was canceled out by a lack of authorial compassion, a too vigorously pursued description of murder and fear. Masuccio's true art, he claimed, was dis-
cernible only in the tales whose style and themes were most similar to those of
Boccaccio's *Decameron*.

This evaluation is by no means unusual. Several decades later, much of the
scholarship on *Il Novellino* still runs along these same lines despite the fact that
measuring Masuccio's style against Boccaccio's leads far too easily to misread-
ings.[6] That Masuccio's stories have often had a lukewarm reception, however, is
not the fault of any particular exegetic school or single individual who was unable
to appreciate the originality of *Il Novellino*'s "squallida ferocia." It is instead the
unexamined result of a critical perspective that was formed in the Renaissance.

Francesco Bonciani, a member of the Accademia Fiorentina and Tuscan by birth, declared in his *Lezione sopra il comporre delle novelle* (1574) that the tragic—and especially the horrible—had absolutely no place in the genre of the short story and supported his notion with a subjective allusion to one of Matteo Bandello's tales of murder and moral outrage.[7] Because the relatively new genre had no Aristotelian codification, as did the epic poem or tragedy, its boundaries were determined for all practical purposes by Boccaccio's model. Although it would be pointless to dispute the privileged literary and cultural position of the *Decameron*, we must acknowledge that Masuccio was writing in a climate very different from Boccaccio's Florence of a century earlier. Fifteenth-century Naples was controlled by the Aragonese monarchy, and its merchant class—unlike that of Florence or Tuscany—was not recognized for its importance to the region's economic stability. Moreover, Masuccio's patron and his fellow courtiers often found themselves in conflict with the upwardly mobile "middle class."[8] Unlike Boccaccio, who had himself been a merchant and whose tales repeatedly reward shrewdness of intellect (especially where characters triumph over their social superiors), Masuccio regularly punishes those merchants or non-nobles who aim to subvert the traditional political and familial hierarchies. Unlike the *Decameron*, *Il Novellino* was written expressly for an aristocratic audience and regularly portrays punishment for social transgressions, as in the story of Martina and Loisi, whose demise can be attributed to their disregard for their parents' refusal to permit their marriage.

With stories like Masuccio's, whose unhappy endings implicitly condemn acts of transgression, we are effectively on new narrative ground. In order to understand this new style properly, we must strive to understand the reasons for his departure from a narrative tradition that had been, from the anonymous *Novellino* to the fifteenth century, fundamentally comic and anecdotal in nature. In the dedication to Ippolita Sforza (*Novellino*, 5), Masuccio specifically situates *Il Novellino* in the comic tradition and underscores the work's entertainment value, but what emerges most clearly in Masuccio's work is that he and Boccaccio (as well as their respective audiences) have different senses of humor. Each aimed to entertain his readers; whereas Boccaccio applauds the triumphs of the underdog, however, Masuccio finds amusement in his debasement and derision. This type of humor, combined with the particularly Masuccian preference for hyperbolic depictions of punishment, lends *Il Novellino* an almost sadistic quality. In other words, where Masuccio's novellas lack humor they are best described as tales of terror, and where he does in fact attempt to make his audience laugh, his predilection for repelling and frightening scenes tends to manifest itself in the grotesque. These are decidedly not Crocean characteristics: indeed, the "aesthetic coherence" of Boccaccio's writing style, which Croce himself so highly praised in his famous essay on the tale of Andreuccio, is purposefully disregarded by Masuccio.[9] *Il Novellino* is unabashedly full of tales that, in their exaggerated insistence upon death, disease, or destruction, were clearly never meant to conform to the *Decameron*'s aesthetic model. This simple fact, fully grasped by Auerbach yet so widely disregarded by even recent scholars of *Il Novellino*, is an essential step toward our adequate understanding of Masuccio's proper place in Italian literary history.

At this point, it would be helpful to consider the question posed by Alberto Del Monte in his intervention in the Neri-Fubini debate: "Ma questi due gusti dissimili, dell'orrido e del grottesco, possono fondersi in un unico, predominante, esclusivo?" (But can these two dissimilar tastes, for the horrifying and for the grotesque, come together in a single, predominant, and exclusive style?)[10] Masuccio's "gusto dell'orrido" (taste for the horrifying) is in fact not separable from his "gusto del grottesco" (taste for the grotesque): they are simply two manifestations of a single underlying narrative mode. Both are manifestations of his preference for hyperbole and of his penchant for play with terror. Terror stories are built upon situations in which the reader witnesses harm befalling the characters of the plot. The reader's participation then becomes an enticing encounter with the fearful and the threatening. The aesthetic pleasure experienced in Masuccio's novellas frequently comes not from reading neat, economically structured narrative units but from a sort of flirtation with death and taboo. We find fascinating, in some unsettling way, scenes of two young lovers trapped in a leper hospital (Novella 31) or of a young woman and a dwarf murdered while having sex (Novella 28). We are curiously interested in the transgressive sexual unions between a noblewoman and a black slave (Novellas 22, 24, and 25), the act of incest (Novella 23), adapted but not surpassed by Giovanni Brevio, and so on.[11]

For any reader who wishes to understand the nature of Masuccio's particular form of grotesque, John Ruskin provides a useful starting point. He explains that any combination of the "ludicrous and the fearful" produces something that can be described as grotesque.[12] As an example, he mentions Dante's amusing demons of *Inferno* XXI–XXII (Ruskin, 11:174–75). In other words, whatever creates a sense of apprehension, anxiety, or terror in daily life becomes grotesque when infused with just enough of the absurd to render it uncannily less harmful. In pure comedy, the fearful is completely quashed, and anxiety is relieved. This is not the case with the grotesque, in which a certain measure of fear or anxiety remains unresolved. Masuccio's *gusto dell'orrido*, when applied to novellistic motifs, produces grotesque scenes of sexual excess and physical danger. What makes this an especially interesting notion is that—unlike Dante, who injects humor into his portrayal of the heretical, the evil, and the demonic—Masuccio inserts the heretical, the evil, and the demonic into the humorous. The eerie result of this technique lies at the root of Neri's comparison of Masuccio to Poe, inasmuch as the reader perceives the characters' actions against the backdrop of a recognizable yet still alien world. When considered in the light of Wolfgang Kayser's important work on the Romantic grotesque and Mikhail Bakhtin's well-known study of Rabelais, the parallelism becomes ever more intriguing. Basing his analysis on the diverse manifestations of the grotesque in the nineteenth century, Kayser—like Ruskin, although in a way less tied to moral ends—sees the grotesque as a self-defensive game with the absurd insofar as it conjures up the demonic chiefly to exorcise it.[13] Bakhtin contradicts Kayser and sees instead a liberating, populist perspective regarding the distortion of reality, one that completely destroys all aspects of the terrible through derisive laughter. Bakhtin thought of the grotesque as being fundamentally subservient to, and derived from, laughter:

> The transformation of the principle of laughter which permeates the grotesque, that is the loss of its regenerating power, leads to a series of other essential differences between Romantic grotesque and medieval and Renaissance grotesque. The differences appear most distinctly in relation to terror. The world of Romantic grotesque is to a certain extent a terrifying world, alien to man. . . . The medieval and Renaissance folk culture was familiar with the element of terror only as represented by comic monsters, who were defeated by laughter. Terror was turned into something gay and comic.[14]

It is Bakhtin's refusal to accept the notion of a terrifying medieval-Renaissance grotesque that allowed him to pursue such an original path in the study of Rabelais and that set his ideas in strict opposition to those of Kayser, who believed that the essential traits of the grotesque are the inhuman, the alienated, and the fearful. Bakhtin, wanting to emphasize the power of the comic, claimed that the Romantic view is "entirely inapplicable" to literature written before 1800 and posits his concept of carnival in strict opposition to Kayser's assertion that the grotesque has to do with the fear of life (*Rabelais*, 48). Naturally, to dismiss the existence of true terror in the medieval-Renaissance imagination requires a certain amount of suspension of disbelief: one need only think of the grim cantos of *Inferno*, various treatments of the *Danse macabre*, the *transis*, the *Trionfo della Morte*, or even Michelangelo's *Last Judgment* in the Sistine Chapel to appreciate the pre-Romantic sensibility to frightening distortions of the human form and character. Although we might never have noticed how similar Masuccio's style is to the Romantic grotesque, there is no question that he did indeed wish to frighten his audience, whether as a moralist, as Salvatore Nigro argues (*Le brache*, 69–87), or as a teller of horror tales.

What the narrative style of *Il Novellino* does not give us, however, is that salubrious reversal of authority that is so often—and so importantly—linked to the grotesque in the works of Bakhtin. Nor does it provide us with the figures of the Rogue, Clown, and the Fool (the vehicles that first suited the grotesque motif for Bakhtin's writings on the chronotope) or the degenerative and regenerative background of social upheaval as does the *Decameron*. Bakhtin identified two contrary literary approaches that he called the "Boccaccio matrix" and the "Poe matrix," the former defined as "the *plague* (death, the grave) as a *holiday* (gaiety, laughter, wine, eroticism)" and the latter in which "these contrasts are static and the dominant of the entire image is, therefore, oriented toward death."[15] This dichotomy can be used to explain the major stumbling block in Masuccio criticism. The static perception of the social structure in *Il Novellino* and the absence of the fool (like Boccaccio's Calandrino or Sacchetti's Gonnella, and for that matter of the *bon mot* so characteristic of other *novellieri*) combine with the eerie *gusto dell'orrido* to produce something very different from the *Decameron*. That something shares a number of characteristics with Poe, especially with regard to Masuccio's insistence on the capacity of evil to be entertaining. In Masuccio, the narrative detachment and the emphasis on the death of the individual—rather than of society—moves his *Novellino* onto a different level from that of the *Decameron*. For Boccaccio, whom we might see as being proto-Rabelaisian, as Bakhtin suggests, life was not strictly divided into neatly delineated rich-poor or aristocrat-commoner binary pairs. It does seem reasonable, however, to categorize Masuccio in this way. Gentile Sermini may have been the first to indulge in lengthy novellas about the disgusting habits and appearance of the plebeians, but it is Masuccio who truly turned them into demonic figures capable of inspiring fear in the aristocratic reader.

In Bakhtin's view, the Rogue and the Fool, stand-ins for the marginalized individual at large, symbolize "the right to be *other* in this world, the right not to make common sense with any single one of the existing categories that life makes available" ("Forms of Time," 159). This class of character is treated very differently by Masuccio, however, who uses the grotesque as a tool for stigmatizing rather than for celebrating alterity: he does not allow for Otherness to become a respectable category in any way. Rabelais's work lends itself much more readily to this type of analysis because it contains so much "bottom-up" laughter that is embodied in Carnival and pivotal to the new world view. Such laughter liberated man to poke fun at the old, medieval concepts (such as the baseness of the body, the devaluation of mortal time, and the ponderous solemnity of death) and to forge a new perspective that was related to the humanistic notion of the importance of the individual. Bakhtin observes that Rabelais "did not adhere completely to any group within the framework of the ruling classes (including the bourgeoisie); he did not adopt any official point of view, nor did he agree with any proceeding or approve any current event" (*Rabelais*, 438). The Soviet scholar describes Rabelais's presentation of the grotesque as "realistic folklore fantasy," the overturning of the established medieval world view, ontological as well as aesthetic, insofar as the old genre (pre-novel) was ill-equipped to comprise this new outlook. Masuccio, who was a respected member of the royal court, clearly would not have found a bottom-up revolution to be socially beneficial. The notion of a "horizontal" change of power, Angevin to Aragonese for example, was not so shocking as a "vertical" populist revolt would have been. Nowhere in *Il Novellino* is there any feeling of social solidarity between the author and his transgressive characters, as there is in Boccaccio and Rabelais. Masuccio's transgressive characters, especially those who inspire fear in the reader, are systematically thwarted. The threats they pose, whether social (as in Novellas 2 and 7) or psychological (as in Novellas 24, 25, and 31), provide the raw material from which Masuccio's *gusto dell'orrido* derives its force. The dangers represented by the Other are no less entertaining when seen in a homeopathic light than when seen in defeat. These tales are meant to excite upper-class readers while implicitly reaffirming their beliefs and values.

If Francesco Bonciani was unable to accept the tragic novella in 1574, it should come as no surprise that a modern reader or critic who defines the entire genre according to the *Decameron* would find it difficult to appreciate Masuccio's extrapolation of grotesque images and situations to produce tales that frighten. Our author's brand of realism, a style that springs from the fantastic possibilities of lived existence rather than from the monotony of daily life, is most artfully reflected in the novella that Neri praised in his review: Novella 31. Considered by a small group of scholars to be *Il Novellino*'s master stroke, the story of Martina and Loisi comes to exemplify those aspects of Masuccio's narrative technique that most clearly set him apart from his contemporaries and that make his particular mode of grotesque narration so appealing to the modern imagination. With the possible exception of some of the bizarre *exempla* of moral corruption written for quite different reasons by Jacopo Passavanti or Domenico Cavalca, this is arguably the most potent tale of horror in the history of medieval and early Renaissance Italian literature. Masuccio opens the narrative in a more or less traditional fashion with a description of two noble lovers whose parents are unwilling to agree to their marriage. Renouncing existing novellistic motifs, he then adds a series of plot twists, intentionally designed to inspire fear and repulsion and terror in the minds of his readers, that ultimately culminate in the bloody scenes of murder, attempted rape, and suicide. The scenes of sexual pollution and violence that had punctuated other tales in the collection are, in Novella 31, distilled into a single, oneiric fantasy that denies the possibility of a cathartic triumph of Good over Evil.

This is not merely a tale that demonstrates the inevitable punishment for evil as in the popular sermons and *exempla* of preceding centuries. Instead, it is a self-indulgent encounter with terror meant to provoke forceful aesthetic and psychological responses in the reader. Wherever the grotesque is employed to define and demonize alterity (as in Masuccio's anticlerical and misogynistic tales), the strict delineation of social groups into categories like noble and commoner, or us and them, naturally produces strong emotional reactions whenever these two poles come into contact with each other.[16] This juxtaposition results in motifs of contamination that feed the fear of sexual pollution in the mind of the reader. In the fourth section of tales, the artistic apex of *Il Novellino*, Masuccio dedicated the even-numbered novellas to comedy and the odd to tragedy and terror, a balance that is the touchstone of the effective implementation of the grotesque style (Ruskin, 11:166–67). Whereas in earlier sections the fearful and the humorous had been combined within a single narrative space, their separation in the fourth allows for a more profound investigation into the chilling possibilities presented by the mixing of high and low. Masuccio tells us:

> Ancora che nel comenciamento de la presente operetta[17] avessi con meco medesmo diliberato, in questa parte non d'altro che de materie lacrimevole e appassionate trattare, nondimeno, da onesta cagione tirato, voglio de tale preposto l'ordene cambiare, e con alquante piacivole novelle le mestuose accompagnando trapassare, a ciò che, con le orrende e infelice le facete e iocunde mescolando, lo avuto dolore de cui legge e de cui ascolta se possa in allegrezza terminare; usando in ciò l'arte de' prudenti fisici, quali, nel dare de loro acute e violente medele, con cose contrarie apposte correggono la malignitá de quelle. (*Novellino*, 251)

> (Although I had made up my mind at the outset of this little work to treat in this section nothing other than heartrending and emotional subjects, I am moved by good reason to change the order that I had originally proposed and to present pleasant tales together with grievous ones. In this way, by mixing sorrowful and horrible stories with cheerful and comic ones such that the sadness of the reader or listener may at last be transformed into happiness, I am employing the art of prudent physicians who in administering keen and violent remedies correct nasty side effects with special contrary measures.)

Although this appears on the surface to be an intentional disarming of what we feel is threatening,[18] the alternation between dark and lighthearted tales works likewise in the opposite direction: on the heels of each funny story comes one with a tragic ending.

One of these "remedies" is, of course, the tragedy of Martina and Loisi. The basic plot line was adapted from a chronicle known as *Floridan et Elvide*, originally written in Latin in around 1424 by Nicolas de Clamanges (c. 1363–1437), Parisian scholar, literary humanist, and moralist. Masuccio probably also knew the legend in Rasse de Brunhamel's French translation, which was completed by 1456.[19] The chief narrative elements of the source text are repeated in *Il Novellino*, albeit with decidedly more sinister tones. In the original tale, two young lovers elope together into the night only to find themselves alone at a small inn in the countryside where four criminals kill Floridan and capture Elvide, whom they plan to rape. The wickedness of the crime comes to the fore in an apostrophe to the reader, which is followed by the description of Elvide's suicide. In closing, the author lays out a brief moral discourse on Elvide's actions, comparing her fate favorably with the legendary martyrdom of Lucretia. Masuccio does away with the quasi-philosophical conclusions and recasts the plot not merely as a case of

rape and virtuous suicide but as a hyperbolic, nightmarish tale. Masuccio's protagonists are, like those of the original, of noble lineage. In Masuccio, however,
the tragedy is deepened by the fact that both Martina and Loisi are the sole heirs
to their families' fortunes. This is the same twist that we see in the stories of
Barbara (Novella 2) and Pino (Novella 23), in which the family legacy depends
exclusively on the fortune of the only child; the risks entailed in a personal
tragedy are in this way extended to include the possibility of the extinction of an
entire family line. Embodied in each of the individual victims of unforeseen catastrophe are the shared hopes of an entire aristocratic class. The torturous events to
which the reader becomes a witness are outrageous offenses to the very stability
of his or her society. These implications are made clear in the dedication of the
tale to Eleonora d'Aragona, firstborn daughter of Ferrante, and in the *exordium* in
which Masuccio writes:

> Se de le cose prospere e gioconde, ornate de facezie giocose e de giocose piace-
> volezze, la natura se ne rallegra, e ne l'ascoltare ne rende graziosi e benigni, non
> altramente me pare, illustrissima madonna, che, leggendo o ascoltando de l'altrui li
> infelici, avversi e orribili casi, da umanitá siamo costretti a dovergli con le nostre piú
> amare lacrime ne le loro miserie piangendo accompagnare. (*Novellino*, 252)

> (If our nature takes delight in propitious and cheerful things made more beautiful by
> playful tales and pleasantries, and if listening to them makes us gracious and kind,
> not otherwise does it seem to me, my most illustrious lady, than that reading or hear-
> ing of the unhappy, adverse, and horrible fates of others shall we be forced by own
> our humanity to shed bitter tears of sympathy for their misery.)

The fate of the "unhappiest of lovers" is meant to affect the reader at an emotional
level; the ghastly conflation of extremes—high and low, noble and ignoble, pure
and diseased, innocent and demonic—is meant throughout to elicit feelings of
disgust and hatred toward the perpetrators of collective debasement. It is a new
phase in the development of the genre of the novella, and one that is realized
exclusively through the vehicles of horror and grotesque.

   Masuccio puts his two young lovers—so pure that they have dutifully
refrained from all sexual contact—into the dark wood where they are separated
from their escort by a sudden and violent hailstorm. The four "grans loudiers"
(big lechers [*Floridan*, 8]) of Brunhamel's translation are transformed into lepers
who provoke in Martina and Loisi a disquieting sense of disgust: "como che la
natura de' dui giovenetti alquanto aborresse la prattica de tali contaminate e
guaste gente, puro, non possedono piú ultre, se ingegnavano darsene pace"
(although the nature of the two youths abhorred to some degree the company of
such polluted and corrupt people, they nevertheless, having no choice in the matter, did their best to put themselves at ease [*Novellino*, 256]). After accentuating
the "natural" contrast between the lovers' regal bearing and the fetid flesh of the

lepers, Masuccio quickens the pace of the narration and thrusts upon the unsuspecting reader a remarkable scene of terror. Whereas in the model Floridan is
killed by a simple lance thrust through the heart, Loisi's murder and the events
that follow it are rather more complex. Brunhamel's protagonist dies quickly and
without much ado: "l'un d'eulz, estans assez loingz, jetta ung dart ayant la pointe
bien acheree, duquel messire Floridan qui point n'estoit armé et qui plus ne se
gardoit comme cuidant estre victorieux, fut assené au coeur et perchiet tout oul-
tre, duquel cop il cheit a terre privé et destabli de toutes ses forces et de toutes ses
vertus; et la morust en la place" (*Floridan*, 16). (One of them, from quite far off,
threw a lance whose tip was very sharp. It struck Sir Floridan who, thinking he
had fought them off, was unarmed and off his guard. Having been pierced straight
through the heart, he fell to the ground, stripped of all his might and virtue, and
died right there on the spot.) Masuccio's version reads:

> 'l fiero ribaldo gli diede una percossa tale con la ditta secura in testa, che, senza pos-
> sere dire omei, il buttò morto a terra; e ancora che cognoscesse, lui veramente essere
> morto, con piú altri dispiatati colpi li andò la testa percotendo. . . . La misera
> Martina rimasta sola, e pur del suo Loisi dimandando, e non gli essendo resposto, a
> la fine l'omicida, fattose avante, con sua gausta e rauca voce gli disse: "Figliola mia,
> a te conviene avere pazienzia, però che in quisto punto abbiamo occiso il tuo uomo,
> e imperciò in lui non piú sperare, ch'io intendo de tua gentile persona, fin che serò
> vivo, goderme." (*Novellino*, 257–58)

> (The fierce rogue gave him such a blow to the head with the aforementioned axe
> that, without uttering a word, Loisi fell down dead. Although the leper knew that
> Loisi was surely dead, he went on delivering several more pitiless blows to his
> head. . . . Meanwhile, poor Martina, who had been left alone, called for her Loisi
> and received no answer. At that point, the murderer appeared and said to her in a
> rough and sickly voice, "Relax, deary. We've just now killed your man so give up on
> seeing him again, because I intend to enjoy that comely body of yours for as long as
> I live.")

The suspense built into the scene is intense and holds the reader firmly until, at
length, it bursts into violence. To attain the desired emotional climax, Masuccio
not only has Loisi die in an undignified manner but also transfers the act of dying
itself into a process of defilement. Although he knows he has already delivered
the decisive axe blow, the leper continues to pound away at Loisi's skull. As if this
were not enough—especially considering that the first redaction of this novella
was dedicated to a seven-year-old girl—Martina discovers that her lover is dead
and that she is to be held there indefinitely as a sex slave. The heroine, trapped
indefinitely within the claustrophobic confines of the leper colony, faces a grim
fate indeed. Martina's punishment for having chosen Loisi against her father's
wishes is incalculably more severe than the reader might have suspected. She and

Loisi, "doe innocente columbe" (two innocent doves [*Novellino*, 257]), are Masuccio's virtuous counterparts of Dante's Paolo and Francesca, the archetypal representatives of bitter justice.[20]

Because the punishment seems incommensurate with the crime, we are compelled to feel compassion for the victim. It is but a short step from compassion to commiseration. We feel a certain identification with Martina, imagine ourselves there in her place, and experience her terror vicariously. Masuccio was looking for just this type of empathetic curiosity and feigns being subjected to it himself:

> me se representano la spaventivole imagine de quei lazari che dintorno a la miserrima giovene stavano, con gli occhi arrobinati e pelate ceglie, li nasi rusi, le guance tumidose e de' piú varii coluri depente, gli labri revolti e marci, le mane fedate paralitiche e attratte, che, como nui viggiamo, piú a diabolica che ad umana forma sono assomigliate, quali sono de tanta forza, che impediscono la mia tremante mano, che scrivere piú ultre non gli è concesso. Voi dunque che con pietá ascoltate, considerate quali pensieri fuorno gli soi, e de quanto spavento, ultre il cordoglio, gli era cagione il vederse tra dui ferocissimi cani, ch'erano si infiammati, che parea che ognuno de essi volesse essere il primo coretore. (*Novellino*, 258)

> (I imagine frightful images of those lepers surrounding the woeful young girl, their bloodshot eyes, hairless brows, and inflamed noses, their swollen cheeks discolored in various hues, their lips upturned and fetid, their filthy hands all twisted and crippled, bodies which, when we sometimes see them, are more demonic than human. The vision is so powerful that my trembling hand is powerless and can write no more. You, therefore, who listen in sympathy, just imagine what she must have been thinking and what terror, in addition to her heartache, she must have felt as she found herself trapped between two ferocious dogs, each aflame with desire and yearning to be the first to rush at her.)

Being gang-raped by lepers might not be among the more common phobias of the twenty-first century, but to contemporary readers or listeners leprosy was a real, if uncommon, part of their world. Masuccio successfully creates the most frightening combination of moral and physical corruption imaginable and pushes his readers into the victim's role.

The fact that leprosy was a disease that carried with it enormous cultural baggage was no doubt essential to Masuccio's decision to transform the rural inn of *Floridan et Elvide* into a leprosarium. Their peeling flesh and putrid limbs, perhaps known to Masuccio through the presence of lepers at the School of Salerno, were often represented in late medieval homilies as punishment for sins; by extension, these poor souls came to personify ungodly behavior and desire. To make matters worse, leprosy was also thought to accentuate the sex drive greatly and, moreover, to be transmitted sexually.[21] In effect, what we have in Novella 31 is another of Masuccio's visions of sexual and moral contamination, this time realized not as the inevitable consequence of female excesses but as an unexpected and overwhelming blow of ill fortune. The arrival at the leprosarium must have been immediately understood by Masuccio's readers as a dangerous combination of events in which the young lovers would be threatened by contagion, a moral as well as a physical peril. The situation's sociological implications, always of interest to Masuccio, are summed up by Henri Hauvette: "Masuccio a rendu en quelques traits saisissants la psychologie de ces infortunés dont les membres se déforments, dont la hideuse maladie ronge les muscles et le visage; du même coup tous leurs sentiments sont dominés par une haine inexpiable pour la société des hommes, qui les livre à leur atroce destin sans les secourir."[22] (Masuccio has depicted in a few powerful lines the psychology of these wretches whose limbs are twisted and whose hideous disease eats away at their muscles and faces. By the same token, all their thoughts are dominated by an implacable hatred for a society that has abandoned them, helpless, to their cruel fate.) The suspense is heightened still further by an almost complete lack of caution on the part of Martina and Loisi who, in their enigmatic innocence, simply seem grateful for shelter. The full impact of this tale of contamination and revenge-lust among the marginalized monsters also depends on the presence of the leper motif in well-known literary texts.

Il Novellino's readers, familiar with Arthurian prose romances, might have recalled the scene of Béroul's *Tristan* in which Yvain convinces King Mark to give Isolde over to a leper colony instead of burning her at the stake.[23] As the deformed men carry the queen away, however, she does not utter a single word of protest. Although the prospect of spending the rest of her life among these creatures would have been a torture in itself, there is no hint of psychological anguish or terror; what is most important to Béroul is that the plot continue smoothly to the narration of her eventual rescue. Similarly, in the Provençal romance known as *Jaufré* we are told the story of a hero who enters a leprosarium to rescue a child whose blood was to be used in the concoction of a cure, only to discover a young girl about to be raped.[24] Despite the gruesome details of Jaufré's victory, including the rescue of the girl (*Jaufré*, 1:82–86) and the liberation of thirty children not yet slaughtered (1:94–98), the genre of knight-errantry permitted no play with terror. The rapidity with which the villains are dispatched leaves no room for suspense, and our almost perfect faith in the hero's valor nullifies all temptation to identify with the virgin's fears. Masuccio's psychological perversion, or psychological realism, stands in contrast to such medieval texts.[25] As Martina learns what the evil lepers have in store for her, she reacts—unlike Isolde or the virgin in *Jaufré*—with intense anguish. She struggles violently, as if trying to awake from a dream, with "immensi gridi e 'l percuoterse de continuo la testa al muro, piú volte tramortita e in sé retornata, con lo suo delicato vulto tutto graffiato e sanguinoso" (powerful cries and pounding her head again and again against the wall; she alternated between dazed and lucid states and clawed her delicate face until it was bloody [*Novellino*, 258]). The lepers drag Martina into the next room and show her the nearly decapitated corpse of her lover. Her once incomparably beautiful face, now stained with blood and tears, erupts in a shrill scream, the signature climax of terror. Masuccio elaborates Brunhamel's description of Elvide's sudden shrieking (*Floridan*, 18–19) into perhaps the first authentic horror-story scream, a timeless emotional trigger to which all readers respond.[26]

The juxtaposition of sex and physical danger, common in some degree to nearly all successful tales of horror, runs throughout Novella 31 and is enhanced with the leitmotif of fire. From the very outset of the tale, Masuccio incorporates images codified in Provençal lyric verse and the *stilnovo* poets to describe the physical beauty of Martina and the power of the couple's desire for one another. The lovers are "innamorati forte e dentro le fiamme d'amore accesi" (deeply in love and warmed by the flames of love [*Novellino*, 253]). "Focosi sospiri" (fiery sighs) are inspired by their "eterno amore acceso da pare fiamme" (eternal love ignited by twin flames), and so on [*Novellino*, 254, 259]. Notably, Masuccio weaves into this thread another of the famous *topoi* of fire, the allusion to leprosy. References to fire and flames were commonly employed in discussions of leprosy both because the disease produced lesions similar to deep sears and because the most frequent punishment for lepers was burning at the stake.[27] The point of contact between these two metaphorical patterns is the actual fire that literally warms Martina and illuminates her radiant features even as it metaphorically stirs up the lepers' sexual desires. Significantly, the retribution that comes at the end of the tale manifests itself in the burning of the leprosarium and all its inhabitants. If, as Guido Guinizzelli once wrote, it is "prava natura" (baser nature) that extinguishes the flames of Love,[28] it is fire itself that puts an end to the depraved lepers. The reality of leprosy, antithetical to the social class that is represented in the figures of Martina and Loisi and recognized by Masuccio's readers, is the vehicle for a powerful inversion of the social order. Punishment is always exacted upon transgressors in the world of *Il Novellino*, even upon the two otherwise pleasant young people who wished to realize a forbidden love. "Per questi due giovani," writes Emilio Pesce, "la condanna viene dal mondo che li circonda, quel mondo dell'istinto e del male che qui assume un volto diabolico."[29] (For these two lovers, punishment comes from the world around them, from the world of instincts and evil that assumes here a diabolical countenance.) Greater than the lovers' "understandable" sin, however, is the abominable crime of the lepers: demonic lust and murder. Masuccio's macabre twists to his model, *Floridan et Elvide*, are a forceful reaction to threats against proper social order.

Modern fans of Gothic fiction are likely to find here all the elements for an exciting, emotional encounter with Evil, including the proverbial "dark and stormy night" as well as a vulnerable virgin, unthinkably monstrous villains, and a frightening rural locale. Although the literary style that featured such elements was not popular until the 1700s, it is useful to apply recent theories on its aesthetic underpinnings to a close examination of Masuccio's *gusto dell'orrido*. The eighteenth and nineteenth centuries' romanticized reelaboration of what seemed "medieval" was not, as we well know, an accurate reflection of anything like the historical Quattrocento Naples. What this perception does allow us, however, is an appreciation of the early horror tale that is based, like several of Masuccio's novellas, upon the fear of transgression and contamination. Let us think not of Walpole, Shelley, or Stoker, but of Masuccio when we read Fred Botting's description of one of Gothic literature's primary themes:

> The terrors and horrors of transgression in Gothic writing become a powerful means to reassert the values of society, virtue and propriety: transgression, by crossing the social and aesthetic limits, serves to reinforce or underline their value and necessity, restoring or defining limits. Gothic novels frequently adopt this cautionary strategy, warning of dangers of social or moral transgression by presenting them in their darkest and most threatening form. The tortuous tales of vice, corruption and depravity are sensational examples of what happens when the rules of social behavior are neglected. Gothic terrors and horrors emanate from readers' identifications with heroes and heroines: after escaping the monsters and penetrating the forest, subterranean or narrative labyrinths of the Gothic nightmare, heroines and readers manage to return with an elevated sense of identity to the solid realities of justice, morality and social order.[30]

What ultimately lies at the root of this comparison is the realization that horror tales (whether in *Il Novellino*, in Gothic fiction, or in films) rely on an ability to make a connection between the known world and the world we fear, one that— today as much as in the Renaissance—is the refuge of Evil. This admittedly anachronistic comparison can apply equally as well to Masuccio, his readers, and their own relationship to moral and social order. Masuccio indulges in exaggerated descriptions of implausibly bizarre and horrible events in order to heighten the social message of his eerie visions. This is a striking innovation in the evolution of fifteenth-century prose. Despite the enduring influence of Crocean criticism, it is often in precisely this innovation that we find what Del Monte called "una novella permeata di poesia" (a novella permeated with poetry [110]).

The subject of the macabre and the fearsome was a motivating factor in Masuccio's redaction of novellas, and this estrangement of reality (a sort of *reductio ad timorem*) is at the heart of Masuccio's literary style. In his gloss to Novella 19, he writes:

> Diverse e strane sono le paure che gli morti sogliono agli vivi donare, sí come ogne dí infinite esperienzie se ne veggono; ove tal volte accade che alcuni, andando de notte ed essendo da tale soverchio timore assaliti, trasvedono in manera che piú volte iudicano una cosa per un'altra, e dopo sopra a quello componeno le piú nove e maravigliose favole, che mai se udessero. (*Novellino*, 167)

(Diverse and strange are the fears that the dead inspire in the living, and we see such things every day. Sometimes it happens that someone, walking at night and being overtaken by excessive fear, sees one thing and takes it to be another and afterwards makes from it the most unusual and fabulous tales you've ever heard.)

To Masuccio, it is clear that fear can awaken our fantasies and vivify our nightmares. It is no less clear to him that these same phobias can be harnessed to a social agenda. His very "un-Boccaccian" privileging of the upper classes and his unwarranted attention to death and dying, as Bakhtin might have said, make him an anomalous figure among Quattrocento novella writers. If Masuccio's critical reception has sometimes suffered on account of his *gusto dell'orrido* and his predilection for images and situations that rely for their artistic impact on our insecurities and apprehensions, his innovative style of storytelling should gain new appreciation from critics and readers who recognize the horror and the grotesque of the *Novellino* not as a failed attempt to mimic the *Decameron* but as a new direction in the novella tradition. Masuccio's psychological distortion of reality, which typically features members of the upper classes being faced with disgusting or dangerous situations, is much more easily understood when seen through the lens of the Romantic grotesque, insofar as so much of it depends upon the individual's reception of the fearful and upon his perception of a threat to accepted concepts of social order and personal safety. The grotesque horror tale is a specific way of addressing a reader's discomfort when faced with characters or situations that expose or accentuate the precariousness of respected social institutions and the often tenuous constructions of his ontological premises. This emphasis on the intensely subjective power of the novella is an odd twist to the well-established patterns of the genre, but one that is born of the most earnest sociological and aesthetic sensibilities. Whether we describe it as Auerbach's "perverse psychology," as Neri's "squalid ferocity," or as Del Monte's *gusto dell'orrido*, this transformation, from the inherited comic style to one that permits the horrible and the grotesque, sets the stage for generations of short-story writers who follow in Masuccio's path. Among these are figures such as Grazzini, Bandello, and Giraldi Cinzio as well as—one might just be tempted to suggest— Edgar Allan Poe.

Notes

An earlier version of this essay was read as part of a session entitled "Transformations of the Novella," at the Modern Language Association Convention held in Toronto, December 29, 1997.

1.   Erich Auerbach, *Zur Technik der Frührenaissancenovelle in Italien und Frankreich*, Verzeichnis der angeführten Literatur (Heidelberg: Carl Winter, 1921), 53. All English translations of original quotations cited in text are mine.

2. Enrico Spinelli, *Masuccio Salernitano: Scrittura della crisi e poetica del diverso* (Salerno: Reggiani, 1980), 35–36; hereafter cited in text as Spinelli.

3. Masuccio Salernitano, *Il Novellino*, ed. Alfredo Mauro, rev. ed. Salvatore S. Nigro, Universale Laterza, no. 530 (1940; reprint, Bari: Laterza, 1979), xx; hereafter cited in text as *Novellino*.

4. Ferdinando Neri, "*Il Novellino* di Masuccio," *La Stampa*. November 24, 1940; reprinted in his *Poesia nel tempo*, Maestri e compagni, no. 10 (Turin: Francesco de Silva, 1948), 28.

5. Mario Fubini, *Studi sulla letteratura del Rinascimento*, Biblioteca Sansoniana critica, no. 11 (Florence: Sansoni, 1948), 50; hereafter cited in text as Fubini.

6. See Michele Cataudella, "Approcci per una formalizzazione della novella di Masuccio," in *Masuccio, novelliere salernitano dell'età aragonese: Atti del Convegno nazionale di studi su Masuccio Salernitano, Salerno, 9–10 maggio 1976*, eds. Pietro Borraro and Francesco D'Episcopo, Collana di saggi e testi, no. 14. Sezione Quarta, Letteratura italiana, no. 1 (Galatina: Congedo, 1978), 1:77–78, hereafter cited in text as Borraro and D'Episcopo; Renzo Bragantini, "La novella del Cinquecento. Rassegna di studi (1960–1980)," *Lettere italiane* 33 (January–March 1981): 83–85; and Salvatore S. Nigro, *Le brache di San Griffone: novellistica e predicazione tra '400 e '500*, Biblioteca di cultura moderna, no. 879 (Bari: Laterza, 1983), 140–47, hereafter cited in text as *Le brache*.

7. Francesco Bonciani, *Lezione sopra il comporre delle novelle. Trattati di poetica e di retorica del Cinquecento*, ed. Bernard Weinberg, 4 vols., Scrittori d'Italia, no. 249 (Bari: Laterza, 1972), 3:135–73. The tale that incensed Bonciani concerns abortion and infanticide (III, 52). See Matteo Bandello, *Tutte le opere*, ed. Francesco Flora, 2 vols., I Classici Mondadori (1934; reprint, Verona: Arnoldo Mondadori Editore, 1966).

8. Although the merchant class was in reality an ever more significant economic presence in the south, the Aragonese consistently strove to limit its power. See Antonio Cestaro, "Per la storia del principato di Salerno nel secolo XV," *Rivista di studi salernitani* 1 (1968): 145–47.

9. Benedetto Croce, "Boccaccio," in *Poeti e scrittori d'Italia*, eds. Floriano del Secolo and Giovanni Castellano, 2 vols. (Bari: Laterza, 1927), 1:54.

10. Alberto Del Monte, "L'arte di Masuccio Salernitano," *Lo spettatore italiano* 2 (1949): 107; hereafter cited in text as Del Monte.

11. Brevio, a Venetian nobleman and friend of Bembo, published his version of the tale in his *Rime et prose volgari* (Rome: Antonio Blaso Asolano, 1545).

12. John Ruskin, *The Stones of Venice*, in *The Works of John Ruskin*, eds. Edward Tyas Cook and Alexander D. O. Wedderburn, 39 vols. (London: Allen, 1903), 11:151; hereafter cited in text as Ruskin.

13. Wolfgang Kayser, *The Grotesque in Art and Literature*, trans. Ulrich Weisstein, McGraw-Hill Paperbacks (New York: McGraw-Hill, 1966), 184–89.

14. Mikhail Bakhtin, *Rabelais and His World*, trans. Hélène Iswolsky (Bloomington: Indiana University Press, 1984), 38–39; hereafter cited in text as *Rabelais*.

15. Bakhtin, "Forms of Time and the Chronotope in the Novel," in *The Dialogic Imagination: Four Essays*, ed. Michael Holquist, trans. Caryl Emerson and

Michael Holquist, University of Texas Press Slavic Series, no. 1 (Austin: University of Texas Press, 1981), 200; hereafter cited in text as "Forms of Time."

16. This notion lies at the root of Peter Stallybrass's and Allon White's study of the social and intellectual imagination of post-Renaissance Europe (*The Politics and Poetics of Transgression* [Ithaca, N.Y.: Cornell University Press, 1986]). Although they do not directly discuss *Il Novellino*, their ideas on the grotesque as a key to boundary construction and the formation of collective identity are useful to understanding the literary consequences of the separation of classes in Renaissance Naples.

17. Concerning the implications of the term *operetta* with regard to the novella genre, see also Note 24 in Christopher Nissen's essay, chapter 11 in this volume.

18. Lee B[yron] Jennings, *The Ludicrous Demon: Aspects of the Grotesque in German Post-Romantic Prose*, University of California Publications in Modern Philology, no. 71 (Berkeley: University of California, 1963), 25–26.

19. Antoine de La Sale commissioned—and perhaps revised—the French translation known as the "Barrois." He included it in a collection of stories that he gave to John of Calabria, the Angevin claimant to the throne of Naples, about a year before Masuccio wrote the early version that was discovered and reprinted by Giorgio Petrocchi ("La prima redazione del *Novellino* di Masuccio," *Giornale storico della letteratura italiana* 129 [1952]: 289–98). Whereas Brunhamel had reported that the story took place "es fins de France" ("at France's borders"), Masuccio moved the setting to Nancy, birthplace of John of Calabria. See *Floridan et Elvide. A Critical Edition of the 15th Century Text, with an Introduction*, ed. Harry Peter Clive (Oxford: Basil Blackwell, 1959), 2–3; hereafter cited in text as *Floridan*.

20. Dante describes his adulterous pair with a dove simile: "Quali colombe dal disio chiamate / con l'ali alzate e ferme al dolce nido / vegnon per l'aere, dal voler portate" (*Inferno* V, 82–84). In the Middle Ages, doves represented concupiscence. See also Cesare De Sio, "Echi danteschi nel *Novellino* di Masuccio Salernitano," in *Dante nel pensiero e nella esegesi dei secoli XIV e XV: Atti del Convegno di studi realizzato dal Comune di Melfi in collaborazione con la Biblioteca provinciale di Potenza e il Seminario di studi danteschi di Terra di lavoro, Melfi, 27 settembre–2 ottobre 1970*, eds. Adalgisa Borraro and Pietro Borraro (Florence: Leo S. Olschki, 1975), 349, 354.

21. Saul Nathaniel Brody, *The Disease of the Soul: Leprosy in Medieval Literature* (Ithaca, N.Y.: Cornell University Press, 1974), 51–59.

22. Henri Hauvette, *La "morte vivante": étude de littérature comparée*, Bibliothèque de la Revue des cours et conférences (Paris: Boivin, 1933), 54.

23. Béroul, *Le roman de Tristan*, ed. and trans. Norris J. Lacy, Garland Library of Medieval Literature, Series A, no. 36 (New York: Garland Publishing, Inc., 1989), ll. 1165–79.

24. *Jaufré. Roman arthurien du XIIIᵉ siècle en vers provençaux*, ed. Clovis Brunel, 2 vols., Société des Anciens Textes Français, no. 74 (Paris: Société des Anciens Textes Français, 1943), 1:78–82; hereafter cited in text as *Jaufré*.

25. See Vito Moretti, "Proposte di lettura del *Novellino*," in Borraro and D'Episcopo, 1:179–84; and Spinelli, 22, 34.

26. An interesting parallel phenomenon appears in modern horror films. The female scream has become an indispensable component in the climactic moment of erotic violence and has been used to heighten our fears since the invention of the sound track. See Anthony Ambrogio, "Fay Wray: Horror Films' First Sex Symbol," in *Eros in the Mind's Eye*, ed. Donald Palumbo, Contributions to the Study of Science Fiction and Fantasy, no. 21 (Westport, Conn.: Greenwood Press, 1986), 128.

27. The recurrence of this motif in literature is analyzed by Laurence Wright, " 'Burning' and Leprosy in Old French," *Medium Ævum* 56 (1987): 101–11.

28. Guido Guinizelli, "Al cor gentil rempaira sempre amore," in *The Poetry of Guido Guinizelli*, ed. and trans. Robert Edwards, Garland Library of Medieval Literature, Series A, no. 27 (New York: Garland Publishing, Inc., 1987), 20–21.

29. Emilio Pesce, *Masuccio Salernitano* (Modena: Società Tipografica Modenese, 1962), 105.

30. Fred Botting, *Gothic*, The New Critical Idiom (New York: Routledge, 1996), 7.

8

Imitation and Subversion of Models in Agnolo Firenzuola's *I Ragionamenti*

Manuela Scarci

Agnolo Firenzuola has always been considered a minor figure among the giants of sixteenth-century Italian culture. The details of his life remain largely unknown, and extant documentation allows for only a partial reconstruction. He was born in Florence in 1493, maternal grandson of Alessandro Braccesi, the renowned humanist, diplomat, and secretary of the Signoria. He spent his youth in Siena and in Perugia, pursued studies in law, joined the Vallombrosan monastic order, and was destined for an ecclesiastical career in the Roman Curia. After attaining the title of abbot, he decided to abandon the legal profession and dedicate himself to the study of literature. This decision was apparently precipitated by his attraction for Costanza Amaretta, a source of poetic inspiration throughout his stay in Rome. In 1526 he was struck by an illness traditionally thought to have been syphilis, and Pope Clement VII dispensed him from his monastic vows. Little is known of his whereabouts during the next eleven years. In 1538 he was living in Prato, where he died in June of 1543.

In a century known for its preoccupation with literary genres, Firenzuola dabbled in all of them. His prose works were written during two short periods of intense literary activity: in Rome, between 1524 and 1525; and in Prato, between 1541 and 1542.[1] His lyric poems, almost all of uncertain date, seem to span his entire life. Although his treatise titled *Discacciamento de le nuove lettere inutilmente aggiunte ne la lingua toscana* is a scathingly sarcastic first rebuttal to Gian Giorgio Trissino's pedantic proposal of orthographical reforms to the vernacular, he is mainly remembered for his *novelle*, written in the style of Boccaccio and frequently anthologized ever since they were first published.

Throughout the centuries, the critical acclaim and popularity of Firenzuola's novellas have coincided with that accorded to the Boccaccian model. His contem-

poraries admired him for the purity of his style and for the elegance that he succeeded in achieving in the vernacular; in the seventeenth century, however, precisely because of the classical elements in his writings, he was nearly forgotten.
The sporadic critical assessments of his writings in this period and the few
reprintings of his texts are proof of a general lack of interest in his work. The situation changed in the eighteenth century when, with the radical revision of literary taste brought about by the Arcadian movement, classical aesthetics were
again sought out and promoted. Nineteenth-century scholarship on Firenzuola is
noteworthy mainly for the philological research done on his works and for the
persistent moralistic preoccupations that permeate critical analyses of his writings. In keeping with the overall Romantic assessment of Cinquecento literary
production, scholars condemned him for the immoral content of his writings, considered especially scandalous in his case because of its strident contrast with his
ecclesiastical profession.

More recent scholarly opinion of this author exhibits little change from that
of previous centuries, despite the more refined tools at the disposal of the literary
critic.[2] Firenzuola's greatest mark of distinction is that he is an able imitator of
Boccaccio's masterpiece, an assessment that fails to recognize his own remarkable literary achievements. Firenzuola was the first writer in the sixteenth century
to take up the novella genre in the vernacular after the virtual stagnation of the
previous century; indeed, he was the first author to readopt the model of the
Decameron in its totality. What is more, far from being a passive appropriation of
some other's literary material, his is an operation on the cultural front with a
broader scope than might at first be suspected.

In this essay, I will examine the six novellas in *I Ragionamenti* and their
importance within the context of an elaborate frame story. A group of young people (three men and three women) retreat to the country for six days where they are
to pass time in pleasant learned conversation: each day, under the rule of their
chosen "queen," Gostanza, they will ponder some philosophical issue, and each
will recite a poem and tell a novella and a *facetia*. On the First Day, the philosophical discussion of the morning revolves around the nature of love. The discussion, which takes place in the afternoon, derives from the poems and is strewn
with poignant observations on literary language and on the poetics of imitation.
Firenzuola abandoned the work upon completion of the First Day and, judging by
the other extant fragments, soon after he had sketched a plan for the Second Day.
The two surviving novellas written for this Second Day have been excluded from
the present investigation since their philosophical content cannot be surmised.

At the time Firenzuola wrote *I Ragionamenti*, the use of different literary
genres in a single work was not without precedent. One thinks of Dante's *Vita
nuova* and the *Convivio*, Boccaccio's *Decameron*, or Bembo's *Gli Asolani*. In
none of these texts, however, is the medley this overstated; in none are the different genres seemingly placed on equal footing. This, together with the fact that the

novellas fail to satisfactorily illustrate the principles of Neoplatonic love, has caused generations of editors and readers to split up the text. In the posthumous publication of *I Ragionamenti* in 1548, the novellas have a separate frontispiece. In later printings (Venice: Griffio, 1552), the dialogue and the novellas are published in different volumes, a practice destined to be repeated through the centuries.[3] Later critical assessments of the work have reproduced the separation iconically figured by the *princeps*.

Some scholars have considered the novellas as a separate body of work, almost an appendix that, at best, has little bearing on the discussions of love itself (Seroni, 25–45). Alternatively, the novellas have been seen as a proof either of the hypocrisy of the social class that the author is said to represent or of his artistic shortcomings.[4] Other critics have dismissed the work as a mere collection of tales modelled on Boccaccio's masterpiece and have relegated the dialogue on love to a mere element of the frame story.[5] They have also viewed Firenzuola as an author who, although intellectually incapable of understanding the deeper structures and meanings of his archetype, lacked any truly original inspiration and was therefore doomed to failure from the start.

I Ragionamenti has rarely been considered as an organic unity whose distinct components gain significance from each other's copresence. Its contradictions—such as the juxtaposition of a dialogue on Neoplatonic love with the licentious novellas written in the style of Boccaccio—are inherent in the text, which is easily deconstructed from within. Numerous elements tend to destabilize its seemingly cohesive structure while at the same time confirming it: for instance, the numerical scheme, and the apparently careful grouping into sixes, is ultimately rendered nonsensical. Every affirmation is negated, but so is every negation: the dialogue on love is developed along the lines of Bembo's *Gli Asolani*, but little space is devoted to an elaboration of the strictly philosophical aspects of love, whereas the ensuing discussion is prolonged to its limits when the interlocutors raise questions and objections of a practical nature. Every component has its exact opposite somewhere else in the text in a *mise en abîme* composition: Celso and Gostanza are depicted as paragons of Neoplatonic lovers, but they are also the ones who tell the most risqué of all the stories; Folchetto, who is openly sensual and irreverently cynical toward every edifying statement made by the queen, tells a truly exemplary story.

The deep-seated contradictions of *I Ragionamenti*, the fundamental restlessness of its poetic material, its apparent inconsistencies, and the dialectic interaction of opposites are far too numerous and systematic to be casual. Provided that one recognizes them not as simple *dégagé* techniques of composition but as ironic structural inversions within the text (and more important, without), it becomes apparent that they represent the governing principle of the novellas.[6] The external point of reference must always be the linguistic and philosophical models promoted by Pietro Bembo, who single-handedly was responsible for most of the conventions of erudite literature in the sixteenth century.[7]

Irony in literature, as Wayne C. Booth tells us in his fundamental *A Rhetoric of Irony*, is not the everyday figure of speech whereby we say the opposite of what we mean to say, fully expecting our audience to reconstruct the true meaning of our statement. That type of irony is merely ornamental, localized, and stable. The ironic processes in literature are far more complex. Booth classifies them according to whether they are overt (when the author actually flags them for the reader) or covert (discovered through the reader's reasonable and justified inference); stable (when the hidden message can be reconstructed) or unstable (when there is no firm reconstruction of that message); local (when irony undermines one specific proposition or belief) or infinite (when the undermining is endless and the author refuses to commit himself to any assertion, including the one diametrically opposite whatever his irony is vigorously trying to negate).[8] In this last category, the reader is invited to decode an infinite number of propositions that manifest themselves as a never-ending series of Chinese boxes. The intention to be ironic often goes hand in hand with the intention to parody another text or set of conventions. "[I]rony is the major rhetorical strategy deployed by the genre [i.e. parody]"; it is "the main rhetorical mechanism for activating the reader's awareness," and it marks that critical distance required a priori between the parodied and the parodying texts.[9] For Mikhail Bakhtin, irony, in more recent literary forms, and laughter, in ancient and popular ones, is the one element that gives parodies their regenerative energies: irony gives the parodic author the power to investigate man and his world freely and fearlessly. It is no less than the means through which artists can demolish old systems and norms of expression and create new ones.[10] Thus parody and imitation—whether Renaissance or modern—can be seen as closely related forms.[11] Parodies can go undetected if the author's intention is not overt or if the reader fails to recognize them.[12] The text survives but in an altered, impoverished, and crippled form, devoid of its deeper significations. It is my contention that such has been the case with Firenzuola's *I Ragionamenti*.

An example of what Bakhtin calls the verbal-ideological center of the text is found in Firenzuola's discussion on literary language and the poetics of imitation that takes place among the group soon after they recite their poems as their first activity in the afternoon of that first day in the country. These pages constitute the most explicit statement of Firenzuola's intent to parody (to repeat with ironic distance) Bembo's "genre," where the term not only stands for a literary form—that is, the love treatise with its prescribed Boccaccian and Petrarchan linguistic influences—but also functions as a code to interpret our reality, "as a zone and a field of valorized perception, as a mode for representing the world" (Bakhtin, "Epic and Novel," 28).

In *I Ragionamenti*, the critical controversy over reliance on prescribed stylistic models begins after one of the *canzoni* is recited by an interlocutor. A female listener in the group remarks that she cannot recall this rhyme scheme being used by any poet, either ancient or modern. To her inquiry about its origins, Selvaggio, the author of the poem, lashes out at modern censors:

"Da me stesso la ho io ritrovata . . . ma qual cagione ti muove a darmene riprensione? Dunque non è egli lecito agli moderni trovar nuovi modi di canzoni, come fu agli antichi? Dunque non ci sarà mai permesso di poter migliorar questa lingua, e arrichirla di nuove cose? Anzi sarà mestieri lasciarla in quegli puri termini che ella si ritrovava quando ella nacque, o almeno in quelli stessi che ella si ritruova al presente? Dimmi, Bianca, per tua fe', sei tu anche tu di quelle che nel riprendere le cose altrui non adduci altra ragione se non 'e' non l'usa il Petrarca?' " (*Opere*, 70)

(I have invented it myself . . . but what would cause you to censure me? Is it not then legitimate for the modern [authors] to invent new ways of composing *canzoni* as it was for earlier ones? Will we never be allowed to improve our language and to enrich it with new things? Or will it instead be necessary to leave it in the pristine state in which it found itself when it was first born, or at least in those in which it finds itself at the present? Tell me, Bianca, in good faith: are you too one of those who, in finding fault with the writings by others, advances no other reason than "Petrarch doesn't use it?")

Later in the discussion, Fioretta is equally militant when she is taken to task for having included in her *canzone* a word found neither in Petrarch nor in any other "good author." Appealing to the twin authorities of Horace and Cicero, who "dicono in più luoghi che doviamo usar parole che sieno nella bocca degli uomini tutto il giorno, e lasciare quelle che son già dimesse e abbandonate" (say in more than one place that we should use words spoken every day by people and leave those already rejected and abandoned), Fioretta argues that "lo uso dei più . . . è l'arbitrio e la regola del parlare" (discretion and rules for speaking rest with the usage by many [*Opere*, 76]). She is incensed by the "nuovi Fallari . . . [che] si sono voluti far tiranni nelle provincie altrui, contro alla voglia dei propri cittadini" (the new Phalarises . . . [who] have set themselves up as tyrants in other provinces against the will of the people [*Opere*, 76]).

Firenzuola's style in these pages is incisive, precise, and energetic. The jokes, the conspiratorial winks, the mischievous looks, and the naughty remarks woven into the morning's discussion on love have disappeared before the seriousness of the remonstrations made by the characters. Even their attitude changes: they become impatient and prone to anger, a behavior that clashes with the courteous manners typical of "valorosi giovani, e . . . onestissime donne" (gallant young men and . . . very honest women [*Opere*, 52]).

If Bembo's system is consistently platonic, Firenzuola's just as consistently is not. Just as in his discussion on love he had shown an interest in the sociological repercussions of the phenomenon rather than in its philosophical aspects, Firenzuola's preferred literary language is to be developed in contact with the real rather than being dictated by already remote models now deemed unchangeable. In arguing for innovations, Firenzuola defended "la tradizione *moderna* . . . che respingeva una perfetta, immobile 'idea' della letteratura" (the *modern* tradition . . . that rejected a perfect, fixed "idea" of literature [Romei, 86–88]), siding with those writers who resisted the rigidity of Bembo's principles. Firenzuola seems well poised to accept the future, were it not for other statements that seem to retract and undermine what he had earlier proposed. For instance, Fioretta, who had earlier repudiated Petrarch's influence, later calls on it so vigorously that Folchetto rebukes her: "Grande è certamente l'autorità del Petrarca, ma non la doverresti allegar tu, che la sprezzasti dianzi, quando la allegò la Reina" (*Opere*, 84). (Petrarch's authority is certainly great, but you should not support it, since you scorned it before when the queen urged its support.) For some critics, such statements exemplify the many contradictions in the text and demonstrate Firenzuola's wavering between a conformist attitude toward the system and fanciful ambitions to overcome it; in Romei's opinion, Firenzuola lacks "un programma maturo e coerente" (a coherent, mature work program [89]). Ultimately, he is incapable of breaking loose, of exorcising all *auctoritates*.

There is, perhaps, a different interpretation. The author is asked to declare himself clearly for one set of proposals or the other, but he might be programmatically unwilling to do so. I would suggest that his project consists of this fundamental ambiguity, of these sudden and constant oscillations from one side of the question to the other, of these position statements that disintegrate the moment we believe he has formulated them clearly. What first appears to be irresolution on the part of the author is but a strategy of textual organization and a *modus operandi* employed in each constituent part of the text.[13] There are two lines of action, both on a formal and a thematic level: he either complies with, or reacts against, Bembo's normative scheme without formulating one of his own. The author is refractory to norms imposed from above that could potentially limit the expressiveness of a language intended not merely as an abstract linguistic code but as the concrete tool of his art; a language that is capable, in its versatility, of interpreting the world as it sees fit, free to choose the perspective from which to contemplate the universe. For Bakhtin, Renaissance parodic forms (such as macaronic poetry) indicated not only "to what extent forms of language, and forms of world views, were inseparable from each other," but also "to what extent the old and new worlds were characterized precisely by their own peculiar languages, by the image of language that attached to each" ("From the Prehistory," 82). Far from proposing new codifications of norms that, no matter how different, would always be restrictive; feeling himself torn between the need to demolish the old system and the desire not to supersede it; conscious that he could not function in its total absence, Firenzuola chooses for himself yet another, absolutely personal alternative: he disavows the validity of the first system by delineating the exigencies of the other while at the same time confirming its authority by refusing to develop and fully articulate his own. From *I Ragionamenti* emerge not only two different linguistic codes, but also two distinct worlds that, in their proximity—to use Bakhtin's term—"interanimate" each other in their dialogic setting.

As we move from the focal point of the text to its outer structure, two things immediately strike the reader in Firenzuola's *cornice*: the numerous explicit references to Boccaccio and his insistence on the senary scheme of the composition. In the *exordium*, he dedicates the book to women for their entertainment. The work opens with the description of "una valletta" (a little valley [*Opere*, 42]) near Florence where Celso owns a *palagio* to which the group retreats. The highly lyrical passage is closely related, both in form and content, to Boccaccio's description of the "valley of women" (la valle delle donne) as well as to Bembo's garden in the *Gli Asolani* (Romei, 49). Furthermore, the idea of passing the time in the country pleasantly conversing and telling stories is occasioned by Boccaccio himself. The queen herself expresses this:

> "Ora mi sovviene, bellissime donne, e voi leggiadri giovani, qual fusse la cagione che movesse quella bella compagnia che, secondo che pone il Boccaccio, assai lieta si passò novellando il pestifero accidente, che affliggeva allor questo paese sì aspramente; ora me ne sovvien, dico, perché queste fontane, queste erbe, questi fiori, tutto questo paese, par che ne invitino a fare il simigliante; e però, quando e' vi paresse seguire in questa parte il mio consiglio, io vi diviserei di maniera la vita nostra quei pochi dì che noi facciam pensier dimorar quassù." (*Opere*, 44–45)

> (Now I recall, most beautiful ladies, and you, graceful young men, what the reason was that prompted that fine group who, according to Boccaccio, very happily passed the time away telling stories during the pestiferous occurrence that then afflicted this country so grievously; now I recall it, I say, because these fountains, this grass, these flowers, all of this countryside seem to invite us to do the same; therefore, if you were to follow my advice in this respect, I would dispose our life in a similar manner during the few days that we plan on sojourning up here.)

This can be neither accidental nor unintentional. Far from wanting or trying to conceal his sources, Firenzuola demands that his models be clearly defined and always borne in mind by his readers.

The frame has a twofold purpose: Displaying at first a general, apparent compliance with Bembo's precepts from which the author later deviates—a pattern typical in Firenzuola—while simultaneously signaling the far-reaching contestations of the same to be found within the text. As for the first purpose, it is important to recall that whereas Bembo accepted the whole of Petrarch (language, style, spiritual and intellectual scenarios), with regard to Boccaccio's literary production he showed a preference for the more solemn language of his frame (the description of the plague, the introductions and conclusions to the stories) from which he drew his examples for the *Prose della volgar lingua*. In that work, Bembo repeatedly rejected the notion that literary language should model itself on popular usage; he rejected any form of language inconsistent with his lofty platonic ideals, insisting on the absolutely elitist nature of it.[14] As for the second

144 Manuela ScarciManuela Scarci

purpose, the stated intention to engage in storytelling foreshadows more profound, unconventional, and daring "enstrangements"[15] on Bembo's cultural apparatus. From the outset, by his deliberate, overstated association with Boccaccio's major work, Firenzuola already implies a challenge to Bembo: through his Platonism and his ethereal concept of love, Firenzuola sets out to oppose the all too earthly loves of the *Decameron*.

The archetypal model for the love treatise in the Cinquecento was Bembo's *Gli Asolani*, which also has six interlocutors, although it is divided into only three days. It was representative of certain tendencies of high culture: for one, an aspiration to order signified by the numerical composition.[16] Firenzuola's *I Ragionamenti*, which takes form through a series of ironic inversions that make the text fluid and seemingly contradictory, suggests the unfeasibility or just the undesirability of those very tendencies. In this sense, Bembo's treatise represents a set of conventions, the norm, where "la norma è l'ordine o la ricerca dell'ordine" (the norm is order or the search for order), whereas Firenzuola's is the opposite; it represents "lo scarto" (the deviation from the norm), where "lo scarto è il disordine" (deviation from the norm is disorder), according to Riccardo Scrivano's formula of investigation for Italian literature in that century.[17] Furthermore, Firenzuola's text has within it the norm explicitly articulated (the backgrounded, parodied text) and the deviation from the norm (the parodying word); their constituent motifs are developed on parallel lines that are so close as to allow their constant interaction.

This brings us to the tales whose presence has traditionally been considered the greatest incongruity in the text, alien to the dialogue on love. The inclusion of the novellas is problematic, and their presence has conditioned readings of the text. When critics such as Fatini take the author at his word and accept the work as a whole, they see in it nothing more than a representation of life in those times. Marziano Guglielminetti and Eugenio Ragni see the elaborate frame as nothing more than a simple-minded mannerist variation on Boccaccio's frame story. Still others fail to see the connection between the dialogue on love and the novellas. Seroni states that whereas in Boccaccio "l'unità fra cornice e novelle . . . è evidente," Firenzuola "per quanto cerchi e ricerchi, non riesce a darci una ragion sufficiente delle sei novelle narrate" (the unity between the frame story and the novellas . . . is obvious; however, as much as [Firenzuola] tries and tries again, he does not manage to provide us with a sufficient rationale for the six novellas he narrates [*Opere*, xv–xvi]. Romei's position is more problematic: he sees the main goal of Firenzuola's work as being the juxtaposition of various unequal genres (95). Even though he acknowledges the contradiction implied by the two genres, the dialogue and the novella, he nevertheless states that the queen's *canzone* brings us back to the beginning, thus closing the circle.[18] But this amounts to excluding the novellas yet again from the economy of the text, to seeing them as a mere appendix to the main text.

It is indeed difficult, if not impossible, to justify the tales if one ignores the double voice of the parodic form. From this perspective, they are not irreconcilable with the rest of the work because, on one plane of textual organization (the figurative, denotative, or parodied one), they establish an ironic connection with it because they constitute yet another ironic inversion of Neoplatonic principles. On another plane (the literal, connotative, or parodying one), the tales establish a consequential link with the rest of the work because they represent the ultimate resting place of the parodic textual strategies employed by the author so far, that is, the contemporization and lowering of the subject matter and the uncrowning of *auctoritates*—processes that Bakhtin theorized in his works on parody. Once again, they constitute an element that both marks a breach in the cohesiveness of the whole and simultaneously strengthens it. The tales are especially significant when one considers the literary establishment's rejection of the novella genre. Bembo, for instance, despite his admiration for Boccaccio, took him to task for having written such tales.[19] They could hardly be expected to harmonize with Bembo's elitist concept of literature: their subject matter, readily adaptable to the present and to reality, was unpredictable and very often lewd, and it belonged to the common people in general.

From a structural point of view, Firenzuola's tales accumulate a rather conspicuous number of traditional motifs, mainly borrowed from Boccaccio, that are combined in a nontraditional manner. The elements of the *fabula* remain the same; what differs is the composition of the plot. This is generally exaggerated, amplified, and lengthened through repetitions, detailed descriptions, direct speeches, and reiterations of schemes and structural units. From a thematic point of view, all but one are contemporary love stories; all but one deal with carnal love; all but one end happily with the illicit relationship merrily consummated. The characters are also typical and, in general, morally reprehensible: the unfaithful wife; the old, impotent husband; the sly trickster; the mischievous servant; the cunning woman; the dishonest, greedy churchman; the lustful priest. Ostensibly the stories should have a didactic function, but in reality the moralistic admonishments, which always follow the praises lavished by the group on the character who pursues and attains sexual fulfillment, acquire a highly ironic nature. Since the ultimate goal is always sexual pleasure, it soon becomes apparent that the novellas not only ironically subvert those truly Neoplatonic theses already rejected during the philosophical debate, but they also subvert those statements concerning love and its concrete manifestations (faithfulness within the institution of marriage, for instance) that appear to be the author's direct discourse rather than the representation of the language of the Other. The latter is, in effect, the essence of parody.

Having invited the group to be decorous in their stories, this is how Gostanza introduces her own:

Poi che i nostri ragionamenti sono stati tutt'oggi d'amore, io non voglio già che la mia novella introduca nuova materia; e dacché con tante ragioni voi avete sentito l'odor de' suoi suavissimi fiori, egli non sarà fuor di proposito che voi cognosciate per isperienza quanto dolci sieno i suoi frutti; e cominceròmmi con quelli di quel ramo, che noi aviamo detto che è di minor perfezione. . . . (*Opere*, 89)

(Since our discussions today have all been about love, I do not wish my novella to introduce a new subject; and since for so many reasons you have smelled the fragrance of its delicate flowers, it will not be out of place for you to get to know by experience how sweet its fruits are; and I will start with those from that branch which we said is less perfect. . . .)

The less perfect branch she refers to is carnal love between man and woman as opposed to purely spiritual love. Her story, the most significant of the six, relates the love story between a beautiful married woman from Tunis and a noble Florentine by the name of Niccolò degli Albizi. They meet after Niccolò, on a voyage to Spain, is shipwrecked off the African coast. Saved by fishermen, he is sold as a slave to her husband, "un gran gentiluomo della terra" (a powerful gentleman of that region [*Opere*, 92]). The woman falls in love with him. For many days she suffers in silence, but in the end "tratto Niccolò in disparte, e narratogli i suoi dolori, gli chiese lo amor suo" (she took him aside, told him of her torments, and pleaded for his love [*Opere*, 95]).

In her oft-cited monologue, the reasons she lists to dissuade herself from loving him—he is a slave, a foreigner, and a Christian; her honor may be irreparably damaged if her unfaithfulness is ever discovered—finally succumb to the power of love. However, she still needs a noble pretext to disguise her surrender: "[E] se pur vuoi macchiar la tua onestà, sieno le cagioni almen tali, ch'elleno non ti arrechin doppia vergogna, ma te ne scusino in conspetto di tutti coloro che avesser mai fumo de' tuoi portamenti" (*Opere*, 93). (And if you do want to stain your honesty, at least let it not be for reasons that may bring shame upon you doubly, but that may excuse you in the eyes of those who ever had an inkling of your behavior.) She finds her pretext, among the many possible ones, in religion: "Chi sa se amando lui ed egli me, io lo persuaderò a credere alle nostre leggi e così ad un tratto farò cosa grata e a me e agli nostri Iddii" (*Opere*, 94). (Who knows if, by loving him and being loved by him, I shall not persuade him to believe in our faith? And thus I will do something at once agreeable to me and to our gods.)

It is, of course, a specious argument that might even appear hypocritical to the modern reader, but not to Firenzuola, who portrays his character as the typical self-deceiver.[20] This character trait extends to Gostanza herself. At the beginning of the dialogue on love, she has given a brief autobiographical sketch: she had been married off to "uno avaro venditor di leggi" (a miserly peddler of laws) who engaged her in discussions that were "libidinosi e brutti" (libidinous and awful [*Opere*, 53]); she was reborn when Love, moved by pity, elected her to his cohort.

But there are no traces in her tale of the ennobling virtues of love she had defended earlier in the day, claiming its goals were "ragionamenti" (discussions) that nurture the soul. Significantly, when Niccolò hesitates at her proposal, the female protagonist of the story, "che altro voleva che parole, gli serrava . . . i basti addosso" (who wanted more than words, fastened the pack saddle on his back [*Opere*, 95]).[21]

The futility of her argument is fully illustrated when the man demands, as a necessary condition of his fulfilling her desires, that she convert to Christianity. He is not acting out of religious zeal, however, but purely for opportunistic reasons, in anticipation of a possible escape. The woman's words of surrender—"Fa di me ciò che ti piace" (Do with me as you please [*Opere*, 96])—blasphemously echo the words of another *ancilla* whose image Gostanza had come to Florence to worship. The climax—pun unintended!—comes soon after:

> E così, per non ve la allungare, il dì medesimo ella si battezzò, e il dì medesimo feceno il parentado, e consumorono il matrimonio il dì medesimo; e così gli [*sic*] parveno dolci i misteri di questa nuova fede, che come già fece Alibec, a tutte le ore riprendeva se stessa d'esser tanto indugiata ad assaggiarla; e sì le piaceva d'esservi dentro profondamente amaestrata, che la non aveva mai bene, se non quando la imprendeva questa nuova dottrina. (*Opere*, 96)

> (So to make a long story short, the same day she was baptized, and the same day they became relatives and consummated their marriage on the same day; and the mysteries of this new faith seemed so sweet to her that, as Alibech had done, she constantly upbraided herself for having delayed so long in tasting it; and she loved so well being deeply instructed in it, that she was never happy except when she was learning this new doctrine.)

Unlike all the other stories, this one is free of all moral interpretations, however artificial they might be. Firenzuola leaves the forum to Folchetto alone, the narrative saboteur par excellence, who for once has nothing to object:

> E nel vero, se tutti i frutti di amore sono come quegli che Niccolò e colui che io vi intendo raccontare al presente colsero sugli arbori delle lor padrone, che la Reina ha avuto mille ragioni a lodarlo tutto dì d'oggi, e io ho avuto torto a biasimarlo. (*Opere*, 104)

> (And in truth, if all the fruits of love are like the ones that Niccolò and the one about whom I am going to tell picked from the trees of their mistresses, the queen has had a thousand good reasons to praise it all day today and I have been wrong in criticizing it.)

If the tale illustrates anything, it is that Love's goal is sexual fulfillment. In the morning, Gostanza had vehemently condemned lustful love—more on sociological than moral grounds, because it brings about transgressions of the social order—and had vigorously preached faithfulness in marriage. It is significant that the philosopher of the group, the paragon of propriety and morality, tells a story centered on an adulteress. The irony is unmistakable and extends to the "ragionamenti" in their totality. We are again in the presence of the fundamental ambivalence of the text: choices are made and repudiated, statements are recanted, and negations are negated.

The tale continues as Niccolò learns that a friend has come all the way from Florence to help him escape. The protagonist is torn between different emotions: love for his country, love for his mistress, fear that if he stays her imprudent passion might betray their secret, and fear of retaliation and vengeance if she gets wind of his plan. Finally, he decides to persuade her to come along because he deems it strategically more efficient to share his scheme with her rather than to conceal it from her and thus risk her undermining his plan or exposing himself to her vengeance. One day, with the friend's complicity, the lovers outwit their entourage, board a ship, and set sail for Italy.

Having reached a logical resolution with the lovers' victory over adverse circumstances, the story could very well end at this point, but it does not. Events repeat themselves in an almost identical fashion. Having landed in Messina, the three are captured by the betrayed husband's emissaries, put on another ship, and sent back to Tunis. They have almost reached the African shore when another fierce storm throws the ship back into the Tyrrhenian Sea where, just off the city of Leghorn, the group falls into the hands of some Pisan corsairs. Held prisoner for a while, they are finally allowed to ransom themselves for a large sum of money, whereupon they set out for Pisa and thence to Florence. There not one but two wedding ceremonies take place, Niccolò having decided to give his sister in marriage to his friend.

The outrageous number of narrative motifs—love, fortune, friendship, honor, courage, intelligence, religion—compressed into a single story is a strategy of textual organization, the technique of "enstrangements" noted earlier. In this regard, however, it is revealing to note that no single theme dominates; none of them becomes the single propelling force of all action. On a structural level, no single factor stands out; all are levelled off; none is more important than the next, but rather all are equally important. From the point of view of the text's ideology, Firenzuola simply abstains from placing the constitutive features of his novella into valorized categories. He refuses to operate within any single ideology. Even so, he is consistent with his initial plan, because to protest against Bembo's linguistic and philosophical totalitarianism means also to abstain from formulating one's own. It implies refraining from articulating any prescriptive hierarchy of values, whether literary or moral.

For Firenzuola, language creates its own reality. It is not by chance that the pivotal turns in this story are entrusted to expertly written passages whose technical merits have been praised through the centuries: the description of the storm, the woman's apostrophe, and the protagonist's speech urging her to leave with him. When events lack a rigorously logical motivation to determine their development, Firenzuola makes up for it rhetorically. In the process, he liberates language, which is now free to create its own contexts, its own logic, and unforeseen situations that might or might not reflect reality. Consequently, it is the act of narration itself that counts. For this reason, this story, like the others, is prolonged well after it reaches its logical conclusion. One voyage is not sufficient, the author needs two; not one storm, one period of captivity, or one wedding, but two of each.

Love as eroticism, the thematic element that constitutes the ironic inversions of platonizing statements made earlier in the day, and the aggregation of traditional novelistic motifs in a nontraditional manner that is equivalent to the liberation of language from all ideologies, are constitutive elements of all the other novellas. The author's source of inspiration is always the *Decameron*, to which Firenzuola's interlocutors often refer. Nowhere is this more evident than in Fioretta's story (*Ragionamenti* I, 5), which is based on both *Decameron* I, 4 and IX, 2. All three tales feature main characters who, having indulged in an illicit sexual relationship, attempt to chastise a subordinate who is guilty of the same thing but are shamed into silence by a witty remark. In this novella, a widow scolds her married daughter Laura for carrying on with another man while she herself enjoys secret rendezvous with her lover, a monk, every night in their home. When confronted by her mother, Laura feigns repentance and asks to make a full confession to the monk locked up in her mother's room. An accord is reached, to the mutual satisfaction of both couples:

> E dette queste parole . . . se ne tornò in camera dal suo Fra Timoteo. Alla quale il giovane andando dietro, non restò mai fin ch'e' non diede ordine che la sera medesima e' cenassero insieme tutt'a quattro, e come parenti si riconoscessero, acciocché poi più agiatamente e senza aver più temenza l'un dell'altro si ritrovassero a fare i fatti loro. E fu tale questo santo accordo, che ciascuna delle donne se ne trovava più contenta l'un dì che l'altro. È ben vero che talvolte la mattina ragionandosi tutt'a due insieme, come accade, delle pruove de' loro amanti, e' si trovava bene spesso che il giovane era stato avanzato dal frate, ancor che e' fusse un poco più attempatello, di più d'un colpo, in modo che Laura portava un poco d'invidia alla madre, e fecene già di grandi rebuffi al suo messer Andreuolo. (*Opere*, 135–36)

> (Having said these words . . . she returned to her room and her Fra Timoteo. But the young man followed her and insisted that the four of them dine together that very same night and acknowledge each other as kinfolk, so that more comfortably and without fearing each other they might go about their business. And this holy accord was such that each of the women was increasingly happier from one day to the next. And it is indeed true that sometimes in the morning, in discussing their lovers' exploits, they often found that the young man had been surpassed by the monk, and

by more than one affray, although the latter was getting on in years, so that Laura was a bit envious of her mother and gave Andreuolo many a good scolding because of it.)

Unlike Boccaccio, who closes his novelle by hinting at future assignations, Firenzuola ends by narrating the eroticism with which he charges his story. In doing so, he exacerbates the lewdness of the tale.

It has often been observed, perhaps to counterbalance the moralistic attacks on the author especially frequent in the nineteenth century, that Firenzuola fails to reify the eroticism of his stories. Although his tales are certainly not notable for their vulgar ostentation of sexual images and coarse language, it is evident that he does not refrain from bawdy allusions and situations. In fact, he often uses them to expand an episode or the epilogue itself. Furthermore, the lubricious component of any text cannot be judged in the abstract but must be related to its context.[22] By the time we read the novellas, we are a long way from the platonizing enunciations of the morning. If we divorce them from the dialogue on love, they lose their contextual referent.

The second novella (I, 2) is narrated by Folchetto and revolves around the *topos* of disguise: Fulvio Macaro is madly in love with the beautiful and young Lavinia, but she is married to "un vecchio rimbambito" (a senile old man [*Opere*, 105]). With the help of a friend, he disguises himself as a young girl named Lucia and goes to work for them in their house. The deception is uncovered by Lavinia, during a thinly veiled lesbian encounter with Fulvio/Lucia (homosexual love had been vehemently condemned in the dialogue on love conducted that very morning). It is also uncovered by the husband who, despite his old age and his sexual near-impotence, lusted after the girl. The husband's gullibility is such that he believes what he is told first by Fulvio/Lucia and later by others: the girl's metamorphosis into a man is a miraculous transformation that presages good fortune because, among other things, it will produce male children, a belief that is strengthened in him when, with her husband's blessing, Lavinia sleeps with the prodigy and gives birth to a male child.

What is striking about the story is Lavinia's characterization—her cold determination to betray her husband as soon as the opportunity presents itself, which amounts to the legitimization of the demands of the flesh:

[Lavinia], veggendosi maritare ad un vecchio rimbambito, e privarsi di quei piaceri Ïper li quali ella aveva bramato tanto tempo di abbandonar la propria casa . . . [si mise] in animo, ogni volta che le venisse in acconcio, prendersi qualcuno che meglio provedesse a' bisogni della sua giovanezza. (*Opere*, 105)

([Lavinia], upon seeing herself married off to a senile old man and deprived of those pleasures for which she had long desired to abandon her own home . . . got it into her head, whenever the opportunity presented itself, to take on somebody who could better satisfy the needs of her youth.)

A carefully orchestrated play of deceits and substitutions is also the topic of the next tale (I, 3). Bianca, who throughout the dialogue had shown a reluctance to love, aptly symbolized by her name, tells a story in which Love seeks and obtains his vengeance. The female protagonist, Agnoletta, is a married woman, scrupulously honest despite being courted by many for her exceptional beauty. For revenge, Love makes her fall for an abbot, Pietro de' Bardi, the handsomest young man in Tuscany. Agnoletta concocts a plan in order to "goder di questo suo amore in modo, che lo Abbate stesso, non che altri, [non] potesse accorgersi di cosa veruna" (satisfy her love in such a way that neither the abbot nor anybody else would suspect anything [*Opere*, 115]). She instructs Laldomine, her maid, to arrange a tryst with the abbot, at which Agnoletta would take her place. The abbot does not notice the attentions Laldomine lavishes on him, although his friend Carlo does. Once smitten with the young girl, Carlo decides to impersonate the abbot to spend a night with her. When they meet, the maid, thinking she is with the abbot, leads Carlo into a darkened room where her mistress takes her place in bed. The result of the tangled plot is that neither partner is aware of the substitution:

> Credendosi adunque questi duoi amanti l'un con Laldomine e l'altra con l'Abbate diacere, senza molte parole, per non si discoprir l'uno all'altro . . . si facevano tante carezze, quante voi potete pensare le maggiori; . . . e mentre che ella godeva di ingannar lui, ed egli godeva di ingannar lei, s'ingannavano tramenduni così dolcemente, che ognun di loro prendeva diletto dello inganno; nel quale senza mai accorgersi l'un dell'altro, egli stettono in tanto sollazzo, in tanta festa, in tanta gioia tutta quella notte, che si sarebbono contentati che la fusse durata tutto un anno. (*Opere*, 120)

> (He believing that he was lying with Laldomine and she believing that she was lying with the Abbot, these two lovers, without saying much in order not to reveal themselves to each other, . . . gave each other the tenderest caresses you can imagine; . . . and while she was enjoying deceiving him and he was enjoying deceiving her, they were deceiving each other so sweetly that each of them was taking delight in the deception; without ever suspecting who the other was, they had such a good time, such fun, such joy the entire night that they would have been happy if it had lasted a year.)

This tale points to nothing but its own internal cohesiveness. It has been noted that in a story of deceptions, there is neither a deceiver nor a deceived; the two protagonists deceive and are deceived at the same time. Thus there is no sense of a just humiliation for the former nor of a just reward for the latter. In Firenzuola, there is no continuation of what Ettore Bonora has termed the "celebration of intelligence" in the manner of Boccaccio.[23] Such a celebration would be tantamount to taking a stand, making a value judgment on his characters; instead, Firenzuola's tone is one of complete neutrality toward the objects of his narration.

The novellas of *I Ragionamenti* make it clear that he has no hypothesis to verify, no behavioral code to promote. He shies away from hierarchical considerations that would impose on himself and others a specific vision of reality that ought instead to be represented in complete freedom.

Celso's tale (I, 4) is perhaps the most famous of the collection, and critics have praised its apparently realistic portrayal of the life of the common people of those times. The characters come alive in their everyday activities, in their caricatured descriptions, in their gestures and, most important, in the vivaciousness and folksiness of their vernacular speech, reminiscent of Machiavelli's *La Mandragola* (Romei, 103–7). We recall that Bembo, when he was not berating Boccaccio for having mimetically represented the language of the populace, in order to reclaim his model from such a conspicuous fallacy, denied that he had any such contaminations.[24] The novella calls to mind another by Boccaccio (*Dec.* VIII, 2) whose main characters, the priest of Varlungo and Monna Belcolore, were the models for Firenzuola's Don Giovanni and Tonia. The first part of the novella is essentially the same as in Boccaccio: a priest lusts after one of his parishioners who consents to his advances when he promises her generous gifts. Whereas in the *Decameron* the miserly clergyman outwits the woman, who in time becomes reconciled with him, to their mutual sexual satisfaction, in Firenzuola the denouement is markedly different. Tonia takes revenge by repeating his indecent proposals to her husband, Giannone, nicknamed Ciarpaglia, who instructs her to lure him to the house; there, Ciarpaglia waits for the priest with one of his brothers. Together, they seize the priest, who is hiding under the bed with his breeches unlaced, and trap him by locking his testicles under the lid of a big, old trunk that they lock. They then leave the room, but not before they have given the priest a rusty old razor. The threat remains unspoken: If the priest wants to free himself, he must exact on himself the husband's vendetta, which in the end he does. The story does not end with the mere announcement of the "penance"; the tools are meticulously, if comically, described, as are later the physical and psychological reactions of the unlucky priest. The atrocious torture becomes itself the object of narration; as a result, the narrative is considerably lengthened.[25]

The sixth and last novella of this first day has an altogether different tone because Selvaggio, whose turn it is to narrate, reserves for himself the right that Dioneo had in the *Decameron*:

> Era lecito a colui, che nel *Decameron* del Boccaccio si trovava l'ultimo a novellare, quanto e' volesse uscire al tutto del ragionato suggetto, che fare il potesse: laonde io, che fra voi sono il sezzo, intendo ora fare il simigliante: perché lasciando le cose d'amore, delle quali s'è parlato tutt'oggi, vi voglio far rider con una novella, che intervenne ad un certo frate. (*Opere*, 136–37)

> (It was granted to the one who in Boccaccio's *Decameron* was the last to tell a tale whenever he wanted to depart entirely from the chosen topic to do so; therefore I,

being the sixth among you, intend to do the same; leaving aside the amorous things about which we have spoken all day long, I want to make you laugh with a story about a certain friar.)

With a final explicit reference to Boccaccio, the model that Firenzuola had so audaciously reintroduced, he brings the cycle to a close.

To conclude, the novellas in *I Ragionamenti* have two main functions. First, they protract, both on a thematic and a formal level, that line of proximity with reality and the present that had started during the course of the dialogue on love and that has its theoretical justifications in the debate on language, and hence literature, where the author's positions are clearly anti-Bemban; and second, on another plane, the novellas constitute the ironic inversions of a platonizing concept of love whose main exponent was also Bembo. The presence of the novellas is tantamount to a rebellion against a given artistic code. Firenzuola's attempts at innovations are of a linguistic order, but only on the surface. On a deeper level, they are intended to have repercussions on the entire cultural apparatus of his times. His target is not only Bembo's linguistic dogmas; he challenges Bembo's concept of literature as well as the very foundations of a culture based on Neoplatonism. To Bembo's vision of life consecrated to the Neoplatonic celestial spheres, Firenzuola opposes an ostentatiously degraded type of naturalism. If Bembo had looked at Boccaccio as a paragon of style and formal excellence, Firenzuola upholds the medieval author's most authentic legacy: the recognition that reality and its constant becoming shun all coercive attempts at being shaped according to some extratemporal ideals.

Like Bembo, Firenzuola values language highly, but he conceives of it very differently. If Bembo prescribed that artists write for posterity,[26] if for him the artistic representation has value only if it is "representation *sub specie aeternitatis*,"[27] then Firenzuola writes for the present and the readers of his own day. If Bembo's concept of language is platonic, insofar as it is a means of communication to be developed in an extratemporal eternity, then Firenzuola conceives of it as necessarily linked to the contingencies of reality, as an element that mediates the world for man. For him, rhetoric is creativity and hence philosophy.[28] Yet, in another irony, such a move ultimately makes this author relevant today. It is this aspect of his writings that can still interest us because modern readers, having abandoned the search for unattainable absolutes, tend to regard philosophy as rhetoric. To the search for essences, Firenzuola opposes the acknowledgment of the real: to the immobility of an idealized present, the unpredictability and dynamism of the historical present; to rhetoric as embellishment or even as means of communication, rhetoric as creativity and mediation between man and his world; to valorized choices and the completeness of the artistic representations of high official culture, the impossibility of formulating any hierarchy of values and the incompleteness of his own literary creations.

Within *I Ragionamenti* as a whole, then, the *novelle* contribute to the most significant feature of the text: its contradictions, ambiguities, incongruities, and conflicts. The dynamic tension between innovative thrusts and complacency with the literary tradition lasts from beginning to end. The double voice of *I Ragionamenti*, one transgressive and censorial, the other traditional and deferentially imitative, is never really unified. Firenzuola's subversive drive simply stops short of formulating a complete alternative system because, ultimately, its effects would be similar to the ones produced by the closed system his work aims to destabilize. *I Ragionamenti* leaves the debate open, both because it offers no final resolution and because the work is incomplete. A work that is unfinished can always be considered somehow imperfect or defective; it implies a project undertaken and later abandoned, and it might denote the writer's inability to accomplish fully what he had set out to do. However, all of Firenzuola's prose works, before and after this one, are incomplete, unfinished. It might be appropriate here to theorize an intentional incompleteness, a programmatic interruption. Recognizing this, however, does not diminish the potential of this work for the renewal of literary conventions; in the name of that freedom that he tirelessly claims for the writer, Firenzuola succeeds in liberating narrative discourse from all possible constraints and ideologies, including his own. In the end, literary discourse is no longer enslaved to anything. It is, instead, free to create its own reality and its own contexts, previously unthinkable and unforeseeable.

Notes

1. In Rome, he composed the *Discacciamento*, the only work published in his lifetime, in 1524; *I Ragionamenti*; the humanist *Epistola in lode delle donne*; and *L'Asino d'oro*, an autobiographical adaptation of Apuleius's *Golden Ass*. In Prato, he wrote the erudite comedies *La trinuzia* and *I lucidi*; two short stories apparently inspired by actual events; *La prima veste dei discorsi degli animali*, a translation of a collection of apologues that originated in India; and the *Dialogo delle bellezze delle donne*, in which Firenzuola constructs the ideal woman by borrowing the most aesthetically pleasing features of his female interlocutors. All his works may be found in *Opere*, ed. Adriano Seroni, Biblioteca Universale Sansoni (1958; reprint, Florence: Sansoni Editore, 1993); hereafter cited in text as *Opere*. All translations from the Italian are my own.
2. Giuseppe Fatini's *Agnolo Firenzuola e la borghesia letterata del Rinascimento* (Cortona: Prem. Tip. Sociale, 1907) is an historical assessment of Firenzuola's works that also provides the most accurate account of his life. The most important names in Firenzuola's criticism are those of Adriano Seroni, who investigated his writings from a stylistic perspective, and of Delmo Maestri and Danilo Romei, whose studies are close to Fatini's in their tendency to analyze his works against the background of the historical and cultural events that occurred during Firenzuola's lifetime. For Seroni, see "Firenzuola novelliere e favolista," in *Apologia di Laura, ed altri saggi. Con alcune questioni di metodo (1940–1946)*, (Milan:

Bompiani, 1958), 25–45; hereafter cited in text as Seroni. For Maestri, see his Introduction to *Opere di Agnolo Firenzuola*, Classici italiani, no. 38 (Turin: UTET, 1977), 9–22. For Romei, see *La "maniera" romana di Agnolo Firenzuola (dicembre 1524–maggio 1525)* (Florence: Edizioni Centro 2P, 1983); hereafter cited in text as Romei.

3. Griffio's two *cinquecentine* bear the following titles: *Ragionamenti di Messer Agnolo Firenzuola fiorentino. Et il discacciamento delle nuove lettere, inutilmente aggiunte alla lingua Toscana. Nuovamente ristampati* (Venice, 1552); and *Le novelle di Messere Agnolo Firenzuola Fiorentino. Nuovamente ristampate e riviste* (Venice, 1552). For early publication history, see *Opere*, ed. Seroni, xliii–xliv.

4. See Luigi Tonelli, *L'amore nella poesia e nel pensiero del rinascimento* (Florence: G. C. Sansoni, 1933), 191–93, 296–97.

5. See Marziano Guglielminetti, *La cornice e il furto: studi sulla novella del '500*, La Parola letteraria, no. 7 (Bologna: Zanichelli, 1984), 7–15; and Eugenio Ragni's introduction to his edition of Firenzuola's *Le novelle*, Novellieri italiani, no. 25 (Milan: Salerno, 1971), 7–31.

6. My analysis contains several points of contact with Romei's arguments, but on the whole it is radically different. From my point of view, Firenzuola's subversive drive and fundamental ambiguity are programmatic, whereas for Romei the destabilizing forces within the text are the inevitable results of a project destined to fail from the very beginning.

7. Bembo had by this time published his *Gli Asolani* (1505) in which he expressed his views that the most noble of loves, the only admissible one, is of a spiritual kind amenable to a desire to contemplate an ideal divine beauty independent of earthly concerns. Between 1522 and 1525 he would codify his project of emulating Boccaccio's prose and Petrarch's verses in *Prose della volgar lingua*, hereafter cited in text as *Prose*. Both texts are found in Bembo, *Opere in volgare*, ed. Mario Marti, I classici italiani (Florence: Sansoni, 1961), hereafter cited in text as *Opere in volgare*.

8. Wayne C. Booth, *A Rhetoric of Irony* (Chicago: The University of Chicago Press, 1974), 233–67.

9. Linda Hutcheon, *A Theory of Parody: The Teachings of Twentieth-Century Art Forms* (New York: Methuen, 1985), 25 and 31; hereafter cited in text as Hutcheon.

10. Mikhail Bakhtin, "Epic and Novel," in *The Dialogic Imagination: Four Essays*, ed. Michael Holquist, trans. Caryl Emerson and Michael Holquist, University of Texas Press Slavic series, no. 1 (Austin: University of Texas Press, 1981), 25; hereafter cited in text as "Epic and Novel."

11. "Parody . . . is a form of imitation, but imitation characterized by ironic inversion" (Hutcheon, 6). "Every creative imitation mingles filial rejection with respect, just as every parody pays its own oblique homage" (Thomas M. Greene, *The Light in Troy: Imitation and Discovery in Renaissance Poetry*, The Elizabethan Club series, no. 7 [New Haven, Conn.: Yale University Press, 1982], 46).

12. "Se la parodia non è svelata, l'opera cambia; così, in sostanza, cambia ogni opera letteraria, strappata dal piano che la costituisce. Ma anche la parodia, il cui elemento principale è dato dai particolari stilistici, quando è strappata dal suo secondo piano (che può essere semplicemente dimenticato), perde naturalmente la

parodicità" (Jurij Tynianov, "Dostoevskij e Gogol [Per una teoria della parodia]," in *Avanguardia e tradizione*, La scienza nuova, no. 4 [Bari: Dedalo Libri, 1968], 171). "We may know that addresser [the author] and its intentions [the text] only in the form of inferences that we, as receivers, make from the text, but such inferences are not to be ignored" (Hutcheon, 23).

13. On Firenzuola's manipulations of Bembo's concept of love, see my "Bembo's and Firenzuola's Contribution to the Renaissance Idea of Literature," *Scripta Mediterranea* 8–9 (1987–1988): 33–42.

14. Consider the following pronouncements by Bembo: "Credete voi che se il Petrarca avesse le sue canzoni con la favella composte de' suoi popolani, che elle così vaghe, così belle fossero come sono, così care, così gentili? . . . Né il Boccaccio altresì con la bocca del popolo ragionò . . . per che, se volete dire, Giuliano, che agli scrittori stia bene ragionare in maniera, che essi dal popolo siano intesi, io il vi potrò concedere non in tutti, ma in alquanti scrittori tuttavia; ma che essi ragionar debbano, come ragiona il popolo, questo in niuno vi si concederà giamai" (*Prose*, 299–301).

15. The term is Viktor Shklovsky's. See his "Art as Device," in *Theory of Prose*, trans. Benjamin Sher (Elmwood Park, Ill.: Dalkey Archive Press, 1990), 6–12.

16. Marti notes that Bembo's *Gli Asolani* is characterized by "lo scolasticismo schematico della composizione" (*Opere in volgare*, xv–xvi).

17. Riccardo Scrivano, *La norma e lo scarto: proposte per il Cinquecento letterario italiano*, L'Ippogrifo, no. 20 (Rome: Bonacci, 1980), 12.

18. "[I] due momenti si pongono come prologo ed epilogo di un segmento dell'opera, ricondotto là da dove era mosso e riassunto dalla storia emblematica di Costanza in circolare unità, così come l'universo per effetto d'amore" (Romei, 72).

19. "Ché quantunque del Boccaccio si possa dire che egli nel vero alcuna volta molto prudente scrittore stato non sia; con ciò sia cosa che egli mancasse talora di giudicio nello scrivere, non pure delle altre opere, ma nel *Decamerone* ancora, nondimeno quelle parti del detto libro, le quali egli poco giudiciosamente prese a scrivere, quelle medesime egli pure con buono e leggiadro stile scrisse tutte; il che è quello che noi cerchiamo" (*Prose*, 343). Carlo Dionisotti points out that Bembo's reservations concern the subject matter, not language or style (Bembo, *Prose e rime*, ed. Dionisotti, Classici italiani, no. 26 [Turin: UTET, 1960], 175, n. 3).

20. Guido Almansi examines the character of the self-deceiver in *L'estetica dell'osceno*, La ricerca letteraria. Serie critica, no. 20 (Turin: Einaudi, 1974), 136–40; hereafter cited in text as *L'estetica*.

21. On the metaphorical relationship of riding and sexual intercourse, see the essay by Susan Gaylard, chapter 2 in this volume.

22. As Almansi states: "Volgarità è . . . concetto squisitamente relativo che trova evidenza solo nella sua opposizione a una norma da trasgredire. . . . Volgarità è dunque trasgressione, e la volgarità sarà dunque una delle possibili maniere in cui l'artista potrà trasgredire le leggi dell'arte, sovvertire le regole del gioco" (*L'estetica*, 205).

23. Ettore Bonora, "La novella," in *Il Cinquecento*, vol. 4, *Storia della letteratura italiana*, dir. Emilio Cecchi and Natalino Sapegno (Milan: Garzanti, 1966), 306.

24. "La lingua delle scritture . . . non dee a quella del popolo accostarsi . . . ella dis-
costare se ne dee e dilinguare, quanto le basta a mantenersi in vago e in gentile
stato. . . . Né il Boccaccio altresì con la bocca del popolo ragionò; . . . Che come
che egli alcuna volta, massimamente nelle novelle, secondo le proposte materie,
persone di volgo a ragionare traponendo, s'ingegnasse di farle parlare con le voci
con le quali il volgo parlava, nondimeno egli si vede che in tutto 'l corpo delle
composizioni sue esso è . . . di belle figure, di vaghi modi e dal popolo non usati,
ripieno" (*Prose*, 299–300).

25. Additional aspects of this novella's eroticism are discussed in the essay by
Domenico Zanré, which follows immediately in chapter 9.

26. "[N]on debbono gli scrittori por cura di piacere alle genti solamente, che sono in
vita quando essi scrivono . . . ma a quelle ancora, e per aventura molto più, che
sono a vivere dopo loro" (*Prose*, 299).

27. This is Bakhtin's definition of epic, which he equated to all genres of high literature, crystallized in its forms and therefore beyond any new elaborations ("Epic
and Novel," 18).

28. A notion articulated in the work of Richard Rorty, *Philosophy and the Mirror of
Nature* (Princeton, N.J.: Princeton University Press, 1979); and id., "Pragmatism
and Philosophy," in *After Philosophy: End or Transformation?*, ed. Kenneth
Baynes et al. (Cambridge, Mass.: The MIT Press, 1987), 26–66.

9

Alterity and Sexual Transgression in the Sixteenth-Century Tuscan Novella

Domenico Zanrè

In recent years, an increasing amount of research has been directed toward the theme of nonconformity and alterity in the literature of medieval and early modern Europe. Interest in this theme has burgeoned, and scholars working on the medieval period in particular have discussed it extensively.[1] The proliferation of interest in this topic is also apparent when one considers studies of fifteenth- and sixteenth-century texts.[2] The present essay will focus upon specific instances of nonconformity as depicted in the novella tradition of Cinquecento Tuscany, an area that has received only a modest amount of critical attention particularly when compared to the novella collections of previous centuries. The emphasis here will be on tales of sexual transgression in the collections of Agnolo Firenzuola and Antonfrancesco Grazzini, and one aim will be to assess the extent to which the personal and professional backgrounds of the authors impacted on the content and style of their writing.

The lives and careers of these two authors have several elements in common. Apart from the fact that both were literati born in sixteenth-century Tuscany—not only contemporaries but actual acquaintances—they were writing at a time of political, social, and cultural upheaval, while Florence and Tuscany were undergoing the dramatic and turbulent transformation from the fall of the Last Republic to the creation and subsequent consolidation of the Medici duchy. The regime that was instituted under Duke Cosimo I in 1537 thereafter rapidly promulgated a policy of hegemonic control.[3] This policy extended to the cultural milieu and was most evident in the formation of the Accademia Fiorentina, an institution that would become the official organ of cultural production in the city.[4]

Despite the fact that Firenzuola and Grazzini were both associated with the recognized cultural community, they were never really a part of it; rather, they were literary figures who stood on the margins of acceptability. This was reflected both in their lives and in their writings. We will begin by discussing Firenzuola, the older of the two men, who was born in 1493. In 1518, at the age of twenty-five, he moved to Rome, where he successfully gained the patronage of Pope Clement VII. While there, Firenzuola became acquainted with literati such as Francesco Berni, Annibale Caro, and Giovanni Della Casa, and he frequented the meetings of several literary circles in the city, including the Accademia Romana and the Accademia della Vigna. It was at this point that he met Pietro Aretino, and together they sought the company of a number of contemporary courtesans. Both of these men were on intimate terms with Camilla Pisana, who had formerly been the mistress of no less an illustrious figure than Filippo Strozzi.[5] In the early 1520s, Firenzuola's name was also linked with Cecilia Veneziana, whom he referred to as "la gran meretrice" (the big whore) in the *Discorso primo* of his *Dialogo delle bellezze delle donne*.[6] He was also associated with Tullia d'Aragona, arguably the most celebrated *cortegiana* of her generation. To judge from Firenzuola's virulent comments about her in his literary works, however, their subsequent relationship was anything but amicable.[7]

In 1526 Firenzuola contracted a debilitating illness that was to afflict him for the next eleven years, and that he described in the poem entitled "Intorno la sua malattia" (*Opere*, 781–88). It appears that this illness was syphilis, which is perhaps not surprising in light of his reputation for numerous sexual exploits. The disease was known to contemporaries, however, as the "mal francese," so called because it was believed to have been brought across the Alps from France by Charles VIII's troops in 1494.[8] A remedy for this affliction was thought to lie in the resin of *guaiacum*, a genus of trees and shrubs that was believed to contain healing properties. *Guaiacum* was native to the West Indies and the more temperate parts of North America, and it was brought to Europe as a result of seafaring expeditions and trading links. Its hard, heavy, brownish-green wood was known as *lignum vitæ* or *lignum sanctum*, and it is to this that Firenzuola refers in the *capitolo* entitled "In lode del legno santo" (*Opere*, 954–57).[9] By the mid-1530s, the illness had worsened to such a degree that he decided to leave Rome and move to Prato for his health. Here he was able to recuperate and to dedicate himself once more to his literary endeavors.

Firenzuola, like Grazzini, was associated with the recognized cultural milieu of his day, in particular with the Accademia Fiorentina. However, Firenzuola's links with the Fiorentina do not appear to have extended to actual membership in the institution. He certainly seems to have been closely connected with some of the founding figures of an earlier intellectual group: the Accademia degli Umidi. This is evinced by Firenzuola's central role in a parodic linguistic debate on the merits of the letter K in the alphabet.[10] The discussion, which took place in the early 1540s, was ostensibly concerned with orthographic reform, but it was transformed by Firenzuola, together with Grazzini and Michelangelo Vivaldi (two of the founders of the Umidi), into a literary *ludus* through the adoption of an ambivalent erotic register.

During this period, Firenzuola's cultural interests extended beyond his participation in acts of intellectual *jouissance*: he was also directly involved in founding the Accademia dell'Addiaccio, which apparently was "quasi in gara con quella fiorentina."[11] The creation of the Addiaccio may have been a response to his failure to assert himself within the official cultural vehicle of Duke Cosimo I. Firenzuola's aim of creating an Arcadian environment, free from the stresses and problems of everyday life, was itself a naïve, short-lived dream. The notion of an idyllic paradise was viewed by some contemporaries as not only impractical but also unacceptable. Within the space of a year, dissent and discord between rival factions caused a split within the Addiaccio that would lead to its downfall.

The strain of nonconformity that was present in Firenzuola's life can also be seen in his collection of novellas, ten of which are extant. This collection was edited by Lodovico Domenichi and Lorenzo Scala and published by Bernardo Giunta in a volume entitled *Le Prose di Agnolo Firenzuola* (1548); the *novelle* were subsequently published as *I Ragionamenti*. Two of the ten tales have been identified as examples of Firenzuola's later literary output, and in modern editions of his work they tend to be published separately from the others and are referred to as the "due novelle del periodo pratese."

As far as *I Ragionamenti* is concerned, it is somewhat surprising to learn that the tales have never been the subject of a satisfactory critical study. This may be due to the fact that the work has traditionally been regarded by scholars such as Benedetto Croce as little more than a bland imitation of Boccaccio's *Decameron*. In his discussion centering on the sixteenth-century novella, Croce reserved his praise almost exclusively for the tales of Bandello, while his judgment on other representatives of this genre was damning. Firenzuola's *I Ragionamenti* was simply dismissed as being "boccaccevole e sensuale ma vacuo" (sensual and Boccaccian in style but lacking in substance).[12] At first sight, there does appear to be compelling evidence to support Croce's claim. In terms of its overall conception, there is a clear link between the *Ragionamenti* and the *Decameron*. Firenzuola's work, like that of Boccaccio, features a group of six aristocratic *giovani* who leave the confines of the city and retire to the countryside near the village of Pozzolatico, where they proceed to engage in storytelling and discussion. Like their Boccaccian counterparts, they are accompanied by their servants who provide all the necessary provisions for the rural sojourn. In essence, the bucolic descriptions and vocabulary used in this frame narrative are very similar to those of the *cornice* of the *Decameron*. So much so, in fact, that Firenzuola makes the comparison explicit by having Gostanza, the appointed queen of his *brigata*, comment that the situation in which they find themselves is very akin to that of Boccaccio's protagonists. Nevertheless, there are some fundamental differences between the two works. For instance, there is no raging plague in Firenzuola's novella collection. The impetus for the presence of the *giovani* in the Tuscan countryside is not survival but *divertimento*: it is Easter time, and they have merely decided to move to more congenial surroundings in order to spend some time together and to enjoy each other's company. Despite this apparent simplicity, Firenzuola's *cornice* is actually much longer and more complex than those of previous collections. Whereas Boccaccio had used his frame narrative to establish the mise en scène, Firenzuola treats his *cornice* as a forum for the discussion of contemporary issues. Hence, the rather inordinate significance given to the protagonists' exegeses on the nature and meaning of love, to *canzoni* written in the Petrarchan manner, and to the *questione della lingua*, in particular to the development and promotion of the *lingua volgare*.[13] It is only at the very end of the frame that the *brigata* return to their original subject matter and begin their storytelling. A close examination of *I Ragionamenti* does reveal instances in which there is a clear departure from the model offered by Boccaccio.

These discrepancies are particularly evident in *I Ragionamenti*, I, 2, which contains elements of Renaissance drama fused to traditional novella motifs. The tale's protagonists are drawn from the stock characters of comic drama: Fulvio plays the role of the lusty young lover; Lavinia, the beautiful and dissatisfied young bride; Cecc'Antonio, the foolish *senex*; and Menico, the resourceful companion who advances much of the action. The plot itself is quite simple: Fulvio is inflamed with passion for Lavinia, the young wife of the elderly Cecc'Antonio of Tivoli. The latter character's name is particularly appropriate because he is in effect "blind" to the events that take place around him. In order to gain access to the house, and ultimately to Lavinia, Fulvio is constrained to disguise himself as the young woman "Lucia," whereupon he succeeds in obtaining employment in the household as a maid.

Firenzuola's inclusion of a cross-dressing tale in *I Ragionamenti* has numerous thematic precedents in the earlier novella collections of Boccaccio, Sacchetti, and Masuccio Salernitano, as well as in Renaissance theater.[14] Stories of cross-dressing and gender confusion offered authors a wealth of possibilities in terms of plot development and interpretation. In the case of women disguising themselves as men, the motivation for such actions was frequently one borne out of necessity. Female characters in novellas who don male apparel invariably do so in order to survive and to resolve a situation of adversity, as Zinevra did in *Decameron*, II, 9. On other occasions, cross-dressing was utilized as a disguise in order to rescue a husband or lover in distress. Furthermore, a man's clothing could provide a woman with relative safety should she be constrained to make a hazardous journey over land (*Dec.* II, 3). The transformations effected by women were often temporary in nature and of a relatively short duration. To some extent, this was also true for men who dressed up in feminine clothing, though their reasons for such behavior were more banal in nature. An author could include descriptions of healthy young men in women's outfits to elicit humor at the resulting confusion and incongruity of the situation in which they found themselves. Alternatively, such stratagems could be employed for more insidious purposes, in order to entice unknowing victims into a trap as part of a *beffa* or practical joke, as in

Grazzini's *Le Cene*, II, 8. The most common occurrence of male cross-dressing, however, was as a means of seduction, in order to gain access to a woman. Such is the case in the present tale of Fulvio/Lucia and Lavinia, which also highlights another aspect of disguise: to provide an opportunity for the *novelliere* to present instances of gender confusion. These encounters can lead to a legitimate variety of both homosexual and heterosexual couplings between bed partners; the fact that the reader is often aware of the true biological sex of the respective partners, unlike the participants themselves, further serves to enhance the erotic *frisson* generated in these scenes.

What is notable in Firenzuola's story of cross-dressing is the way in which Lucia is portrayed and how the characters react to "her" in turn. The first sexual encounter occurs when Cecc'Antonio is called away from the city on business, and Lavinia invites Lucia to share her bed. At this point, the tale diverges from previous literary models. The usual scenario was for the female character to despair because she believed that she was lying in bed with another woman; when she subsequently discovered all too plainly that the person she was with was a man, she was delighted, and the couple would enjoy each other sexually. Such instances of mistaken identity might seem quite implausible to the modern reader, but was familiar to contemporaries; the theme of disguise and discovery was very common in fifteenth- and sixteenth-century literature. In *I Ragionamenti* I, 2, the credibility of Fulvio's transformation is no doubt aided by his true physical features, which, according to his friend Menico Coscia, are quite feminine. As they plan the disguise together, Menico tells him:

> "E a tutto questo ci aiuterà l'esser tu di *pel bianco, e sanza segno alcuno di avere a metter barba* . . . e l'avere *il viso femminile*, in modo che i più, come tu sai, credono che tu sia una femina [*sic*] vestita da uomo." (*Opere*, 106, emphasis added)

> (And in all of this we will be helped by the fact that you have a *pale complexion, are beardless without any hint of stubble*, and that you have *a woman's features*, to the extent that most people, as you yourself know, believe you to be a woman dressed as a man.)[15]

What is even more important than the fact that Lucia is actually a man in disguise is that Lavinia has asked "her" to share her bed precisely because she thinks she is a woman. As soon as they are lying together, Lavinia begins to embrace and kiss Lucia "con grandissimo disio" (with very great desire), as Firenzuola intimates, in an effort to find the kind of sexual relief that she is unable to obtain from her aging husband. It is only when she reaches down Lucia's body—"là dove si conosce il maschio dalla femmina" (in that place where one can discriminate between a man and a woman [*Opere*, 107])—that she comes to realize that the "she" is in fact a "he."

At this juncture, it will be useful to compare the present tale with two of its most likely sources: Boccaccio's tale of Alessandro and the Abbot (*Dec.* II, 3) and

Masuccio Salernitano's story of Madonna Francesca and the innkeeper's wife (*Novellino*, XII), both of which involve cross-dressing.[16] Boccaccio's storyteller recounts how a young man named Alessandro spends the night at an inn where, due to a lack of accommodations, he is forced to sleep in the same room as an abbot with whom he is traveling. The abbot, whom the novella presents as a man, calls Alessandro to his bed, and within a very short time Alessandro discovers that his seducer is in fact a woman. In Masuccio's story, the lover disguises himself as "Madonna Francesca" so that he can spend the evening with the young wife of an innkeeper from Amalfi. As soon as the two "women" are alone, the lover reveals his true identity, and the wife's initial indignation gives way to acceptance and pleasure. Firenzuola's version differs from both of these antecedents because it is the seduced, not the seducer, who has undergone an apparent gender transformation in the Lavinia-Lucia encounter. Lavinia also undergoes a transformation of sorts; in this case, it involves a transformation of gender roles, as she assumes the traditionally patriarchal position of active instigator in the sexual liaison. The assigned roles are reversed—the seducer is the mistress of the house, not the master, while the seduced is a man disguised as a woman.

An additional layer of sexual nonconformity is provided by the female homoerotic resonances apparent in the encounter.[17] Lavinia is initially aroused by the biological sex of her bed partner, whom she assumes to be female. It is significant here that stimulation occurs before discovery: the intimate acts initiated by Lavinia are performed before she becomes aware of the actual sex of her maid. Often, in the Renaissance novella, foreplay occurs once the real identity of the person has been established and the disguise has been revealed; however, this is not the case in Firenzuola's tale. Here, Lavinia is in a state of erotic excitement precisely because she thinks that her partner is a woman, of her own gender, and not because "she" is in fact a "he." Thus what is being performed here is an act of genuine lesbian desire.

The appropriation of terminology such as "lesbian" or "homosexual" within the context of the early modern period has been a contentious issue among academics working in the field of gender studies and queer theory.[18] According to the hypothesis enunciated by those scholars who adhere to the social constructionist school of thought, "homosexuality" as a distinct sexual orientation only began to feature in a discursive manner in the latter half of the nineteenth century.[19] Constructionists have been notoriously reticent about applying such a term to premodern contexts in which the recently formulated concept of a binary division of people's sexual proclivities would have been alien. The constructionist argument maintains that to classify someone who was associated with, or who actually indulged in, erotic encounters with members of the same sex in the Cinquecento as a "lesbian" or "homosexual" would be to misconstrue sixteenth-century configurations of human sexuality. Scholars such as Alan Bray have pointed to the difficulty of articulating a distinctive homosexual matrix in early modern England.[20] By contrast, "the opposing 'essentialist' school looks for evidence of a distinct, historically constant homosexual personality."[21] Hence the position taken by John Boswell, an advocate of this theoretical critique, who perceived the existence of "gay" individuals during the early Christian period.

Whichever ideological standpoint one adheres to in this debate, it is undeniable that both erotic desire and physical union between members of the same sex played a part in human relationships during the Renaissance. Such relationships were categorized under the heading of *sodomia*, a wide-ranging and all-embracing term used to refer to a number of particular sexual acts that were declared morally and socially unacceptable by the Church. Already, in the Middle Ages, *sodomia* was applied to every kind of behavior that did not constitute sexual intercourse between a married heterosexual couple for the express purpose of procreation.[22] *Sodomia* may have been referred to by contemporaries as "the unspeakable vice," but the many allusions to it nevertheless testify to the fact that the practice must have occurred. For instance, the existence of "female homogenital activity" was generally acknowledged in the medieval and Renaissance periods by both theological and medical doctors (Mormando, 117). Same-sex unions between women received scant attention in the legal documentation of the Quattrocento and Cinquecento,[23] but they obviously took place, as the actions of Lavinia in the present story indicate.

Upon discovering the real biological sex of her bed partner, Lavinia's initial reaction is one of amazement. She concludes that there must be some kind of "spirito incantato" (magical spirit) at work that is ultimately responsible for transforming Lucia from a female into a male. Her reference to the spirit as "malo" (evil) is perhaps indicative of the fact that what she really wanted was a woman and not a man in disguise. However, superstition gives way to pragmatism: now that she has a handsome young man in her bed, she decides to take advantage of this and continues to enjoy herself with him in order to assure herself of the fact that she was not mistaken the first time about his biological sex. An arrangement is reached between the couple that will involve daily sexual transformations: "Lucia" will help Lavinia during the day, and Fulvio will make love to her during the night.

The fact that Lucia is actually a man does not resolve the sexual nonconformity of the situation. This is especially true once the husband becomes involved in the relationship. Like his wife, he also wants to seduce Lucia. The phrase used to register Cecc'Antonio's desire to possess her sexually—"si era diliberato di scaricarne una soma al suo palmento" (he had decided to unload a quantity of grain into her millstone [*Opere*, 109])—is reminiscent of the rural and agricultural double entendres used in the *Decameron*, especially in the tale of the elderly Ricciardo di Chinzica and his young wife (II, 10, 32): "E dicovi che se voi aveste tante feste fatte fare a' lavoratori che le vostre possession lavorano, quante faciavate fare a colui che il mio piccol campicello aveva a lavorare, voi non avreste mai ricolto granel di grano." (And I tell you that if you had given the laborers who work on your lands as many holidays as you gave to the man who had to plough my own little field, you would never have harvested a single grain of corn.) In

Boccaccio's story, Ricciardo, like Firenzuola's character Cecc'Antonio, is a foolish old man who becomes embroiled in a love triangle. In the former case, the relationship involves his young wife and the dashing pirate Paganino da Monaco; here, however, the outsider is the maid.

In some respects, the scene in which Cecc'Antonio attempts to seduce Lucia parallels his wife's initial sexual encounter, because in both instances a surprising discovery is made. Cecc'Antonio seizes his opportunity some months later while Lucia is asleep and the mistress of the house has gone to attend a friend's wedding celebrations. When Cecc'Antonio lifts the maid's skirt to find what he so ardently seeks, he is confronted by an unexpected sight. Lucia has to rely on some fast thinking to explain away her apparent physical abnormality. Her excuse, accompanied by a suitably contrite performance complete with tears, is that she has experienced a growth in her private parts. As she herself declares at the climax of her speech, "mi pare esser la più impacciata cosa del mondo a sentir batter questo presso ch'io non dissi tra gambe" (it seems the most embarrassing thing in the world to feel this thing, about which I would rather not speak, swinging between my legs [*Opere*, 111]).

This mistake in sexual identity is clearly meant to elicit a humorous response from the reader, yet it also embodies more serious corollaries. Lucia's decision to present herself as a sexual other, as an androgyne, reflected a well-established discourse on biological nonconformity. In addition to the tales of transformation in Ovid's *Metamorphoses*, readers in the medieval and early modern periods had access to a host of material relating to this topic. Ancient accounts of hermaphroditism were available to them, thanks to the Latin translations of Hippocrates, Aristotle, Paul of Aegina, and other Greek writers by Arabian scholars such as Avicenna and Albucasis. The anatomical studies of Aetius and Caelius Aurelianus provided further contributions to the debate. Part of the reason for the fascination in this subject matter was to the fact that hermaphrodites were seen as challenging and, indeed, crossing the traditional boundaries of gender construction. Sexual identity has been seen as one of the most overt denominators of selfhood; scholars such as Stephen Greenblatt, for example, have argued for the emergence of a conscious need among individuals in the fifteenth and sixteenth century to fashion their own identities. Hermaphroditism, however, threatened the very concept of selfhood by subverting the conventional model of a binary division of sexual identity. In the latter half of the sixteenth century, it was to become associated with overt forms of sexual trangression, such as sodomy, cross-dressing, and pornography.

The transgressive aspects of hermaphroditism were thought by some medieval and early modern authors to extend beyond "an unseemly cross-mixture of gender" in the physical sense and to involve also an alteration in behavior.[24] One might argue that such characteristics are apparent in Firenzuola's delineation of Lucia's demeanor. The reader has already been informed of Fulvio's feminine appearance; in his actions as Lucia there is a similar mode of comportment more traditionally associated with women. His attempt at seduction is a case in point. The whole motivation for his transformation into a maid is ostensibly to gain access to Lavinia. However, it is actually she who assumes the traditionally masculine active role and who initiates their sexual affair: Fulvio, as Lucia, is the passive partner in the encounter. Later, during the confrontation with Cecc'Antonio, Fulvio's reaction is in keeping with that of a normative female maid more than a young male lover in disguise. Readers of the novella have to keep reminding themselves that the maid is in fact a man, and the character's true gender is deliberately blurred through the constant use of feminine pronouns to describe or refer to "her."

Firenzuola's familiarity with both classical and contemporary texts that dealt with the question of hermaphroditism is apparent in the precise bibliographical references that he incorporates into the novella. When Cecc'Antonio comes to terms with the ambivalent identity of his housemaid, he subsequently journeys to Rome for medical advice and by chance encounters Menico, who is well aware of the actual situation since it was he who had originally introduced Lucia to Cecc'Antonio. Menico directs him to the bookshop of Giacomo Giunta,[25] where— Firenzuola is careful to tell us—they consult specific passages regarding sexual transformation in both the vernacular translation of Pliny's *Historia naturalis* and in Battista Fregoso's *De dictis factisque memorabilibus.*

The denouement of the novella is similar in certain respects to the conclusion of Machiavelli's *La Mandragola*. Menico counsels Cecc'Antonio not to terminate Lucia's employment, insisting that her presence in the house will ensure male children. This prediction is soon confirmed when Lavinia becomes pregnant. Cecc'Antonio's delight on being informed of his role as a prospective parent, and his subsequent self-congratulation on siring a son, echoes Messer Nicia's deluded pride in his sexual prowess. In both of these stories, the husbands are blind to their own impotence as well as to the fact that the people responsible for the conceptions are outsiders who have performed their duties by means of a disguise; in Firenzuola's novella, the event is made even more transgressive since the real father of the child is the (apparently) female maid.

Firenzuola was not the only *letterato* who chose to deal with tales of sexual transgression and transformation; this subject matter was utilized by other contemporary writers in their own *novella* collections. One such author was the Florentine Antonfrancesco Grazzini (b. March 22, 1503). First employed as an apprentice in a pharmacy, he subsequently dedicated himself to a career in writing and publishing. Grazzini is a good example of a Florentine literary figure with an ambivalent political past. We know that he remained in Florence during the siege of 1530 and thus had witnessed the fall of Republic and the establishment of the Medici duchy. In addition, he had numerous friends and acquaintances who were sympathizers, if not actually members, of the Florentine political exiles known as the *fuorusciti*.[26] There is no solid evidence of any direct involvement with the *fuorusciti* on Grazzini's part, although he was placed under suspicion by the authorities. Grazzini's nonconformist reputation was not only founded on his chosen political affiliations, but also on his friendships with men such as Pandolfo Pucci and Giovanni Fantini, who had been arrested by the *Otto di Guardia e Balìa* (the Eight on Public Safety) on charges of sodomy. In terms of his own sexual activity, Grazzini, like Firenzuola, had a penchant for the company of both culti- vated courtesans and more common prostitutes. His poetry reflects this, with a variety of works that catalogue his relationships with women such as Tullia d'Aragona, Milla Capraia, Nanina Zinzera, and Giulia Napoletana. He was ulti- mately to pay the price for his promiscuity when he contracted a venereal disease, just as Firenzuola had done.[27]

Grazzini and Firenzuola were clearly acquaintances, if not actually close friends. Both were closely associated with the Accademia Fiorentina, and their poetic and dramatic works were published together on more than one occasion. Bernardo Giunta asked Grazzini to write the preface to the anthology entitled *Il primo libro dell'opere burlesche* (1548), which contained some of Grazzini's own compositions, together with those of Firenzuola and others. In the following year, examples of Grazzini's verses were included in Firenzuola's volume of *Rime*.

Grazzini, like his colleague, was unable to carve a permanent niche for him- self in the formal cultural ambit despite the fact that he, too, was instrumental in the establishment of a literary academy: in this case, the Accademia degli Umidi. The Umidi, essentially a loosely knit literary group, was founded on November 1, 1540, by twelve like-minded dilettanti whose intention was to create a relaxed forum in which they could read sonnets and exchange poetic compositions. Within the next three months, however, the Umidi was to become the victim of a cultural takeover sanctioned by Cosimo I. The original ideals that had led to the formation of this institution were swiftly pushed aside by a series of restrictive statutes and a cultural program designed to provide the duke with control over the city's writers and intellectuals.

Grazzini was arguably the most vociferous critic of this cultural transforma- tion and was not slow to voice his dissent concerning the systematic changes that were being put into place. He was one of the few members who dared to oppose the takeover of the Umidi. Furthermore, on February 11, 1541, he alone voted against the imposition of new statutes that included such measures as changing the name of the institution from *Umidi* to *Fiorentina*. He continued to express his disapproval by resigning from the post of *cancelliere* (chancellor) of the Acad- emy, a position he had held since January first of that year. When he was asked to give a lecture to the Academy in November 1542, he categorically refused, thus directly contravening the statutes of the Fiorentina. Additional acts of dissent included his refusal to submit his works to the Academy's authorities for supervi- sion and censorship, as well as his decision in 1546 not to perform the ceremony of presenting the outgoing consul with a silver cup. Given his history of complaints and infringements, it is not surprising that Grazzini was eventually expelled from the Accademia Fiorentina following the reforms of 1547.

Grazzini's reaction at being sent into cultural isolation was one of anger and frustration. His expulsion was made even more unpalatable by the fact that he was denied access to an institution that he had helped to create. It was only through his literary output that he was able to vent his feelings adequately, and during this period of personal rejection he wrote some of the novellas that would form the basis of his collection of tales known as *Le Cene*.[28] Grazzini's original intention had been to incorporate thirty tales into his collection, which were to be recounted by ten *giovani fiorentini* over the course of three separate Thursday evenings during Carnival time, culminating in *Berlingaccio* (Fat Thursday). Unfortunately, the work is incomplete, consisting of only the first two "evenings" and one novella for the third, making a total of twenty-one novellas.

Le Cene is very much a product of its times. One might even go so far as to suggest that the wintry landscapes in the opening pages of the *cornice* evoke the bleakness of Grazzini's own situation in the cultural cold. The first meeting of the young storytellers takes place on the evening of January 31, 1540. When this date is converted from *stile fiorentino*, by modern standards the year would actually have been 1541. The significance of this date for Grazzini becomes clear when we consider the cultural events that were taking place in Florence at the time: on that very day—January 31, 1541—the Accademia degli Umidi was dissolved by ducal decree to be replaced by the newly created, Medici-sponsored Accademia Fiorentina.

Grazzini's inability to integrate himself into the official cultural setting was reflected in his choice of unconventional subject matter in his novellas; nonconformity and alterity, particularly in relation to sexuality, are prevalent features of *Le Cene*. Several critics have commented on the inordinate emphasis that seems to be placed on tales of sexual violence within this small collection. This appears to have been an aspect of contemporary Florentine culture and was not unique to Grazzini himself; for instance, sadism, sodomy, and excessive cruelty permeate the *Vita* of Benvenuto Cellini.[29] Nevertheless, the *beffe* perpetrated in the novellas are particularly vicious in nature, a feature of *Le Cene* that has been singled out by Michel Plaisance.[30] Plaisance hypothesized that the acts of sexual transgression and the graphic depictions of physical disfigurement are indicative of masochistic and homosexual tendencies on the part of the author; however, in the light of recent research in the fields of gender studies and queer theory in the Renaissance, his statements need to be reassessed. Despite the incidents of sexual violence between men that occur in several of the novellas in *Le Cene*, and despite the fact that Grazzini was acquainted with Florentines who had been arrested on charges of sex crimes, there is no explicit proof that the author participated in same-sex acts himself. Even if there were evidence of sodomitic activity

on Grazzini's part, this would not necessarily imply an exclusive sexual preference for other men because, as we have seen, *sodomia* was not limited to sexual
intercourse between partners of the same sex.

In light of these caveats, what can be said of Grazzini's novellas? They
clearly contain references to behavior that we would today term "sexually transgressive." A number of his tales are also notable for their focus on the themes of
punishment and revenge, and the heightened levels of graphic violence inherent
in them separates Grazzini's novella collection from earlier exemplars of the
genre. Such is the case of *Le Cene*, I, 2, whose plot centers on the humiliation and
physical torture of a pedagogue portrayed as the archetypal pedant *in extremis*.
The vilification of such individuals was part of a well-established literary theme.
The pedagogue was a figure traditionally associated with sexual nonconformity,
in particular the practice of pederasty. Classical sources provided numerous
examples of *paiderastia*, or the homoerotic relationship between a pedagogue and
his young male charge. This model was to form the basis for much of the physical
interaction between men in Renaissance Florence, as the prevalent form of all-
male sexual behavior was one based on age difference and a rigid distinction in
roles between the partners.[31]

In Grazzini's story, the pedagogue is tricked by one of his former pupils,
Amerigo Ubaldi. After having lived in Lyon for some years, this young Florentine
nobleman returns to Florence upon the death of his father, only to discover that
the pedant is by this time instructing his younger brothers. Significantly, Lyon
was the center of a large community of Florentine expatriates in the Cinquecento,
many of whom resided there due to political incompatibility with the contemporary Medici regime. Beyond this political gibe, the story is notable for its strong
erotic overtones. There are definite allusions to a pederastic relationship in Grazzini's *Le Cene*, I, 2. As the narrator points out at the beginning of the story, when
Amerigo was very young, he was carefully watched over by his pedagogue, who
treated him as if he were a girl: "Messer lo precettore non aveva altro struggi-
mento che menarselo dietro e stargli appresso, e lo guardava com' una fanciulla in
casa" (*Le Cene*, 29). (Monsieur Private Tutor had no other yearning than to take
himself behind him and to stay close to him, and he watched over him as if he
were a girl at home.) Not only does this detail support the contemporary perception of young boys as androgynous beings, but it also contains a clear sexual allusion, since the term *menare dietro* was equated with sodomitic copulation ("to
take from behind") in the ambivalent erotic lexis of the early modern period
(Rocke, 103). Grazzini also explicitly notes the pedagogue's selfish refusal to let
his young pupil form any attachments with friends his own age so as "not to pick
up any bad habits" from them. In what could be seen as a form of homoerotic tit-
illation for older men, however, Amerigo is encouraged to frequent the company
of the pedant's own circle of adult acquaintances. The narrator deliberately
informs us of the precise age of the young boy at this point: "E in questa maniera

lo tenne da gli undici per infino a i diciassette anni" (*Le Cene*, 29, emphasis added). ([The pedagogue] *kept him* in this manner from the age of eleven until he was seventeen years old.) Once again, Grazzini's choice of lexicon is significant, since the verb *tenere*, or more specifically *tenersi*, had a particular meaning in pederastic circles and was used in the sense of "to keep" or "to maintain" a young boy (Rocke, 167). By the time Amerigo returns to Florence, however, he is no longer an adolescent; having spent ten years in Lyons, he is now twenty-seven years old and in a position to exact revenge on the pedagogue.

The *beffa* is perpetrated one evening while Amerigo and his former pedagogue are walking through the center of the city. Grazzini provides the reader with precise geographical landmarks in order to facilitate visualizing their route. Having attended the performance of a comedy by the Compagnia del Lauro in the Palazzo Pitti—not coincidentally the seat of the Medici—the two men head back across the Ponte Vecchio towards the *quartiere* of San Giovanni. The site of transgression takes place in the heart of the *centro storico*: on the corner of Via Vacchereccia, between Porsantamaria and the Piazza della Signoria. As they pass through this area, Amerigo jokingly suggests that they urinate through the crack in a shop door. When the pedagogue inserts his penis into the hole, in an act suffused with all too obvious sexual connotations, it is seized by the shop-owner Giovanni Piloto, a gold-smith and sculptor who is part of the group of *beffatori*. The sharp-toothed implement that Piloto uses to skewer the member of the unfortunate pedagogue naturally causes excruciating pain for the victim. The humor at this point derives from the suffering pedagogue's belief that the aggressor on the other side of the door is a cat; while he tries to talk to it and calm it down, Piloto perpetuates the deception with his feline meowing. The suffering victim cries out to his former student:

> "O Amerigo, misericordia! aiuto! ohimè, ch'io son diserto! Una gatta mi si è attac-
> cata al membro, e hammelo morso e trafitto, e per disgrazia no llo lascia: io non so
> come mi fare: ohimè! consigliatemi in qualche modo." (*Le Cene*, 33)

> (Oh Amerigo, have pity on me! Help me! Oh my, I'm ruined! A pussycat has
> attached herself to my member; she has bitten into me and unfortunately she won't
> let me go. I don't know what to do: oh my, advise me in some way!)

There might very well be an additional erotic element present here; the word *gatto* had an ambivalent meaning in the contemporary sexually equivocal register and was used to denote the penis.[32] Could it be that the feminine variant of this noun—*gatta*—was used to refer to the female genitalia? If this were the case, then on another interpretative level the pedagogue's desperate pleas for advice could reflect the widespread perception in society that pedants were unaccustomed to indulging in vaginal intercourse.

As if this violent punishment were not enough, Amerigo and a companion give a prearranged signal and are quickly joined by a group of fellow conspirators who proceed to pelt the helpless pedagogue with stones. The only thing that the suffering *beffato* (victim of the trick) can do is to try and extricate himself from the crack. He succeeds in doing this, but not without leaving half his penis behind. Prompt medical attention is not enough to save what remains of his manhood, and in order to avoid infection it is surgically removed. The concluding image in the novella is a pathetic one: As a result of his operation, the pedant is left with a mere stump and is henceforth obliged to urinate through a small brass tube. Amerigo's decision to throw him out of the house leads the former pedagogue to seek the life of a hermit, while the *beffatore* himself returns to Lyon to share the joke with his expatriate friends.

Like Grazzini's brigata of *giovani novellieri*, the reader is perhaps taken aback at the sheer vindictiveness of the trick. This instance of excessive cruelty is by no means unique among his tales: a pedant is once more the object of humiliation in *Le Cene*, II, 7. Here, however, the *beffa* is instigated not for any underlying instances of sexual alterity on his part, but rather because the pedant, called Taddeo, is seen to be going against the traditionally perceived behavior of someone in his profession when he attempts to court and to seduce a young woman called Fiammetta. This punishment arises out of sexual conformity as opposed to transgression; however, the treatment that he receives at the hands of the woman's brother, Agolante, is anything but conventional. On discovering Taddeo's love for his sister, Agolante assumes the role of Fiammetta and writes a letter to Taddeo, inviting him to the house. Upon arriving, Taddeo is immediately seized and beaten. Part of the *beffa* involves the construction of an effigy of the pedant, which is tied to a column in the Mercato Vecchio; there is a notice around its neck that reads: "Per aver falsato la sodomia" (For having given sodomy a bad name). Not only does this highly visual display underline the public nature of the humiliation, because the effigy is seen by everyone in the light of day, but it also points to the fact that the pedant has gone against traditional sexual expectations.

The particular form of punishment meted out by Taddeo's captors also reflects contemporary penalties that were inflicted on anyone found guilty of committing sodomy. "After fines, the penalty . . . inflicted most often on sodomites was public humiliation" (Rocke, 77). This usually took place in the Mercato Vecchio and normally involved the offender being tied to a column and whipped in public. Often a notice would be placed around the offender's neck with the word "sodomita" inscribed on it. The form of emasculation that has taken place in this novella is a symbolic one; public mockery, together with the physical beating that Taddeo receives from Agolante and his *brigata*, succeeds in eradicating any semblance of respectability that the pedant might have had.

Sexual violence and actual castration appears in Grazzini's portrayal of clerics. The mockery of ecclesiastical figures, often in relation to the theme of sexual incontinence, was a traditional motif of the medieval novella genre; here, however, it is taken to extremes. In *Le Cene*, II, 8, a country priest who has fallen in love with a young noblewoman from his parish is brutally punished by her brothers and their friends for his romantic intentions. The priest is portrayed in the worst possible terms as the most wretched hypocrite that ever lived, and the virtuous young woman informs her brothers of his amorous advances. They duly orchestrate a plot to teach him a lesson. The cleric is given false information that the object of his desire will be alone at home on a particular evening. When he arrives at the house, they capture him and enact their revenge. After leaving him naked and bound, the brothers go to his house and rob him of all his valuables, including 200 *fiorini d'oro*. The victim is subsequently led into the cloister behind the church and is tied to a tree with his arms raised above him in a mock crucifixion. One of the brothers secures the cleric's testicles with a rope that is attached to a high branch of the tree and then pulled tight so that the priest is forced to stand in a most uncomfortable position to avoid suffering extreme pain in his genitalia. After almost three hours of being left in this position, the poor man can last no longer and is forced to place his feet fully on the ground. The resulting movement tugs on his genitalia to such an extent that his scrotum is torn, and he understandably faints from the pain. He is not discovered until the following morning when some parishioners arrive to attend Mass. Apart from the public shame at being seen in such a condition, he must contend with the loss of both his property and his manhood.

Despite the fact that the priest remains poor and disfigured, the conclusion of the novella is nevertheless somewhat lighthearted, *à la* Boccaccio's tale of Frate Cipolla (*Dec.* VI, 10). Having decided to say the second Mass, the cleric uses the sermon as an opportunity to restore his reputation and even to profit from the apparently terrible situation in which he finds himself. His attackers were three demons, he explains, who had abused him and had stolen money that he had been intending to use for the good of the church. Like the verbal *tour de force* delivered by his counterpart in Certaldo, the oral performance of Grazzini's priest successfully persuades his parishioners to accept his story and to feel compassion for him, so much so that they are willing to give him both money and clothing. Within two years, the cleric is able to recoup all the money he had lost and, in addition, has cultivated the reputation of being a saint. The brothers who robbed and attacked him, meanwhile, give the 200 *fiorini d'oro* to their sister as a dowry and laugh together about the priest's ability to turn adversity into triumph.

Clerical castration is not a theme that is unique to Grazzini: Firenzuola features a similar tale in his *I Ragionamenti*, I, 4, where Don Giovanni trades sexual favors with a certain Tonia in exchange for the promise of clothes. The archetype for the ensuing comic scenes of rustic wooing is clearly the story of Monna Belcolore and the Prete da Varlungo (*Dec.* VIII, 2). Firenzuola explicitly cites Boccaccio's character in his own tale: "[I] buon prete . . . averebbe pur voluto fare a credenza, come quel da Varlungo" (*Opere*, 125). (The good priest . . . would have liked to have been granted credit, like the one from Varlungo.) In Firenzuola's version, however, the priest's treachery at breaking the arrangement is dealt with in an extreme manner that departs from Boccaccio's good-natured tale. Tonia convinces her husband, Giannone, that the priest has attempted to compromise her honor; in revenge, her furious husband and his relatives seize the priest, remove his trousers, and forcefully place his testicles over the edge of a trunk and then close and lock it, so that he is physically trapped. Before departing, they leave a razor on the lid. The meaning is clear: If the priest wants to free himself of the pain of having his testicles trapped in the trunk, he can literally cut himself clear, castrating himself in the process. The fact that his testicles are caught in the trunk is a fitting punishment, because the trunk contains Tonia's clothing. Thus, the theme of sex as a mode of transaction to obtain material goods is encapsulated in the brutal conclusion to this tale, which ends with Don Giovanni's desperate act of self-mutilation. Although Firenzuola's tale draws on the Boccaccian source in its general outlines, its transgressive denouement clearly sets it apart from any exemplars found in the *Decameron*.[33]

What conclusions can be drawn from the *novelle* surveyed here? It is evident that the novella collections of the sixteenth century merit a far greater degree of study than was suggested by Croce. Despite their adherence to some aspects of style and structure contained in the *Decameron*, the tales of Firenzuola and Grazzini are notable for their own features. This is particularly the case in the stories of sexual nonconformity, of which there are examples in both *I Ragionamenti* and *Le Cene*. The transgressive actions of the protagonists in both Firenzuola's and Grazzini's stories are an appropriate reflection of their authors' own eventful lives. What is notable in both their collections is that, in the novellas involving incidents of sexual violence, the *beffe* are perpetrated against figures in traditional positions of authority or respectability. The reference by Grazzini to the former professions of the country priest in *Le Cene*, II, 8, should not be viewed as merely incidental: "[E]ra stato prima pedagogo, poi birro e doppo frate, il piú tristo e il maggior ipocrito che fusse già mai." (First of all he had been a pedagogue, and then a police officer, and finally a cleric, and he was the greatest and most wretched hypocrite that ever lived.) By portraying members of the recognized establishment as the victims of violent practical jokes, Grazzini and Firenzuola were able to undermine effectively their credibility and portray them as ludicrous. The culmination of physical violence is epitomized in the act of castration. This brutal gesture not only deprives the victim of the possibility of future sexual activity, but on a symbolic level it also signifies the permanent loss of masculine power and authority.

Tales of transgressive behavior were an appropriate inclusion in the collections of two authors who were themselves on the margins of social and cultural conformity. The sexual transgression and the often violent *beffe* that typify *I Ragionamenti* and *Le Cene* could be interpreted as an aggressive response by the authors to the contemporary cultural transformations that were taking place in

Florence at the time of their composition. Such tales can be read as a way of making subversive attacks on authority figures at a time when both Firenzuola and Grazzini were unable to secure a permanent position for themselves in the official cultural milieu. In the case of Grazzini, the instances of brutality carried out against various representatives of the official establishment might be viewed as a form of literary catharsis, because they allowed him vent his frustration at his lack of success in the cultural life of the city. In the light of these conclusions, Michel Plaisance's findings need to be reexamined: Grazzini is perhaps not so much the *beffato*, but the *beffatore*.

Notes

1. For examples, see J. A. Burrow, " 'Alterity' and Middle English Literature," *Review of English Studies* 50 (1999): 483–92; Paul Freedman and Gabrielle M. Spiegel, "Medievalisms Old and New: The Rediscovery of Alterity in North American Medieval Studies," *American Historical Review* 103 (1998): 677–704; Michael Goodich, ed., *Other Middle Ages: Witnesses at the Margins*, The Middle Ages Series (Philadelphia: University of Pennsylvania Press, 1998); Évelyne Berriot-Salvadore, ed., *Les Représentations de l'Autre du Moyen Âge au XVIIe siècle: Mélanges en l'honneur de Kazimierz Kupisz* ([Saint-Étienne]: Publications de l'Université de Saint-Étienne, 1995).

2. See Lucia Folena, *"Mirrours More Than One"*: *Fables of Alterity in Renaissance Culture* (Padua: Unipress, 1990); M.-T. Jones-Davies, ed., *L'Étranger: Identité et alterité au temps de la Renaissance* (Paris: Klincksieck, 1996); Sergio Zatti, ed., *La Rappresentazione dell'altro nei testi del Rinascimento*, Morgana, no. 3 (Lucca: Maria Pacini Fazzi, 1998).

3. See, for example, Elena Fasano Guarini, *Lo Stato mediceo di Cosimo I*, Archivio dell'Atlante storico italiano dell'età moderna, Quaderno no. 1 (Florence: Sansoni, 1973); Giorgio Spini, *Cosimo I e l'indipendenza del principato mediceo*, Collana storica (1945; Florence: Vallecchi, 1980); and Rudolf von Albertini, *Firenze dalla repubblica al principato: storia e coscienza politica*, Biblioteca studio, no. 12 (1970; Turin: Einaudi, 1995).

4. On the Accademia Fiorentina and the Accademia degli Umidi, see Michel Plaisance, "Une première affirmation de la politique culturelle de Côme Ier: la transformation de l'Académie des 'Humidi' en Académie Florentine (1540–1542)," in *Les Écrivains et le pouvoir en Italie à l'époque de la Renaissance*, ed. André Rochon et al., First Series, Centre de recherche sur la renaissance italienne, no. 2 (Paris: Université de la Sorbonne Nouvelle, 1973), 361–438; id., "Culture et politique à Florence de 1542 à 1551: Lasca et les *Humidi* aux prises avec l'Académie Florentine," in *Les Écrivains et le pouvoir . . . 2° série*, ed. A. Rochon et al., Centre de recherche sur la Renaissance italienne, no. 3 (Paris: Université de la Sorbonne Nouvelle, 1974), 149–242; and id., "Les leçons publiques et privées de l'Académie florentine (1541–1552)," in *Les Commentaires et la naissance de la critique littéraire. France/Italie, XIVe–XVIe siècles. Actes du Colloque international sur le commentaire, Paris, mai 1988*, eds. Gisèle Mathieu-Castellani and

M. Plaisance (Paris: Aux Amateurs de Livres, 1990), 113–21. See also Judith Bryce, "The Oral World of the Early Accademia Fiorentina," *Renaissance Studies* 9.1 (1995): 77–103.

5. Aretino recalled some of their youthful adventures with Camilla Pisana in a letter to Firenzuola from Venice, dated October 26, 1541. See *Lettere*, ed. Paolo Procaccioli, 2 vols., I classici della BUR, no. 1803 (Milan: Biblioteca Universale Rizzoli, 1990), 1:471–72.

6. *Dialogo*, in *Opere*, ed. Adriano Seroni, Biblioteca Universale Sansoni (1958; reprint, Florence: Sansoni Editore, 1993), 542; hereafter cited in text as *Opere*. Cecilia Veneziana's name appears in a catalogue of Rome's most famous *cortegiane*, compiled by Aretino and included in Day Three of his *Sei Giornate*, ed. Giovanni Aquilecchia, Universale Laterza, no. 576 (Bari: Laterza, 1969), 127.

7. See Firenzuola's stinging sonnet "Mentre che dentro a le nefande mura" (*Opere*, 941). There is another biting reference to Tullia in *L'asino d'oro*, Book IX: "Tu meriteresti una femina, come è la Tullia, che si pascesse di adultèri, lasciando morir di fame il marito" (*Opere*, 383).

8. See Alessandro Luzio and Rodolfo Renier, "Contributo alla storia del malfrancese ne' costumi e nella letteratura italiana del secolo XVI," *Giornale storico della letteratura italiana* 5 (1885): 408–32.

9. John Boswell suggested that expressions involving wood "had a sexual significance in the later Middle Ages comparable to that of leather in the modern West" (*Christianity, Social Tolerance, and Homosexuality: Gay People in Western Europe from the Beginning of the Christian Era to the Fourteenth Century* [Chicago: The University of Chicago Press, 1980], 261–62, n. 66; see also 253); hereafter cited in text as Boswell.

10. Domenico Zanrè, " 'Che K.[zo] vuol dire?' A Re-Reading of Mid-Sixteenth-Century Linguistic Debates in the Accademia Fiorentina," *Italian Studies* 53 (1998): 20–37.

11. Giuseppe Fatini, *Agnolo Firenzuola e la borghesia letterata del Rinascimento* (Cortona: Prem. Tipografia Sociale, 1907), 23.

12. Benedetto Croce, *Poesia popolare e poesia d'arte: studi sulla poesia italiana dal Tre al Cinquecento*, 2d ed. (Bari: Laterza, 1946), 499.

13. Firenzuola's *Discacciamento delle nuove lettere, inutilmente aggiunte nella lingua toscana* (1524) was intended as a vehement response to Gian Giorgio Trissino's *Epistola de le lettere nuovamente aggiunte ne la lingua italiana*. Both of these treatises appear in *Trattati sull'ortografia del volgare, 1524–1526*, ed. Brian Richardson, Testi italiani di letteratura e di storia della lingua, no. 5 (Exeter: University of Exeter Press, 1984), 13–35 and 1–12, respectively.

14. For other examples of men disguised as women, see D. P. Rotunda, *Motif-Index of the Italian Novella in Prose*, Indiana University Publications, Folklore series, no. 2 (Bloomington: Indiana University Press, 1942), 104, motifs K1321, K1321.1, K1321.1.1, K1321.1.2, and K1321.4. See also Christopher Nissen's discussion of Giulia Bigolina's *Urania* in chapter 11 of this volume. On the treatment of this theme within the theatrical context, see Peter Brand, "Disguise, Deception, and Concealment of Identity in Ariosto's Theatre," in *Renaissance and Other Studies:*

Essays Presented to Peter M. Brown, ed. Eileen A. Millar (Glasgow: University of Glasgow, 1988), 129–43; and id., "Disguise and Recognition in Renaissance Comedy," *Journal of Anglo-Italian Studies* 1 (1991): 16–32.

15. All translations from Italian sources are my own.

16. For these texts, see Giovanni Boccaccio, *Decameron*, ed. Vittore Branca, 2 vols., Einaudi Tascabili. Classici, no. 99 (1980; reprint, Turin: Einaudi, 1992); hereafter cited in text as *Decameron*; and Masuccio Salernitano, *Il Novellino*, ed. Salvatore S. Nigro, Universale Laterza, no. 530 (1940; reprint, Bari: Laterza, 1979); hereafter cited in text as *Novellino*.

17. Firenzuola discusses the question of same-sex relations between women in the *Discorso primo* of his *Dialogo delle bellezze delle donne* (*Opere*, 542). For general considerations, see Jacqueline Murray, "Agnolo Firenzuola on Female Sexuality and Women's Equality," *Sixteenth Century Journal* 22 (1991): 199–213; and Judith C. Brown, "Lesbian Sexuality in Medieval and Early Modern Europe," in *Hidden from History: Reclaiming the Gay and Lesbian Past*, ed. Martin Bauml Duberman et al. (New York: New American Library/Penguin, 1989), 67–75.

18. For definitions of the terms *gay* and *homosexual*, see Boswell, 41 ff.

19. Charles Gilbert Chaddock was credited by the *Oxford English Dictionary* with having introduced the term *homo-sexuality* into the English language in 1892 (David M. Halperin, *One Hundred Years of Homosexuality and Other Essays on Greek Love* [New York: Routledge, 1990], 15).

20. Alan Bray, *Homosexuality in Renaissance England* (London: Gay Men's Press, 1982), 13–17.

21. James M. Saslow, "Homosexuality in the Renaissance: Behavior, Identity, and Artistic Expression," in *Hidden from History*, 96, and see also 504, n. 14; hereafter cited in text as Saslow.

22. For definitions of the term *sodomia*, see Franco Mormando, *The Preacher's Demons: Bernardino of Siena and the Social Underworld of Early Renaissance Italy* (Chicago: The University of Chicago Press, 1999), 111–15; hereafter cited in text as Mormando. See also Jacques Chiffoleau, "Dire l'indicible: remarques sur la catégorie du *nefandum* du XIIᵉ au XVᵉ siècle," *Annales ESC 45* (1990): 289–324.

23. On the various reasons for this lack of documentation, see Mormando, 118–19; and Saslow, 95.

24. Lorraine Daston and Katharine Park, "The Hermaphrodite and the Orders of Nature: Sexual Ambiguity in Early Modern France," in *Premodern Sexualities*, ed. Louise Fradenburg and Carla Freccero (New York: Routledge, 1996), 122.

25. The bookseller mentioned in this tale (*Opere*, 113) was a member of the famous Florentine family of printers responsible for publishing a number of Firenzuola's own works. These included a selection of his sonnets in the anthology entitled *Il primo libro dell'opere burlesche* (1548); his *Rime* (1549); and his two plays, *La trinutia* and *I lucidi* (both 1549).

26. See Plaisance, "La Structure de *la beffa* dans les *Cene* d'Antonfrancesco Grazzini," in *Formes et significations de la 'beffa' dans la littérature italienne de la Renaissance . . .* , ed. A. Rochon (Paris: Université de la Sorbonne Nouvelle, 1972), 51–52; hereafter cited in text as "La Structure."

27. This is the subject of Grazzini's *Canzone* III as well as of his *Sonetti* XLII and LXXXIX, in *Le rime burlesche edite e inedite di Antonfrancesco Grazzini detto Il Lasca*, ed. Carlo Verzone, Raccolta di opere inedite o rare di ogni secolo della letteratura italiana (Florence: G. C. Sansoni, 1882), 143–48; 37–38; 73–74. The effects of venereal disease are mentioned in *Le Cene*, ed. Riccardo Bruscagli, I Novellieri italiani, no. 27 (Rome: Salerno Editrice, 1976), I, 9; hereafter cited in text as *Le Cene*.

28. *Le Cene* was first published in 1743, almost two centuries after its initial composition. Grazzini also wrote three separate, additional tales, known collectively as the *novelle magliabechiane*, which survive in the Biblioteca Nazionale Centrale di Firenze, Magl. MS VI, 190; these are included in Bruscagli's edition of *Le Cene*.

29. For sodomy in Cellini's life and writings, see Margaret A. Gallucci, "Cellini's Trial for Sodomy: Power and Patronage at the Court of Cosimo I," in *The Cultural Politics of Duke Cosimo I de' Medici*, ed. Konrad Eisenbichler (Aldershot, U.K.: Ashgate, 2001), 37–46. For Cellini's violent behavior, see Paolo L. Rossi, "The Writer and the Man. Real Crimes and Mitigating Circumstances: *Il caso Cellini*," in *Crime, Society and the Law in Renaissance Italy*, eds. Trevor Dean and K. J. P. Lowe (Cambridge: Cambridge University Press, 1994), 157–83.

30. Plaisance, "La Structure," 55–57.

31. For a detailed discussion on questions of age and gender, see Michael Rocke, *Forbidden Friendships: Homosexuality and Male Culture in Renaissance Florence*, Studies in the History of Sexuality (Oxford: Oxford University Press, 1996), 87–111; hereafter cited in text as Rocke.

32. See Jean Toscan, "Le carnaval du langage: Le lexique érotique des poètes de l'équivoque de Burchiello à Marino (XVᵉ–XVIIᵉ siècles)," 4 vols., diss., Université de Lille, 1981, 3:1537.

33. The terrible choice that the priest has to make in this tale is similar to the fate of another cleric, Giacomo da Gandino, in Matteo Bandello's Novella II, 20, in *Tutte le opere*, ed. Francesco Flora, 2 vols., I Classici Mondadori (1934; reprint, Verona: Arnoldo Mondadori Editore, 1966).

10

Animal Anxieties: Straparola's "Il re porco"

Suzanne Magnanini

In mid-sixteenth-century Italy, one could read marvellous novellas of a queen who gives birth to a pig, of a marchioness who gives birth to a snake, and of a princess accused of having given birth to three mongrel pups; these stories all appear in Giovanfrancesco Straparola's *Le piacevoli notti*, an extremely popular two-volume collection of novellas first printed in Venice in 1550 and 1553. Such tales of monstrous births clearly appealed to Straparola's readers, because *Le piacevoli notti* was reprinted more than twenty times in the sixty years following the *princeps*. These stories of bestial offspring distinguish Straparola's work from countless other collections of novellas published in the same period, while simultaneously likening it to the early modern scientific discourse on the monstrous. For example, in one of the novellas in his collection, Straparola narrates the story of an enchanted tuna that magically impregnates a haughty young princess at the behest of a foolish lad. A similar case of ichtyo-human hybridization can be found in Juan Huarte's *Essame* [sic] *degl'ingegni degli huomini* (1586), in which the Spanish physician relates what he held to be the true episode of a woman who, "andando a spasso lungo la riva del mare, un pesce uscì dell'acqua e impregnolla" (while she was wandering along the seashore, a fish left the water and impregnated her).[1] In another one of Straparola's novellas, a noble woman gives birth to mismatched twins: a normal child and a serpent. Serpent siblings, however, were not merely the fantastic inventions of storytellers used to entertain their audiences or readers. In his 1573 treatise *Des monstres et prodiges*, the French surgeon Ambroise Paré repeats Lycosthenes' 1494 account of a woman in Cracow who delivered a stillborn child "who had a live snake attached to its back."[2] Similarly, in his book of secrets, the Neapolitan humanist Giambattista Della Porta purports that corrupt menstrual blood, when mixed with human seed in the womb, has been known to generate "rospi, lucerte, e altri simili animali" (toads, lizards, and other similar animals).[3] In the early modern collective consciousness, Straparola's *favole*, as he refers to his novellas, dwelt in closer proximity to scientific discourse than they do in our imagination. In our own day, stories of bestial births have been eliminated from scientific discourse and are most often relegated to those genres a majority of readers recognize as popular fictions: children's stories, horror films, and supermarket tabloids. For many of Straparola's contemporaries, however, the line dividing the fantastic tale from the scientific case history was both penetrable and ever shifting.

In his *Dialogo del tempo del partorire delle donne* (1542), for example, Venetian author Sperone Speroni marvels over the ability of the female body to deliver forth creatures that blur the boundaries between what was thought to be fact and what was known to be fiction. He depicts the female body as hovering at the edge of the biologically possible, as capable of dragging creatures once thought possible only in fairy tales and myths into the category of the real. He asks his readers,

> Quante sono hora, quante furono per lo passato, che, tre, e quattro e cinque, e sette figliuoli vivi, e sani partorirono in una volta? Similmente, tale ve n'hebbe, ch'in una volta dieci, dodici, trenta, e settanta ne disperdette. Tal serpenti, tale elefanti, *e per far vere le favole*, tal minotauri, e hippocentauri si partorì.[4]

> (How many are there now, and how many were there in the past who gave birth to three, four, five, or even seven live, healthy children at once? Similarly, there have been those that at one time sent into the world ten, twelve, thirty, even seventy of them. Some serpents, some elephants, *and making fables come true*, some minotaurs and centaurs were born.)

Although this crescendo of anomalous offspring, which spirals upward from multiple births, to serpents, to minotaurs and centaurs, might appear to our modern eyes to be a gross distortion of biological reality, undoubtedly many sixteenth-century Italian readers would have agreed with Speroni's assessment that the marvelous issues from the female body could "far vere le favole": make fictions come true. Despite the shared content in Straparola's novellas and contemporary scientific treatises, and despite the permeability of the border between fact and fiction in this period, literary critics of early modern texts have consistently ignored the contiguity of science and *favola*.

During the twentieth century, *Le piacevoli notti* was more likely to be catalogued, to figure as an element in a literary list or folklore index, than to be read or studied. Since the collection contains material that was later reworked into what we recognize today as fairy tales, including the earliest known written version of classics like "Puss in Boots," Straparola's work has figured prominently in nineteenth- and twentieth-century folklore and comparative narratology studies. Such analyses, from the brothers Grimm to later formalist critics, limited the interpretation of monstrous births by dismissing them as fantastic elements intrinsic to the fictional genre. Furthermore, influential theoretical works in the field of folklore studies, like Vladimir Propp's *Morphology of the Folktale* and Max Lüthi's *The European Folktale: Form and Nature*, focused attention on the common narrative elements across cultures, thus displacing culturally specific concerns.[5] Such folklore and formalist approaches tend to argue for a cross-cultural uniformity through a reduction of the narrative to the most basic elements (whether they be the motifs of folklore studies or the basic narrative elements of structural analysis), thus stripping the work of its details and peculiarities—what Italo Calvino calls the "la polpa *storica* sul nocciolo *morfologico*" (the *historical* fruit around the *morphological* pit).[6] By removing the historical fruit, however, such analyses discard those portions of the work that betray its ties to the cultural milieu in which it was written. Thus, within folklore studies Straparola's tales are often simply categorized, according to motif or type, as "animal-bridegroom tales" or "dragon-slayer tales."

Outside of folklore and formalist circles, few critics have paused to study this work and its author in any detail, and those who have dedicate scant space to the interpretation of individual tales.[7] In general, critics have approached Straparola as belonging to a long line of sixteenth-century *novellieri* who, with greater or lesser success, reworked Boccaccio's *Decameron*. Inasmuch as Straparola is the author of a collection of novellas with a frame tale in which a *lieta brigata* convenes each night to recount *favole*, he does owe a certain debt to the Boccaccian model. Yet such comparisons tend to be overly reductive, limiting the scope of critical analysis to a particular innovation or variation that distinguishes the author under examination from his contemporaries and his work from the Trecento model. As is the fate of many *minori*, Straparola shrinks under the reductive gaze of the literary historian and the anthologist, catalogued as a mere *novelliere* who reworked popular stories in his collection. Indeed, some of Straparola's critics refer to his use of popular tales—stories of dragon slayers, talking animals, and monstrous births—as the author's only notable contribution to the novella tradition.[8] Only recently have critics begun to recognize Straparola's "assoluta singolarità letteraria e culturale" (absolute literary and cultural uniqueness).[9]

The present study continues down this recently blazed critical trail. This essay focuses on the three novellas in Straparola's work in which women give birth to animals, and it presents a close reading of *Notte* II, 1, in which a queen gives birth to a pig who must marry three times in order to transform into a human. The representations of the birth of animal-human hybrids differ significantly from depictions of other types of monstrosity in *Le piacevoli notti* because, unlike the dragons and sirens in other novellas, these interspecies beings provoke terror and instill a need for interpretation in those who view them. Once the novella of the pig boy is restored to its cultural context—the sixteenth-century debate on the monstrous—it becomes evident that Straparola's human-swine hybrid evokes the early modern anxieties surrounding bestiality and the perceived encroachment on the limits of the human. Through a comparative reading of Straparola's novella and the humanist Benedetto Varchi's scientific account of a woman who was thought to have given birth to a dog, we can explain how these fears of interspecies unions are allayed at the end of the novella by the destruction of the monster and the reconstruction of the boundary between man and beast. Finally, the pig child, whose monstrous birth interrupts the royal lineage and menaces the fate of the realm, can be interpreted as a symbol for those who were perceived to be destabilizing elements in Straparola's Venetian milieu: the young, unmarried male patricians.

The first volume of *Le piacevoli notti* consists of twenty-five tales distributed evenly over five evenings; the second volume contains forty-eight novellas distributed over eight evenings. This work marks the first instance in which a substantial number of popular tales were included in a collection of Italian novellas. The frame tale describes a *lieta brigata* composed of ten fictional *damigelle* (maidens) and many unnamed gentlemen, as well as a number of historical personages. These include Chiara, the wife of the Ferrarese gentleman Girolamo Guidiccione; Veronica, wife of Santo Orbat, a nobleman from Crema; Pietro Bembo and his cousin Antonio; Giambattista Casali, ambassador to the king of England; prelate Vangelista Cittadini; merchant Ferier Beltramo; and poets Bernardo Capello, Benedetto Trivigiano, and Antonio Molino. This group of friends meets each evening for thirteen nights during Carnival on the island of Murano at the home of Lucrezia Sforza and her father Ottaviano, both of whom have been recently exiled from Lodi. As in the *Decameron*, the members of Straparola's *brigata* entertain each other with songs, stories, and dancing. A madrigal opens each evening, and after each tale the narrator presents an enigma in the form of an octave for the group to solve.

The *damigella* Isabella begins the first *favola* of the second night by informing her listeners that King Galeotto of Anglia (England) and his virtuous bride Ersilia lacked only an heir to complete their otherwise happy union. Despite what his name might suggest, this Galeotto was no panderer or go-between, but a faithful husband and wise ruler. One day after having gathered flowers in the garden, Queen Ersilia reclined in the shade of a tree and fell fast asleep. Three fairies (*fate*) happened upon the dozing queen and, moved by her beauty, decided to render her "inviolabile ed affatata" (inviolable and enchanted).[10] The first fairy granted that Ersilia would become pregnant the next time she slept with her husband. The second fairy declared that the son born to her would be the most handsome in the world. The third fairy inexplicably swore that Ersilia herself would be the richest, wisest woman in the world, but that her son would be born with the appearance and manners of a pig and that he would be liberated from this curse only after having married three times. With no knowledge of what had occurred as she slept, Ersilia awoke and returned to the castle. Upon discovering a short time later that the queen was pregnant, the whole kingdom rejoiced. This joy gave way to terror the moment the child arrived, for it more closely resembled a pig than a human. After initially resolving to murder the monstrous newborn, Galeotto ordered that it be raised as a rational being. Even though the pig boy behaved like a swine, rooting through garbage and rolling in manure, he did at least possess the power of speech, an ability that humanists held distinguished humans from beasts.[11] One day he demanded that his parents find him a bride. Since his monstrous appearance and behavior rendered him an undesirable match for a noble woman, he chose to marry the eldest of a poor woman's three daughters. When he overheard his bride's plot to kill him on their wedding night rather than endure his bestial ways, the pig prince brutally murdered her. He then married the poor woman's second daughter who, like her sister before her, met a violent end after conspiring to kill her husband. It was the third daughter's unconditional love, a love that blinded her to the excrement-encrusted skin of her spouse, that permitted the pig prince to become human. At the end of the novella, he peels off his pig skin and metamorphoses into a handsome youth.

Folklorists like Stith Thompson and D. P. Rotunda catalogue this novella under the animal-bridegroom tale type, a group of stories that trace their origins to Apuleius's Cupid and Psyche and include Beauty and the Beast tales among their variations.[12] Modern critics, regardless of their theoretical framework, tend to read animal-bridegroom tales as revealing a given society's anxieties surrounding sex and marriage. Specifically, child psychologist Bruno Bettelheim views animal-bridegroom tales as narratives that work through the psychological aspects of the process of sexual maturation. In *The Uses of Enchantment*, he notes that in these tales "the male's anxieties that his coarseness will turn off the female are juxtaposed with her anxieties about the bestial nature of sex" (298). Undoubtedly, such post-Freudian psychological mechanisms can be identified in this tale; if we insert the novella into the context of the sixteenth-century debate on the monstrous, however, it becomes clear that Straparola has written it in such a way as to highlight a very different set of anxieties. What Straparola writes is not so much a story of Beauty and the Beast but a tale of Beast and the Beauty, one in which the narrative focus is on the male protagonist. The pig king's own identity as a hybrid creature becomes storyteller Isabella's primary concern while the fate of the "beauties," his three brides, and the scenes of their sexual initiation assume a secondary importance.

After having concluded her tale with a happy ending, Isabella poses an enigma to her listeners that recalls a central motif of the animal-bridegroom tale: the patriarchal figure who provides a husband for the young female protagonist. She challenges those gathered before her with this puzzle:

Vorrei che tu mi desti, o mio Signore,
Quel che non hai, nè sei per aver mai,

S'avesti andar al mondo con tuo onore
Mill'anni, e più, di vita ancor assai.
E se tu 'l pensi aver, vivi in errore,
E come cieco per la strada vai:
Ma se, come mi mostri, il mio ben vuoi,
Dammel, non tardar più; chè dar me 'l puoi. (*Piacevoli*, 1:79)

(I would like you to give me, o my Lord, / That which you don't have, nor are you ever about to have / If you had to go about the world with your honor for a thousand years or more, still very much alive. / And if you think that you have it, you live in error, / And like a blind man down the street you go / But if, as you show me, you want what is good for me / Give it to me, do not delay any longer; because give it to me you can.)

When her companions cannot solve this enigma, Isabella reveals that a husband is that which a man can give to a woman but can never have himself. In this way, Straparola shifts the traditional marriage discourse to a space outside the limits of the *favola*, fixing it in the frame tale of *Le piacevoli notti*. This displacement permits Straparola to concentrate on what was for him and the Venetian *brigata* a more compelling component of the animal-bridegroom tale: the animal-human hybrid. What preoccupies the narrator of the tale is the pig king's uncertain morphology, which challenges the boundaries of human identity and threatens the stability of the state by disrupting the royal lineage.

Isabella's lengthy description of the royal couple's negative reaction to the birth of their bestial son reveals these preoccupations:

[A]ggiunta al desiderato parto, partorì un figliuolo, le cui membra non erano umane, ma porcine. Il che andato alle orecchie del Re e della Reina, inestimabile dolore ne sentirono. Ed acciò che tal parto non ridondasse in vituperio della Reina che buona e santa era, il Re più fiate ebbe animo di farlo uccidere e gettarlo nel mare. Ma pur rivolgendo nell'animo e discretamente pensando che 'l figliuolo, qual che si fusse, era generato da lui ed era il sangue suo, deposto giù ogni fiero proponimento che prima nell'animo aveva, e abbracciata la pietà mista col dolore, volse al tutto, non come bestia, ma come animal razionale allevato e nodrito fusse. (*Piacevoli*, 1:72)

(Having arrived at the moment of the much awaited birth, she gave birth to a son whose limbs were not human but porcine. Upon hearing this, the king and queen felt an inestimable grief. And in order that this birth would not redound to the shame of the queen, who was good and pious, the king more than once got it into his head to have it killed and thrown into the sea. But, turning this over in his mind and prudently thinking that his son, such as he was, was generated by him and was of his blood, he put aside all cruel resolutions that he had had before in his mind, and

embracing mercy mixed with sorrow, wanted him to be raised and nurtured entirely,
not as a beast, but as a rational animal.)

Although Galeotto never doubts his wife's virtue, because he knows her to be
good and pious ("buona e santa"), he fears that this monstrous birth might
besmirch the queen's reputation. Isabella, however, never precisely articulates
why this birth would discredit the mother. In this period, abnormal births were
often perceived as signs of the sins of the parents regardless of the nature of a
child's deformity. Pierre Boaistuau, for example, asserted that "il est tout certain
que le plus souvent ces creatures monstrueses procedent du iugement, iustice,
chastisement, e malediction de Dieu, lequel permet que les peres e meres pro-
duisent telles abominations, en l'horreur de leur péché."[13] (It is quite certain that
most often such monstrous creatures arise from the judgment, justice, chastisement, and curse of God, who allows the fathers and mothers to produce such
abominations, horrified by their sin.) For medieval Europeans, as for Straparola's
society, there was always the risk that the bodies of children that appeared to unite
the human and the bestial would be (mis)interpreted as a sign of the creatures'
sinful origins, as the physical evidence of their mothers' wicked couplings with
brute beasts. In Straparola's novella, not only does the monstrous body create the
possibility for misinterpretation, but it also initially resists interpretation. Moved
by the desire to protect the queen, the king repeatedly resolves to have the child
murdered and its body thrown into the sea. Confused and not completely convinced of this decision, the king refrains from acting in order to reflect more
deeply on the situation. Reasoning through the dilemma, Galeotto finally arrives
at an interpretation of the child's abnormal body: since his wife was virtuous and
chaste, then the pig child must somehow have been generated by their union ("era
generato da lui ed era il suo sangue"). Unable to explain the child's anomalous
form, yet convinced that it is his own flesh and blood, the king decides to raise the
pig boy as a rational being.

Isabella's account of this animal-human hybrid marks the *brigata*'s first of
many encounters with monstrosity in *Le piacevoli notti*; the novellas that follow
teem with monstrous phenomena. A talking tuna grants Pietro Pazzo's wishes in
Notte III, *Favola* 1; Doralice saves her husband from a siren who has swallowed
him whole (III, 4); Costanza captures and subdues a satyr (IV, 1); siblings
Acquirino, Fulvio, and Serena possess jewel-generating locks (IV, 3); Guerrino
frees a wildman (V, 1); and Cesarino slays a dragon (X, 3). Yet none of these monstrosities evoke the intense horror and anxiety of interpretation that the pig boy
generates in his father. In fact, the characters in Straparola's novellas most often
accept the monstrous as quotidian. Without expressing fear nor pausing to reflect,
the majority of his characters react immediately to the monstrosities that appear
before them, viewing these creatures either negatively as obstacles to overcome,
or positively as helpers in their quest.

Galeotto's grief and his need to contemplate and interpret the abnormal body of his son, however, can be considered the paradigmatic reaction to a monstrous birth in *Le piacevoli notti*. In *Notte* IV, 3, King Anciolotto's mother fakes a monstrous birth in order to discredit her daughter-in-law. At the moment of their birth, the king's mother secretly replaces her daughter-in-law's newborn triplets with three mongrel pups. When King Anciolotto learns of this monstrous birth, he almost swoons. His wife denies the charge but is unable to explain the creatures at her side. Anciolotto, confused and unsure of what to believe, "molto si turbò, e quasi da dolore in terra caddè [*sic*], ma poscia ch'egli rinvenne alquanto, stette gran pezza tra il sì e 'l no suspeso, ed al fine diede piena fede alle parole materne" ([h]e became very upset and almost fell to the ground from the grief; but he revived somewhat, was for a long time suspended between "yes" and "no," and in the end put his complete faith in the words of the mother [*Piacevoli*, 1: 219]). As in the novella of the pig king, these alleged animal offspring initially resist interpretation and engender in the king an overwhelming sense of grief. In III, 3, when a woman gives birth to a serpent and a beautiful girl, the midwives were quite frightened: "si paventarono molto" (they got very frightened [*Piacevoli*, 1: 154–55]). The horror produced by this bestial birth dissipates quickly when the snake slithers off into the garden, thus removing the burden of interpretation from those present. Why do animal-human hybrids terrify those who witness their births, whereas dragons, talking animals, and satyrs do not? Why do these hybrid births both demand and then initially resist interpretation, whereas other monstrosities are merely accepted as givens? To answer these questions, we must look beyond the novella of the pig king and search for interpretive clues first in the contiguous space of the frame tale and then in scientific texts of the period that depict similar monstrous births.

Isabella introduces her story not with an observation on matrimony nor with banalities about the transforming power of love, but with a call to her listeners to thank God that they were created humans instead of beasts. Her tale, she tells her companions, will make them realize

> [q]uanto l'uomo . . . sia tenuto al suo creatore che egli uomo e non animale brutto l'abbia al mondo creato, non è lingua sì tersa nè sì faconda, che in mille anni a sofficienza il potesse isprimere. (*Piacevoli*, 1: 71)

> ([h]ow much man . . . is beholden to his creator that he was created man in the world and not a brute animal, there is not a tongue so clear and prolific that would be able to express it sufficiently in a thousand years.)

With these words, Isabella simultaneously recalls for her listeners and praises the Christian hierarchy in which man stood above the beasts. In their writings and teachings, the early Church fathers endeavored to shape a Christian culture that defined itself against the pagan culture from which it had emerged. Part of this effort involved the reconfiguration of the relationship between the human and the animal.[14] Whereas in pagan culture the boundary between these categories was tenuous and permeable, the Christian fathers forged a deep divide between them. Ambrose, Augustine, and later Thomas Aquinas held that reason, intellect, and rational capacity, and the fact that they had been created in the image of God, placed men above the beasts (Salisbury, 5). Isabella temporarily upsets this hierarchy by relating an episode of monstrous birth that calls into question the division between the human and the animal: although the pig king is capable of speech and reason, he possesses the body of a beast. By the time we arrive at the happy ending of her novella, however, the monster will be undone and the threat to the existing order removed. Evidently Straparola anticipated that the ambiguous category introduced by Isabella's novella would be so disturbing to her listeners as to necessitate a verbal reassurance of the fixity of the boundaries circumscribing the human. The same mechanism is at work in the novella of King Anciolotto and the three mongrel pups. Here, too, the diegetic narrator begins by reminding her listeners of the privileged and distinct position of man in relation to the animals:

> Io ho sempre inteso . . . l'uomo esser il più nobile e il più valente animale che mai la natura creasse; perciò che Iddio lo creò alla imagine ed alla similitudine sua, e volse ch'egli signoreggiasse e non fusse signoreggiato. (*Piacevoli*, 1: 214)

> (I have always understood man . . . to be the most noble animal that Nature ever created; for this reason God created him in his image and likeness, and wanted him to rule, and not to be ruled over.)

These words echo the verses in Genesis often cited by Church fathers as justification for the human domination of other species: "Let us make man in our image and likeness to rule the fish in the sea, the birds of heaven, the cattle, all wild animals on earth, and all reptiles that crawl upon the earth. . . . Be fruitful and increase, fill the earth and subdue it, rule over the fish in the sea, the birds of heaven, and every living thing that moves upon the earth" (Genesis, 1:26, 28).[15] As in the novella of the pig king, the birth of the three mongrel pups—albeit a fraudulent birth—requires the verbalization of the superiority and separateness of the human. The concern with maintaining distinct divisions between the human and other species links these novellas to what was a broader cultural debate in early modern Europe on the nature of the monster and the limits of humanity.

Straparola lived and wrote in monstrous times. His was an age of great turmoil during which what had seemed stable categories in the collective consciousness underwent revision, and many "facts" were challenged. Jeffrey Jerome Cohen has written that the monster is the "harbinger of category crisis"[16] and that which shows "that 'fact' is subject to constant reconstruction and change" (Cohen 14–15). Cohen's thesis helps us understand the proliferation of monsters in this period as a sort of cultural by-product of the steady erosion of the "facts" on which early modern European society founded various beliefs. The certainties that the classical authorities and the Church had once offered no longer seemed to exist, for, as Paula Findlen has noted, "In the wake of the political and religious upheavals of the Reformation era that called into question other forms of authority, the 'old' no longer had the security of meaning it had formerly enjoyed."[17] New World discoveries challenged the ancients' geographical, anthropological, and biological assumptions and proved to be doubly destabilizing. First, explorers brought back from their travels plants and animals that were considered monstrous inasmuch as, like all monsters, they defied categorization in existing taxonomies and threw "doubt on life's ability to teach us order."[18] Second, many monsters that classical authors had placed at the margins of civilization, such as the Plinian monstrous races, were never found during subsequent explorations. This led early modern authors to reassign what had previously been considered materially real creatures into the realm of the fantastic. In short, this century was not only one of many monsters, but also one in which the very category of the monstrous came under revision. Since monsters dwell at the borders of the human and thus serve to define the limits of the human, the reconsideration of the monster necessitated a reconsideration of the human. With her introductory remarks, Isabella seeks to overcome this taxonomic instability by shoring up the walls between man and beast.

As physicians, philosophers, natural scientists, and the clergy struggled to define the monster, to explains its origins, and to determine its purpose in nature, they created a canon of teratalogical literature. This canon was not created *ex novo* but was founded on the writings of earlier authorities: Aristotle explained monsters to be aberrations of nature; in their works on divination, Cicero and Julius Obsequens presented monsters as portents; in Pliny's *Historia naturalis* monsters became marvels and wonders.[19] As the authors of the early modern teratological canon debated the validity and merits of each of these theories—monster as aberration, portent, or marvel—they discussed examples of monstrosity gleaned from classical sources, medieval chronicles, personal observation, and literary works. For example, in his discussion of the power of the imagination to deform the fetus, Paré (38–42) offers as evidence accounts from the works of Aristotle and Hippocrates, a citation from Heliodorus' *History of Ethiopia*, as well as a contemporary case history recorded by a fellow surgeon. In the texts of the teratalogical canon, what was thought to be fact and what was known to be fiction dwelt side by side.

Virtually every teratalogical treatise of the period, regardless of the author's theoretical stance, included a few cases of human mothers who delivered what were perceived to be animals or animal-human hybrids. Accounts of such hybrids could be found in texts as varied as the Swiss humanist Conrad Lycosthenes's prodigy book *Prodigiorum ac ostentorum chronicon* (1557), the naturalist Ulisse

Aldrovandi's encyclopedia of monstrosity *Monstrorum historia* (1642), and the medical treatises of Paduan physician Fortunio Liceti (1634).[20] Among the plethora of case histories, Benedetto Varchi's account of a woman who gives birth to a canine-human hybrid offers the richest point of comparison for analyzing Straparola's novellas because of the similarity of content and its chronological proximity to *Le piacevoli notti*. Varchi's account appears in his "Della generazione de' mostri," a lecture presented to the Florentine Academy in July 1548, two years before the publication of Straparola's work.

As he stood before his fellow academics, Varchi recounted the story of a woman from Avignon who brought forth a "monster" three days after having given birth to a daughter. The girl perished only an hour after entering the world, but her monstrous twin lived. Varchi described the surviving child to his audience in detail, lingering over the description of his hybrid form:

> [Q]uel mostro che nacque l'anno 1543 in Avignone, il quale nacque dopo tre dì che era nata della medesima donna una bambina, la quale non visse un'ora, era così fatto. Egli aveva la testa d'uomo dagli orecchi in fuori, i quali insieme col collo, colle braccia e mani erano di cane, e così il membro virile: le gambe ed i piedi con un picciol segno di coda di dietro.[21]

> (That monster that was born in the year 1543 in Avignon, that was born three days after the same woman had given birth to a girl who didn't live but an hour . . . was made like this. He had a human head except for the ears, which, along with the neck, arms, and hands were those of a dog, and similarly the virile member, the legs, and feet with the hint of a tail behind.)

Like the pig king, the dog boy confounded the boundary between the human and the animal; he exhibited a horrifying blend of canine and human features, emitting cries that more closely resembled the whine of a dog than human speech. The public reaction was one of great anxiety. Varchi continues:

> tutte le membra canine erano coperte di pelo lungo e nero come era il cane, col quale confessò poi essersi giacciuta quella tal donna che l'aveva partorito: il restante del corpo infino alla cintura, era tutto d'uomo, colle coscie e le gambe bianchissime. (*Opere*, 2:666)

> (All of the limbs were covered by long black fur like that of a dog, with which that same woman who had given birth to it confessed to having lain. The remainder of the body, up to the waist, was completely human, with very white thighs and legs.)

Those who viewed the dog child interpreted its body not as a portent of some future event, nor as a marvel of nature, but as a sign of the mother's past sin of bestiality, a charge to which she confessed. Mother and child were transported from Avignon to Marseilles, where the "most Christian" (*cristianissimo*) King

Francis I ordered that both be burned. On the last day of July 1543, mother and dog—as Varchi refers to the woman's offspring—perished at the stake.

Varchi's lesson provides insight to both those anxieties that initially spur Straparola's fictional king to contemplate infanticide and those that then cause him to reconsider his murderous plan. The teratalogical text also illuminates those aspects of hybrid births that render them more terrifying than other forms of monstrosity in *Le piacevoli notti*. Although the woman of Avignon confessed to unnatural sexual relations with a dog, the reference to this sin simmers just under the surface of Straparola's tale, threatening to burst forth. King Galeotto worries that the pious queen will be "vituperata" on account of her abnormal offspring. Although he does not dare to utter a precise term, what Galeotto fears is not merely that "people would talk" but that people would interpret the birth of the pig king as a sign of some act of bestiality on the part of the queen, a charge so serious that it moved the French King Francis to condemn both mother and child to death.

The fear of damaging accusations in the novella and King Francis's order of execution reflect the early modern perception of the sin of bestiality as far worse than other sexual transgressions. The prohibition against human-animal intercourse was an ancient one set down in Leviticus: "A man who has sexual intercourse with any beast shall be put to death, and you shall kill the beast. If a woman approaches any animal to have intercourse with it, you shall kill both woman and beast" (Leviticus, 20:15–16). The Christian penitentials, texts that were "central to the compilation and transmission of a comprehensive code of sexual ethics in the early Middle Ages,"[22] upheld this proscription. Over the centuries, the gravity of the sin of bestiality, and the corresponding duration and severity of the penance necessary to expiate it, increased dramatically. All of the early penitentials (datable before 813) had "at least one provision covering this activity" (Payer, 44). In the course of the eleventh and twelfth centuries, bestiality came to be seen as a more serious crime, a form of sodomy or unnatural sex that went against nature and offended God (Salisbury, 94). By the thirteenth century, Thomas Aquinas wrote that among all the types of unnatural vice, which included homosexuality, masturbation, and unacceptable sexual positions, " 'the most grievous is the sin of bestiality, because use of the due species is not observed' " (quoted in Salisbury, 99). According to one of Aquinas's contemporaries, the Franciscan theologian Alexander of Hales, both the human and the animal partner involved in unnatural acts must be killed in order to "erase the memory of the act with the participants" (Salisbury, 99). As Varchi's academic lesson attests, those found guilty of bestiality in Straparola's day also risked execution.

Clearly, the desire to erase the abnormal body in order to stave off rumors of bestiality motivates Galeotto to contemplate the murder of his offspring, but his murderous impulse also betrays his need to maintain order. The pig boy's apparent hybridity taints the purity of humankind and dismantles the sanctioned hierarchy of species lauded by Isabella at the beginning of the novella. Although to some degree all monsters stand between categories, animal-human hybrids are especially disturbing because they challenge our own identity. Even in cases where the mother was not accused of bestial acts, these abnormal births threatened the epistemological order. Such creatures were destabilizing radicals within the carefully constructed system of classification erected in order to make sense of the surrounding world and humankind's position within it. If allowed to live, such hybrids raised vexing questions. Should they be baptized? What was their legal status?

In Straparola's day, as before, the desire to restore order was often fulfilled by violence.[23] Midwives in early modern Europe, in fact, were described in teratalogical treatises as smothering those newborns that they judged to lie outside the category of the human and that were thus unfit for baptism. The encyclopedist Tommaso Garzoni recounts the physician Levinius Lemnius's chronicle of an incredible monster that, upon leaving the womb, ran about the room wildly, "ma le donne ch'erano quivi presenti pigliano i guanciali, e gettandogliene adosso, l'affogarono" (but the women who were present there grabbed the pillows and, throwing them on, smothered it).[24] The practice became so widespread that the German physician Martin Weinrich, who believed that physical deformity did not necessarily preclude the existence of a soul, felt compelled to remind the readers of his *De ortu monstrorum* that "num lecito occidere monstra" (it is forbidden to kill monsters).[25] Weinrich's interdiction did not apply to all monstrous births, however, and he argued that one could kill those children thought to be born from unions with brute beasts or devils, or those who, due to the intervention of the maternal imagination, were born more animal than human.[26] As no specific guidelines or standards existed, it was no simple task to distinguish between those births that could be declared human, and thus fit for baptism, and those that were to be killed. King Galeotto's hesitation, his reflection prior to committing the act, and his ultimate rejection of infanticide also reflect the difficulty in this period of determining which monstrous births could justly be considered human and therefore spared and which were to be eliminated.

Galeotto's deliberation is rendered even more complex because there was no consensus in scientific writings as to whether the coupling of two disparate species could produce offspring. Although he seems to believe that his wife would never commit such a sin, Straparola's protagonist lacks the security of the scientific knowledge that such unions are always sterile, knowledge that would dismiss any doubts that the malformed newborn might be the product of a bestial act. Accounts of such hybrid births had been recorded since classical times. In Book VII of his *Historia naturalis*, a favorite source for early modern naturalists and scientists, Pliny claimed to have seen the remains of a hippocentaur (half-man, half-horse) and noted the astounding case of Alcippe, who gave birth to an elephant.[27] Many classical authors, however, dismissed the idea that such unions could be fertile, although they recognized that similar species, such as horses and donkeys, did crossbreed in real life and produce live, but sterile, offspring. Varchi, like many Renaissance humanists, adhered to this theory. He observed that those in Avignon and Marseilles who thought they were viewing a canine-human hybrid had been fooled by appearances. Citing the laws set forth in Aristotle's *On the Generation of Animals*, Book II, Chapter 5, Varchi states that unions between species with differing gestation periods and disparate somatic types were necessarily infertile (*Opere*, 2:666). On such grounds, he concludes that the French woman's offspring could not have been generated through her copulation with a dog. Yet for every author like Varchi who refuted the generative possibility of such unions, there was another like Paré who argued that such abominable "joinings"—the mixing or mingling of seed—could indeed produce monstrous hybrids:

> There are monsters that are born with a form that is half-animal and the other [half] human, or retaining everything [about them] from animals, which are produced by sodomites and atheists who "join together" and break out of their bounds—unnaturally—with animals, and from this are born several hideous monsters that bring great shame to those who look at them or speak of them. Yet, the dishonesty lies in the deed and not in words; and it is, when it is done, a very unfortunate and abominable thing, and a great horror for a man or a woman to mix with or copulate with brute animals; and as a result, some are born half-men and half-animals. (Paré, 67)

Paré continues by offering proof of his assertion in the form of case histories and illustrations. His evidence includes a canine-human hybrid, not unlike Varchi's dog boy, born in 1493, and a child born in Antwerp possessing the body of a dog and the head of a fowl, as well as instances of animals thought to have been inseminated by men. For Paré, the aberrant form of these offspring, fusions of man and beast in a single body, replicated the sinful joining that led to their generation.

By reinserting Straparola's tale into its cultural milieu, by juxtaposing the novella of the pig king with Varchi's and Paré's teratological writings, the submerged causes of Galeotto's distress at the birth of his bestial boy and the motivations for his behavior rise to the surface. Unlike the dragons, sirens, and talking animals in *Le piacevoli notti*, the pig king raises the specter of bestiality. So great was the fear of the disintegration of the boundaries between animals and humans in this period that the birth or alleged birth of animal-human hybrids rent the fantastic fabric of the novella, allowing the extreme terror that this particular monstrosity evoked in early modern Italy to penetrate the realm of make-believe. In the end, the animal-human hybrids in both the novella and the teratalogical treatise, like those found guilty of acts of bestiality in this period, must be erased.

In her seminal study *Purity and Danger*, anthropologist Mary Douglas posits that all cultures possess mechanisms intended to remove any radical elements that might dismantle their classificatory systems. She explains, "Any given system of classification must give rise to anomalies, and any given culture must confront events which seem to defy its assumptions. It cannot ignore the anom-alies which its scheme produces, except at risk of forfeiting confidence. This is why . . . we find in any culture worthy of the name various provisions for dealing with ambiguous or anomalous events."[28] Douglas describes five distinct order-enforcing reactions to those events that defy collocation in existing schema, but the first two of these are the most relevant to our argument here. The first provi-sion involves reducing ambiguity through interpretation, while the second requires physically controlling (destroying) the anomaly. So powerful is the destabilizing force of the hybrid creature that both Straparola and Varchi must employ not one but both of these provisions in their texts in order to neutralize it.

Before the reader arrives at the happy ending that reinstates the clear divi-sion between animals and humans, which Isabella enthusiastically endorses at the beginning of the novella, the monster must undergo a double-erasure. The first of these is a sort of intellectual cancellation that occurs when Galeotto concludes, by scholastic reasoning, that the pig progeny must be his own flesh and blood. Despite all appearances, and even though no rational explanation can be found for the child's irregular form and behavior, Galeotto decides that his malformed prog-eny is not a beast but a rational creature. The second erasure of the monster regards its physical nature and begins shortly after the pig boy's marriage to his third wife, Meldina. Her accepting love quite literally transforms the pig from a dirty swine into an affectionate spouse. One evening soon after the wedding, the pig king peels off his pigskin, drops it beside the bed, and reveals himself to be a handsome young man, a metamorphosis he reverses each morning. When Mel-dina becomes pregnant, Galeotto's fear of interspecies transgression resurfaces, for he knows nothing of his son's temporary nocturnal metamorphoses. The deliv-ery of a normal (human) son dispels these anxieties: "al Re e alla Reina fu di grandissimo contento, e massimamente che non di bestia, ma di creatura umana teneva la forma" (the king and queen were very happy and chiefly because he did not have the form of a beast, but of a human [*Piacevoli*, 1:78]). The agnatic line, seemingly interrupted by the birth of the pig boy, continues with the birth of his human son.

One day Meldina confesses to the queen that she has not married a beast but a handsome and virtuous youth. That night when the queen and king steal into the young couple's bedroom, they are overcome with joy to see their son, no longer a swine but a man, dozing beside his wife. The queen quickly seizes the pigskin, and the king orders that this hide be shredded into tiny pieces: "tutta minutamente stracciata" (*Piacevoli*, 1:79). Galeotto's order to shred his son's animal hide elim-inates the pig boy's monstrosity by physically destroying its outward sign. Not surprisingly, it is ultimately the action of the king—the male—that removes the final traces of the disorder created by the female body. The novella concludes with the pig king's ascension to the throne, after which he and his family live hap-pily ever after ("lungo tempo felicissimamente visse" [*Piacevoli*, 1:79]). The monster is undone, the threat to the division between the animal and the human is removed, and the natural order is restored.

In Varchi's lecture, the first erasure of the monster was physical, occurring when the canine-human hybrid perishes at the stake. The French king's order, like Galeotto's command to shred his son's skin, restores epistemological and civil order by physically destroying the offending bodies. The second erasure occurs in Varchi's commentary on the events and is essentially an intellectual negation of the hybrid's double nature. Varchi tells his audience that the notion of such monstrous hybrids

> è tanto lontano da' filosofi, che una spezie perfetta possa generare un'altra spezie diversa da sè, che essi non vogliono ancora che si possa generare mostro alcuno di due spezie diverse, come molti affermano di aver veduto, come, esempi grazia, un fanciullo col capo di bertuccia, o di cane, o di cavallo, o d'altro animale, o un vitello, o cane, o bue col capo d'uomo. (*Opere*, 2:666)

> (is so far from the teachings of the philosophers, that a perfect species can engender another species different from itself, that they do not yet admit that any such monster can be engendered by two species, as many attest to having seen: for example, a lad with the head of a monkey, or of a dog, or of a horse, or of another animal; a calf or dog or ox with the head of a man.)

With this appeal to ancient philosophers, the humanist Varchi neutralizes the threat that the dog boy posed to the Christian hierarchy of being. Furthermore, he moves beyond this specific case to summarily dismiss the possibility that any animal-human hybrid could be formed in nature. Like Galeotto, Varchi declares that the anomalous birth was human. Thus two texts that at first appear to belong to drastically different genres—one an academic lecture based on humanist philosophy, the other a narrative that attributes monstrous births to fairy spells—perform the same double-erasure, intellectual and physical, of the animal-human hybrids depicted in their pages.

Once we understand the cultural anxieties that inform the scenes of monstrous births in *Le piacevoli notti*, we can clearly see that a coherent interpretation of the entire novella of the pig king forces us to shift our critical focus from issues of sexual initiation, seen by critics like Bettelheim as central to the interpretation of animal-bridegroom tales, and to redirect our gaze toward issues of generation and lineage. Isabella sets her novella in the recent past in "England," but a close analysis of the events that follow Galeotto's rejection of infanticide reveals that this novella is an apt reflection of the interactions of gender, family, and politics unique to the *brigata*'s own cultural milieu: sixteenth-century Venice. The preoccupation with lineage, the intertwined fates of the family and the state, and the difficulties of arranging a suitable marriage for the pig boy in this novella replicate the social realities of the young, unmarried patrician male. The Venetian

Republic was an aristocratic oligarchy in which "the Venetian noblemen . . . are the state itself."[29] The Great Council that governed the Republic was composed of patrician males who acquired the privilege and responsibility of governance through agnatic descent. Male identity lay at the heart of the establishment of entitlement, and young male patricians were required to present detailed documentation of their ancestry in order to be inducted into the Great Council.[30]

Guido Ruggiero demonstrates that in early modern Venice young, unmarried male patricians were often perceived as destabilizing elements capable of upsetting societal order, a description that we could also apply to the pig boy in Straparola's novella. Whereas women tended to be married off at puberty or shortly thereafter, men married much later, granting them a period of "adolescence." "This period was viewed with ambivalence; these young males—attractive as future scions of their families—were also feared in practice, as well as often uneasily laughed about in literature for their tendencies to deflower daughters, commit adultery with wives, and disturb the calm disciplined flow of business in urban society."[31] The rulers of the Venetian Republic feared that these young men, lacking a licit outlet for their sexual energy, would turn to illicit and unnatural activities, including fornication or sodomy, in order to satisfy their urges. Because "[a]dultery, fornication, rape, homosexuality, and other sexual acts labeled criminal threatened the stability and order of family and community,"[32] already in the fifteenth century the Republic began to enact stricter laws and enforce them with greater vigor in an effort to regulate sexual practice and thus maintain civic order. Marriage offered a means by which to satisfy the disruptive sexual desire of the young patrician male; however, "the strong pressure on nobles to marry within their rank," coupled with fewer marriageable women due to skyrocketing dowries, led to a tightening of the marriage market and a subsequent decline in patrician marriages beginning in the latter half of the sixteenth century (Sperling, 19). As a result, patrician males occasionally "lowered their standards," so to speak, by marrying the non-noble daughters of wealthy merchants (Sperling, 20).

In *Le piacevoli notti* animal-human hybrids are born only to noble couples whose marriages have not yet produced an heir. At the outset of each of these novellas, the fate of the aristocratic line, and thus the fate of the state, remains uncertain as the noble spouses await the birth of a child. The symbiosis of family and government in these novellas mirrors the interrelationship of these very institutions in the Venetian Republic. In both the historical maritime republic and the fictional English kingdom of the novella, any interruptions in the aristocratic lineage erodes the very foundations of the state.

In a world in which the public and private are inextricably bound together, it would be naïve to think that Galeotto's desire to preserve his wife's reputation and the need to maintain order would be sufficient motivation to contemplate infanticide. Any rumors of bestiality would raise doubts regarding the purity of the royal line and in turn would threaten the pig boy's right to the throne. What

sways Galeotto from his initial resolve is the conviction that the pig boy "era generato da lui ed era il suo sangue" (was generated by him and was his blood
[*Piacevoli*, 1:72]). The patriarch's word discounts the pig boy's monstrosity and
testifies to his royal heritage, thus securing him the right to govern. Galeotto's
assertion of paternity, however, does more than simply attest to his son's noble
ancestry. In early modern Venice, as throughout most of Europe, the "prevailing
values tied man's honor to control over their womenfolk's sexuality" (Chojnacki,
175). Thus such rumors of an impure coupling would not only defile Ersilia's reputation, but it also—and perhaps more important—would put Galeotto's masculinity into question by implying that he was unable to control his wife's
perverse appetite. The articulation of genealogy, while preserving the king's masculinity, does not completely annul the destructive power of the pig boy's existence: it is not simply a rumor that threatens to undermine the king's authority.

Although the pig king "parla umanamente" (speaks like a human), his
porcine morphology and comportment seem to contest the validity of the pater-
nal word, for the pig boy appears better adapted to the dung heap than to the
court. Instead of dedicating himself to the study of statecraft, this prince spent
his days wandering about the city, and "dove erano l'immondizie e le lordure, sì
come fanno i porci, dentro se li cacciava" (he got into wherever there was
garbage and filth, just as pigs do [*Piacevoli*, 1:73]). When the pig boy demanded
that his parents find him a bride, his mother responded by pointing out the
impossibility of her son's request: "O pazzo che tu sei, chi vuoi tu che per marito ti prenda? Tu sei puzzolente e sporco, e tu vuoi che un barone o cavaliere sua
figliuola ti dia?" (*Piacevoli*, 1:73) (Oh, are you crazy? Who do you think would
take you as a husband? You are smelly and dirty, and you want a baron or
courtier to give you his daughter?). It appears that, even if the pig ascends the
throne, he will do so alone; Galeotto and Ersilia's line will end with their malformed son, because the pig boy's stench and his uncivilized behavior drastically
restrict the pool of available brides. He finds a bride in this tight marriage market
by marrying below his station, perhaps comforted by the fact that his own offspring, although born to a common mother, will be able to prove their nobility
through their father's line. Like some Venetian patricians in Straparola's day, the
pig boy adopts the strategy of "marrying down" as a means for continuing his
family line despite the dearth of noble brides. The pig boy's diminished
prospects for a bride also indirectly harm the realm by removing the possibility
of creating politically fruitful alliances through marriage. Whereas his parents'
marriage served to unite two nations—Ersilia is the daughter of King Mattias of
Hungary—the pig boy's betrothal creates no advantageous political ties. Eventually, the pig boy's sexual desire, like that of the young male patricians described
by Ruggiero, becomes a direct threat to the security of the kingdom. After having gored his first wife to death, the pig boy demands a second one, a request initially refused by his mother. He reacts violently, "minacciando di porre ogni cosa

in roina" (threatening to destroy everything [*Piacevoli*, 1:75]). This overt challenge to authority so riles Galeotto that he once again contemplates killing his son, but Ersilia's maternal love diffuses her husband's murderous rage and they eventually cede to their son's demand. Only after the pig boy has been civilized through his marriage and his bestial hide destroyed do the threats to the security of the kingdom cease.

The pig boy is both a biological and a social monster who simultaneously menaces taxonomy and civic order. In Straparola's novella, the unmarried patrician pig boy's desire, frustrated in a restricted marriage market—albeit limited by his own deformity—becomes a disruptive force that challenges the throne and leads to acts of uxoricide. Whereas Galeotto erases the biological monster through scholastic theory and the physical destruction of the pig's hide, the social monster is erased through marriage to a woman who, although not of noble blood, succeeds in fulfilling her husband's desires and perpetuating the agnatic line. The pig king, like many social monsters, is "transgressive, too sexual, perversely erotic, a lawbreaker; and so the monster and all that it embodies must be . . . destroyed" (Cohen, 16). Isabella's story delights the *brigata*, and they can laugh at "messer lo porco tutto inlordato che accarezzava la sua diletta moglie, e, così impiastracciato da fango, con lei giaceva" (Monsieur Pig, completely filthy, who was caressing his dear wife and so smeared with mud lay with her [*Piacevoli*, 1:79]), precisely because the need for the destruction of the monster is fulfilled by the end of the novella. Ultimately, Isabella's novella functions to assuage not only early modern anxieties concerning the instability of the boundary between the animal and the human, but also to allay the *brigata*'s fear of the unmarried patrician male whose unbridled sexual desire threatens Venetian society. Like Varchi and Galeotto, Isabella performs a sort of double erasure at the end of her novella by eliminating both the biological and social monstrosity that the pig boy represents.

Notes

1. Juan Huarte, *Essame* [sic] *degl'ingegni degli huomini*, trans. Camillo Camilli (Venice: Aldo Manuzio, 1586), 347. Except as noted, all translations are my own.

2. Ambroise Paré, *On Monsters and Marvels*, trans. Janis L. Pallister (Chicago: The University of Chicago Press, 1982), 58; hereafter cited in text as Paré.

3. Giambattista Della Porta, *De' miracoli et meravigliosi affetti della natura prodotti* (Venice: Gio. Giacomo Carlino, 1611), 86r.

4. Sperone Speroni, *Dialoghi* (Venice: Domenico Gigli, 1558), 47r, emphasis added.

5. Vladimir Propp, *Morphology of the Folktale*, trans. Laurence Scott, 2nd rev. ed. Louis A. Wagner (Austin: University of Texas Press, 1996); Max Lüthi, *The European Folktale: Form and Nature*, trans. John D. Niles, Translations in Folklore Studies (Philadelphia: A Publication of the Institute for the Study of Human Issues, 1982).

6. Italo Calvino, "La tradizione popolare nelle fiabe," in *Sulla fiaba*, ed. Mario Lavagetto, Saggi brevi, no. 1 (Turin: Einaudi, 1988), 114, emphasis in original.

7. See, for example, Giorgio Bàrberi Squarotti, "Problemi di tecnica narrativa cinquecentesca: Lo Straparola," *Sigma* 5 (1965): 85–108; Stefano Calabrese, "L'enigma del racconto. Dallo Straparola a Basile," *Lingua e stile* 18.2 (1983): 177–98; Marziano Guglielminetti, *La cornice e il furto: studi sulla novella del '500*, La Parola letteraria, no. 7 (Bologna: Zanichelli, 1984), 79–99; and Mario Petrini, *La fiaba di magia nella letteratura italiana*, Università degli Studi di Trieste, Facoltà di Magistero, 3ª ser., no. 10 (Udine: Del Bianco Editore, 1983), 153–65.

8. See Letterio Di Francia, *La novellistica*, 2 vols., Storia dei generi letterari italiani (Milan: F. Vallardi, 1924), 2:716; and Alberto Chiari, "La fortuna di Boccaccio," in *Questioni e correnti di storia letteraria*, ed. Umberto Bosco, Problemi ed orientamenti critici di lingua e di letteraria italiana, no. 3 (Milan: C. Marzorati, 1949), 327, n. 80.

9. Renzo Bragantini, *Il riso sotto il velame: la novella cinquecentesca tra l'avventura e la norma*, Saggi di "Lettere italiane," no. 37 (Florence: Leo S. Olschki, 1987), 11.

10. Giovanfrancesco Straparola da Caravaggio, *Le piacevoli notti . . . nelle quali si contengono le favole con i loro enimmi* [sic] *da dieci donne e duo giovani raccontate*, ed. Giuseppe Rua, 2 vols., Collezione di opere inedite o rare dei primi tre secoli della lingua, [nos. 81 and 97] (Bologna: Romagnoli-Dall'Acqua, 1899 and 1908), 1:72; hereafter cited in text as *Piacevoli*.

11. Erica Fudge, *Perceiving Animals: Humans and Beasts in Early Modern English Culture* (New York: St. Martin's Press, 2000), 64.

12. Stith Thompson, *Motif-Index of Folk Literature: A Classification of Narrative Elements in Folktales, Ballads, Myths, Fables, Mediaeval Romances, Exempla, Fabliaux, Jest-Books, and Local Legends*, rev. and enlarged ed., 6 vols. (Bloomington: Indiana University Press, 1966), vol. 1:461, motif B601.8; D. P. Rotunda, *Motif-Index of the Italian Novella in Prose*, Indiana University Publications, Folklore Series, no. 2 (Bloomington: Indiana University Press, 1942), 5, motif B601.8; Marina Warner, *From the Beast to the Blonde: On Fairy Tales and Their Tellers* (New York: The Noonday Press/Farrar, Straus, and Giroux, 1996), 274. See also Bruno Bettelheim, *The Uses of Enchantment: The Meaning and Importance of Fairy Tales* (1976; reprint, New York: Vintage Books, 1977), 282; hereafter cited in text as Bettelheim.

13. Pierre Boaistuau, *Histoires prodigieuses* (Paris: Pour Vincent Norment et Jehanne Bruneau, 1564), 18.

14. Joyce E. Salisbury, *The Beast Within: Animals in the Middle Ages* (New York: Routledge, 1994), 4; hereafter cited in text as Salisbury.

15. All citations from the Bible follow readings found in *The New English Bible with the Apocrypha: Oxford Study Edition*, gen. ed. Samuel Sandmel (Oxford: Oxford University Press, 1979).

16. Jeffrey Jerome Cohen, "Monster Culture (Seven Theses)," in *Monster Theory: Reading Culture*, ed. Jeffrey Jerome Cohen (Minneapolis: University of Minnesota Press, 1996), 6; hereafter cited in text as Cohen.

17. Paula Findlen, *Possessing Nature: Museums, Collecting, and Scientific Culture in Early Modern Italy*, Studies on the History of Society and Culture, no. 20 (Berkeley: University of California Press, 1994), 71.

18. Georges Canguilhem, "Monstrosity and the Monstrous," *Diogenes* 40 (1962): 27.

19. On the interpretations of the monster in the teratatological canon in these and other classical sources, see Zakiya Hanafi, *The Monster in the Machine: Magic, Medicine, and the Marvelous in the Time of the Scientific Revolution* (Durham, N. C.: Duke University Press, 2000), 6–14.

20. Conrad Lycosthenes, *Prodigiorum ac ostentorum chronicon* (Basle: Per Henricum Petri, 1557); Ulisse Aldrovandi, *Monstrorum historia* (Bologna: Nicolai Tebaldini, 1642); Fortunio Liceti, *De monstrorum caussis, natura, et differentiis*, 2nd rev. ed. (Padua: Paulum Frambottum, 1634).

21. Benedetto Varchi, "Della generazione de' mostri," *Opere*, ed. A[ntonio] Racheli, 2 vols., Biblioteca classica italiana. Secolo XVI, no. 6 (Trieste: Sezione letterario-artistica del Lloyd austriaco, 1858–1859), 2:666; hereafter cited in text as *Opere*.

22. Pierre J. Payer, *Sex and the Penitentials: The Development of a Sexual Code 550–1150* (Toronto: University of Toronto Press, 1984), 5; hereafter cited in text as Payer.

23. On the use of violence to restore order in the novellistic as well as the social worlds, see the essays by Cormac Ó Cuilleanáin and Michael Papio, chapters 3 and 7 in this volume.

24. Tommaso Garzoni, *Il serraglio degli stupori del mondo* (Venice: Ambrosio et Bartolomeo Dei Fratelli, 1613), 41.

25. Martin Weinrich, *De ortu monstrorum commentarius* (n.p.: Sumptibus Heinrici Osthusii, 1595), 56v.

26. Ottavia Niccoli, "Menstruum quasi Monstrorum: parti mostruosi e tabù mestruali nel '500," *Quaderni storici* 44 (1980): 404.

27. Pliny the Elder, *Natural History: A Selection*, trans. John F. Healy, Penguin Classics (London: Penguin Books, 1991), 80.

28. Mary Douglas, *Purity and Danger: An Analysis of the Concepts of Pollution and Taboo*, 2nd ed. (New York: Routledge, 1999), 40.

29. Jutta Gisela Sperling, *Convents and the Body Politic in Late Renaissance Venice*, Women in Culture and Society (Chicago: The University of Chicago Press, 1999), 2; hereafter cited in text as Sperling.

30. Stanley Chojnacki, *Women and Men in Renaissance Venice: Twelve Essays on Patrician Society* (Baltimore: The Johns Hopkins University Press, 2000), 30–31; hereafter cited in text as Chojnacki.

31. Guido Ruggiero, "Marriage, Love, Sex, and Renaissance Civic Morality," in *Sexuality and Gender in Early Modern Europe: Institutions, Texts, Images*, ed. James Grantham Turner (Cambridge: Cambridge University Press, 1993), 17.

32. Ruggiero, *The Boundaries of Eros: Sex Crime and Sexuality in Renaissance Venice*, Studies in the History of Sexuality (Oxford: Oxford University Press, 1985), 9.

11

The Motif of the Woman in Male Disguise from Boccaccio to Bigolina

Christopher Nissen

The Italian fascination for literary works that include female characters who dress and act as men is remarkably pervasive in the Middle Ages and Renaissance, spanning a variety of genres including *cantari*, epic poems, comic plays, and novellas.[1] The popularity of the motif in the late medieval and Renaissance novella is attested by D. P. Rotunda, who lists no fewer than thirty-one instances in his *Motif-Index of the Italian Novella in Prose*. This preponderance becomes all the more remarkable when one considers the fact that Rotunda's list is rather inaccurate and fails to include a considerable number of relevant stories.[2]

For the most part, the early Italian novellas employing this motif fall into two broad categories. The first category includes tales of amorous intrigues and *beffe*, the practical jokes that are so common in the Italian novella; here the disguised characters are rarely well developed, and often their disguised state is of relatively brief duration.[3] In the second category, which includes the type of love story that Mario Baratto has called *novella-romanzo* in the context of the narrative modes of Boccaccio's *Decameron*, the motif is much more amply developed and tends to confer far greater power and freedom of movement on the disguised character.[4] Such stories typically follow narrative patterns that derive from the ancient Greek romances, including pairs of separated lovers or spouses who become involved in a series of disasters and journeys marked by abrupt shifts in fortune, often ending with a recognition scene and a joyful reunion. In many of these stories, heroines must disguise themselves as men as a result of danger or desperate need in order to facilitate their movements in male-dominated social spheres. I will begin this essay by tracing some of the salient aspects of this motif as it appears in various *novelle-romanzi* from Boccaccio to the sixteenth century. I will then seek to demonstrate how the motif attains the apex of its development—with truly unique social implications—in the works of Giulia Bigolina, the first woman to have gained any renown for her contributions to the Italian novella and romance in prose.[5]

Early examples of male disguise in *novelle-romanzi* appear in two tales of Boccaccio's *Decameron*, Day Two, Stories 3 and 9. It is altogether appropriate that these stories appear in the second day, which bears a theme conducive to plots with romance elements: protagonists suffering from the effects of adverse fortune ultimately arrive, after many adventures, at a happy ending that they could not have foreseen. *Decameron* II, 3 tells of a young man who shares a bed with an abbot, only to find he is lying beside the daughter of the king of England in disguise; ultimately he marries her and regains his lost fortune. With respect to the present study, *Dec.* II, 9, the tale of Zinevra and Bernabò, is the more important of the two, because it contains a type of disguised female character that will recur in many subsequent narratives, including Bigolina's.

Bernabò Lomellin, a Genoese merchant conducting business in Paris, wagers with the unscrupulous Ambruogiuolo that the latter will not succeed in seducing Bernabò's wife, Zinevra, left behind in Genoa. Ambruogiuolo soon finds out that Bernabò's claim is true, for Zinevra is far too virtuous; nonetheless, he manages through trickery to acquire apparent proof of his success, whereupon Bernabò pays his part of the wager and then orders a servant to take Zinevra to a remote spot and murder her. However, Zinevra is able to convince the servant to spare her life. She also has the presence of mind to obtain male garments from him that allow her to create a male persona for herself in the midst of the harsh world in which she has been abandoned. Boccaccio underscores this process of transformation: he describes the fashioning of her costume and the cutting of her hair in great detail. In fact, as Guido Almansi has noted, he devotes far less space to many of her subsequent actions in order to impress upon the reader that this character is a model of cleverness and self-control.[6] It might also be said that this description stresses the completeness of her transformation to the extent that by the time she has assumed a masculine name and hired herself out as a seaman to a Catalan ship owner, on a grammatical level the text has subtly changed her from a woman into a man:

> Col quale *entrata* in parole, con lui s'acconciò per servidore e salissene sopra la nave faccendosi chiamare Sicuran da Finale. Quivi, di miglior panni *rimesso* in arnese dal gentile uomo, lo 'ncominciò a servir sì bene e sì acconciamente, che egli venne oltre modo a grado. (*Dec.* II, 9, 43, emphasis added)

> (Having engaged him in conversation, she made an arrangement with him to work as his servant and went aboard the ship, calling herself Sicuran da Finale. Then, having been fitted out with better clothes by the gentleman, he began to serve him so well and so properly that he made himself exceedingly pleasing to him.)[7]

The change of participle agreement from one sentence to the next (*entrata*, *rimesso*) marks the final phase of the transformation. Once Zinevra has assumed a new name for herself, it is complete: the woman has become a man, free to act in a world completely dominated by men. Sicuran not only survives; "he" even flourishes, ultimately commanding the guards attached to a group of merchants serving the Sultan of Alexandria and acquiring what Almansi calls a "supreme masculine and mercantile attribute," that is, the ability to hoodwink another merchant, none other than Ambruogiuolo himself (Almansi, 136–37). When Sicuran meets Ambruogiuolo in a bazaar and sees that the latter owns items stolen from Zinevra's room in Genoa, Sicuran presses him for his story and at last learns why Bernabò acted so cruelly. Only here, when Sicuran thinks back to past events, does the text slip a bit and describe him with a feminine pronoun: "Sicuran, udendo questo, prestamente comprese qual fosse la cagione dell'ira di Bernabò verso *lei*" (*Dec*. II, 9, 55, emphasis added). (Sicuran, hearing this, immediately understood the reason for the wrath Bernabò had shown *her*.) By now Zinevra is fully able to exploit the advantages of her male disguise, for in prompting Ambruogiuolo to tell his boastful tale of adulterous triumph "man to man" and in pretending to find such an account immensely entertaining, she shows that she has truly learned the finest points of how to mimic men.[8]

In the end, Sicuran/Zinevra brings all the participants in the intrigue together for a dramatic public revelation of long-hidden truths. Zinevra now sheds both her male disguise and her false identity—even baring her breasts before the Sultan's astonished court—and, after all the care Boccaccio has lavished on making us believe the original transformation, he shows us that nothing less than this will suffice for undoing the illusion. Zinevra's transformation into a man, like many that will follow in subsequent narratives, has been a temporary trespass, conceived in a moment of desperation and essential for revealing the hidden strengths and moral steadfastness of the female protagonist who must flee to a strange place and make a new life for herself. As in later stories containing this motif, the transformation must also be carefully done away with as soon as the proper state of things has been restored, so that the false man can once more become a woman and rejoin her place in society.

It is hard not to see a more or less explicit commentary on the roles of the sexes in this story. The story shifts from hard-headed pragmatism (the debate between the merchants and their wager) to the marvelous and fantastic (the adventures of Zinevra in disguise, when she can accomplish great deeds), only to resolve itself in the restoration of Zinevra's and Bernabò's quite traditional and proper marriage, almost as if the betrayal and exile in disguise never took place. We are not told how Zinevra reflects upon her accomplishments, nor how they might have changed her life, after her six-year exile in disguise has ended. Nonetheless, in a marvelous interlude that employs many romance conventions, the character has been allowed to realize her true potential for action. Such characters can also be found in older stories with similar plots, such as the anonymous *Roman dou roi Flore et de la belle Jehanne*. Here Jehanne, after being falsely accused of adultery, disguises herself and finds employment as a squire to her own husband, serving him so cleverly that in the course of several years she makes him quite wealthy.[9]

Although Zinevra and Jehanne are clearly cut from similar cloth, not all the characters of this type exhibit their remarkable strengths and abilities. In Shakespeare's *Cymbeline*, another narrative involving a wager leading to exile in disguise, the woman's accomplishments become considerably less noteworthy. Here, the disguised Imogen scarcely flourishes as a man. She does not engineer her own disguise, commits no extraordinary deeds, and plays only a small role in the final dramatic unmasking of all disguises and deceptions; her cleverness does not lead her to root out and prosecute her betrayer, for instance. Moreover, the text does not go to any lengths to make her truly "become" a man: unlike Boccaccio's tale, we get the impression that Imogen does not really like her disguise, and in any event she is not made to wear it for long. Nonetheless, Boccaccio and Shakespeare have this much in common: they both appreciate the potential for the male disguise to provide a new perspective on relations between the sexes and on sexual roles in the social order.[10]

In the best of these tales, the male disguise serves as a commentary on the distinction between the sexes. What does it mean for a woman to become a man? What can a woman learn and accomplish once she has created this illusion? The late medieval novella and *cantare* provide many examples of women disguised as men who, like Zinevra, find themselves suddenly endowed with remarkable powers. Another type of early tale depicts women as solvers of unresolvable problems, disguised as judges or doctors in order to accomplish things their society would never believe possible for a woman. Examples of this can be found in Ser Giovanni Fiorentino's *Il Pecorone* (IV, 1) and Giovanni Sercambi's *Il Novelliere* (*Exemplo* 4), as well as in Antonio Pucci's *Il Cantare di Madonna Lionessa*. In the first we meet the mysterious and powerful Lady of Belmonte, a character clearly descended from the enchantresses of folklore and medieval romance and one who would later inspire Shakespeare to create his character Portia in *The Merchant of Venice*.[11] In Ser Giovanni's story, the Lady dresses as a judge and alters her features with magic herbs in order to rescue her lover's benefactor from the doom of a pound of flesh imposed on him by a Jewish moneylender; ultimately her task is not only to restore her hapless lover's fortune but also to test his constancy as a lover. In Sercambi's *Exemplo* 4, a fourteen-year-old girl named Calidonia, who has a stupendous capacity to resolve mysteries, dresses as a doctor in order to cure the king of Portugal's supposedly incurable ailment. In a moment of high drama, the girl has the whole court undress, revealing the queen's adulterous union with a man disguised as a female attendant: thus a "proper" gender disguise proves its worth by unmasking an "improper" one. Once the queen and her lover have been executed, Calidonia throws off her disguise and asks to be made the new queen as her reward; to this the king assents, and all live happily ever after. Typically enough for the unsentimental Sercambi, all traces of a tender love story are rejected in favor of an emphasis on practical values: the king is able to get rid of his treacherous wife and at the same time gain a new one whose loyalty, as well as her virginity, are quite manifest. But one feature does link tales of this sort with the model established by Boccaccio's tale of Zinevra: the disguise still functions as an aid to uncovering unjust deeds and rooting out malefactors; in other words, it is perceived to work toward the good of society. A judicial element, including executions or threats of execution, is present in all of these stories, and the person promoting it is always a disguised woman. In Pucci's *cantare*, Madonna Lionessa disguises herself as no less a judge than Solomon himself, allegedly come back to earth in order to rescue her husband from a sentence of mutilation.[12] In Boccaccio's case, however, the injustice has not been committed against others but against the woman herself, who must employ her wiles, as well as her disguise, to restore her good name.

In the novellas of the fifteenth and sixteenth centuries, authors put the male disguise to a wide variety of uses, in both *novelle-romanzi* and tales of *beffe* and adulterous intrigue. If Zinevra's story turned on a false accusation of adulterous love, then the Renaissance novellas that follow its pattern tend to tell of disguised flights from the grave consequences of actual amorous relationships, typically those of young people who are not yet married. The anonymous fifteenth-century "Novella di Ottinello e Giulia," written in verse, might be considered a classic of this type: here a pair of royal lovers elope, but when Ottinello is kidnapped by pirates Giulia is forced to dress as a man, call herself Giulio, and establish a hospice that she runs for many years until a miraculous concatenation of events brings Ottinello to the hospice and allows for a tender recognition scene and eventual marriage.[13] Masuccio Salernitano, in his *Il Novellino*, provides an oddly contrasting pair of tales on this theme, one tragic and grim (Novella 39), the other joyous and triumphant (Novella 43). The first also reveals the influence of the "rescuing woman in disguise" motif of Ser Giovanni and Sercambi, but in this case all is doomed to failure despite the heroic efforts of the disguised heroine Susanna, who attempts to defy her evil fortune and rescue her lover from Moorish pirates. In the end, her lover is killed and, after the customary scene of public revelation of her true gender, Susanna kills herself for grief in the court of the Moorish king. Masuccio's tale of Veronica and Antonio (Novella 43) follows the tale of Zinevra in several details, including the female protagonist's escape from murder at the hands of sympathetic servants and her subsequent employment, disguised as a male courtier, in the service of a duke who values her ability to look after his falcons. However, her accomplishments as a man are nothing like Zinevra's, and indeed she has no legal battle to win nor any cause to outwit men through superior intelligence. Her eventual good fortune is just that, good fortune, little influenced by her own machinations; in that regard her situation stands as part of a diptych on the ways of fortune, a counterpart to the tale of the ill-fated Susanna.

Many sixteenth-century Italian *novellieri* made occasional use of the motif of the male disguise, but no author showed a greater predilection for it than the

Paduan *novelliera* Giulia Bigolina. Although only two of her narratives have survived, they contain no fewer than three female characters disguised as men, including both of her principal protagonists. In her hands, especially in her magnum opus, the prose romance *Urania*, the motif of the male disguise attains its fullest expression and becomes a vehicle for the reexamination of the status of women and the roles of the sexes in society.

Very little is known about Giulia Bigolina, and only since the late 1990s has any biographical research been done on her. She was a married woman of the noble family Bigolino, also known as Bigolin in the Paduan dialect. In accordance with a custom for distinguished women of the Veneto during the Cinquecento, she was given the feminine form of the family name. She apparently lived all her life in and around Padua. Various documents in the Archivio di Stato of Padua give us tantalizing pieces of this author's life. Two notarial documents help us establish a rough time frame for Bigolina's birth: in one, dated 1543, we are told that her father, Girolamo Bigolino, had received a dowry from her mother, Aldovisa Soncin, in 1516; in another, we find Bigolina already married to a certain Bartolomeo Vicomercato in 1534.[14] Thus she was likely born after 1516, but probably not much past 1520, even if we take into consideration the young age at which girls of the time were typically married. Two lists of Bigolina's dowry goods appear in another document.[15] The first of these, dated May 1561, was presented by Bigolina herself ("Beni stabili, li quali possedo io Giulia Bigolina di mia dote" [ASP, *Estimo 1518*, 142r]). In the second list, which is dated March 1569 and was witnessed by her son Silvio Vicomercato, Bigolina is referred to as *quondam*, that is, already deceased (ASP, *Estimo 1518*, 143v). Therefore, we can conclude that the author's life span might be placed sometime between the years 1516 and 1569, and that she could not have been much past the age of fifty when she died.[16]

Contemporary literary texts indicate that Bigolina attained a considerable local reputation as a writer of poems and prose novellas during her life, yet she never managed to see any of her works in print. Two Paduan poets, Giovanni Maria Masenetti and Angelo Leonico, mention her in their works. She is called "dotta" (learned) and given a place of honor in the tenth canto of Leonico's poem *L'amore di Troilo et Griseida*, published in 1553. She is also most likely the Bigolina who appears in a triumphal procession in Masenetti's poem of 1548, *Il divino oracolo*.[17] Bigolina also appears as an interlocutor in an unpublished dialogue, *A ragionar d'amore*, written in around 1554 by another Paduan, Mario Melechini, which is preserved in Besançon, Bibliothèque Municipale, MS 597. The Paduan historian Bernardino Scardeone speaks highly of her, and Pietro Aretino included among his published correspondences three letters he had addressed to her in 1549.[18] One of Bigolina's works was finally printed in 1794 when another Paduan, Anton Maria Borromeo, published her "Novella di Giulia Camposanpiero e di Tesibaldo Vitaliano" in an anthology. This novella includes elements of a frame story that reveal that it was probably meant to be part of a lost or planned novella collection.[19]

"Giulia Camposanpiero" has several remarkable characteristics, including one of the few secret marriages in Renaissance literature that ends well. Bigolina's surviving works indicate her preference for fantasies of love in which female protagonists are endowed with an almost limitless ability to choose the objects of their affection without consulting their families or running grave risks to their honor. Nonetheless, whenever they find it necessary to move about outside their native towns, they invariably decide to dress as men. Giulia Camposanpiero, an aristocratic maiden of fifteenth-century Padua, chooses as her consort the unattainable Tesibaldo Vitaliani, a nobleman who does great deeds yet scorns the company of women. Despite Tesibaldo's attitude, Giulia wins his heart through a combination of boldness and her reputation for virtue. After their secret marriage, Tesibaldo goes to Vienna to serve the Emperor, only to be falsely accused of having an affair with the Emperor's daughter. When he is subsequently condemned to death, Giulia dresses as a man and rides over the Alps, planning to disrupt the execution and bring about her own death at the same time as her husband's. On the day Tesibaldo and the Emperor's daughter are about to be burned at a single stake, Giulia draws a sword and attacks the guards, wounding and killing several of them. Tesibaldo is released when the truth about his alleged crime is revealed. Subsequently the Emperor pardons Giulia for her attack and allows the couple to live happily in great wealth, their marriage no longer kept secret.

As a character, Giulia Camposanpiero clearly belongs to the type of the disguised rescuing wife or lover, exemplified by Pucci's Madonna Lionessa, Ser Giovanni's Lady of Belmonte, Masuccio's Susanna, and others.[20] As in the case of so many of her literary predecessors, Bigolina's character finds her disguise to be a source of unimagined strength and ability, despite the fact that her ultimate goal is not rescue but suicide as a grand gesture of love in the face of hopeless odds. In creating this character, Bigolina sets the stage for a tour de force of male disguise in her only other surviving work, the far more amply developed narrative *Urania*.

Urania has never been published. It exists today in two manuscripts, Trivulziana MS 88 of the Trivulziana Library in Milan, and Patetta MS 358 of the Vatican Library, which is a diplomatic eighteenth-century copy of the Trivulziana codex. Giulio Porro notes that the undated sixteenth-century Trivulziana manuscript might well be an autograph, since the brush-gilded impressions on the leather cover include the initials of the jurist Bartolomeo Salvatico, the person to whom Bigolina dedicated the work; thus it was in all likelihood the presentation copy she sent to him personally.[21] In her dedication, Bigolina refers to Salvatico as "Dottor di Legge" (Doctor of Law) and stresses his youthfulness. Since Salvatico is known to have received his law degree from the University of Padua in

1552, when he was around nineteen years old, this record provides evidence for dating the completion of *Urania*.[22]

Given its length (176 folios in Triv. MS 88) and its subdivision into an introduction and six chapters, *Urania* cannot be called a novella, Borromeo's judgment notwithstanding (Borromeo, 6–7). Instead, it properly belongs in an exiguous and little-studied category of Italian Renaissance literary types, that of the prose romance.[23] Nonetheless it reveals considerable links to the novella tradition, especially in terms of plot, style, and concern for verisimilitude. Bigolina herself refers to it as an "operetta," a little work, and it would seem at this point that she is indifferent to the genre distinctions that she otherwise emphasizes in her proem to "Giulia Camposanpiero." At first she calls the shorter work a novella, only to say later it is really more of an *istoria* because it purports to tell of real historical events (Borromeo, 119–20).[24]

The introduction to *Urania* begins with an allegorical vision, the only depiction of the supernatural in the entire book. Here we find the authorial persona musing over how to leave some token of remembrance to the youthful Bartolomeo Salvatico, of whom she is exceedingly fond. She decides she will leave him a painted portrait of herself, but no sooner has she resolved to do this than she is visited in her room by an allegorical figure, a naked homunculus with a single huge eye who calls himself Judgment. Looking at him in terror, Bigolina's narrative persona also sees her naked reflection in the creature's eye, even though she is actually dressed. She sees stains on her body, which the little man says represent the vices that stain her soul. He claims he has the power to reveal such things to anyone who looks within his eye.

Now the homunculus chides Bigolina's narrative persona for planning to have her portrait painted because it would show bad judgment on her part: it would be a vain and useless gesture for communicating the chaste and heartfelt love she bears Salvatico.[25] In an extended passage, he explains to her how she would do better to leave Salvatico something that she has created herself, within her own Intellect. At this point, the little man disappears in a flash before the narrative persona has even had a chance to thank him. Following his advice, she says she then looked within herself and spontaneously conceived the entire story of Urania, which she will recount as her gift to Salvatico.

Now begins the actual story, the tale of Urania, a young unmarried woman living in Salerno. As in the case of her character Giulia Camposanpiero, Bigolina takes pains to present Urania as someone free to make her own choices in life. Her mother, said to be her only guardian, appears in the story only twice, each time quite briefly (Triv. MS 88, 25v; 170v–71r). Urania loves virtue and rejects all offers of love from men until she meets a certain Fabio who so impresses her with his manners and person that she permits herself to fall in love. For some time, Fabio visits her chastely and they exchange poems; eventually, however, he forgets his love of virtue, allows himself to become attracted to another woman, and finally abandons Urania. Urania is so grief-stricken that she expects to die:

Per lo grande affanno si pensava di certo morire: et perciò per non incorrere in così grande scandalo, com'era di dover così vilmente lasciarsi condure à morte, et per non far del suo male allegra colei, per la quale d'ogni suo contento, et d'ogni sua gioia era priva, deliberossi che che incontrar di ciò le ne potesse di volere sanza indugio vestita da huomo, et sola fuor di Salerno partirsi, et andar pe 'l mondo errando sin tanto che il lungo partire et molti disagi che per lo camino harrebbe sofferti, il soverchio amor che à Fabio portava, anzi più tosto la insania le levasser del cuore, et di se stessa la facesser pietosa: imperciò che di là dove amor scolpito nel cuor le lo haveva, per accidente che incontrar le potesse, non conosceva di poterlosi altrimente levare. (25r–v)[26]

(She felt such boundless grief at this state of affairs that she thought she would surely die. Yet she desired to avoid the great scandal that would arise if she allowed herself to die in such a vile fashion; moreover, she did not wish to give her rival, the one who had deprived her of all her joy and happiness, any cause to rejoice at her demise. Therefore she resolved, no matter what might come from this course of action, to flee Salerno without delay, dressed as a man, and wander the world until such a time as the great suffering and considerable discomfort that she would undergo along the way might free her heart from its excessive, indeed insane, love for Fabio; only thus could she prove merciful to herself. She could think of no other way to remove love from her heart, once it had become engraved therein, unless it be by some accident.)

The motif is old and established, but the motivation is not. Urania's decision to escape her city dressed as a man does not arise from a need to avoid imminent catastrophe or to elope with her beloved, as in the typical *novella-romanzo* going back to the time of Boccaccio. Her choice is partly ethical, to avoid the scandal her death would cause, but more essentially it is therapeutic: she must undergo sufferings in order to free herself from a love that has become insanity. Only in this way can she "prove merciful to herself." The period of self-imposed introspection while wandering, which only the male disguise can make possible, is meant to cure her psychological distress, to cause the "accident" that is necessary to remove Fabio's graven image from her heart.

Separation and wandering are common motifs in the romance tradition, and at times they are associated with the temporary insanity of lovers, as Chrétien de Troyes's Yvain, Tristan of the prose *Tristan*, or Ariosto's Orlando illustrate. Bigolina's Urania is clearly descended from such creations, but she adds thereto a unique dimension: a woman incognito, so she will not be disturbed as she gives vent to grief and undergoes hardships calculated to cure her insanity. Her disguise allows her to do something denied to women of her time: to wander alone in wild places as a cure for the depression caused by lost or unattainable love. What Petrarch does so easily in a lyric context—"Solo e pensoso i più deserti campi / vo mesurando a passi tardi e lenti"[27] (Alone and thoughtful I measure out the most deserted fields, with footsteps lingering and slow)—Bigolina would have her character do as well, but inasmuch as her literary context is that of romance and her protagonist is female, the male disguise becomes an essential component.

Urania composes a long letter to Fabio in which she explains why he has been a fool not to realize she was the best of all possible women and excoriates him for abandoning her for a woman who is more attractive than she is, yet less virtuous. (This passage reveals yet another distinctive aspect of this work: Bigolina's Urania is quite possibly the only heroine of the romance tradition who is not said to be of surpassing beauty!) After sending her letter, Urania wanders off in a daze, letting her horse go where it will, while she weeps and utters bitter laments. North of Naples she encounters a group of young aristocratic women who have met in a wood to debate a *questione d'amore*: How should women choose the best man as a lover? This question is clearly one that is dear to Bigolina, because the search for its answer pervades both of her surviving works. There is no question that in Bigolina's narrative world women should be able to choose the man they wish to fall in love with, and thus she has Urania talk frequently about how a woman should do this properly. The women who listen to her are convinced that Urania is a young man in love who can give them good advice.

Urania's transformation into a man is not as abrupt as Zinevra's. The reader is not expected to forget she is simply a woman in disguise, especially in those passages that describe her as alone and weeping for love of Fabio. Once she is in the company of the women and they ask her name, however, she finds she must call herself Fabio and, just as in the case of Zinevra/Sicuran, the name works like a charm; the narrative ambiguity of identity is supported by grammatical shifts in gender, and the text completes the illusion by referring to her consistently by that name and switching her pronouns and adjectives from feminine to masculine (Triv. MS 88, 41v–42r). The text then makes this sleight of hand official with a bold declaration, unseen in any of the stories of male disguise that we have examined: "Fabio, che di tal nome *la* chiameremo per hora. . . ." (Fabio, as we will call *her* from now on [Triv. MS 88, 42v, emphasis added]). This new Fabio says he has been abandoned by the woman whom he loves and then goes on to give the ladies advice for nearly twelve folios concerning how to choose the best-suited and most virtuous lover (Triv. MS 88, 42v–54r). The irony of all this is quite apparent: in order to teach women how to select lovers, Urania assumes the very identity of the man who failed her and forced her to flee in disguise in the first place. The women imagine this Fabio to be the best of men, especially since he makes many feminist pronouncements and takes the side of women in the love debate. As a result, they invite him to spend the night in their castle. Once more, Bigolina seems intent on creating female characters whose lives are remarkably free and uncircumscribed by convention.

As soon as she is alone again, the text resumes regarding Urania in purely feminine terms. As long as she was thought to be a man by other characters and spoke as one, the reader was made to see her in that guise; the transformation was quite temporary, however, far shorter than Zinevra's. This is underscored by the way she appears on the following day when she subsequently encounters five young men in another woodland setting. She is still in disguise, still riding aimlessly about in a fit of melancholy. These men, who are in love with the five women Urania met the day before, are likewise convinced that she is a man who can dispense good advice, and thus they urge her to hold forth on the differences between men and women. Urania rises to the challenge and defends the female sex quite vehemently, citing numerous examples of great women from ancient history and legend. The men are portrayed as boors: they have gathered in the woods to engage in falconry, not to debate *questioni d'amore*, and they rouse Urania from her reverie by pounding on her with their fists and the pommels of their swords. Moreover, they soon reveal a variety of misogynistic opinions, whereupon Urania gives them a long speech about how women are so often mistreated by men and are scarcely the cause of all evil in the world, as these men are disposed to believe. The men respect her because they believe her to be a very wise young man, and in time she sways them with her arguments. However, it must be noted that throughout this episode Urania does not call herself Fabio, and the text no longer contains any grammatical shifts in gender. The reader is not allowed to forget another supreme irony at work here: women are being artfully and eloquently defended by a woman, but she is only taken seriously because she is thought to be a man. Midway through her discourse Urania makes a declaration that, by the story's conclusion, will take on great significance because the man in question is clearly meant to be the faithless Fabio and the woman none other than Urania herself: "Et conchiudiamo ancora potersi beato chiamar quell'huomo, al quale da Cieli fu dato in sorte, che valorosa Donna gli fosse compagna" (Triv. MS 88, 70v). (And let us also conclude that any man may call himself blessed, if by chance the heavens have given him an excellent woman as a consort.)

These digressions from the main action are quite extensive, filling some thirty-six folios of the manuscript (Triv. MS 88, 40r–76v), and must be seen as central to the work as a whole. They belong to a romance tradition established in the fourteenth century by Boccaccio in the fourth book of *Il Filocolo*, which contained a famous sequence of similar love debates or *questioni d'amore*. They also show the influence of the didactic love dialogues that were so much in vogue in Bigolina's own time. In his dialogue *A ragionar d'amore*, Melechini makes Bigolina one of his spokespersons for various notions originally expressed in one of the best-known love dialogues, the *Dialoghi d'amore* of Leone Ebreo;[28] in point of fact, however, *Urania* does not appear to have been particularly influenced by Leone's rather abstruse philosophical pronouncements. To date, I have not found any dialogue that appears to have directly inspired her.[29] Nonetheless, similar conversations on the nature and ethics of love had, by her time, already become commonplace in literature, either in dialogue form or as *questioni d'amore* in works of prose fiction.

Urania has now become a teacher, imparting advice to young people who need to learn how to act virtuously and make wise choices. I know of no other work in which a female character fulfills such a role while disguised as a man, and indeed she is all the more successful in the role because she is so disguised. Originally, she assumed a male persona for the simple reason that she needed to wander about alone as a means of preserving her sanity. As her character develops, she realizes the full potential of her disguise as a means of communicating with others, of teaching virtue and correct attitudes. The full didactic scope of the work is taking shape through a unique exploitation of an old novella motif.

Urania has provided comfort to others with her words but has found none for herself. Sadder than ever, she rides on to Tuscany where she collapses in a faint before an inn when she is denied lodging. She is rescued by a young Florentine widow named Emilia, who is staying at the inn with her retinue. Again, Urania assumes the identity of Fabio, more out of convenience than didactic intent, and concocts a story of how "he" was forced to flee Salerno because his lover, a woman named Urania, had betrayed him. Convinced that this Fabio is the best and most courtly of men, Emilia soon falls in love with him and offers him her considerable wealth in marriage, much to the disguised Urania's distress.[30] Speaking as Fabio, Urania says she cannot reciprocate this love in good conscience until she has returned to Salerno to determine once and for all how her affairs stand. Emilia agrees but insists on putting on men's clothing herself and accompanying her beloved, and to this Urania must accede. Thus the two women ride to Salerno both disguised as men, with one of them believing the other actually is a man; clearly Bigolina means to exploit fully the ironic potential of the male-disguise motif.

They arrive in Salerno to find the city in turmoil. This story contains a series of subplots too complicated to recount fully here, but pertinent portions of the main plot can be summarized. Briefly, the real Fabio who abandoned Urania is about to be executed for a bizarre crime that he, driven by his misguided love for the new woman, has committed against the Prince of Salerno. The Prince has proclaimed that Fabio will be released from his doom if any maiden might be found who can kiss a bestial Wild Woman ("la Femina Salvatica") whom he keeps chained up in his palace.[31] The fearsome Wild Woman despises women and will not let one near her; thus, the Prince has imposed a nearly impossible task on the maidens of Salerno. The one who succeeds will be given Fabio's hand in marriage. Many of them risk their lives trying to approach the Wild Woman, some disguised as men (the Wild Woman is very fond of men), but none can succeed in kissing her. All of these women yearn to rescue the dashing Fabio and have him as a husband.

When Emilia and Urania ride up in their disguises, Emilia is confused to hear of this second, apparently doomed Fabio. Her companion is forced to make up another story, explaining that this Fabio is the brother of the fictional Urania with whom "he" is supposedly in love. Emilia boldly says she will rescue this man who clearly means so much to her beloved by kissing the Wild Woman herself. However, when she attempts to do this, she finds she is too terrified of the bestial woman to approach her, despite her professed love for the disguised Urania and her claim that she will undergo any danger for this love. This gives Urania a chance to make yet another didactic pronouncement, because now she can chide Emilia for not being a true lover nor really understanding what it means to be one (Triv. MS 88, 148r–149r). She then dons filthy, foul-smelling men's clothing and goes to the Wild Woman who is fooled by the stench into thinking Urania must be a real man. Thus she kisses Urania many times with great passion and vigor, in front of witnesses.

Bigolina has one last didactic use for this male disguise. Urania now calls for an audience with the Prince and his whole court and asks for Fabio to be present as well. Inventing a third male persona for herself, she claims to be a merchant from Bologna who met the depressed Urania during her travels and heard her tale of woe just before the unfortunate woman killed herself for love of Fabio. Fabio, grief-stricken, says that at last he knows what true love really is and admits what Urania had always been yearning for him to understand: that she was the best of all women. Now Urania finally unmasks herself and invents a final story to preserve the astounded Emilia's honor and good name. Urania, having reassumed her feminine aspect in all ways, is at once betrothed to Fabio, and a suitable match is found for Emilia as well. They all live happily ever after.

Originally, the male disguise in Zinevra's story had served a twofold purpose, allowing a woman to escape danger and simultaneously realize her strengths and abilities by outwitting an unscrupulous man; thus she regains her proper identity and good name. In another early narrative form, women in disguise come to the rescue of the social order by solving crimes or legal questions. In *Urania*, Bigolina seems clearly inclined to conjoin these two categories of novella because her protagonist resembles both Zinevra and the Lady of Belmonte (or perhaps a more successful Susanna) in her escape from danger and in her use of her wits and disguise to right wrongs and rescue her man. Bigolina then goes on to develop the motif to an extent far exceeding that of any narrative in the tradition. Initially, her heroine dons the disguise only to avoid personal scandal and to save herself from a nervous crisis, itself an innovation; in time, other, more useful purposes manifest themselves. First, Urania finds her disguise permits her to hold forth in extended didactic sequences as a lecturer on the proper ways that men and women in love can relate to one another. Through the heartfelt pronouncements of her disguised protagonist, Bigolina clearly hopes to reform and even rescue society from its tendency to demean women. Later, in the climax of the tale, Urania modifies her disguise in order to dupe the Femina Salvatica, thereby symbolically conquering all traces of dangerous feminine "wildness" that must be rejected by any woman who aspires to true virtue. At the same time, she provides yet another demonstration of the powers of a resourceful woman in love. In this fashion, while acting like a man, she rescues her true love from certain death, and thereby finally resolves the personal psychological crisis that prompted her flight in the first place.

Ten years before the birth of Shakespeare, Giulia Bigolina had already embarked on the course the great playwright would follow, that is, to reveal the degree to which a clever writer might exploit the full creative and expressive potential of the old Italian novella motifs. In Bigolina's hands, the motif of the woman in disguise becomes a grand vehicle for pronouncements on social reform, as well as a means for reexamination of the roles of the sexes and the status of women in society.

Notes

An earlier version of this essay was read at the Thirty-Fifth International Congress on Medieval Studies, Western Michigan University, Kalamazoo, Michigan, on May 6, 2000.

1. For the prevalence of this motif, especially in romances and novellas antedating the *Decameron* or contemporaneous with it, see Maria Bendinelli Predelli, "Lettura in filigrana della novella di Zinevra (*Decameron* II.9)," in *Da una riva all'altra. Studi in onore di Antonio D'Andrea*, ed. Dante della Terza (Fiesole: Cadmo, 1995), 175–76, 185–86; and Valerie R. Hotchkiss, *Clothes Make the Man: Female Cross-Dressing in Medieval Europe*, The New Middle Ages, no. 1 (New York: Garland, 1996), 83–124; hereafter cited as Hotchkiss.

2. D. P. Rotunda, *Motif-Index of the Italian Novella in Prose*, Indiana University Publications, Folklore Series, no. 2 (Bloomington: Indiana University Press, 1942), 125, motif K1837. Novellas that Rotunda fails to mention for this motif include Boccaccio's *Decameron* (ed. Vittore Branca, 2 vols., Einaudi Tascabili. Classici, no. 99 [1980; reprint, Turin: Einaudi, 1992]), II, 9; Simone Prodenzani's "Il Sollazzo e il Saporetto *con altre rime*" (ed. Santorre Debenedetti, *Giornale storico della letteratura italiana* 15 [1913]: 3–208), Novella 1; Giovanni Sabadino degli Arienti's *Le Porretane* (ed. Bruno Basile, I Novellieri italiani, no. 13 [Rome: Salerno Editrice, 1981]), Novella 11; Masuccio Salernitano's *Il Novellino* (ed. Alfredo Mauro, rev. ed. Salvatore S. Nigro, Universale Laterza, no. 530 [1940; reprint, Bari: Editori Laterza, 1979]), Novella 40; and Giovanfrancesco Straparola's *Le piacevoli notti* (ed. Giuseppe Rua, 2 vols., Collezione di opere inedite o rare [nos. 81 and 97], [Bologna: Romagnoli-Dall'Acqua, 1899 and 1908]), IV, 1; hereafter cited in text as *Decameron*, *Sollazzo*, *Novellino*, and *Piacevoli*, respectively. Rotunda also includes some stories that do not display the motif, such as *Novellino* 34; *Piacevoli*, III, 4; and Giovanni Sercambi's *Il Novelliere* (ed. Luciano Rossi, 3 vols., I Novellieri italiani, no. 9 [Rome: Salerno Editrice, 1974]), *Exemplo* 56; hereafter cited in text as *Novelliere*. Rotunda does not include Giulia Bigolina in any part of his study, despite his evident familiarity

with *Notizia di Novellieri italiani posseduti dal conte Anton Maria Borromeo, gentiluomo padovano, con alcune novelle inedite*, ed. A. M. Borromeo (Bassano: Remondini, 1794)—hereafter cited in text as Borromeo—in which Bigolina's "Novella di Giulia Camposanpiero" was published (119–46) and which he cites in his bibliography (Rotunda, xx).

3. Examples of this type include *Sollazzo*, 1; *Novelliere, Exemplo* 7; *Novellino*, 11 and 40; and Matteo Bandello's Novellas III, 47 and IV, 7 (*Tutte le opere*, ed. Francesco Flora, 2 vols., I Classici Mondadori [1934; Verona: Arnoldo Mondadori Editore, 1966]).

4. For the term *novella-romanzo*, see Mario Baratto, *Realtà e stile nel* Decameron, Nuova biblioteca di cultura, vol. 244 (Rome: Editori Riuniti, 1984), 129; and Guido Guglielmi, "Una novella non esemplare del *Decameron*," *Forum Italicum* 14.1 (1980): 33. For an extensive discussion of the relationship between novella and romance, see Paul Zumthor, *Toward a Medieval Poetics*, trans. Philip Bennett (Minneapolis: University of Minneapolis Press, 1992), 285–334.

5. See Giambattista Passano, *I novellieri italiani in prosa*, Part 1 (Turin: Paravia, 1878), 325–26, 414–15, for mention of two other sixteenth-century Italian women active after Bigolina who occasionally wrote novellas: Moderata Fonte and Lucrezia Marinella.

6. See Guido Almansi, "Lettura della novella di Bernabò e Zinevra (II, 9)," *Studi sul Boccaccio* 7 (1973): 135–36; hereafter cited in text as Almansi.

7. All translations from Italian are mine. The evolution of the treatment of Zinevra's transformation by Boccaccio's various translators could be a study in itself, ranging from John Payne's painstaking footnotes documenting the shift in grammatical gender to the remarkable decision on the part of Musa and Bondanella to keep Sicuran feminine throughout the entire episode. See *The Decameron of Giovanni Boccaccio*, trans. John Payne (New York: Black, n.d.), 116–17; and *The Decameron*, trans. Mark Musa and Peter Bondanella (New York: Penguin/New American Library/Mentor, 1982), 146–51.

8. For the notion of Sicuran as Zinevra's "masculine double," which permits her to reveal her true qualities, see Elisabetta Menetti, *Il Decameron fantastico* (Bologna: Cooperativa Libraria Universitaria Editrice Bologna, 1994), 60. For a study of how this novella emphasizes Zinevra's masculine attributes both before and after assuming her disguise, and the fleeting nature of her "challenge to cultural gender," see Hotchkiss, 89–91.

9. Under the name Jehan, and with pronouns altered, this woman shows great skill both in baking bread and in running a hostelry; see *Théatre français au moyen âge*, ed. Francisque Michel (Paris: Firmin-Didot, 1885), 417–30. On the further implications of Jehanne's cross-dressing, see Hotchkiss, 91–95.

10. See Almansi, 136. Imogen, in her first soliloquy as a boy, finds a man's life uncomfortable and later expresses a fear of swords and fighting; see William Shakespeare, *Cymbeline. The Complete Pelican Shakespeare*, ed. Robert B. Heilman (New York: Penguin Books, 1969), Act III, Scene 6, ll. 1–4, 25–27.

11. For the sources of this tale, see Ser Giovanni Fiorentino, *Il Pecorone*, ed. Enzo Esposito, Classici italiani minori, no. 1 (Ravenna: Longo Editore, 1974), 87, n. 1;

and Gianfranco Contini, ed., *Letteratura italiana delle origini* (Florence: Sansoni, 1970), 846.

12. See Antonio Pucci, *Madonna Lionessa*, in *Fiore di leggende. Cantari antichi*, ed. Ezio Levi, Scrittori d'Italia [no. 64], Series 1: Cantari leggendari (Bari: Laterza, 1914), 217–27.

13. See Goffredo Bellonci, ed., *Novelle italiane, Vol. I: Dalle origini al Cinquecento* (Milan: Lucarini, 1986), 558–69.

14. See Padua, Archivio di Stato, *Archivio notarile*, vol. 4830: 697r, and vol. 4830: 827r; archive hereafter cited in text as ASP. I am grateful to the Gladys Krieble Delmas Foundation for a grant that allowed me to examine documents in Padua that pertain to Bigolina's life.

15. See ASP, *Estimo 1518, Polizze della città, busta* 34.

16. For a Bigolino family tree that includes Giulia, see Vincenzo Mancini, *Lambert Sustris a Padova. La Villa Bigolin a Selvazzano*, Quaderni di storia locale, no. 5 (Selvazzano: Comune di Selvazzano/Biblioteca Comunale/Centro Culturale, 1993), 148; hereafter cited in text as Mancini.

17. See Angelo Leonico, *L'Amore di Troilo, et Griseida, ove si tratta in buona parte la guerra di Troia* (Venice: Gerardo, 1553), 53v–54r; and Giovanni Maria Masenetti, *Il divino oracolo in lode dei nuovi sposi del 1548 e di tutte le belle gentildonne padovane* (Venice: n.p., 1548), 23r. For Bigolina's role in Leonico's and Masenetti's poems, see Marisa Milani's Introduction to *Il soldato*, by Angelo Leonico, *Quaderni veneti* 13 (June 1991): 15, n. 18, and Mancini, 132, n. 30, respectively.

18. See Bernardino Scardeone, *Historiae de Urbis Patavii* (1560; reprint, Bologna: Forni, 1979), 418–20; and Letters 338, 339, and 353 in Pietro Aretino, *Lettere*, ed. Paolo Procaccioli, 5 vols., Edizione nazionale delle opere di Pietro Aretino, no. 4 (Rome: Salerno Editrice, 1997–), 5:261–62, 276–77. Bigolina is briefly mentioned in the works of many Italian literary critics from the sixteenth to the twentieth centuries, but only Borromeo's research is substantial.

19. See Borromeo, 6–7, 119–46. Padua, Biblioteca Civica, MS 1451 VIII preserves a sixteenth-century exemplar of this novella (improperly described as an eighteenth-century work) which was most likely the source for Borromeo's edition. On the importance of the Camposanpiero and Vitaliani families in medieval Padua, see Padua, Biblioteca Civica, MS 2134, Marcantonio Calza, *Cronica di Padova con l'origine di tutte le notabili famiglie che in quella al presente s'attrovano: 1556*, 5r, 8v; and Theodor Zwinger, *Methodus apodemica in eorum Gratiam, qui cum fructu in quocumque tandem vite genere peregrinari cupiunt* (Strasbourg [Argentinae]: Zetznerum, 1594), 278–79. Although Bigolina makes much of the historical foundations of her story, Borromeo (120–21, 126) finds part of her account inaccurate.

20. For the prevalence of disguised wives who rescue their husbands in medieval German and French literature, see Hotchkiss, 83–89.

21. See Giulio Porro, *Catalogo dei codici manoscritti della Trivulziana*, Biblioteca storica italiana, no. 2 (Turin: Fratelli Bocca, 1884), 31.

22. See Emilia Veronese and Elisabetta della Francesca, eds., *Acta Graduum Academicorum ab anno 1551 ad annum 1565*, Fonti per la storia dell'Università di Padova, no. 16 (Rome/Padua: Antenore, 2001), 79.

23. On the paucity of Italian prose romances in this period and their characteristics, see Adolfo Albertazzi, *Romanzieri e romanzi del Cinquecento e del seicento* (Bologna: Zanichelli, 1891), 3–6; Gino Raya, *Il romanzo*, Storia dei generi italiani (Milan: Vallardi, 1950), 91; and Ginetta Auzzas, "La narrativa veneta nella prima metà del Cinquecento," *Storia della cultura veneta*, eds. Girolamo Arnaldi and Manlio Pastore Stocchi, 6 vols. (Vicenza: Neri Pozza, 1976–1986), 3:134–36.

24. In the preceding century, Masuccio Salernitano had referred to his own collection of novellas as an "operetta" (*Novellino*, 251). For the contemporary use of the term *operetta* to define a prose romance, see Ludovico Corfino, *Istoria di Phileto Veronese*, ed. Giuseppe Biadego (Livorno: Raffaello Giusti, 1899), 5.

25. For a discussion of Bigolina's motif of portraiture, see my "Subjects, Objects, Authors: The Portraiture of Women in Giulia Bigolina's *Urania*," *Italian Culture* 18.2 (2000): 15–31, hereafter cited in text as Nissen.

26. All citations of *Urania* are taken from Milan, Biblioteca Trivulziana, Trivulziana MS 88. The accent marks, punctuation, and spellings in this transcription are those of the manuscript. I have regularized the use of *v* for *u* according to modern norms and have expanded abbreviations without comment. My own edition of Bigolina's works is at press.

27. Francesco Petrarca, *Canzoniere*, ed. Gianfranco Contini, Nuova Universale Einaudi, no. 41 (Turin: Einaudi, 1991), 35, lines 1–2.

28. Besançon, Bibliothèque Municipale, MS 597, 57v–58v, 60r. As an interlocutor in Melechini's text, Bigolina's pronouncements often repeat, almost verbatim, words of the speaker Sofia at the beginning of Leone Ebreo's *Dialoghi d'amore* (ed. Santino Caramella (Bari: Laterza, 1929), 5–6.

29. On the relationship between *Urania* and Renaissance love dialogues, see Nissen, 22–23.

30. On the motif of the cross-dressed woman who unintentionally attracts other women in medieval French romances, see Hotchkiss, 105–24.

31. On the motif of the Wild Man or Wild Woman in art, literature, and history from the Middle Ages to modern times, see Roger Bartra, *The Artificial Savage: Modern Myths of the Wild Man*, trans. Christopher Follett (Ann Arbor: University of Michigan Press, 1997). A fresco by Lambert Sustris in the Villa Bigolin includes a pair of wild men who resemble satyrs (Mancini dustjacket and plate 74). I am grateful to Renzo Bragantini for his suggestion that the Femina Salvatica might well be a role-reversing pun on the name Bartolomeo Salvatico.

Contributors

Gloria Allaire teaches Italian at the University of Kentucky. She is the author of numerous articles and encyclopedia entries on medieval Italian manuscripts, literature, and culture. She has published *Andrea da Barberino and the Language of Chivalry* (University Press of Florida, 1997) and edited the collection of essays *Modern Retellings of Chivalric Texts* (Ashgate, 1999). She has recently completed the first edition with translation of *Il Tristano panciatichiano* (D.S. Brewer, 2002).

Cathy Ann Elias holds the Ph.D. in musicology from the University of Chicago. A violist who studied at Julliard and an Assistant Professor in the School of Music at DePaul University in Chicago, she has presented papers on medieval and Renaissance music. Publications include "Musical Performance in Sixteenth-Century Italian Literature: Straparola's *Le piacevoli notti*" in the journal *Early Music*.

Susan Gaylard is a Ph.D. candidate in the Department of Italian Studies, University of California-Berkeley, where she has already earned her M.A. She has translated entries for *The Dante Encyclopedia*, edited by Richard Lansing (Garland, 2000).

Suzanne Magnanini is Assistant Professor in the Department of French and Italian at the University of Colorado at Boulder. She holds the Ph.D. from the University of Chicago, where she wrote a dissertation on monsters and monstrous births in Straparola's and Basile's tales. Her essays on Basile appear in *Corpi: Storia, metafore, rappresentazioni fra Medioevo ed età contemporanea* (Marsilio, 2000) and in *Seminario sulla poesia* (Longo, forthcoming).

Christopher Nissen is Associate Professor of Italian at Northern Illinois University in De Kalb. His dissertation treated the Italian novella and was later published as *Ethics of Retribution in the Decameron and the Late Medieval Italian Novella: Beyond the Circle* (Mellen, 1993). His articles include studies of Boccaccio, Ser Giovanni Fiorentino, Simone Prodenzani, and Gentile Sermini. His critical edition with translations of the works of Giulia Bigolina is forthcoming.

Cormac Ó Cuilleanáin is a Senior Lecturer and Head of the Department of Italian at Trinity College Dublin. Among his research interests are Boccaccio, narrative literature, and translation studies. He is the author of *Religion and the Clergy in Boccaccio's* Decameron (Edizioni di Storia e Letteratura, 1984) and of "Boccaccio's *Decameron*: The Plot Thickens," in *Italian Storytellers* (Irish Academic Press, 1989), which he coedited. He is currently completing a new translation of the *Decameron* based on John Payne's 1886 version for the Wordsworth Classics of World Literature series (Wordsworth Editions, forthcoming).

Michael Papio holds degrees in Italian Studies from the University of Virginia and Brown University. He is Assistant Professor of Italian in the Department of Modern Languages at College of the Holy Cross. He has published several articles on Boccaccio's *Decameron* and is the coeditor of the Decameron Web. His dissertation has been published as *"Keen and Violent Remedies": Social Satire and the Grotesque in Masuccio Salernitano's* Novellino (Lang, 2000).

Maria Bendinelli Predelli was the Chair of the Department of Italian Studies at McGill University from 1990 to 1999. Her research interests lie primarily in the relationship between French and Italian chivalric literature of the Middle Ages. Her extensive publications include *Alle origini del Bel Gherardino* (Olschki, 1990) and *Cantari e dintorni* (Euroma, 2000).

Myriam Swennen Ruthenberg is Associate Professor of Italian and Comparative Literature at Florida Atlantic University where she heads the program in Italian Studies. Her dissertation at New York University was on Sercambi; recent publications have focused on rereadings of medieval and Renaissance texts in contemporary Italian literature and on the Neapolitan writer, Erri De Luca.

Manuela Scarci is Senior Lecturer in Italian Studies at the University of Toronto. Her research interests include medieval narrative, computer pedagogy, and the Italian Canadian immigrant experience. She has presented or published numerous papers on Bandello, Firenzuola, and the novella tradition after Boccaccio, and she is currently editing a collection of essays entitled *Portraits of Women: Paradigms of Femininity in Italian Literature and Culture*.

Ernesto Virgulti is Assistant Professor of Italian at Brock University, where he teaches courses devoted to language, the literature of various periods, cinema studies, and pedagogy. The same breadth of experience is reflected in his publications. These include the essays "Literary Semiotics in Italy," "Narratology as a Pedagogical Strategy," and "Idiomatic Expressions in English and Italian" and a critical edition of Luigi Pirandello's *Così è (se vi pare)* (Éditions Soleil, 2000).

Domenico Zanrè is a Lecturer in Italian at the University of Glasgow. His papers and publications focus on the literature and cultural institutions of Cinquecento Italy. He is currently preparing for publication *Cultural Non-Conformity in Mid-Sixteenth-Century Ducal Florence*.

Author/Title Index

Alain de Lille, 41, 48n. 24
Albertazzi, Adolfo, 217n. 23
Albertini, Rudolf von, 175n. 3
Aldrovandi, Ulisse (naturalist), 188–189
Alexander of Hales, 190
Allaire, Gloria, 41
Almansi, Guido, 29n. 4, 46n. 1, 65n. 3,
    156nn. 20, 22; 202, 203
Ambrogio, Anthony, 136n. 26
Ambrose, 187
Amore di Troilo et Griseida, L' (Leonico),
    206
Andreas Capellanus, 112–113
Apuleius, 38–39, 48n. 23, 154, 183
Aretino, Pietro, 160, 176nn. 5, 6, 206
Ariosto, Ludovico, 209
Aristotle, 166
    generation, theory of, 4, 11, 35–36, 41,
        188, 192
    poetics, 121
Asolani, Gli (Bembo), 138, 139, 143, 144,
    155n. 7, 156n. 16
Auerbach, Erich, 119, 133
Augustine, 23, 187
Auzzas, Ginetta, 217n. 23

Bakhtin, Mikhail, 8, 122–124, 133, 140,
    142, 145, 157n. 27
Bandello, Matteo, 121, 133, 134n. 7, 161,
    178n. 33, 215n. 3
Baratto, Mario, 30n. 9, 32nn. 23, 24, 201
Barlaam and Josaphat, legend, 23
Barolini, Teodolinda, 4, 33, 80n. 15
Barr, Cyrilla, 85, 102n. 11
Bartra, Roger, 217n. 31
Basile, Giambattista, 1, 53
Beck, Eleonora M., 95, 102
Bellonzi, Fortunato, 46n. 8
Bembo, Pietro, 1, 8–9, 134n. 11, 140
    linguistic precepts, 140, 152, 153,
        156nn. 14, 19, 157n. 24
    literary precepts, 2, 31n. 18, 142, 143,
        144, 145
    neoplatonic ideals of love, 141, 143,
        153, 155n. 7, 156n. 13.
    See also Asolani, Gli; *questione della
        lingua*; *Prose della volgar
        lingua*
Berni, Francesco, 160
Bettelheim, Bruno, 183, 194, 198n. 12
Bible, 1, 70

Genesis 1:26, 28: 187
Gen. 2:7: 35
Gen. 19:24: 40
John 1:1–3: 35
Leviticus 20:15–16: 190
Romans 1:25: 46
Bigolina, Giulia, 11, 202, 205–214
    biography, 206, 216nn. 14, 16
    as interlocutor, 211, 217n. 28
    status as writer, 206.
    See also "Novella di Giulia
        Camposanpiero," *Urania*
Blackburn, Bonnie J., 101
Boaistuau, Pierre, 2, 185
Boccaccio, Giovanni, 1, 2, 3–4, 6, 7, 11,
        12, 15–32, 82, 83, 86, 87, 95, 144,
        152, 157n. 24, 162, 211. *See also*
        characters in *Decameron*; *De
        mulieribus claris*; *Decameron*;
        Filocolo, Il
Boethius, 64
Boiardo, Matteo Maria, 115
Bonciani, Francesco, 121, 125, 134n. 7
Bondanella, Peter, 215n. 7
Bonora, Ettore, 151, 156n. 23
Bonvesin della Riva, 70, 78n. 3
Booth, Wayne C., 8, 30n. 10, 49–50, 140
Bornstein, Daniel, 6, 29n. 6, 87, 93
Borromeo, Anton Maria, 12, 206, 208,
        214–215n. 2, 216nn. 18, 19
Boswell, John, 165, 176n. 9
Botting, Fred, 132
Braccesi, Alessandro, 137
Bracciolini, Poggio, 2
Bragantini, Renzo, 198n. 9, 217n. 31
Branca, Daniela Delcorno, 37
Branca, Vittore, 29n. 5, 30n. 8, 40, 44, 48n.
        23, 64n. 1, 66n. 18
Brand, Peter, 176n. 14
Bray, Alan, 164
Brevio, Giovanni, 122, 134n. 11
Brody, Saul Nathaniel, 135n. 21

Brown, Howard Mayer, 6, 83–85
Brown, Judith C., 177n. 17
Brunhamel, Rasse de, 126, 127–128, 131,
        135n. 19
Bruni, Francesco, 47n. 18
Bryce, Judith, 175–176n. 4
Burrow, J. A., 175n. 1

Calabrese, Stefano, 198n. 7
Calvino, Italo, 181
Calza, Marcantonio, 216n. 19
Canguilhem, Georges, 199n. 18
Cantare di Madonna Elena (anon.), 117n. 1
Cantare di Madonna Lionessa, Il. See
        Pucci, Antonio
Cantarella, Eva, 66n. 14
Capello, Bernardo, 182
Caro, Annibale, 160
Cataudella, Michele, 134n. 6
Catherine of Siena, 85
Cavalca, Domenico, 24, 125
Cavalcanti, Guido, 18, 19, 36, 37
Cellini, Benvenuto, 169, 178n. 29
Cene, Le (Grazzini), 10, 169
    I, 2: 170–172
    II, 7: 172
    II, 8: 163, 172–174
    publishing history, 178n. 28
Centonovelle. See Decameron
Certeau, Michel de, 80n. 17
Cestaro, Antonio, 134n. 8
Chaddock, Charles Gilbert, 177n. 19
Chiffoleau, Jacques, 177n. 22
Chojnacki, Stanley, 196
Chrétien de Troyes, 209
Cino da Pistoia, 18, 19, 44
Cinzio, Giraldi, 133
Clamanges, Nicolas de, 126
Clements, Robert John, 78n. 7
Cohen, Jeffrey Jerome, 187–188, 197
Confessions (Augustine), 23
Corfino, Ludovico, 217n. 24

Croce, Benedetto, 121, 134n. 9, 161, 174, 176n. 12.
  See also aesthetics, Crocean
Cronaca della venuta dei Bianchi e della moria, 87, 92
Croniche di Luccha, Le (Sercambi), 69–72, 79n. 10, 81, 82, 89–90, 92, 93
Cymbeline (Shakespeare), 204

D'Accone, Frank A., 85
Dante Alighieri, 18, 19, 35–36, 39, 44
  Commedia, 17
  Inf.: 39, 41, 123
    V: 37, 60, 65n. 7, 129
    XV: 41–43
    XVI, 124: 78n. 4
    XXI–XXII: 65n. 7, 122
  Purg. XVII, 51: 33
  Par. VI, 127–42: 65n. 7
  Convivio, 138
  Epistle to Cangrande della Scala, 17
  Vita nuova, 138
Daston, Lorraine, 177n. 24
De amore. See Andreas Capellanus
De dictis factisque memorabilibus (Fregoso), 167
De institutione musica (Boethius), 64
"Della generazione de' mostri" (Varchi), 189. *See also* Varchi, Benedetto
De Matteis, Maria C., 47n. 11
De mulieribus claris (Boccaccio), 45
De nugis curialium (Map), 106, 107, 109, 110, 112
De ortu monstrorum (Weinrich), 191
De peccatore cum virgine (Bonvesin della Riva), 78n. 3
De Sanctis, Francesco, 17, 30n. 12. *See also* aesthetics, Romantic
Decameron (Boccaccio), 9, 12, 33–48, 49–67, 86, 95, 123
Del Monte, Alberto, 122, 132, 133
Della Casa, Giovanni, 160

Della Porta, Giambattista, 179
Des monstres et prodiges (Paré), 179
Di Francia, Letterio, 106, 198n. 8
Dialoghi d'amore (Leone Ebreo), 211, 217n. 28
Dialogo del tempo del partorire delle donne (Speroni), 180
Dinucci, Alberto, 72
Dionisotti, Carlo, 156n. 19
Divino oracolo, Il (Masenetti), 206
Dolce Stil Nuovo. See stilnovism
Domenichi, Lodovico, 161
Dominici, Luca, 87, 92
Douglas, Mary (anthropologist), 192–193
Duby, Georges, 29–30n. 6
Durling, Robert M., 41, 47n. 13

Eakin, Paul John, 69
Elias, Cathy Ann, 6, 8, 103n. 18
Eliot, T. S., 65n. 5
Essame degl'ingegni degli huomini (Huarte), 179
European Folktale: Form and Nature, The (Lüthi), 181

Faidit, Gaucelm (troubadour), 111–112, 113
Fantini, Giovanni, 168
Fatini, Giuseppe, 144, 154n. 2, 176n. 11
Fido, Franco, 37
Filocolo, Il (Boccaccio), 114, 211
Findlen, Paula, 188
Firenzuola, Agnolo, 8–9, 10, 159
  aggregation of motifs, 148
  anti–Bemban, 9, 153
  avoids formulating own system, 142, 148, 152, 154
  biography, 137, 159–161
  contradictions in, 143, 147–148, 154
  departure from models, 143, 150, 162, 163, 174
  imitative, 9, 138, 139, 143, 144, 145, 149, 152, 154, 161, 173–174

innovations in, 145, 153, 154, 162, 174
language of, 141–142, 148, 153
licentious elements in, 139, 144, 150
literary production of, 137, 154n. 1, 168,
    176nn. 7, 13
subversion of models in, 9, 139, 141,
    144, 145, 149, 153
texts
    Asino d'oro, L', 154n. 1, 176n. 7
    Dialogo delle bellezze delle donne,
        154n. 1, 160, 177n. 17
    Discacciamento delle nuove lettere,
        137, 154n. 1, 155n. 3, 176n. 13
    Epistola in lode delle donne, 154n. 1
    "In lode del legno santo," 160
    Lucidi, I, 154n. 1, 177n. 25
    "Mentre che dentro a le nefande
        mura," 176n. 7
    *Prima veste dei discorsi degli
        animali, La*, 154n. 1
    Primo libro dell'opere burlesche, Il
        (anthology), 168, 177n. 25
    Prose di Agnolo Firenzuola, Le, 161
    Rime, 168, 177n. 25
    Trinuzia, La, 154n. 1, 177n. 25.
    See also *Ragionamenti, I*
Floridan et Elvide (Brunhamel), 126, 128,
    129, 131
Folena, Lucia, 175n. 2
Fonte, Moderata, 215n. 5
Fontes, Anna, 67n. 21
Forni, Pier Massimo, 31n. 17, 32n. 24,
    66n. 20
Forster, E. M., 65n. 3
Freedman, Alan, 36
Freedman, Paul, 175n. 1
Fregoso, Battista, 167
Fubini, Mario, 7, 120, 122
Fudge, Erica, 198n. 11

Gallo, F. Alberto, 102n. 16
Garzoni, Tommaso, 191

Gaylard, Susan, 4
Gemma ecclesiastica (Giraldus
    Cambrensis), 106–107, 108, 109,
    110, 111, 113
Gibaldi, Joseph, 78nn. 3, 7
Gillaume de Lorris, 47n. 16, 48n. 25. *See
    also Roman de la Rose*
Gillespie, Gerald, 78n. 3
Giovanni Fiorentino, Ser, 6, 11, 106, 108,
    204, 205
Giraldus Cambrensis, 6, 106–107, 108,
    109, 111, 112, 113
Giunta, Bernardo, 161, 168
Giunta, Giacomo, 167
Grazzini, Antonfrancesco, 9, 10, 133, 159,
    160, 163, 167–175
Greenblatt, Stephen, 166
Greene, Thomas M., 64–65n. 1
Grendler, Paul F., 13
Griffio (Venetian printer), 139, 155n. 3
Grimm, brothers, 180
Guardati, Tommaso. *See* Masuccio
    Salernitano
Guarini, Elena Fasano, 175n. 3
Guglielmi, Guido, 215n. 4
Guglielminetti, Marziano, 144, 198n. 7
Guinizzelli, Guido, 131

Halperin, David M., 177n. 19
Hanafi, Zakiya, 199n. 19
Hastings, Robert, 28n. 2, 31n. 17
Hauvette, Henri, 130
Hinton, James, 106, 117–118n. 8
Historia naturalis (Pliny), 167, 188, 191
Hollander, Robert, 34, 35, 41, 43
Hotchkiss, Valerie R., 214n. 1, 215n. 9,
    216n. 20, 217n. 30
Huarte, Juan, 179
Hutcheon, Linda, 155–156nn. 9, 11, 12

Iser, Wolfgang, 30n. 10

Jacopo da Varagine, 23
Jacques de Vitry, 24
James, Henry, 50, 65n. 6
Jaufré (anon. romance), 130
Jauss, Hans Robert, 118n. 13
Jean de Meun, 41, 47n. 16, 48n. 25
Johansson, Warren, 40, 47n. 20
John of Damascus, 23

Kayser, Wolfgang, 122–123
Kirkham, Victoria, 29n. 5
Kolve, V. A., 37

La Sale, Antoine de, 135n. 19
Lavagetto, Mario, 32n. 23
Leggenda Aurea (Jacopo da Varagine), 23
Lejeune, Philippe, 69, 78n. 1
Lemnius, Levinius, 191
Leone Ebreo, 211, 217n. 28
Leonico, Angelo, 206
Lezione sopra il comporre delle novelle (Bonciani), 121
Libro delle rime, Il (Sacchetti), 87
Libro di novelle e di bel parlar gentile, Il. See *Il Novellino* (anon.)
Liceti, Fortunio (physician), 189
Lüthi, Max, 181
Luzio, Alessandro, 176n. 8
Lycosthenes, Conrad, 179, 188

McKee, Robert, 65n. 4
McWilliam, G. H., 51
Maestri, Delmo, 154–155n. 2
Magnanini, Suzanne, 8, 10
Mancini, Vincenzo, 216nn. 16, 17
Mandragola, La (Machiavelli), 152, 167
Map, Walter, 6, 106, 109, 110–111, 112, 113, 114, 117n. 3
Marcus, Millicent, 23, 29n. 4, 31n. 17, 32n. 24
Marinella, Lucrezia, 215n. 5
Marti, Mario, 156n. 16

Martinez, Ronald L., 41
Masenetti, Giovanni Maria, 206
Masuccio Salernitano (Tommaso Guardati), 3, 6, 7, 11, 106, 108, 110, 114, 115, 119–136, 162, 164, 207
  audience, 121, 124–125, 131
  changes to models, 107, 121, 124, 126–128, 131, 133
  effect on reader, 122, 125, 128, 129
  hyperbole, use of, 121, 122, 127
  mixed registers in, 126–127
  place in literary history, 119, 122, 133
  psycological perversion, 119, 130, 133
  realism in, 125, 130
  sadistic quality in, 106, 121
  structural balance in, 125–126, 205. *See also* grotesque, horror, *Il Novellino* (Masuccio), terror
Mauro, Alfredo, 119, 134n. 3
Mazzacurati, Giancarlo, 31n. 17
Mazzotta, Giuseppe, 29n. 4, 30n. 7, 32n. 24
Melechini, Mario, 206, 211, 217n. 28
Menetti, Elisabetta, 215n. 8
Merchant of Venice, The (Shakespeare), 204
Milani, Marisa, 216n. 17
Molino, Antonio, 182
Monstrorum historia (Aldrovandi), 189
Moravia, Alberto, 32n. 24
Moretti, Vito, 135n. 25
Mormando, Franco, 177n. 22
Morphology of the Folktale (Propp), 181
Motif–Index of the Italian Novella in Prose (Rotunda), 201
Mouzat, Jean, 111
Murray, Jacqueline, 177n. 17
Musa, Mark, 215n. 7

Narrationes (Odo of Shirton), 24
Neri, Ferdinando, 119, 120, 122, 125, 133

Niccoli, Ottavia, 199n. 26
Nigro, Salvatore, 123
Nissen, Christopher, 6, 8, 11, 217nn. 25, 29
"Novella di Giulia Camposanpiero" (Bigolina), 12, 206–207, 208, 214–215n. 2
"Novella di Ottinello e Giulia" (anon.), 205
Novelliere, Il (Sercambi), 5–6, 31n. 16, 69–80, 81–103
  Exemplo 1: 72
    4: 72, 204
    7: 215n. 3
    56: 214n. 2
    79: 5, 69–70, 73–77
    131: 72
    155: 74
Novelliere, Il (Sermini), 115
Novellino, Il (anon.), 1, 24, 121
Novellino, Il (Masuccio), 7, 119–136
  Novella 2: 125, 127
    7: 125
    11: 215n. 3
    12: 164
    19: 132
    21: 106, 110, 114–116
    22: 122
    23: 122, 127
    24: 122, 125
    25: 122, 125
    28: 122
    31: 119, 122, 125, 129, 131
    33: 119
    34: 214n. 2
    39: 205
    40: 214n. 2, 215n. 3
    43: 205

Ó. Cuilleanáin, Cormac, 4–5, 29n. 4, 66n. 14, 67nn. 23, 27, 29
Odo of Shirton, 24

Origo, Iris, 51–52
Orlando Innamorato (Boiardo), 115
Ortega y Gasset, José, 49
Ovid. *See* metamorphoses

Pabst, Walter, 70, 78n. 3
Padoan, Giorgio, 31n. 14
Pagnamenta, Roberta Bruno, 33
Papio, Michael, 7, 8
Paré, Ambroise (surgeon), 179, 188, 192
Park, Katharine, 177n. 24
Passano, Giambattista, 215n. 5
Passavanti, Jacopo, 27, 125
Payer, Pierre J., 190
Payne, John, 31n. 19, 66n. 15, 215n. 7
Pecorone, Il (Ser Giovanni), 106, 108–109, 110, 204
Pentamerone (Basile), 53
Percy, William A., 40, 47n. 20
Perrault, Charles, 53
Perrot, Michelle, 29–30n. 6
Pesce, Emilio, 131
Petrarch (Francesco Petrarca), 8, 12, 18, 31n. 13, 141, 155n. 7, 156n. 14, 209. *See also* Bembo, Pietro
Petrini, Mario, 198n. 7
Petrocchi, Giorgio, 79n. 11, 117n. 6, 135n. 19
Petrucci, Armando, 13
Phaedrus. See Plato
Piacevoli notti, Le (Straparola), 10, 53
  Notte II, *favola* 1: 179–199
    III, 1: 185
    III, 4: 185
    IV, 1: 185, 214n. 2
    IV, 3: 185, 186
    V, 1: 185
    X, 3: 185
  place in literary history, 10, 181
  printing history of, 179
  structure of, 182
Pirrotta, Nino, 84

Plaisance, Michel, 169, 175, 175–176n. 4, 177n. 26

Plato, 67n. 27

Pliny the Elder. *See Historia naturalis*; hybrids, Plinian

Poe, Edgar Allen, 120, 122, 123–124, 133

Porretane, Le (Sabadino degli Arienti), 214n. 2

Porro, Giulio, 207

Predelli, Maria Bendinelli, 6, 7, 117n. 2, 214n. 1

Prencipe Galeotto. See Decameron, Galeotto

Prodenzani, Simone, 214n. 2

Prodigiorum ac ostentorum chronicon (Lycosthenes), 188

Proemio: 16, 17, 22, 24, 26, 27, 29n. 5, 33, 34

 I, Intro.: 33, 54

 I, 1: 47–48n. 22

 I, 4: 52, 149

 I, 7: 29n. 5, 67n. 31

 I, 8: 67n. 31

 II, 1: 67n. 31

 II, 2: 51, 60–61, 67nn. 22, 27

 II, 3: 162, 202

 II, 5: 57, 59

 II, 6: 66n. 11

 II, 9: 11, 51, 59, 70, 162, 202–203, 214n. 1, 215n. 6

 II, 10: 165–166

 III: 16, 18, 26

 III, 1: 20, 27, 28

 III, 2: 37

 III, 4: 37

 III, 9: 57

 III, 10: 15, 20, 26, 28

 IV, Intro: 3, 5, 15–32, 33, 36, 43

 IV, 1: 15, 25–26, 28, 32n. 24, 52, 59, 67n. 23

 IV, 5: 25, 28, 32n. 23

 IV, 6: 65n. 8

 IV, 9: 32n. 25, 59

 IV, 10: 57

 V, rubrics: 36, 46

 V, 1: 21

 V, 5: 67n. 25

 V, 7: 59, 67n. 28

 V, 8: 67n. 25

 V, 9: 67n. 23

 V, 10: 4, 33–48, 67n. 24

 V, Concl.: 42, 44, 45

 VI, Intro.: 44, 45, 55, 66n. 12

 VI, 1: 4, 33, 36–38, 41, 46, 47n. 14, 73

 VI, 2: 57

 VI, 4: 56

 VI, 5: 35, 43

 VI, 9: 37

 VI, 10: 51, 53, 62–64, 173

 VI, Concl.: 55

 VII: 16

 VII, 1: 67n. 25

 VII, 2: 37

 VII, 3: 58

 VII, 7: 61

 VII, 8: 53, 57

 VIII, 1: 66n. 17

 VIII, 2: 152, 173–174

 VIII, 4: 37, 57

 VIII, 7: 58–59

 VIII, 10: 53, 67n. 25

 IX, 2: 52, 149

 IX, 4: 67n. 28

 IX, 9: 66n. 17, 70

 IX, 10: 37

 X, 4: 115

 X, 5: 52, 114–116

 X, 8: 115

 X, 9: 66n. 17, 115

 X, 10: 59, 62

 Author's Concl.: 34, 35, 43

 disguise in, 61, 201–204, 205, 213, 214n. 2

 as feminist text, 3, 16, 21,

innovation in, 16, 17, 19, 28, 30n. 12
language of, 17–18, 156n. 14
as normative model, 1, 2, 3, 7–9, 31n.
    18, 86, 115–116, 120–121, 125,
    137–139, 140, 143, 145, 151–152,
    153, 156n. 14, 19, 161, 173–174,
    181, 182, 205
proto–Rabelaisian, 124
realism in, 4, 22, 51, 53
structure of, 1, 3, 24, 33, 83
translations of, 31n. 19, 66n. 15, 215n.
    7.
See also Boccaccio, Giovanni;
    characters in *Decameron*;
    dedications, authors'; frame story;
    Galeotto; ladies in love
Propp, Vladimir, 181
Prose della volgar lingua (Bembo), 1, 143,
    155n. 7, 156nn. 14, 19, 157nn. 24,
    26
Prunster, Nicole, 65n. 8
Pucci, Antonio, 11, 204, 205, 207
Pucci, Pandolfo, 168
Purity and Danger (Douglas), 192
"Puss in Boots," 53, 180. *See also* cat,
    fairy tales

questione della lingua, 9, 17, 137, 141,
    143, 153, 155n. 7.
    See also Bembo, Pietro; *Decameron* as
    normative model; Petrarch
questioni d'amore, 9, 12, 111, 138, 141,
    146, 149, 162, 210, 211. *See also*
    Andreas Capellanus, courtly ideals,
    Neoplatonism

Radcliff–Umstead, Douglas, 28n. 1
Ragionamenti, I (Firenzuola), 8–9, 138, 139
    I, 1: 145–148
    I, 2: 150, 162–163, 164, 165–167
    I, 3: 151

    I, 4: 173–174
    I, 5: 149–150
    dialogic components, 142, 154
    parodic intent of, 140, 142, 144
    printing history, 139, 155n. 3, 161
    structure of, 139, 143, 145
A ragionar d'amore (Melechini), 206, 211
Ragni, Eugenio, 144, 155n. 5
Ramat, Raffaello, 19, 31nn. 15, 17
Raya, Gino, 217n. 23
"Re porco, Il" (Straparola). *See Piacevoli
    notti, Le*, II, 1
readership
    aristocratic, 121, 124–125
    bourgeois, 1–2, 17, 22, 30n. 8
    female, 2, 4, 15, 17, 18, 24–25, 28, 29n.
      5, 30n. 9, 34, 37, 128
    "implied," 17.
    See also Boccaccio, Giovanni; cultural
      milieu, literary impact of;
      dedications, authors'; ladies in
      love; reception
Renier, Rodolfo, 176n. 8
Rhetoric of Fiction, The (Booth), 49
Rocke, Michael, 170, 171, 172, 178n. 31
Roman de la rose (Jean de Meun), 37, 41,
    43, 118n. 17
Roman dou roi Flore et de la belle Jehanne
    (anon.), 203–204
Romei, Danilo, 142, 144, 152, 154n. 2,
    155n. 6, 156n. 18
Romeo and Juliet (Shakespeare), 50, 119
Rorty, Richard, 157n. 28
Rossi, Luciano, 72, 86, 89
Rossi, Paolo L., 178n. 29
Rotunda, D. P., 176n. 14, 183, 201, 214n. 2
Ruggiero, Guido, 195, 196
Ruskin, John, 122–123, 126
Russo, Luigi, 32n. 24
Ruthenberg, Myriam Swennen, 4, 5, 7,
    79n. 9, 82, 102n. 4

Sabadino degli Arienti, Giovanni, 214n. 2
Sacchetti, Franco, 87, 162
Salisbury, Joyce E., 187, 190
Salvatico, Bartolomeo, 207–208, 217n. 31
Salwa, Piotr, 79n. 12
Sanguineti, Federico, 31n. 17
Sannazaro, Jacopo, 12
Saslow, James M., 177n. 21
Scaglione, Aldo D., 31n. 17
Scala, Lorenzo, 161
Scarci, Manuela, 8, 156n. 13
Scardeone, Bernardino, 206
Scrivano, Riccardo, 144, 156n. 17
Sei Giornate (Aretino), 176n. 6
Sercambi, Giovanni, 5, 7, 11, 31n. 16,
    69–80, 81–103, 205, 214n. 2. *See
    also Croniche di Luccha, Le*;
    Novelliere, Il
Sermini, Gentile, 115, 124
Seroni, Adriano, 139, 144, 154nn. 1, 2
Shakespeare, William, 2, 12, 64, 119, 204,
    214
Shklovsky, Viktor, 156n. 15
Singleton, Charles S., 31n. 19
Smarr, Janet Levarie, 30n. 7
Soldanieri, Niccolò, 83, 87, 92
Sollazzo, Il (Prodenzani), 214n. 2, 215n. 3
Specchio della vera penitenza (Passavanti),
    27
speculum principis, 72
Sperling, Jutta Gisela, 195
Speroni, Sperone, 180
Spiegel, Gabrielle M., 175n. 1
Spinelli, Enrico, 134n. 2, 135n. 25
Spini, Giorgio, 175n. 3
Squarotti, Giorgio Bàrberi, 198n. 7
Stallybrass, Peter, 135n. 16
Stewart, Pamela, 80n. 13
Stocchi, Manlio Pastore, 40
Storia della dama bolognese (anon.),
    105–118

Straparola, Giovanfrancesco, 1, 10, 53,
    179–199.
    See also Piacevoli notti, Le
Strozzi, Filippo, 160

Thomas Aquinas, 187, 190
Thompson, Stith, 183
Todorov, Tzvetan, 28n. 3
Tonelli, Luigi, 155n. 4
Toscan, Jean, 178n. 32
Tourney, Leonard, 65n. 4
Trionfo della Morte, 123
Trissino, Gian Giorgio, 137, 176n. 13
Tristan (Béroul), 130
Tristan, anon. prose, 209
Trivigiano, Benedetto, 182
Twelfth-Night (Shakespeare), 64
Tynianov, Jurij, 155–156n. 12

Urania (Bigolina), 12, 206, 207–209,
    210–213, 217n. 31.
    See also Bigolina, Giulia; manuscripts,
    Milan, Bibl. Trivulziana, Triv. MS
    88
Uses of Enchantment, The (Bettelheim),
    183

Varchi, Benedetto, 182, 189–190,
    191–193, 194
Vega, Lope de, 2
Vespasiano da Bisticci, 2
Villani, Giovanni, 2
Vincent de Beauvais, 24
Virgulti, Ernesto, 3–4, 5, 7, 32n. 25
Vita (Cellini), 169
Vivaldi, Michelangelo, 160

Wallace, David, 66n. 19
Warner, Marina, 198n. 12
Weinrich, Martin, 191
Welter, Jean-Thiébaut, 117n. 3

Wetzel, Hermann H., 80n. 16
White, Allon, 135n. 16
White, Hayden V., 77
Wright, Laurence, 136n. 27

Zanrè, Domenico, 8, 9–10, 176n. 10
Zumthor, Paul, 215n. 4
Zwinger, Theodor, 216n. 19

Subject Index

Accademia dell'Addiaccio, 161
Accademia Fiorentina, 9, 121, 159, 160,
    161, 168–169, 175n. 4, 189
Accademia Romana, 160
Accademia degli Umidi, 10, 160, 168–169,
    175n. 4
Accademia della Vigna, 160
acrostic, author's, 74, 82
action, gendered male, 4, 11, 33–36,
    42–43, 45.
    See vengeance, male; word–deed
    dichotomy
adultery. *See* sexual relations, adulterous
aesthetics,
    Crocean, 7, 120, 121–122, 132
    Romantic, 7–8, 123, 131.
See also Croce, Benedetto; De Sanctis,
    Francesco; Gothic fiction;
    grotesque; horror; sublime
agency, 4, 36, 43–44
alterity, 9, 124, 125, 145, 166, 169, 172.
    See also nonconformity
analogues, 6, 10, 23, 47n. 18, 107
animal–human divide, 182, 186–189, 192,
    193–194, 197

animal offspring, 179–180, 181, 184,
    186–188, 191. *See also* monstrous
    births
anxiety, 122, 182–184, 185, 190, 193, 194,
    197
apologues, 3, 16, 20, 22, 24, 26
Aragonese monarchy, 7, 121, 124, 134n. 8.
    See also Naples
Arcadian movement, 138, 161
asceticism, 19, 21, 26–27, 28
Asinaio, Mount, 19, 21, 22
autobiography, 5, 12, 69, 70–72, 78n.
    1, 82

ballata (verse form), 6, 83–84, 87, 88, 89,
    95
Beauty and Beast, 183. *See also* fairy tales
beffa. *See* practical jokes
beffato (victim of trick), 36, 172, 175
beffatore (trickster), 171, 175
bestiality, 10–11, 182, 184–185, 189–190,
    192, 195. *See also* sodomy
Bianchi movement, 86, 92
bisticci (verse form), 93
Black Death. *See* plague

brigata (group of storytellers), 1–2, 3, 9,
    15, 17, 19, 42, 44, 54, 56, 66n. 19,
    74, 76, 82, 83, 86–87, 91, 93, 94,
    95, 138, 140, 161–162, 172, 181,
    182, 184, 185, 194, 197. *See also*
    frame story

caccia (verse form), 87, 95
cameo by author, 31n. 16, 73–74
cantare (genre), 7, 106, 107, 110, 114,
    201, 204, 205
canzone morale. See songs, didactic
canzone (Petrarchan), 9, 140, 141, 144,
    156n. 14, 162.
canzonetta (verse form), 87, 89, 91
carnal love. *See* sexual desire
Carnival
    Bakhtinian, 119, 123–124
    as setting, 73, 75, 77, 169, 182
castration, 10, 152, 172, 173–174, 178n.
    33
cat, 35, 46, 53, 171. *See also* Puss in Boots
cavalcare. See metaphors, sexual
centrality, structural, 33, 45, 73
characters in novella
    aristocratic, 1, 4, 23, 36–37, 56, 61, 127,
        133, 146, 170, 173, 182, 195, 205,
        207, 210
    Arthurian, 37, 45, 60, 130, 209
    artisans, 1
    author's relation to, 29n. 5, 120, 125,
        151
    children, 57, 59, 62, 86–87, 88–89
    clergy, 1, 10, 52, 57, 58, 86, 119, 145,
        149, 151, 164, 172–173, 178n. 33
    elderly, 1, 19, 27, 34–36, 43–45, 57,
        67n. 24, 86, 145, 150, 162, 165
    merchants, 52, 61, 76, 182, 203, 215n. 9
    minor, 4, 44, 50, 58, 65nn. 5, 7, 67n. 24
    monstrous, 7, 10–11, 119, 122, 123,
        130–131, 179, 181–186, 189–199
    Muslims, 1, 51, 66n. 17, 119, 146, 205

    nuns, 27, 52
    pedants, 10, 170–171, 172
    reader's relation to, 49–50, 65n. 4, 127,
        129, 132, 210–211
    servants, 4, 44, 49–67, 145, 161
        kitchen–maid, 51, 53, 63, 67n. 23
        maidservants, 5, 50–52, 53, 57, 58,
            61, 65n. 8, 151, 162, 164–165, 166,
            167, 204
        menservants, 5, 51
        merciful, 50–51, 59–60, 67n. 22, 202,
            205
    slaves, 51–52, 122, 146
    wild woman, 12, 212–213, 217n. 31
    young, 1, 4, 19, 27, 34, 35–36, 44, 73,
        75, 86, 120, 122, 127, 130, 149,
        150, 151, 162, 164, 165, 183, 205

in *Decameron*
    Alessandro, 164
    Alibech, 15, 26, 27, 147
    Ambruogiuolo, 59, 202–203
    Andreuccio, 59, 121
    Andreuola, 65n. 8
    Anichino, 61
    Ansaldo, 114–115
    Balducci, Filippo, 15, 16, 18, 19–20,
        22–23, 25, 27, 28
    Balducci son, 15, 19–23, 25, 26
    Beatrice de' Galuzzi, 61
    Belcolore, Monna 152
    Bergamino, 67n. 31
    Berlinghieri, Arriguccio, 53, 57
    Calandrino, 124
    Cecco Angiolieri, 67n. 28
    Cecco Fortarrigo, 67n. 28
    Cepparello, 16, 29n. 4, 41, 42, 43,
        47–48n. 22
    Chichibio, 56
    Cimone, 21
    Cipolla, Frate, 41, 42, 43, 51, 62–64,
        173

Ciutazza, 57
Dioneo, 42, 44–45, 54–55, 152
Dianora, 52, 114–115
Efigenia, 21
Egano de' Galuzzi, 61
Elissa, 44–45
Ercolano, 38–40, 48nn. 23, 28
Federigo, 67n. 23
Fiametta, 38
Filippa, 16
Filomena, 36, 37
Gentile de' Carisendi, 115
Ghismonda, 15, 16, 25–26, 28, 32n. 24,
    52, 60, 67n. 23
Gianfigliazzi, Currado, 56
Gisippo, 115
Gostanza, 16
Griselda, 16, 62
Gualtieri of Saluzzo, 62
Guardastagno, 32n. 25
Guccio, 51, 53, 63–64
Guglielmo Borsiere, 67n. 31
Guiscardo, 25–26, 32n. 25, 52, 60
Gulfardo, 66n. 17
Licisca, 44–45, 54–56, 66n. 20
Lisabetta, 25, 26, 28, 32n. 23
Lodovico, 61
Lomellin, Bernabò, 11, 51, 59, 202–203,
    215n. 6
Lorenzo, 25
Oretta, 16, 33, 36–38, 43, 45, 47n. 14,
    73, 80n. 13
Piccarda, 57
Sismonda, 57
Marchesana di Monferrato, 16
Martellino, 67n. 31
Masetto da Lamporecchio, 20, 27, 28
Nuta, 53, 63
Paganino da Monaco, 166
Pampinea, 17, 33, 54
Pietro di Vinciolo, 38–44, 45, 47n. 18,
    48n. 23

priest of Varlungo, 152, 173
Primasso, 67n. 31
Ricciardo di Chinzica, 165
Rinaldo d'Asti, 50–51, 60–61, 67n. 22
Rinaldo of Siena, 58
Rinieri, 58
Rossiglione, 32n. 25
Roussillon, Countess of, 57
Rustico, 15, 20, 26, 27, 28
Salabaetto, 52–53
Saladin, 66n. 17, 115
Sicuran da Finale, 202–203, 215nn. 7, 8
Tancredi, 15, 25, 32nn. 24, 25
Teodoro, 67n. 28
Tindaro, 66n. 12
Tito, 115
Torello, 66n. 17, 115
Zinevra, 11, 51, 162, 202–204, 205,
    210, 211, 213, 214n. 1, 215nn. 6, 7,
    8

in *Il Novellino*, 120, 122, 124, 125, 127,
    130, 133
in *I Ragionamenti*, 145, 150, 162.
See also Boccaccio; heroines, unfortunate;
    ladies in love; lepers

chivalric ideals, 7, 113–115
chronicle, 5, 69–70, 72, 74–77, 82, 90,
    188, 191. *See also Croniche di
    Luccha, Le*
chronicler, 5, 69, 71–72
Church (moral authority), 11, 23–24, 42,
    48n. 29, 111, 165, 186–188, 190
ciance. See songs, bawdy
classical authorities, 8, 18, 19, 67n. 27,
    141, 166, 167, 188, 191, 194, 211.
    See also Neoplatonism
Clement VII (pope), 137, 160
comedy, 62, 126
composers, 6, 81–82, 83–85, 87, 94–95
    Andrea da Firenze, 101n. 3

Bartolino da Padova, 85, 90, 101n. 3,
     102n. 17
Donato da Cascia, 85–86, 88, 94, 101n.
     3
Egidio di Francia, 101n. 3
Gherardello da Firenze, 83, 84–85, 88,
     94, 101n. 3
Giovanni da Cascia, 101n. 3
Guiglielmo di Francia, 101n. 3
Guillaume de Machaut, 101n. 3
Jacopo da Bologna, 101n. 3
Landini, Francesco, 85, 86, 95, 101n. 3
Lorenzo da Firenze, 101n. 3
Maestro Piero, 84, 101n. 3
Masini, Lorenzo, 85, 94
Niccolò da Perugia, 85, 101n. 3, 102n.
     17
Pagliaresi, Neri, 85
Paolo da Firenze, 101n. 3
Vincenzo da Rimini, 101n. 3
Zaccaria da Teramo, 101n. 3
confinement, 28
     of children, 21, 23, 24–25
     of women, 11, 12, 16, 24, 29n. 6, 33
     gothic use of, 128
contamination
     moral, 129–130
     physical, 125, 127, 129–130, 132, 179.
     See also disease
cornice. *See* frame story
Cosimo I (de' Medici), 10, 159, 161, 168,
     178n. 29
Courtesans
     Camilla Pisana, 160, 176n. 5
     Cecilia Veneziana, 160, 176n. 6
     Costanza Amaretta, 137
     Giulia Napoletana, 168
     Milla Capraia, 168
     Nanina Zinzera, 168
     Tullia d'Aragona, 160, 168, 176n. 7
courtly ideals, 6–7, 50, 62, 105, 109–111,
     118n. 17.

See also Andreas Capellanus; *Roman de
     la rose*
courtly tales, 1, 6, 105–118.
     See also characters in novella,
          Arthurian; Chrètien de Troyes;
          romance, medieval
creation (Christian paradigm), 4, 35, 41
criminal acts, 5, 57, 129, 131, 169, 178n.
     29, 195.
     See also bestiality, sodomy, violence
cronaca. See chronicle
cross–dressing, 9, 11–12, 51, 162–164,
     166, 176–177n. 14, 201–217
cruelty. *See* violence
cultural dissent. *See* nonconformity
cultural milieu, literary impact of, 3, 4–5,
     7–8, 10, 21, 71, 105–107, 113–116,
     168–170, 174–175, 182, 192,
     194–196

dance, 6, 83, 86, 87, 88, 91, 94, 182
death, 7, 51, 122, 124, 128, 133, 196, 214.
     *See also Danse macabre, transis,
          Trionfo della Morte*
debates on love. *See questioni d'amore*
deception, 15, 16, 28n. 3, 59, 67n. 26, 69,
     78n. 4, 150, 151, 186, 204,
     212–213.
     verbal, 3–4, 5, 20, 23, 25, 26, 28, 29, 39,
          45–46, 76–77.
     See also cross–dressing; disguise; false
          identity; fact–fiction dichotomy;
          motifs, false servant; gender
          confusion
decorum, 5, 11, 54–56, 57, 63, 145
dedications, authors', 3, 16, 30n. 7, 127,
     128, 207
defense,
     of author, 15, 18, 22, 30n. 9, 44
     of women, 3–4, 211
deformity, 120, 130, 169, 185, 191, 197.
     See also hybrids, lepers

deformation. *See* deformity

demons, 23–24, 65n. 7, 122

dialogue on love, 8, 144, 146, 217n. 29.
 See also Neoplatonism, *questioni
 d'amore*

didacticism, 1, 7, 9, 23, 110, 113–114,
 115, 117n. 3, 145, 212, 213

diletto. See entertainment; pleasure of text;
 pleasure, verbal

dire (verb), 42, 103n. 18

disease, 122
 venereal, 160, 168, 178n. 27.
 See also contamination, leprosy,
 plague

disguise, 11–12, 28n. 3, 77, 162–165
 functions of, 167, 204, 209, 212.
 See also cross–dressing; *Decameron*,
 disguise in; false identity; motifs,
 false servant; transformation

drama
 Elizabethan, 119
 Renaissance, 9, 11, 162, 176–177n. 14

entertainment, 6, 12, 16, 22, 33–34, 71–72,
 76, 81, 83, 86–87, 89, 93, 117n. 3,
 138, 161, 182. *See also* brigade;
 dance; music; songs; storytelling

entrare in novelle, 70, 75, 76. *See also*
 deception, verbal; *novellare*,
 storytelling

eroticism, 5, 9, 18, 26, 30n. 7, 46n. 8, 124,
 139, 150, 157n. 25, 160, 163

Exemplo ("tale"). *See Novelliere, Il*
 (Sercambi)

exemplum, 1, 3, 4, 6, 9, 12, 16, 22, 24,
 27, 28, 70, 106, 110, 111, 114,
 115, 117n. 3, 125. *See also*
 didacticism

expatriots, Florentine, 168, 170, 172

fabliaux, 1. *See also* folk tales

facetia, 138

fact–fiction dichotomy, 5, 11, 69, 77–78,
 79n. 12, 82, 180, 188

fairy tales, 1, 10, 12, 179, 180, 182–183.
 See also folk tales, Puss in Boots.

false identity, 61, 67n. 28, 203, 204, 212

favole. See Piacevoli notti, Le (Straparola)

fear, 120, 122, 123, 125, 132, 148, 185,
 193, 197.
 See also anxiety; horror; Masuccio
 Salernitano, effect on reader; social
 order, threats to; terror

female body, 11, 128, 180, 193

Florence
 fictional, 1, 19, 21, 73, 76, 143, 147–148
 historical, 1, 2, 3, 8, 17, 40, 54, 81–82,
 85, 87, 95, 121, 137
 under Medici dukes, 159, 167–169, 170,
 171, 174–175, 178n. 29. *See also*
 Cosimo I

folk tales, 1, 10, 123, 124, 182, 204.
 See also fairy tales, folklorists

folklorists, 10, 180–181, 183, 201. *See
 also* fairy tales; folk tales

frame story, 1, 5, 9, 12, 51, 54, 56, 66n. 18,
 69, 72, 81, 82, 86, 138, 139, 143,
 144, 161–162, 169, 181, 182, 184,
 207

frame tale. *See* frame story

Francis I (king of France), 189–190, 194

fraud, 39, 41, 51. *See also* deception

frottola (verse form), 95

fuorusciti. See expatriots, Florentine

Galeotto (go–between),
 function of book, 4, 36, 42, 44, 45, 60
 function of character, 34, 36, 43–44,
 67n. 24
 name of character, 37, 45, 182–183,
 185–186, 190–197
 subtitle of *Decameron*, 10, 36, 46, 60.
 See also characters in novella; servants
 as facilitators

gender
    confusion, 36, 162–164, 167, 202–203,
        210, 211, 215nn. 7, 9
    construction of, 4, 16, 33, 163, 166,
        215n. 8
    roles examined, 204, 206, 211, 213, 214.
    See also action, gendered male;
        misogyny; transformation; words,
        gendered female
gender studies, 164–165, 169
genres, literary, 1, 2
    conflation of, 5, 9, 69–80, 82, 138–139,
        144, 162.
    See also exemplum; fabliaux; fairy tales;
        folk tales; novella;
        novella–romanzo; sermons,
        popular; romance
gestures
    chivalric, 4, 28, 37, 114
    religious, 40, 43, 44
go–between. *See* Galeotto
Gothic fiction, 7, 131–132
grotesque, 7, 119, 122–124, 125, 131, 133,
        135n. 16.
    See also horror; Masuccio Salernitano;
        Bakhtin, Mikhail
Guinigi (rulers of Lucca), 71, 72, 82, 86,
        87
gusto dell'orrido. See grotesque, Masuccio
        Salernitano

Henry II (king of England), 106, 112
hermaphroditism, 166–167
heroines, unfortunate, 12, 25–26, 67n. 23,
        128, 131, 205, 207, 209–210, 212.
    See also ladies in love; novella,
        tragic; suicide
hierarchy of species, 186–187, 190, 194
historiography. *See* chronicle
homosexuality, 41–42, 164–165, 195.
    See also sexual relations, homosexual
AIN1:horror, 7, 122, 185

— films, 132, 136n. 26, 180
— tales, 119, 123, 125, 131, 132, 133.
    See also fear, Masuccio Salernitano,
        terror
horseback riding. *See* metaphors, sexual
humor, 1, 3, 22, 25, 28, 36, 56, 121, 122,
        162. *See* also disguise; gender
        confusion; parody; satire; witty
        retort
hybrids, Plinian, 10, 188
    animal–human, 11, 179, 181–186,
        188–197
hypocrisy, 21, 39, 42

impotence, 167
incest, 122
infanticide, 11, 134n. 7, 183, 184, 190,
        191, 194, 195
irony, 8, 9, 12, 41, 46, 47n. 22, 48n. 29,
        140, 148, 153, 210, 211, 212

jongleurs, 7, 106

knights, 7, 36–37, 41–43, 45, 105, 112,
        130

ladies in love, 2, 3, 10, 11–12, 16–17, 29n.
        5, 30n. 7, 34, 210.
    See also questioni d'amore
laude, 84, 85, 89, 92, 93
laughter (Bakhtinian theory), 123–124, 140
lay spirituality, 22, 85. *See also* Bianchi
        movement
lepers, 120, 127, 128–130
leprosy, 129.
    See also contamination, disease, lepers
lesbianism, 150, 163–165, 177n. 17
lies. *See* deception, verbal
lineage, extinction of. *See* social order,
        threats to
love treatise. *See Asolani, Gli*; dialogue on
        love

Lucca, 8, 71, 73, 74, 75, 81, 82, 95.
   See also Croniche di Luccha, Le;
   Guinigi; Sercambi, Giovanni
lust. *See* sexual desire
lyric, Provençal, 111, 113, 131. *See also*
   courtly ideals, jongleurs

macabre, 25–26, 132.
   See also *Danse macabre*, death, fear,
   horror, terror
madness due to love, 12, 209
madrigal, 84, 87, 88, 95, 182
male disguise. *See* cross–dressing
manuscripts, 2, 74, 81, 84, 117n. 6, 118n. 9
   Besançon, Bibl. Municipale, MS 597:
      206, 217n. 28
   Cortona, Bibl. del Comune, MS 91:
      84
   Florence, Bibl. Medicea Laurenziana,
      Med. Pal. MS 87: 82, 85–86,
      87–88, 101n. 2
      Bibl. Naz. Centrale, Magl. MS
      II.I.122 (*Banco Rari* MS 8): 84
      Magl. MS VI, 190: 178n. 28
      Panc. MS 26: 82, 101n. 3
   London, Brit. Lib., Add. MS 29987:
      82
   Milan, Bibl. Trivulziana, Triv. MS 88:
      207, 208–209, 210, 211, 213, 217n.
      26
      Triv. MS 193: 79n. 10
   Oxford, Bodley, Bod. MS 851: 106
   Padua, Archivio di Stato (documents),
      Archivio notarile, vol. 4830: 216n.
      14
      Estimo 1518: 206, 216n. 15
      Bibl. Civica, MS 1451 VIII: 216n. 19
      MS 2134: 216n. 19
   Paris, Bibl. Nat., it. MS 568: 82
      it. MS 482: 37
   Perugia, Bibl. Augusta, MS C43: 6–7,
      105, 106

Vatican City, Bibl. Apostolica Vaticana,
   Patetta MS 358: 207
   Bibl. Apost. Vat., Rossi MS 215:
      83–84
melancholy, 12, 209, 211, 213
menare dietro (sodomitic copulation), 170
menstrual blood, 179
merchants, 2, 22, 30n. 8, 69, 121, 134n. 8,
   195
metalanguage, 4, 37
metamorphoses, Ovidian, 10, 166.
   See also transformation
Metamorphoses. See Apuleius
metanarrative, 38
metanovella, 5, 69, 73, 76
metaphors
   Eucharistic, 67n. 23
   for narrating, 4, 33, 36–38, 42–43
   musical, 64
   sexual, 4, 33, 36–38, 42–43, 45, 46, 147,
      165
mimesis, 35
mise en abime, 139
misogyny, 3–4, 7, 11, 17, 20, 23–24,
   38–39, 42, 106, 109–110, 125, 160,
   176n. 7, 193, 211
monstrous births, 11, 179, 182–183, 185,
   186, 189, 191, 194.
   See also animal offspring; bestiality;
   hybrids, animal–human
monstrous, discourse on. *See*
   animal–human divide; characters in
   novella, monstrous; monstrous
   births
Moors. *See* characters in novella, Muslims
moralità. See songs, didactic
moralizing. *See* didacticism
motifs,
   animal–bridegroom, 181, 183–184
   burning, 40–41, 130–131
   chess game, 61
   Clown (Bakhtinian), 123

coining, 41
courtly, 113
Danse macabre, 123
discovery, 9, 53, 163, 166, 213
dog and whipping, 47–48n. 22
doves, 135n. 20
dragon–slayer, 181
falconry, 56, 67n. 23, 107–109, 211
eaten heart, 32n. 25, 67n. 23
false servant, 9, 61, 67n. 28, 162
Fool (Bakhtinian), 123–124
Fortune, 17
locus amoenus, 76
mistaken identity, 9, 151, 163
nakedness, 50–51, 58, 60–61, 62
rescue of husband / lover, 12, 162, 205,
    207, 213, 214, 216n. 20
Rogue (Bakhtinian), 123, 124
scream, female, 131, 136n. 26
secret marriage, 207
solitary wandering, 209
sulphur, 40–41, 48n. 23
tournament, 107, 108, 109
wood, sexual significance of, 176n. 9
women as geese, 20, 23, 24, 26.
    See also courtly ideals, cross–dressing,
    misogyny
motto. See witty retort
murder, 7, 26, 28, 32n. 25, 38, 51, 59, 62,
    120, 121, 125, 127, 128, 131, 183,
    190, 196–197, 202, 205. *See also*
    criminal acts; vengeance, male;
    violence
music, medieval
    amateurs and, 6, 87, 95
    extant, 81–82, 83–84, 87, 88, 89, 90
    instrumental, 6, 81, 88, 89, 90, 91, 93
    performance practice, 5–6, 81–82, 88,
        81–95
    monophonic, 6, 83–4, 85, 88, 89, 93,
        94–95

polyphonic, 83, 85, 87, 91, 94–95
vocal (*see* singers). *See also* composers;
    metaphors, musical; songs

names, significance of, 21–22, 23, 40, 43,
    45, 48n. 29, 66nn. 18, 20
Naples (narrative setting), 7–8, 121, 124,
    132, 135n. 16, 19, 210.
See also Aragonese monarchy
narrare (verb), 5, 71. *See also* storytelling
naturalism, 20, 31, 153
nature, base human, 20–21, 26, 61, 62–64,
    131, 144.
    See also bestiality, sexual desire
Neoplatonism, 8, 9, 139, 141, 143–144,
    149, 150, 153.
    See also Bembo, Pietro; *questioni
    d'amore*
nonconformity, 9, 161, 164–165, 168, 174.
    See also alterity
notare (verb), 5, 70, 71
novella (genre)
    anticlerical, 125
    comic elements in, 22, 28, 126
    dark settings, 5, 25, 75–76, 120, 126,
        127, 131
    defined, 2–3, 5, 70
    development of, 1–3, 12, 119, 124, 127,
        132, 133, 154, 182, 208, 210, 214
    innovations in, 3–4, 7, 9, 10, 12, 16, 77,
        154, 181, 182
    place in literary history, 2, 12
    pragmatism in, 165, 203, 204
    realism in, 1, 4, 12, 21, 75–76, 108,
        208
    sources of, 1, 16, 47n. 18, 66nn. 18, 20,
        106–107, 126, 203, 215n. 11
    as social critique, 1, 12, 28, 132
    tragic, 25, 28, 125, 126.
    See also Decameron, normative model;
        didacticism; eroticism; genres,

literary; conflation of; misogyny; practical jokes; reception; singers; violence

novella–romanzo (genre), 201, 202, 205, 209, 215n. 4

novellare (verb), 2, 46, 71, 75, 77. *See also entrare in novella*; deception, verbal; storytelling

novellas of Firenzuola. *See I Ragionamenti*

novelletta. See Decameron IV, Intro

novelliere (novella writer), 7, 181, 205
   women, 11, 202, 215n. 5. *See also* Giulia Bigolina

operetta (literary term), 126, 135n. 17, 208, 217n. 24

Orlando (Ariostan), 209

Ovid. *See* metamorphoses

Paolo and Francesca. *See* Dante Alighieri, *Inferno* V

parody, 4, 8, 9, 20, 140, 142, 144, 145, 155nn. 11, 12, 160

pederasty, 170–171

penitentials, 190

plague, 5, 9, 17, 124, 143, 161

pleasure
   of action, 42
   of text, 1, 7, 12, 22, 34, 49, 71–72, 122, 125, 133, 166
   sexual, 34, 37, 44, 151, 163, 164
   verbal, 36, 37, 42–43.
   See also entertainment

plot construction, 50–51, 122, 125, 130, 145, 162

practical jokes, 1, 10, 11, 62, 67n. 21, 119, 162, 169, 171, 172, 174, 201, 205.
   See also beffato, *beffatore*, violence

procreation, 11, 41, 43, 45, 165

pronta risposta. See witty retort

proverbs, Italian, 34, 35, 46n. 8

"Puss in Boots," 53, 180. *See also* cat, fairy tales

queer theory, 164–165, 169

questione della lingua, 9, 17, 137, 143, 153, 155n.7.
   See also Bembo, Pietro; *Decameron*, normative model; Petrarch

questioni d'amore, 9, 12, 111, 138, 141, 146, 149, 162, 210, 211. *See also* Andreas Capellanus; Bembo, Pietro; courtly ideals; dialogue on love; Neoplatonism

rape, 7, 125, 127, 129, 130, 195

readership
   aristocratic, 121, 124–125
   bourgeois, 1–2, 17, 22, 30nn. 8, 9
   female, 2, 4, 15, 17, 18, 24–25, 28, 29n. 5, 34, 37, 128
   "implied," 17. *See also* Boccaccio; cultural milieu, literary impact of; dedications, authors'; ladies in love

reception,
   bourgeoisie, 1, 30n. 8
   critical, 2, 5, 7–8, 9, 10, 12, 119, 133, 169
   popular, 10, 17, 106, 133, 137, 153, 179, 181, 187
   modern, 146, 153
   of *Decameron*, 15, 17–19, 22, 30n. 12, 31n. 13, 42
   of *Le piacevoli notti*, 180–181, 183
   of *I Ragionamenti*, 137–139, 140, 144, 150, 161
   of *Il Novellino*, 120–121, 125, 133

rhetoric, 4, 51, 63, 153

roman (genre). *See* romance

romance, 3
   ancient Greek, 11, 201
   chivalric, 1, 12

medieval, 113, 130, 203, 204, 209, 211,
    214n. 1, 217n. 30
prose, 208, 217n. 23. *See also* Chrètien
    de Troyes; *Urania*
romanzo (genre). *See* romance
Rome, 137, 160
Rossi Codex. *See* manuscripts, Vatican
    City, Biblioteca Apostolica
    Vaticana, Rossi MS 215

Saracens. *See* characters in novella,
    Muslims
satire, 7
scientific discourse
    classical, 166, 188
    medieval and Renaissance, 165, 166
    early modern, 10–11, 12, 165, 166,
        179–180, 188–189, 191, 194.
    See also teratalogical canon
seduction, 27, 58, 61, 76, 163, 164, 167.
    See also characters in novella; servants
sermons, popular, 1, 3, 111, 125, 129
servants
    as accomplices, 57–59, 61
    as conveyors of status, 4, 52–53
    duties of, 54–55, 67n. 23
    as facilitators, 50–51, 60, 67n. 25
    historical, 52
    as metaphors, 50
    punished, 53, 56, 58.
    See also characters in novella
service to lady. *See* courtly ideals
sexual desire, 3, 7, 15, 20–21, 23, 26, 27,
    29n. 5, 51, 113, 128, 131, 144,
    145, 146, 147, 150, 165, 195, 196,
    197.
    See also Andreas Capellanus
sexual pollution. *See* contamination
sexual relations
    adulterous, 11, 38–41, 53, 56, 149, 195,
        203, 204, 205
    heterosexual, 4, 41, 151, 163, 164, 165,
        172

homosexual, 4, 9, 38, 40–41, 47, 150,
    163–164, 170
non–normative, 7, 9, 122, 185.
    See also bestiality, lesbianism,
    pederasty, sodomy
sexuality, 23, 28n. 3, 38, 44, 196
Sforza, Ippolita, 121
Sforza, Lucrezia, 182
silencing, 38, 42–43, 44, 45, 77, 149
sin without words. *See* homosexuality
singers
    accompanied, 89
    children, 87, 88, 89, 91
    female only, 88, 91
    male only, 91
    mixed gender, 88, 93–94
    religiosi (clerics), 71, 89, 91, 93
    unaccompanied, 90, 91
social hierarchy, 4–5, 49, 52, 57, 60
social order, threats to, 10–11, 54–55, 123,
    124–125, 127, 132, 133, 147–148,
    159, 182–184, 187–188, 191, 193,
    195–197, 199n. 23, 213. *See also*
    plague
social upheaval. *See* social order, threats to
    socioeconomic classes, 1, 6, 54–55,
    83, 84, 92, 95, 124, 125, 131, 135n.
    16. *See also* characters in novella;
    merchants
sodomia. See sodomy
sodomites. *See* sodomy
sodomy, 4, 38–42, 43, 45, 47–48n. 22,
    165, 166, 168, 169–170, 172, 177n.
    22, 178n. 29, 190, 192, 195. *See
    also menare dietro*, pederasty,
    sexual relations
songs
    bawdy, 44
    didactic, 6, 92–93 (*see also* didacticism)
    improvisatory, 84, 85, 89, 91
    texts of, 81, 83
    titles of
        "L'aguila bella nera pellegrina," 90

"Ama chi t'ama," 89
"Ami tu, donna, me come dimostri?" 93–94
"Ciascun faccia per se," 85, 89
"Chi ama, in verità," 85
"Colui pover non è che di' c'ha pogo," 92
"Come da lupo pecorella presa," 88
"Cosí del mondo e stato alcun ti fida," 92
"Dà, dà a chi avansa pur per sé," 90
"La fiera biscia che d'uman si ciba," 88, 102n. 17
"I' servo e non mi pento, ben che a 'ngrato," 91
"I' vo' bene a chi," 83, 85, 88
"Musica son," 95
"Non formò Cristi," 84
"Quando l'aire comença," 84
"Quotiescunque claudicat Justitia," 93
"Roma fu già del secol la colonna," 92
"Stabat mater dolorosa," 93
"Tu che biasmi altrui, guarda in te prima," 91
"Un bel giffalco scese alle miei grida," 88
"Virtú luogo non ha perché gentile," 89
"Vita non è piú misera e piú ria," 89.
See also ballata, caccia, canzone, composers, entertainment, *laude, madrigal,* music, singers
Squarcialupi, Antonio, 101n. 3
Squarcialupi Codex. *See* Florence, Biblioteca Medicea Laurenziana, Med. Pal. MS 87
stilnovism, 18, 21, 131. *See also* Cino da Pistoia, Dante Alighieri, Guido Cavalcanti
storytelling, 1, 3, 4, 16, 17, 18, 21, 36–38, 41–43, 46, 56, 70, 71, 72, 76, 82, 86, 133, 143, 144, 162, 179.

See also brigade, *entrare in novelle,* fairy tales, *novellare*
sublime, 7
substitution, 53, 57, 151. *See also* servants, punished
subversion of authority
cultural, 7–8, 9, 10, 22, 139, 153
familial, 16
moral, 28, 46
parental, 24, 121, 125, 128, 197
social, 121.
See also Church; cultural milieu, literary impact of; Firenzuola; Grazzini; vengeance, male
suicide, 45, 125, 205, 207
suspense, 128, 130
suspension of disbelief, 123
swearing oaths, 40, 43, 44, 45

taboo, 7, 122
tenere, tenersi (pederastic), 171
teratalogical canon, 188, 190–192, 199n. 19
terror, 120, 121, 122, 123, 126, 129, 130, 131, 183, 192. *See also* fear; Gothic fiction; grotesque; horror; motifs, scream
textual tradition, 6, 105–107, 110, 116
textual transmission
oral, 1, 7, 84, 87, 106
written, 1, 106
torture, 130, 152.
See also castration, violence
tragedy, 126–127.
See also heroines, unfortunate; novella, tragic; murder; suicide
transformation, 9, 11, 150, 162–167, 183, 193, 202–203, 210
See also cross–dressing, gender confusion, metamorphoses
transgression, 53, 132, 135n. 16, 193, 197
sexual, 9, 11, 122, 159, 166, 167, 169, 172, 174, 203

social, 121, 125, 147.
   See also cross–dressing,
      hermaphroditism
transgression, punishment for, 10, 39–41,
   42, 45, 51, 56, 61–62, 121,
   128–129, 152, 204, 205, 207.
   See also vengeance, male
transis, 123
Trionfo della Morte, 123
Tuscany, 1, 2, 51–52, 121
twins. *See* animal offspring, monstrous
   births

utile consiglio (useful counsel), 17, 22, 27,
   34, 43, 46.
   See also didacticism
uxoricide, 183, 197. *See also* infanticide,
   misogyny, violence

Venetian Republic, 182, 194–196
vengeance, male, 25, 53, 58, 59, 62, 173,
   174
vernacular Italian
   2–4, 12, 17, 18.

   See also Bembo, Pietro; *questione della
      lingua*
violence, 5, 10, 25, 39, 51, 53, 58–59, 61,
   125, 128, 169, 171, 174, 175, 178n.
   29, 183, 191, 196–197, 199n. 23.
   See also castration; murder; practical
      jokes; servants, punished;
      vengence, male

witty retorts, 36, 56, 67n. 21, 124, 149
women novella writers. See *novelliere*
Word, the (Christ), 35–36, 40, 41, 42, 44,
   46, 48n. 29
word–deed dichotomy, 4, 11, 33, 36,
   41–42, 44–45
words, gendered female, 3, 4, 33–36, 38,
   42, 45.
   See also Bembo, Pietro; *questione della
      lingua*; word–deed dichotomy
writer, role of, 5, 29n. 4, 41, 64, 67n. 31,
   72–73
writing process, 4, 41, 64, 77–78

For Product Safety Concerns and Information please contact our EU
representative GPSR@taylorandfrancis.com
Taylor & Francis Verlag GmbH, Kaufingerstraße 24, 80331 München, Germany